大学英语情境式教学教材

（全二册）

上册

马纳琴　原　嫄　主　编
杨晓娅　梁玉娟　副主编

中国社会科学出版社

图书在版编目(CIP)数据

大学英语情境式教学教材：全二册／马纳琴，原嫄主编．-- 北京：中国社会科学出版社，2024.8

ISBN 978-7-5227-3342-5

Ⅰ.①大… Ⅱ.①马…②原… Ⅲ.①英语—高等学校—教材
Ⅳ.①H319.39

中国国家版本馆 CIP 数据核字(2024)第 065626 号

出 版 人 赵剑英
责任编辑 党旺旺
责任校对 马婷婷
责任印制 王 超

出 版 中国社会科学出版社
社 址 北京鼓楼西大街甲 158 号
邮 编 100720
网 址 http://www.csspw.cn
发 行 部 010-84083685
门 市 部 010-84029450
经 销 新华书店及其他书店

印 刷 北京明恒达印务有限公司
装 订 廊坊市广阳区广增装订厂
版 次 2024 年 8 月第 1 版
印 次 2024 年 8 月第 1 次印刷

开 本 710×1000 1/16
印 张 37.25
字 数 535 千字
定 价 188.00 元(全二册)

Content I

Unit One
Friendship

Part One: Phonics
Part Two: Dialogue
Part Three: Text
Part Four: Play — I am Hungry
Part Five: Language Skills

Part One: Phonics

I. Letter name and letter sound 字母名和字母音

A. ABC Song 字母歌

Aa Bb Cc Dd Ee Ff Gg

Hh Ii Jj Kk Ll Mm Nn

Oo Pp Qq Rr Ss Tt

Uu Vv Ww Xx Yy Zz

Now you see I can sing my ABC.

B. Letter name 字母名

26 个英文字母的字母名(Name)发音表：

A a	[ei]	**N n**	[en]
B b	[bi:]	**O o**	[əu]
C c	[si:]	**P p**	[pi:]
D d	[di:]	**Q q**	[kju:]
E e	[i:]	**R r**	[ɑ(r)]
F f	[ef]	**S s**	[es]
G g	[dʒi:]	**T t**	[ti:]
H h	[eitʃ]	**U u**	[ju:]
I i	[ai]	**V v**	[vi:]
J j	[dʒei]	**W w**	['dʌblju:]
K k	[kei]	**X x**	[eks]
L l	[el]	**Y y**	[wai]
M m	[em]	**Z z**	[zi:]/[zed]

C. Letter Sound 拼读音

拼读音和字母音是不一样的，下面通过韵律英语让大家感受拼读音和字母音的不同。在这些韵律英语中，前面单独重复朗读的是字母音（如 a，a，a），后面出现在单词中的便是该字母的拼读音（如 apple）。

a a a [ei]	Aa is for	apple
a a a [ei]	Aa is for	ant
b b b [bi:]	Bb is for	ball
b b b [bi:]	Bb is for	black
c c c [si:]	Cc is for	cool
c c c [si:]	Cc is for	cat
d d d [di:]	Dd is for	dad
d d d [di:]	Dd is for	duck
e e e [i:]	Ee is for	elephant
e e e [i:]	Ee is for	egg
f f f [ef]	Ff is for	five
f f f [ef]	Ff is for	fish
g g g [dʒi:]	Gg is for	gift
g g g [dʒi:]	Gg is for	good
h h h [eitʃ]	Hh is for	hello
h h h [eitʃ]	Hh is for	horse
i i i [ai]	Ii is for	Indian
i i i [ai]	Ii is for	ink
j j j [dʒei]	Jj is for	Jack

j j j [dʒei]	Jj is for	juice
k k k [kei]	Kk is for	kiss
k k k [kei]	Kk is for	kite
l l l [el]	Ll is for	light
l l l [el]	Ll is for	lion
m m m [em]	Mm is for	mother
m m m [em]	Mm is for	map
n n n [en]	Nn is for	no
n n n [en]	Nn is for	nose
o o o [əu]	Oo is for	ox
o o o [əu]	Oo is for	open
p p p [pi:]	Pp is for	panda
p p p [pi:]	Pp is for	pig
q q q [kju:]	Qq is for	queen
q q q [kju:]	Qq is for	question
r r r [ɑ(r)]	Rr is for	rock
r r r [ɑ(r)]	Rr is for	room
s s s [es]	Ss is for	sun
s s s [es]	Ss is for	sit
t t t [ti:]	Tt is for	time
t t t [ti:]	Tt is for	foot
u u u [ju:]	Uu is for	under
u u u [ju:]	Uu is for	up
v v v [vi:]	Vv is for	voice
v v v [vi:]	Vv is for	very
w w w ['dʌblju:]	Ww is for	window
w w w ['dʌblju:]	Ww is for	warm
x x x [eks]	Xx is for	fox
x x x [eks]	Xx is for	box
y y y [wai]	Yy is for	yes
y y y [wai]	Yy is for	yellow
z z z [zi:]/[zed]	Zz is for	zebra
z z z [zi:]/[zed]	Zz is for	zoo

Part Two: Dialogue

Dialogue 1

Alice: Glad to see you again.

Barbara: Me too. It’s been a long time, hasn’t it?

Alice: I should say so. How have you been?

Barbara: Quite well. Thank you, and you?

Alice: Good. Thanks. How did you spend your holiday?

Barbara: I went to Canada for sightseeing.

Alice: That's nice. I will go there next holiday.

Barbara: Best wishes.

Words and Expressions

quite [kwaɪt] *adv.* 非常

spend [spend] *v.* 度过；花（时间）

holiday ['hɒlədeɪ] *n.* 节日

sightseeing ['saɪtsiːɪŋ] *n.* 观光

Decide whether the following statements are True (T) or False (F).

(　　) 1. Alice and Barbara haven't seen each other for a long time.

(　　) 2. Barbara goes to America to spend her holiday.

(　　) 3. Barbara goes to Canada for a meeting.

(　　) 4. Alice will go to Canada next holiday.

(　　) 5. This is a dialogue about how to study English.

Dialogue 2

Alice: Good morning!

Barbara: Good morning! How are you doing?

Alice: Fine, thanks. And you?

Barbara: The same as usual. How are your parents?

Alice: They're pretty well.

Barbara: Say hello to them for me.

Alice: Of course. They will be happy you asked about them. I have to go to work immediately. See you!

Barbara: See you!

Words and Expressions

pretty ['prɪti] *adv.* 相当

immediately [ɪ'mi:diətli] *adv.* 立即

Decide whether the following statements are True (T) or False (F).

(　　) 1. This dialogue happens in the morning.

(　　) 2. Alice and Barbara greet each other.

(　　) 3. Barbara gives her regards to Alice's parents.

(　　) 4. Barbara's parents are very well.

(　　) 5. Alice has to go to wok at once.

Dialogue 3

Mr. Johnson: Good evening, Mrs. Brown. It's a nice night out, isn't it?

Mrs. Brown: Oh, hello, Mr. Johnson. Yes, it is. Are you out for a walk?

Mr. Johnson: In a way. I'm showing Mr. Green some of the sights of our city. Let me introduce you. Mrs. Brown, this is Mr. Green.

Mrs. Brown: How do you do, Mr. Green. I hope you like our city.

Mr. Green: Oh, yes, I'm enjoying my stay here very much.

Words and Expressions

show [ʃəʊ] *v.* 展示

sight [saɪt] *n.* 景象

introduce [ˌɪntrə'dju:s] *v.* 介绍

enjoy [ɪn'dʒɔɪ] *v.* 喜欢

Decide whether the following statements are True (T) or False (F).

(　　) 1. This dialogue happens in the afternoon.

(　　) 2.Mrs. Brown thinks it is a nice night out.

(　　) 3.Mr. Johnson is showing Mrs. Brown some of the sights in the city.

(　　) 4. Mr. Green knew Mrs. Brown before.

(　　) 5.Mr. Green is enjoying his stay here very much.

Dialogue 4

Alice: Hello, May I speak to Mary?

Mary: Hi, who's that? Speaking, please.

Alice: This is Alice, how's your feeling now? I heard that you feel not very well today.

Mary: Oh, Alice, thanks, I feel much better now.

Alice: Okay, take care of yourself and I promise that I will come to see you with some fruit tomorrow afternoon.

Mary: That's very kind of you. Thanks very much. I'll expect you.

Alice: Okay, see you.

Mary: See you.

Words and Expressions

speak [spiːk] *v.* 讲

feel [fiːl] *v.* 感觉

promise ['prɒmɪs] *v.* 许诺

expect [ɪk'spekt] *v.* 期望

take care of 照顾

Decide whether the following statements are True (T) or False (F).

(　) 1. This dialogue happens in the telephone.

(　) 2. Alice makes a call to Barbara.

(　) 3. Alice calls Mary to ask if she has time to see a movie.

(　) 4. Mary tells Alice that she feels much better.

(　) 5. Alice promises that she will come to see Mary with some fruit tomorrow afternoon.

Part Three: Text

This is a Silk Scarf. It is a greeting gift of Chinese Women.

This is Qipao. It is traditional costume for Chinese Women.

This is Nang. It is traditional food in Xinjiang.

That is water-ink picture. It is a traditional painting in China.

That is Dongbula. It is a musical instrument in Xinjiang.

This is a passport. It is used for travelling abroad.

Words and Expressions

greeting ['griːtɪŋ] *n.* 问候

Eg. 1. His greeting was familiar and friendly.

他的问候亲切而友好。

2. I'm greeting the students.

我在问候学生。

gift [gɪft] *n.* 礼物

Eg. 1. I really like this gift.

我真的很喜欢这个礼物。

2. He accepted my gift.

他收下了我送给他的礼物。

traditional [trə'dɪʃən(ə)l] *adj.* 传统的

Eg. 1. They sang and danced for peace in traditional native dress.

他们身着传统服装，为祈祷和平唱歌跳舞。

2. Do you like the Chinese traditional silk?

你喜欢中国传统的丝绸吗？

costume ['kɒstjuːm] *n.* 服装

Eg. 1. The costume in Paris broadened his outlook.

巴黎的服装使他大开眼界。

2. This is the best costume design.

这是最佳服装设计。

painting ['peɪntɪŋ] *n.* 绘画

Eg. 1. He gave me a painting with his name.

他送给我一张他署名的绘画。

2. His painting is on the wall.

他的绘画在墙上。

musical ['mjuːzɪk(ə)l] *adj*. 音乐的

Eg. 1. If you have a musical ability, you should use it.

如果你有音乐的能力，你可以使用它。

2. He was my musical partner and my friend.

他是我音乐上的搭档，也是我的朋友。

instrument ['ɪnstrəmənt] *n*. 仪器

Eg. 1. Language is an instrument.

语言是一种工具。

2. This instrument is new.

这个工具是新的。

Language Focus

I. Make a sentence with the words given below.

1. a / This / book / is
2. red / This / a / is / bag
3. is / That / yellow / a / table
4. student / is / a / chinese / That
5. beautiful / It / box / a / is

II. Translating

Put Chinese into English.

1. 这是一张桌子。
2. 那是一把椅子。
3. 这个房间很大。
4. 这是一条可爱的狗。
5. 它是一只猫。

Put English into Chinese.

1. This is my classmate, he is diligent.

2. This is my boyfriend, he is friendly.

3. That is a wonderful birthday party.

4. It is a beautiful garden with many flowers.

5. It is a big city. There are many high buildings in the city.

III. Reading Comprehension

Choose the best answer to each of the following questions or incomplete sentences.

This is Jim's room. It's not big, but it's very clean. There is a bed in the room. It's near the door. Under the bed, there are two balls. There is a desk and a chair near the window. There is a bookcase beside the desk. On the bookcase, there are many books and newspaper(报纸). There are two pictures in the room, too. They are on the wall.

1. The balls are ______.

A. near the window

B. on the desk

C. under the bed

D. beside the desk

2. Jim's bed is ______.

A. near the door

B. near the window

C. on the bookcase

D. on the wall

3. ______ are on the wall of Jim's room.

A. The books

B. The balls

C. The newspapers

D. The pictures

4. Jim's ______ are on his bookcase.

A. books

B. newspaper

C. pictures

D. A and B

5. Jim's room is ______.

A. big

B. not clean

C. dirty

D. not big

Part Four: Play

I am Hungry

Characters:

Lion 狮子(小狮子的爸爸)

Little Lion 小狮子

Rabbit 兔子

Bear 熊

Squirrel 松鼠

Monkey 猴子

Little Girl 小女孩

Scene 1

Lion: Roar, roar! I am a lion, the king of the forest. No one is stronger than me. Roar, roar!

Little Lion: Daddy! I'm hungry!

Lion: You are old enough now. Be brave! Go and find your own food.

Little Lion: Oh! Daddy, but… but I don't know how.
Lion: Follow me! Roar, roar!
Little Lion: Roar, roar!
Lion: Rush to the small animals and bite them with your sharp teeth. Go and do it now.
Little Lion: Yes, daddy.

Scene 2

Little Lion: Hi, rabbit! I am hungry. Roar, roar!
Rabbit: Do you want some carrots?
Little Lion: Yes, please! Oh, thank you!
Rabbit: Carrots are the best food ever.
Little Lion: Yuck! I don't like it. Anyway, thank you, rabbit.
Rabbit: You are welcome.

Scene 3

Little Lion: Hi, bear! I am hungry. Roar, roar!
Bear: Do you want some porridge?
Little Lion: Yes, please! Oh, thank you!
Bear: Porridge is the best food ever.
Little Lion: Yuck! I don't like it. Anyway, thank you, bear.
Bear: You are welcome.

Scene 4

Little Lion: Hi, Squirrel! I am hungry. Roar, roar!
Squirrel: Do you want some peanuts?
Little Lion: Yes, please! Oh, thank you!
Squirrel: Peanuts are the best food ever.
Little Lion: Yuck! I don't like it. Anyway, thank you, squirrel.
Squirrel: You are welcome.

Scene 5

Little Lion: Hi, Monkey! I am hungry. Roar, roar!

Monkey: Do you want some peaches?

Little Lion: Yes, please! Oh, thank you!

Monkey: Peaches are the best food ever.

Little Lion: Yuck! I don't like it. Anyway, thank you, monkey.

Monkey: You are welcome.

Scene 6

Little Lion: Hi, little girl! I am hungry. Roar, roar!

Little Girl: Oh, a lion! Help, help!

Little Lion: What is it on the grass? Oh, an apple. Mmm..., delicious! I like it, lalala...

（师生改编剧本）

Words and Expressions

hungry ['hʌŋgri] *adj*. 饥饿的

lion ['laɪən] *n*. 狮子

little ['lɪt(ə)l] *adj*. 小的

rabbit ['ræbɪt] *n*. 兔子

bear [beə(r)] *n*. 熊

squirrel ['skwɪrəl] *n*. 松鼠

monkey ['mʌŋki] *n*. 猴子

roar [rɔː(r)] *v*. 吼叫，咆哮

king [kɪŋ] *n*. 国王

forest ['fɒrɪst] *n*. 森林

enough [ɪ'nʌf] *adv*. 足够地

follow ['fɒləʊ] *v*. 跟随

rush [rʌʃ] *v*. 冲

small [smɔːl] *adj*. 小的
animal ['ænɪm(ə)l] *n*. 动物
bite [baɪt] *v*. 咬
teeth [tiːθ] *n*. 牙齿
carrot ['kærət] *n*. 胡萝卜
please [pliːz] *v*. 请
anyway ['enɪweɪ] *adv*. 不管怎样
welcome ['welkəm] *v*. 欢迎
porridge ['pɒrɪdʒ] *n*. 麦片粥
peanut ['piːnʌt] *n*. 花生
peach [piːtʃ] *n*. 桃子
grass [grɑːs] *n*. 草地
delicious [dɪ'lɪʃəs] *adj*. 美味的

Listening Practice

I. Bingo game

Work in groups, one student read about the script of *I am Hungry*, other students listen carefully, when they hear the adjective from the script, say "Bingo", and write the word in the form quickly, and then he/she wins. And take turns, and change the words into Verbs, Nouns, etc.

words	adjective	verbs	nouns	prepositions	adverbs	conjunctions
student 1						
student 2						
student 3						
student 4						
student 5						

II. Dictation

Listen to the passage three times and supply the missing information.

One day, a lion, the ___1___ of the ___2___, teaches his son how to find food. He tells his son that he should ___3___ to the small ___4___ and ___5___ them with his sharp ___6___. The little lion meets a rabbit, and the rabbit gives him some___7___ to eat. And then he meets a bear, and the bear gives him some ___8___. After that, he meets a squirrel, and the squirrel gives him some peanuts. He meets a monkey, and the monkey gives him some ___9___. Finally, he knows that ___10___ is his favorite food.

Reading Practice

I. Read and choose

1. Which of the following statement is True?

A. The little lion bites the rabbit.

B. The lion likes to eat banana.

C. The monkey drops peach on the grass.

D. The lion asks the little lion to find his own food.

2. The rabbit offers the little lion ________ to eat.

A. orange

B. apple

C. carrots

D. peach

3. What is squirrel's favorite food?

A. peach

B. apple

C. peanut

D. carrot

4. Who do you think likes to eat peach?

A. monkey

B. little girl

C. bear

D. rabbit

5. What does the little lion like to eat?

A. apple

B. peach

C. carrot

D. porridge

II. Read and answer

1. Who was the little lion? Is he the lion's friend?
2. Why does the lion ask the little lion to find food on his own?
3. Where does the little girl drop the apple?
4. If you were the little lion, which would you like to eat, the little girl or an apple?
5. What does the little girl drop on the grass?

Speaking Practice

I. Role Play

Suppose you were the little lion, would you run after the little girl, or just eat the apple the girl dropped on the grass? Use the following functional sentences, you have to add your own expressions when it is necessary.

- Hi, I'm a lion.
- Will you make a friend with me?
- I like eating apples.
- Listen to me, otherwise I will eat you!
- Bye for now.
- Remember me!
- So long.

II. Problem-Solving

Think of appropriate lines for the animal in the picture above.

III. Delivery Game

The teacher divides the whole class into four or five groups, queue the students. The teacher writes a long sentence from the script in a piece of paper, just let the first student read and recite it for one minute, and let the student retell the sentence to the second student, the second to the third, when the sentence is delivered to the last student, he/she should write it on the blackboard, and translate it into Chinese. The group which has got great speed and relative accuracy wins.

Translating Practice

I. Translate the sentences into Chinese.

Work in pairs, one student reads the following sentences, and the other translates the sentences into Chinese in spoken way. (Add extra sentences from the scripts if necessary.)

1. Roar, roar! I am a lion, the king of the forest. No one is stronger than me. Roar, roar!
2. Go and find your own food.
3. Rush to the small animals and bite them with your sharp teeth. Go and do it now.
4. Do you want some carrots?
5. Peach is the best food ever.

II. Translate the sentences into English.

Work in pairs, one student reads the following sentences, and the other translates the sentences into English in spoken way. (Add extra sentences from the scripts if necessary.)

1. 勇敢一点！
2. 我饿了。
3. 跟我来！
4. 谢谢！

5. 我不喜欢。

Writing Practice

Write a summary of *I am Hungry* in 50 words.

"Ws" / "Who"	doing what	whom	where	when

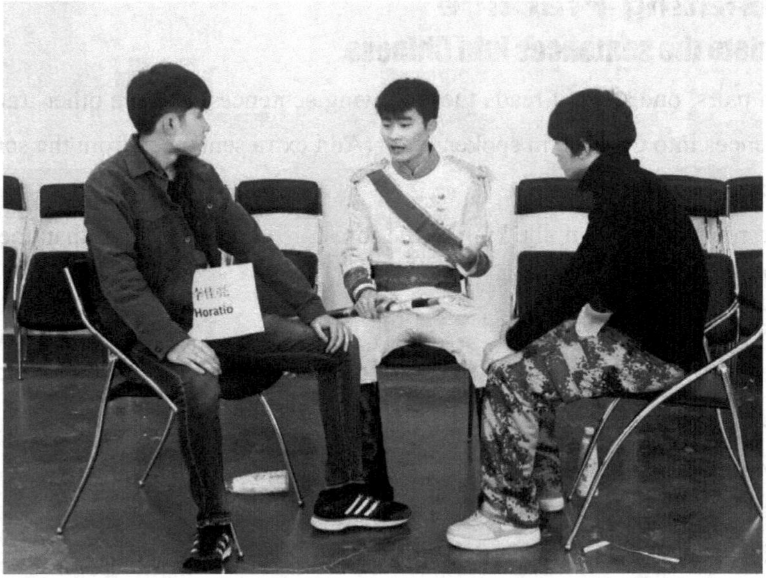

Part Five: Language Skills

1. 指示代词 This, That, It

（1）this 指这个，that 指那个，it 是代词，可以用来指代东西、动物、植物和未确定身份的人，还可以指时间、天气、距离等。

（2）离说话人近的人或物用 this，离说话人远的人或物用 that。

如：

This is a book.　　这是一本书。(距说话人较近的)

That is a pencil. 那是一只笔。(距说话人较远的)
如两样东西放在一起，介绍的时候先说 this，后说 that。
如：
This is a dog. That is a cat. 这是一只狗。那是一只猫。
向别人介绍某人时说 This is…，
如：
This is my friend, Judy. 这是我朋友，朱迪。
it 做代词时没有远近之分。
如：
It is good. 很好。
It is five o'clock. 五点了。
需要注意：This is 不能缩写，而 that is 可以缩写成 that's。
如：
This is a bus. That's a car. 这是一辆公共汽车。那是一辆轿车。

2. these 和 those 用法

this, that, these 和 those 都是指示代词，these 是 this 的复数形式，指时间、距离较近的或下面要提到的人或事；those 是 that 的复数形式，指时间、距离较远或前面已经提到过的人或事。结构如：this is — these are+名词的复数形式 / that is — those are +名词的复数形式。
如：
This is a beautiful flower. 这是一朵漂亮的花。
These are beautiful flowers. 这些是漂亮的花。
That is a story-book. 那是一本故事书。
Those are story-books. 那些是故事书。

Exercises

A. Multiple Choice

1. ________ is an apple tree. (近处)

A. Those B. These C. This D. That

2. ________ is a bird. (远处)

A. Those B. These C. This D. That

3. Hi, Ann! _______ is Jack.

A. It B. These C. This D. That

4. Mum, _______ is my friend Tom.

A. it B. these C. this D. that

5. —Look at ________Barbies. Are they Nacy's?

—No, those are hers._______ are mine.

A. these, These B. those, These C. those, Those D. these, Those

6. _______ is a ruler, ________ is a pen.

A. This, that B. Those, these C. That, that D. These, these

7. Jane, _______ are my parents.

A.this B. that C. those D. these

8. — Are _______your books? (近处)

— Yes, _______ are.

A. this, this B. that, that C. these, they D. those, it

9. — Are _______ butterflies?

— No, _______are not.

A. this, this B. that, it C. this, it D. these, they

10. These clothes are mine. ______________ are yours.

A. It B. Those C. This D. That

11. What _______ this?

A. be B. are C. is D. will

12. That is ______ orange.

A. some B. an C. a D. any

13. It is my ______.

A. book B. apples C. papers D. pens

14. This_______ my friend.

A. are B. is C. one D. be

15. That is ______ cute dog.

A. some B. many C. a D.one

16. —Hello! Is______ Miss Green?

—Yes, ______is. Who's _____?

A. this, this, this B. that, this, that C. this, it,this D. this, that,that

17. These keys are mine. _______ are yours.

A. This B. Those C. This D.That

18. —What's that?

—______ a cat.

A. This is B. It's C. That is D.They are

19. —What is this in English?

—________

A. They are a ruler. B. It's a ruler. C. Those are a ruler. D. It's rulers.

20. —Are these Tim's books?

—________

A. Yes, it is. B. No, they are. C. No, it is. D. Yes, they are.

B. Complete each of the following sentences with a proper demonstrative pronoun.

1. — What's ________?

— It's a pencil box.

— What's ________ over there?

— It's a gift.

2. — Are_______ your friends?

— Yes, they are.

3. I like _____ toys. ______ toys are cute.

4. I don't like ____ shirt. ____shirt is too small.

5. I want _____ sweater. I don't want________ sweater. _____ is too big.

6. These keys are mine. ______ are yours.

7. I like_____better than that.

8. He is going to marry_____ girl.

9. ______is Mr. White and _____ is my father.

10. ______two boys are Mr. Green's sons.

C. Translating Practice

I. Translate the sentences into English.

1. 这是我的尺子。

____

2. 那是你的书。

____

3. 这些是你的铅笔。

____

4. 这位是我的好朋友，海伦。

____

5. 今天是个好天气。

____

II. Translate the sentences into Chinese.

1. This is an orange.

____

2. These are bicycles.

____

3. These are yellow cups.

____

4. That is a fox.

____

5. Those are exercise-books.

____

Unit Two
Gratitude

Part One: Phonics
Part Two: Dialogue
Part Three: Text
Part Four: Play — The Fisherman and the Goldfish
Part Five: Language Skills

Part One: Phonics

I. Short Vowel

A. 短音“a”　　Short “a” Sound

1. 拼读发音方式。

字母“a”有字母音和拼读音，字母音就是在字母“ABCDE...”中的读音，而它的拼读音与字母音不同。它的拼读短音发音是这样的：舌端靠近下齿，舌前部抬高，唇形扁平，嘴唇开口可容纳食指和中指，是开口最大的音，介于半开半闭之间，下巴往下拉，嘴角的肌肉紧张。就像在 apple，cat，act，back，land 等单词中的发音。

2. 仔细听并朗读以下单词、短语和句子，找出其中的短音“a”，学一学字母“a”的拼读发音短音。

(1) Names

Boys	Girls
Dan	Angela
Mac	Ann

Jack	Candy
Sam	Samantha

(2)

Fruits— apple banana mango

Animals— cat rat rabbit bat panda

Foods— pancake carrot

(3)

ant pan fan man lamp nap mat jam fat ham

bad man in a hat ants in your pants gas cans in the van

hand and jam in a bag

(4)

The cat sat on the mat.

Dan is a fat man.

He can nap in the van.

Can a cat in a hat and a bat in a cap flag a man with a bag in a van?

B．短音 “e” **Short “e” Sound**

1. 拼读发音方式。

字母 “e” 有字母音和拼读音，字母音就是在字母 “ABCDE…” 中的读音，而它的拼读音与字母音不同。它的拼读短音发音是这样的：舌端靠近下齿，舌前部抬高，唇形扁平，嘴张开可容纳一个食指尖那么大。字母 “e” 的拼读音就像在 bed，best，west，help，leg，bet 等单词中的发音。

2. 仔细听并朗读以下单词、短语和句子，找出其中的短音“e”，学一学字母 “e” 的拼读发音短音。

(1) Names

Boys	**Girls**
Ben	Wendy
Ted	Penny
Fred	Kelly
Den	Peg

(2)

Countries—	Denmark	Mexico
Jobs—	Dentist	vet
Fruits—	lemon	berry
Animals—	hen	

(3)

leg jet pen bell web red rest well bell

elephant in the room end in the smoke step on the best sled

(4)

There are seven bird's eggs in the birds nest.

Peg's leg is red.

Betty likes pet dog.

Len and Ben are best friends.

Len has a pet hen called Meg.

C. 短音"i" Short "i" Sound

1. 拼读发音方式。

字母"e"有字母音和拼读音，字母音就是在字母"ABCDE…"中的读音，而它的拼读音与字母音不同。它的拼读短音发音是这样的：舌端靠近下齿，舌前部抬高，唇形扁平，嘴张开可容纳一个小指尖，声带振动。字母"i"的拼读音就像在 tip，fill，bit，igloo，thin，pig 等单词中的发音。

2. 仔细听并朗读以下单词、短语和句子，找出其中的短音"i"，学一学字母"i"的拼读发音短音。

(1) Names

Boys	**Girls**
Mick	Vicky
Dick	Jill
Rick	Ivana
Jim	Ingrid

(2)

Countries—	India	Italy	Iran
Jobs—	instructor	inventor	

(3)

Big fig kid win Jim tin hit his dish fish pig

(4)

a fish in a dish a pig in a wig fill in the pit

(5)

A prince gave a princess a kiss on the lips.
The king gave the princess a ring.
The princess hid the ring in a big pink tin,
and the king asked the princess to sing.

Bill is slim but he isn't thin,
Jill can think but she cannot wink,
Mick is sick but he's very quick,
Phil is ill and he's taken a pill.

D. 短音"o" Short "o" Sound

1. 拼读发音方式。

字母"o"有字母音和拼读音，字母音就是在字母"ABCDE…"中的读音，而它的拼读音与字母音不同。它的拼读短音发音是这样的：舌端离开下齿，舌头尽量降低、后缩，舌头后部抬高，嘴唇收圆，开口大。字母"o"的拼读音就像在 lot，fox，box，mop 等单词中的发音。

2. 仔细听并朗读以下单词、短语和句子，找出其中的短音"o"，学一学字母"o"的拼读发音短音。

(1) Names

Boys	**Girls**
Tom	Polly
Ron	Dorothy
John	Constance

(2)

Countries—	Holland	Columbia	
Jobs—	photographer	postman	policeman

Fruits— orange melon

Animals— dog hog frog fox donkey

(3)

Don had a lot of cod.

The dog and the donkey have gone to Hong Kong.

The fox is on the box.

The top of Ron's body is orange and the bottom is not.

E．短音"u" Short "u" Sound

1. 拼读发音方式。

字母"u"有字母音和拼读音，字母音就是在字母"ABCDE…"中的读音，而它的拼读音与字母音不同。它的拼读短音发音是这样的：舌头后部靠前部分稍稍抬起，舌头两侧抵下齿。双唇扁平，放松。字母"u"的拼读音就像在 just，but，plus，hut，pub 等单词中的发音。

2. 仔细听并朗读以下单词、短语和句子，找出其中的短音"u"，学一学字母"u"的拼读发音短音。

(1) Names

Boys	**Girls**
Buster	Sunny
Rusty	Bunny
Duncan	Dusty

(2)

It's fun to chew gum.

The puppy is under the umbrella.

Butter a currant bun.

Brush the dust under the rug.

(3)

ugly duckling Uncle Sam under a cloud up in the air upper hand

upset the apple cart until the last dog is shot cub runs after mum

Part Two: Dialogue

Dialogue 1

Alice: Hello, do you have a public phone here?

Clerk: Of course, do you need the local or long-distance phone?

Alice: What are the prices?

Clerk: Four jiao for the first three minutes for local calls; and two jiao per minute for long-distance calls.

Alice: I need to make both kinds of calls.

Clerk: Okay. Make the call, please. The timer will start automatically after you dial the number.

Words and Expressions

public ['pʌblɪk] *adj.* 公共的

phone [fəʊn] *n.* 电话

long-distance [ˌlɒŋ 'dɪstəns] *adj.* [通信]长途的

call [kɔːl] *v.* 打电话

timer ['taɪmə(r)] *n.* 计时器

start [stɑːt] *v.* 开始

automatically [ˌɔːtə'mætɪkli] *adv.* 自动地

dial ['daɪəl] *v.* 打电话，拨电话号码

Decide whether the following statements are True (T) or False (F).

(　　) 1. Alice wants a public phone.

(　　) 2. Clerk tells Alice that there is no long-distance phone.

(　　) 3. Four jiao for the first three minutes for local calls.

(　　) 4. Alice needs to make the local call.

(　　) 5. The timer will start automatically before Alice dials the number.

Dialgoue 2

Cindy: Good morning, ABC Company, Cindy speaking. Can I help you?

Customer: This is Tom Stevens. May I speak to your customer service manager?

Cindy: I'm sorry, he is in a meeting. May I take a message?

Customer: When will he be available?

Cindy: I don't know, sir. Would you like to leave a message?

Customer: No, that's OK. I will call back.

Words and Expressions

company ['kʌmpəni] *n.* 公司

customer ['kʌstəmə(r)] *n.* 顾客，客户

service ['sɜːvɪs] *n.* 服务

available [ə'veɪləbl] *adj.* 可获得的；可使用的

customer service manager 客户经理

take a message 捎个口信

Decide whether the following statements are True (T) or False (F).

( ) 1.Cindy works in ABC Company.

( ) 2.Customer, Tom Stevens, wants to speak to the customer service manager.

( ) 3.The customer has a talk with the customer service manager.

( ) 4.Customer service manager is in a meeting.

( ) 5.Customer leaves a message to the customer service manager.

Dialgoue 3

Tom: Hi, mother. I may go home late tonight.

Mum: Overtime again?

Tom: Yes, I have just taken a new project.

Mum: But you've already logged in three days of overtime, take care of your body.

Tom: I will, mother. Three days later, I will have to go on business. Help me book train ticket to Shanghai.

Mum: Ok, I will. Relax about your work.

Words and Expressions

tonight [tə'naɪt] *n.* 今晚

overtime ['əʊvətaɪm] *n.* 超出的时间

project ['prɒdʒekt] *n.* 项目，工程

log [lɒg] *v.* 把……载入正式记录

book [bʊk] *v.* 预订

relax [rɪ'læks] *v.* 轻松

Decide whether the following statements are True (T) or False (F).

( ) 1. This is a dialogue between mother and child.

( ) 2. Tom tells his mother that he will not go home tonight.

( ) 3. Tom has just taken a new project.

( ) 4. Mum worries about Tom's health and hope he could take care of his body.

( ) 5. Tom will have to go on business a week later.

Dialgoue 4

Tom: Jim, is there anything wrong with this telephone? Why can't I make a call?

Jim: It's ok. There is nothing wrong with it.

Tom: But why haven't I gotten through after dialing for such a long time?

Jim: Did you dial zero? You need to dial zero first to get an outside line.

Tom: Why didn't you tell me earlier? No wonder I haven't been able to make a call. I'll give it another shot.

Words and Expressions

wrong [rɒŋ] *n.* 故障，错误

zero ['zɪərəʊ] *num.* 零

outside [ˌaʊt'saɪd] *n.* 外面

shot [ʃɒt] *n.* 尝试，努力

Decide whether the following statements are True (T) or False (F).

( ) 1. Tom wants to make a call.

( ) 2. Jim thinks there is something wrong with the telephone.

( ) 3. Tom dials for a long time but he does not get through.

( ) 4. Jim tells Tom that he needs to dial zero first to get an outside line.

(   ) 5. Tom will try it again.

Part Three: Text

Is this a yak?   Yes, it is.

Is the yak a mammal?   Yes, it is.

Is the yak white?   Yes, it is.

Is that a great musuem?   Yes, it is.

Is the great museum in Xi'an?   Yes, it is.

Is the great museum one of the oldest and best-preserved museums in China?   Yes, it is.

Is the picture of grassland in Sichuan?   No, it isn't. It is in Gansu Province.

Is the big lake in Xinjiang?   No, it isn't. It is in Qinghai.

Words and Expressions

yak [jæk] *n.* 耗牛

Eg. 1. The yak is well adapted to the harsh conditions of the Hinalayas.

耗牛很好地适应了喜马拉雅山脉的恶劣条件。

Eg. 2. Yaks are known for their thick fur.

耗牛以其厚实的毛发而闻名。

mammal ['mæməl] *n.* 哺乳类动物

Eg. 1. Elpehants are the largest mammals on land.

大象是陆地上最大的哺乳动物。

Eg. 1. Mammals have hair or fur on their bodies.

哺乳动物身上有毛发和皮毛。

preserved [prɪ'zɜːvd] *adj.* 保藏的；腌制的

Eg. 1. These books are well preserved.

这些书保存得很好。

2. It must be preserved.

它必须被保护住。

grassland ['grɑːslænd] *n.* 草原

Eg. 1. There is a large grassland in the distance.

远处是一大片草原。

2. There is a sheep and some cows on the grassland.

草原上有一只羊和几头牛。

Language Focus

I. Make a sentence with the words given below.

1. a / this / car / is / big / ?
2. white / that / a / is / bird / ?
3. is / that / tall / a / boy / ?
4. river / is / a / long / that / ?
5. colorful / it / bird / a / is / ?

II. Translating

Put Chinese into English.

1. 这是一个电脑吗？是的。
2. 那是一个日本姑娘吗？不，她是一个中国姑娘。

3. 这是一个很大的学校吗？是的。
4. 那是一幅美丽的图画吗？是的。
5. 那是一本小说吗？不，那是一本杂志。(novel, magazine)

Put English in to Chinese.

1. Is this the famous tower?　Yes, it is.
2. Is that a river?　No, it isn't.　It is a lake.
3. Is this book very difficult to understand?　No, it isn't.　It is easy to understand.
4. Is it a big house with many rooms?　Yes, it is.
5. That is the Great Wall.　It is one of the wonders in the world.

III. Reading Comprehension

Choose the best answer to each of the following questions or incomplete sentences.

My name is Gao Ping. My English teacher is Julia. She is from England. She has two children, a son and a daughter. Her daughter is Betty. Her son is Dick. Julia and her daughter are in China, but her husband Paul Smith is in England. Her son is in America. Paul is a policeman. Dick is a college student. Betty and I are in the same school. We are classmates, and we are good friends. I teach her Chinese and she teaches me English.

1. The writer's name is___________.

A. Julia

B. Betty

C. Paul

D. Gao ping

2. Julia and Paul are Betty's___________.

A. teachers

B. students

C. parents

D. classmates

3. Betty and Dick are___________.

A. sisters and brothers

B. sister and brother

C. sister and brothers

D. sister and father

4. Betty's father is a___________.

A. teacher

B. policeman

C. worker

D. farmer

5. Julia is a___________in China.

A. housewife in England

B. teacher

C. worker

D. player

Part Four: Play

The Fisherman and the Goldfish

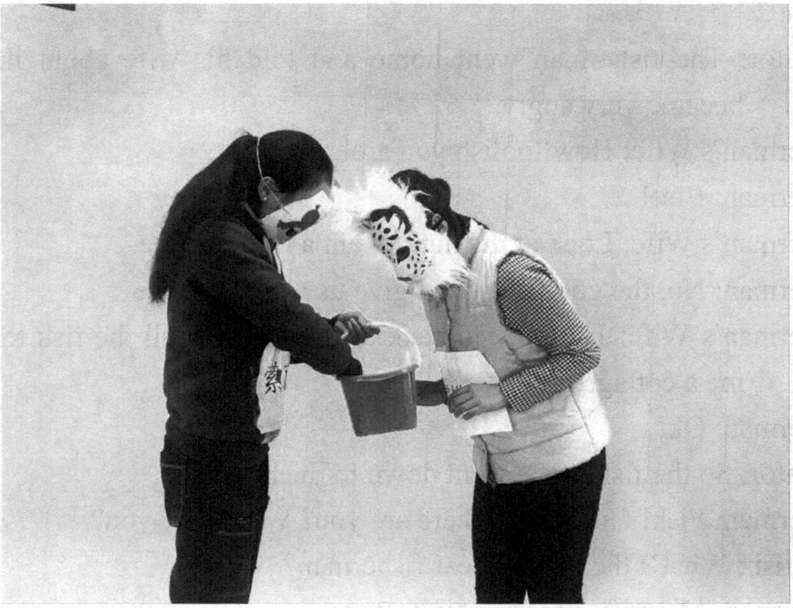

Characters:
Narrator 旁白
Goldfish 金鱼
Fisherman 渔夫
Fisherman's wife 渔夫的妻子

Scene 1

Narrator: Once, there was a fisherman. He had an ugly wife. They were very poor. One day, the fisherman caught a goldfish. But the goldfish could talk.
Goldfish: Please let me go!
Fisherman: Oh, my god! You can talk.
Goldfish: Yes, yes! Please let me go! I will reward you!
Fisherman: Oh! Don't worry! I have no wish to eat a talking fish.
Goldfish: Thank you! I will reward you! Bye.
Fisherman: Bye.

Scene 2

Narrator: The fisherman went home and told his wife about it. She became very angry.
Fisherman's Wife: How foolish you are!
Fisherman: But I …
Fisherman's Wife: Look at the hut. I want a new cottage.
Fisherman: No, the goldfish won't give us a new cottage.
Fisherman's Wife: Just go! Go back to the sea and tell the fish to give me a cottage.
Fisherman: Ok!
Narrator: So the fisherman went down to the beach.
Fisherman: Fish! Goldfish! Where are you? Where are you?
Goldfish: What's the matter, dear fisherman?
Fisherman: My wife wants a new cottage.

Goldfish: Don't worry! She will have it.

Fisherman: Thank you, goldfish.

Goldfish: You're welcome. Bye. Dear Fisherman.

Fisherman: Bye.

Narrator: So the fisherman's wife had her cottage.

Scene 3

Narrator: But after a few days, fisherman's wife became tired of it.

Fisherman's Wife: How foolish you are!

Fisherman: But I …

Fisherman's Wife: Look at the cottage. I don't like it anymore. I want a palace.

Fisherman: No, the goldfish won't give you a palace.

Fisherman's Wife: Just go! Go back to the sea and tell the fish to give me a palace.

Fisherman: Ok!

Narrator: So the fisherman went down to the beach.

Fisherman: Fish! Goldfish! Where are you? Where are you?

Goldfish: What's the matter, dear fisherman?

Fisherman: My wife wants a palace.

Goldfish: She will have it.

Fisherman: Thank you, goldfish. Bye.

Narrator: So the fisherman's wife had her palace.

Scene 4

Narrator: But she soon got tired of it, too.

Fisherman's Wife: You, stupid Fisherman.

Fisherman: But I …

Fisherman's Wife: I don't like the palace anymore. I want to be a queen.

Ask the fish to be my servant.

Fisherman: No, it's impossible. I won't go.

Fisherman's Wife: Just go! Go back to the sea and ask the fish to be my servant, and I want to be a queen.

Fisherman: Oh…

Narrator: So the fisherman went down to the beach again.

Fisherman: Fish! Goldfish! Where are you? Where are you?

Goldfish: What's the matter?

Fisherman: My wife wants to be a queen, and… and ask you to be her servant.

Narrator: This time, the fish got angry. It said nothing and swam away. The fisherman waited and waited, but the goldfish didn't come back. When he went home, he found his wife back in their old hut.

（师生改编剧本）

Words and Expressions

fisherman ['fɪʃəmən] *n.* 渔夫

goldfish ['gəʊldfɪʃ] *n.* 金鱼

narrator [nə'reɪtə(r)] *n.* 叙述者

once [wʌns] *adv.* 曾经

ugly ['ʌgli] *adj.* 丑的

wife [waɪf] *n.* 妻子

poor [pɔ:(r)] *adj.* 贫穷的

catch [kætʃ] *v.* 抓住

reward [rɪ'wɔːd] *n.* 报答

worry ['wʌri] *v.* 担心

become [bɪ'kʌm] *v.* 成为，变得

angry ['æŋgri] *adj*. 生气地，愤怒的

foolish ['fuːlɪʃ] *adj*. 愚蠢的

hut [hʌt] *n*. 小屋

cottage ['kɒtɪdʒ] *n*. 村舍

beach [biːtʃ] *n*. 海滩

anymore [ˌeni'mɔː(r)] *adv*. 不再

stupid ['stjuːpɪd] *adj*. 愚蠢的

queen [kwiːn] *n*. 女王

servant ['sɜːvənt] *n*. 仆人

impossible [ɪm'pɒsəb(ə)l] *adj*. 不可能的

go back 回去

go down to 延续至

What's the matter? 怎么了？

become tired of 变得厌倦

look at 看

get tired of 疲倦

swim away 游开

come back 回来

Listening Practice

I. Bingo game

Work in groups, one student read about the script of *The Fisherman and the Goldfish*, other students listen carefully, when they hear the adjective from the script, say "Bingo", and write the word in the form quickly, and then he/she wins. And take turns, and change the words into Verbs, Nouns, etc.

words	adjective	verbs	nouns	prepositions	adverbs	conjunctions
student 1						
student 2						
student 3						
student 4						
student 5						

II. Dictation

Listen to the passage three times and supply the missing information.

Once, there was a ___1___. He had a ___2___ wife. One day, the fisherman ___3___ a goldfish. The goldfish promised to ___4___ him if he put it back to the sea. The fisherman's wife was very ___5___ and ordered her husband to ask a ___6___ from the goldfish. But after a few days, fisherman's wife became ___7___ of it. She asked a ___8___ from the goldfish, and after that she became even greedier, she wanted to be a ___9___. At this time, the goldfish got ___10___ and swam away. When the fisherman went home, he found his wife back in their old hut.

Reading Practice

I. Read and choose

1. Which of the following statement is True?

A. The fisherman's wife asked for 3 things altogether.

B. The goldfish did not give anything to the greedy woman.

C. The fisherman took the goldfish back to the home.

D. The goldfish was very foolish.

2. The fisherman's wife asked for a ______ for the first time.

A. hut

B. cottage

C. goldfish

D. palace

3. The goldfish got angry when the fisherman's wife asked to become a _______.

A. queen

B. hut

C. palace

D. cottage

4. How do you think about the fisherman's wife?

A. greedy

B. kind

C. warm-hearted

D. outgoing

5. At last, what did the old woman have?

A. a palace

B. a cottage

C. goldfish

D. nothing

II. Read and answer

1. Who was the old woman? Was she the fisherman's neighbor?
2. Why did the goldfish promise to reward the old fisherman?
3. Where did the fisherman catch the goldfish?
4. If you were the goldfish, what would you do, satisfy the old woman or just ignore her?
5. How do you think about the fisherman?

Speaking Practice

I. Role Play

Suppose you were the goldfish, would you satisfy the old woman or just ignore her? Use the following functional sentences, you have to add your own expressions when it is necessary.

- Hi, I'm a goldfish.
- I will give you…
- I want a ...
- I want another …
- Bye for now.
- See you!
- So long.

II. Problem-Solving

Think of appropriate lines for the animal in the picture above.

III. Delivery Game

The teacher divides the whole class into four or five groups, queue the students. The teacher writes a long sentence from the script in a piece of paper, just let the first student read and recite it for one minute, and let the student retell the sentence to the second student, the second to the third, when the sentence is delivered to the last student, he/she should write it on the blackboard, and translate it into Chinese. The group which has got great speed and relative accuracy wins.

Translating Practice

I. Translate the sentences into Chinese.

Work in pairs, one student reads the following sentences, and the other translates the sentences into Chinese in spoken way. (Add extra sentences from the scripts if necessary.)

1. One day, the fisherman caught a goldfish.
2. Go back to the sea and tell the fish to give me a cottage.
3. But after a few days, fisherman's wife became tired of it.
4. I want to be a queen. Ask the fish to be my servant.
5. The fisherman waited and waited, but the goldfish didn't come back.

II. Translate the sentences into English.

Work in pairs, one student reads the following sentences, and the other translates the sentences into English in spoken way. (Add extra sentences from the scripts if necessary.)

1. 这次，金鱼生气了。
2. 你在哪儿？
3. 我不喜欢它了。
4. 你真蠢！
5. 不要担心。

Writing Practice

Write a summary of *The Fisherman and the Goldfish* in 50 words.

"Ws" / "Who"	doing what	whom	where	when

Part Five: Language Skills

Grammar

指示代词 **This**，**That** 和 **It** 的否定及疑问

A. This，That 和 It 的肯定句变为否定句：

在系动词 am / is / are 后面直接加 not，其余的按顺序照抄。

如：

指示代词	肯定句	否定句
This	This is a cat.	This is not a cat.
That	That is a book.	That is not a book.
These	These are pencils.	These are not pencils.
Those	Those are apples.	Those are not apples.
It	It is a nice day.	It is not a nice day.

B. This，That 和 It 的疑问句

将 this，that 和 it 的陈述句变为疑问句时须将系动词 am / is / are 提到句首并将首字母大写，其他语序不变，并且需要以 yes 或 no 来作答。

如：

指示代词	陈述句	疑问句
This	This is a cat.	Is this a cat?
That	That is a book.	Is that a book?
These	These are pencils.	Are these pencils?
Those	Those are apples.	Are those apples?
It	It is a nice day.	Is it a nice day?

在回答 this 和 that 做主语的疑问句时，常用 it 代替 this 和 that。

如：

—Is this / that a dog? —这/那是一只狗吗？

—Yes,it is./No,it isn't. —是的，它是。/不，它不是。

—What's this / that? —这/那是什么？

—It's a ruler. —这/那是一把尺子。

Exercises

A. Multiple Choice

1. ________ pen is red. ________ pencil is green.

A. this, that B. These, Those C. That, Those D. This, That

2. — Look, what is _____?

— It's an eraser.

A. this B. that C. these D. those

3. — What is this?

— ____is a cake.

A. That B. This C. It D.One

4. Is _____ a panda over there?

A. this B. That C. those D. that

5. ______this your teacher?

A. Be B. Are C. Is D. Were

6. Are ______ her parents?

A. this B. these C. that D. he

7. — Is that Mary's schoolbag?

— _________

A. Yes, it isn't. B. No, it is. C. Yes, it's. D. No, it isn't.

8. — What are _____ in English?

— They are _______.

A. these, boxes B. these, box C. this, boxes D. this, box

9. — Is this your friend?

— _______

A. Yes, he is. B. Yes, it is. C. No, its not. D. Yes, I am.

10. — Helen, ________ is my cousin Andy.

— Nice to meet you, Andy.

A. he B. she C. that D. this

11. — Are these Helen's pencils?

— _______

A.Yes, they're. B. No, they are. C. Yes, they are. D. No, it is.

12. — What are those?

— ______

A. They are box. B. They are boxes. C. It's a box. D. Yes, they are.

13. The weather in Shenzhen is hotter than _______ in Beijing.

A. that B. it C. this D. one

14. I found _______ necessary to learn English well.

A. that B. this C. it D. one

15. We find ______ impossible for us to finish this work in a short time.

A. it B. this C. one D. that

16. — I need something for cutting the paper.

— Oh, you want a knife? Ok, I'll get ______ for you.

A. it B. that C. this D. one

17. ______those his dictionaries?

A. is B. Are C. Is D. are

18. —What is this in English?

— ___________

A. It an eraser. B. It's an eraser. C. It's my an eraser. D. It's my eraser.

19. Are _____ your books over there?

A. this B. that C. these D. those

20. —Is this your English teacher?

— __________

A. No, it isn't. B.Yes, it is. C. Yes, he is. D. No, he is.

B. Complete each of the following sentences with a proper word.

1. This is ______ apple.
2. These _______ cars.
3. _______ are yellow bananas over there.
4. That _______ a fox.
5. It _______ a story-book.
6. Is_____ your grandpa?

7. These are _______ （pencil）.
8. ______ is picture of my family.
9. ______ this a pencil?
10. These ______ Chinese.

C. Translating Practice

I. Translate the sentences into English.

1. 那是什么？

____

2. 这些是什么？

____

3. 那些是西兰花（broccoli）吗？

____

4. 这些是你的作业本（exercise book）吗？

____

5. — 这是什么？
   — 是 Lucy 的风筝（kite）。

____

II. Translate the sentences into Chinese.

1. — Are these your books?
   — Yes, they are.

____

2. — Are those bears?
   — No, they are not.

____

3. — What's this in English?
   — It is a toy.

____

4. — What are those in English?
   — They are roses.

____

5. — Is this your umbrella?
   — No, it isn't.

____

Unit Three
Growing Up

Part One: Phonics

Part Two: Dialogue

Part Three: Text

Part Four: Play — The Little Tadpoles Looking for Their Mother

Part Five: Language Skills

Part One: Phonics

A. 元音字母 a；e；a + silent e；e+silent e

元音字母“a”和“e”的拼读发音及各自加上不发音字母“e”的拼读音

1. 拼读发音方式。

当一个单词只有一个元音时，该元音应该发短音，但是，当这个单词后面加上字母“e”，则该元音就要读它本身的字母音，而字母“e”只起到让前面的元音发其字母音的作用，自己是不发音的。例如，hat—hate，其中单词“hate”的元音字母“a”读作其字母音，即在字母“ABCDE...”中的发音。也就是说，字母“e”只起到了使“a”从其短音拼读音到字母音转化的作用。我们把母“e”叫作不发音“e”。同样，字母“e”后面有不发音“e”时，第一个字母“e”读作其本身的字母音，而不是读成拼读音中的短音。例如，单词“can”，其中的“a”发短音，如果结尾加上“e”，变为 cane，元音“a”就发其字母音了，而“e”不发音。同样，单词“gene”中，第一个字母“e”读作字母音。其他这样拼读的单词如 date，cake，gate，name，athlete 等。

2. 听一听，学一学字母“a”和“e”的拼读发音。

(1) cat dad fat sad ham hat

(2) pet get red ten hell well

(3) cake gate mate name game grape
(4) Pete gene delete eve these Chinese

3. 仔细听，然后做句子一口气快读练习。

(1) This cat likes jam and ham with apple.
(2) Dad is mad and sad for he is too fat.
(3) The bell fell into the well.
(4) Teddy has ten elephants.
(5) The plane at the gate is late.
(6) Cane and Jane make milkshakes and cup cakes.
(7) Steve and Pete compete at music.
(8) It's a beautiful scene in the dene.

4. 听一听下列的韵律英语，并熟练朗读。

Pat-a-cake, pat-a-cake,
Baker's man,
Bake me a cake
As fast as you can.
Roll it and pat it
And mark it with a B
And put it in the oven for baby and me.

Just look at Dave.
Can you see him wave
As he comes out of the cave?

Did you forget my name?
What a shame!
What a shame!

Hurry, hurry, Kate!
Don't be late
For your date.

We are Chinese,
If you please.
Whose are these?
They belong to the Japanese.

B. 字母 i； i + silent e，元音字母“i”加上不发音字母“e”的拼读音

1. 拼读发音方式。

当一个单词只有一个元音时，该元音应该发短音，但是当这个单词后面加上字母“e”，则该元音就要读它本身的字母音，而字母“e”只起到让前面的元音发其字母音的作用，自己是不发音的。例如，mik—mike，“mike”中的元音字母“i”读其字母音。即在字母“HIJKL…”中的发音。也就是说，字母“e”只起到了使“i”从其短音拼读音到字母音转化的作用。我们把字母“e”叫作不发音“e”。例如，pin，其中的字母“i”发短音，如果结尾加上“e”，变为 pine，元音“i”就发其字母音了，而“e”不发音。其他这样拼读的单词如 time，fine，wine，hide 等。

2. 听一听，学一学字母“i”和 i + silent e 的拼读发音。

(1) ink infant igloo Indian big pig hill ill kid

(2) kite white line like site pine bite fine

3. 仔细听，然后做句子一口气快读练习。

(1) Here is a big hill and there is a mill on the hill.

(2) The little kid is kidding with rich Bill.

(3) The grapes on the vine are used to make wine.

(4) Mike is riding his fine bike.

4. 听一听下列的韵律英语，并熟练朗读。

Silly Billy! Silly Billy!
Silly Billy loves lily.
Why is Silly Billy silly?
Why does Silly Billy love lily?
Silly Billy isn’t silly.

Three blind mice,
Three blind mice.
See how they run,
See how they run.
They all ran after the farmer's wife,
Who cut off their tails with a carving knife.
Did you ever see such a thing in your life,
As three blind mice?

C. 字母 o；o + silent e，元音字母“o”加上不发音字母“e”的拼读音

1. 拼读发音方式。

当一个单词只有一个元音时，该元音应该发短音，但是当这个单词后面加上字母“e”时，则该元音就要发它本身的字母音，而字母“e”只起到让前面的元音发其字母音的作用，自己是不发音的。例如，cop—cope，“cope”中的元音字母“o”读作其字母音，即在字母“...MOPQ...”中的音。也就是说，字母“e”只起到了使“o”从其短音拼读音到字母音转化的作用。我们把字母“e”叫作不发音字母“e”。同样，字母“o”后面有不发音的字母“e”时，字母“o”读作其本身的字母音，而不是拼读音中的短音。例如，cod，其中的“o”发短音，如果结尾加上“e”，则变为 code，元音“o”就发其字母音了，而“e”不发音。其他这样拼读的单词如 hope，stone，note 等。

2. 听一听，学一学字母“o”和 **o + silent** e 的拼读发音。

(1) ox box fox hot pot hop top cop not pop

(2) rose smoke joke coke hole mole pose nose home

3. 仔细听，然后做句子一口气快读练习。

(1) I can hop, hop, hop and I can hop to the top.

(2) My pot is not so hot.

(3) Put a rose on your nose and make a pose.

(4) My home is in Rome.

4. 听一听下列的韵律英语，并熟练朗读。

Pease porridge hot

Pease porridge hot,
Pease porridge cold.
Pease porridge in the pot
Nine days old.
Some like it hot.
Some like it cold.
Some like it in the pot
Nine days old.

Little Bo Peep

Little Bo Beep
Has lost her sleep,
And can't tell where to find them;
Leave them alone,
And they'll come home,
Wagging their tails behind them.
Little Bo Peep
Fell fast asleep,
And dreamt she heard them bleating;
But when she awoke,
She found it a joke,
For they were still all fleeting.

D. 字母 u； u + silent e，元音字母"u"加上不发音字母"e"的拼读音

1. 拼读发音方式。

当一个单词只有一个元音时，该元音应该发短音，但是当这个单词后面加上字母"e"，则该元音就要读它本身的字母音，而字母"e"只起到让前面的元音发其字母音的作用，自己是不发音的。

例如，mat—mate，“mate”中的元音字母“a”读作其字母音，即在字母“ABCDE…”中的发音。也就是说，字母“e”只起到了使字母“a”从其短音拼读音到字母音转化的作用。我们把字母“e”叫作不发音“e”。同样，元音字母“u”后面有不发音的字母“e”时，字母“u”就读作其本身的字母音，而不是拼读音中的短音。例如，单词 cut，其中的“u”发短音，如果结尾加上字母“e”，变为 cute，元音“u”就发其字母音了，而“e”不发音。其他这样拼读的单词如 use，mule，huge，rude 等。

2. 听一听，学一学字母“u”和 **u + silent** e 的拼读发音。

(1) run sun bug hug cut nut umbrella underwear upset

(2) use fuse muse cute mute mule duke

3. 仔细听，然后做句子一口气快读练习。

(1) I run in the sun and hug my bug.

(2) She can cut the nut but don't cut the thumb.

(3) He sat down to muse about how to use a fuse.

(4) They are cute when they are mute.

4. 听一听下列的韵律英语，并熟练朗读。

Up, up, umbrellas.
Up, up, up!
Uu says u, u.
Up, up,up!

Humpty Dumpty

Humpty Dumpty sat on a wall.
Humpty Dumpty had a great fall.
All the king's horses
And all the king's men
Couldn't put Humpty
Together again.

From Head to Toe

I use my eyes to see.
I use my mouth to talk.
I use my ears to hear
And my feet to walk.
I use my nose to smell.
I use my teeth to bite.
I use my head to nod
And my hand to write.

Part Two: Dialogue

Dialogue 1

Jim: Tom, be careful! Drive slowly.

Tom: Ok, It's so foggy today.

Jim: I haven't seen such heavy fog for months.

Tom: I hope it will be fine by 10.

Jim: So do I. I hate the foggy day.

Tom: Tomorrow will be a sunny day.

Words and Expressions

careful ['keəf(ə)l] *adj*. 仔细的，小心的

foggy ['fɒgi] *adj*. 有雾的，雾气朦胧的

sunny ['sʌni] *adj*. 和煦的，照到阳光的

Decide whether the following statements are True (T) or False (F).

( ) 1.Jim asks Tom to drive quickly.

( ) 2.It's rainy today.

( ) 3.Jim hasn't seen such heavy fog for months.

( ) 4.Tom hopes that the fog will disappear by 10 o'clock.

( ) 5.Tomorrow will be a sunshine day.

Dialogue 2

Jim: It's raining heavily outside.

Tom: I didn't take my umbrella. It's so bad.

Jim: I took mine, you can go with me.

Tom: Thanks. Shall I wait for a moment?

Jim: Sure, it's so heavy now.

Tom: It's good for the crops anyway.

Words and Expressions

heavily ['hevɪli] *adv.* 大量地

umbrella [ʌm'brelə] *n.* 雨伞

crop [krɒp] *n.* 农作物，庄稼

be good for 对……有好处

Decide whether the following statements are True (T) or False (F).

( ) 1.It's snowing heavily outside.

( ) 2. Tom takes his umbrella with him.

( ) 3. Jim would like to share his umbrella with Tom.

( ) 4.Tom will go with Tim together to use one umbrella.

( ) 5.Tom thinks the heavy rain is not good for the crops.

Dialogue 3

Jim: It's already spring and flowers smell so good.

Tom: Yes, the weather is sunny.

Jim: And the grass turns green.

Tom: It's very warm now.

Jim: I don't have to wear the thick clothes any more.

Tom: Let's go to the park to have a walk.

Jim: OK.

Words and Expressions

smell [smel] *v.* 嗅，闻

weather ['weðə(r)] *n.* 天气，气象

turn [tɜ:n] *v.* 使变为

warm [wɔ:m] *adj.* 暖和的，温暖的

wear [weə(r)] *v.* 穿着，戴着

thick [θɪk] *adj.* 厚的

have a walk 散步

Decide whether the following statements are True (T) or False (F).

(　　) 1. It's spring now.

(　　) 2. The weather is sunny.

(　　) 3. The grass turns yellow.

(　　) 4. Jim doesn't have to wear the thin clothes any more.

(　　) 5. Tom asks Jim to have a walk in the park.

Dialogue 4

Mary: The weather outside couldn't be better.

Jenny: How about bringing a camera with us? We could take some photos of flowers.

Mary: Brilliant idea!

Jenny: By the way, we could invite some friends to join us.

Mary: Excellent. That's exactly what I have in mind.

Jenny: I'll give Jim and Nancy a call.

Mary: OK. Tell them we meet at the school gate.

Words and Expressions

camera ['kæm(ə)rə] *n.* 照相机，摄影机

photo ['fəʊtəʊ] *n.* 照片，相片

flower ['flaʊə(r)] *n.* 花

brilliant ['brɪliənt] *adj.* 才华横溢的，明亮的

invite [ɪn'vaɪt] *v.* 邀请

join [dʒɔɪn] *v.* 加入，参加

excellent ['eksələnt] *adj.* 优秀的，太好了

exactly [ɪg'zæktli] *adv.* 恰恰，确切地，精确地

gate [geɪt] *n.* 门

Decide whether the following statements are True (T) or False (F).

( ) 1.Mary thinks the weather outside will be better.

( ) 2.May advised bringing a mobile phone with them.

( ) 3.Mary thinks that it's a good idea to take a camera.

( ) 4.Jenny wants to invite some friends to join them.

( ) 5.Their friends will meet them at the park gate.

Part Three: Text

What is it? It is a palace for Emperors.

Is it the oldest palace in China? Yes, it is./No, it isn't.

What is that? That is a yak.

What color is the yak? It is white.

What is this? This is Peking Opera.

Is it terrific? Yes, it is. /No, it isn't.

What is that? That is Qipao.

Is it elegant? Yes, it is. /No, it isn't.

What is this? This is Dongbula.

Is it a musical instrument? Yes, it is. /No, it isn't.

What is that? That is Jiangshui.

Is it a kind of drink in Gansu Province? Yes, it is./No, it isn't.

Words and Expressions

palace ['pæləs] *n.* 宫殿

Eg. 1. It seems to be an abandoned palace.
这似乎是一座废弃的宫殿。

2. But what about the room in the palace?
那宫殿里的那间屋子怎么办？

emperor ['empərə(r)] *n.* 皇帝

Eg. 1. However he was not advisable and welcome in politics as an Emperor.
然而，作为一个皇帝，他在政治上并不明智，也不受人欢迎。

2. He must be the poorest emperor ever.
他肯定是世上最可怜的皇帝。

people ['piːp(ə)l] *n.* 人，人类

Eg. 1. I like friendly people.
我喜欢友善的人。

2. Some people are always lucky.
有些人总是很幸运。

terrific [tə'rɪfɪk] *adj.* 极好的

Eg. 1. This is a terrific gift.
这是一个极好的礼物。

2. The beer is terrific.
这啤酒太棒了。

elegant ['elɪgənt] *adj.* 优雅的

Eg. 1. She is elegant.
她很优雅。

2. He is one of the richest and most elegant gentlemen.

他是最富有、最优雅的绅士之一。

popular ['pɒpjələ(r)] *adj.* 受欢迎的

Eg. 1. The song has become very popular.

这首歌正在广泛流行开来。

2. She is popular in China.

她在中国很受欢迎。

Language Focus

I. Make a sentence with the words given below.

1. an / story / it / is / interesting / ?

is / it / yes

2. it / what / is / ?

is / a / boring / it / book

3. is / that / what / ?

that / a / tree / is / tall

4. what / it / is / ?

it / a / rope / long / is

5. it / a / restaurant / is / ?

no / is / it / not / , / is / it / hotel / a

II. Translating

Put Chinese into English.

1. 这是什么？ 这是一本有趣的书。
2. 那是什么？ 那是一把椅子。
3. 这是一个银行吗？ 是的。
4. 那是这个城市最高的楼吗？ 是的。
5. 那是你妈妈吗？ 不，那是我的小姨，她是我妈妈的妹妹。

Put English into Chinese.

1. What is that? That is a colorful kite.
2. Is it the only river in this country? Yes, it is.

3. What is that building over there? It is Eiffel Tower.

4. What is this? It is a lamp.

5. What is that? It is a boat.

III. Reading Comprehension

Choose the best answer to each of the following questions or incomplete sentences.

At school I have a good friend. He is an English boy. His name is Tom. He is twelve. We are in No. 3 Middle School. We are not in the same class. He is in Class 2, Grade1. Tom's sister is not a student. Her name is Jane. She is five. She is a nice girl.

Miss Gao is my English teacher. She is thirty. Mr Wang is Tom's Chinese teacher. He is thirty, too. They are good teachers.

1. Tom is _________

A. English

B. American

C. Chinese

D. French

2. Tom is in_________

A. Class four, Grade Two

B. Class Two, Grade One

C. Class four, Grade One

D. Class Three, Grade One

3. How old is Jane? _________

A. four

B. five

C. twelve

D. six

4. Miss Gao is my _________ teacher.

A. English

B. Chinese

C. math

D. French

5. Tom and I _________ in the same class, we _________ in the same school .

A. are, aren't

B. are, are

C. aren't, are

D. aren't, aren't

Part Four: Play

The Little Tadpoles Looking for Their Mother

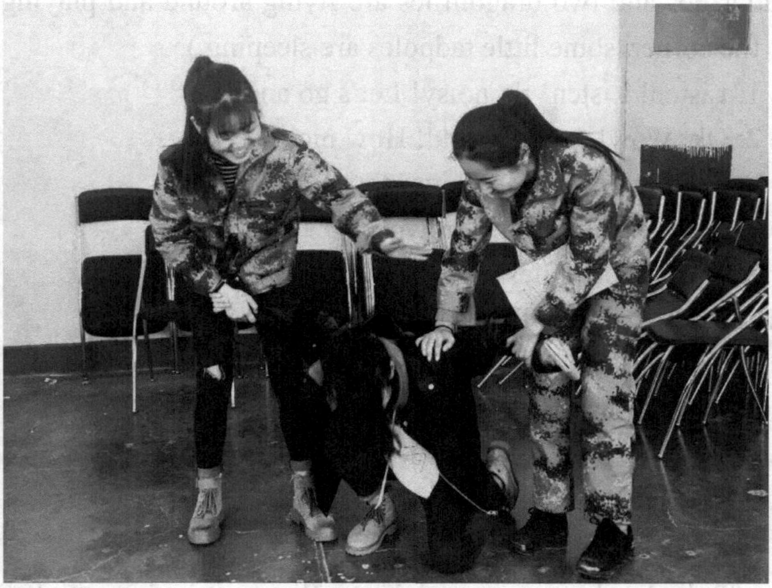

Characters:

Narrator 旁白

Butterfly 小蝴蝶

Dragonfly 小蜻蜓

Tadpole 小蝌蚪

Fish 鱼

Duck 鸭子

Frog 青蛙

Scene 1

Narrator: This is a big and nice pool. The water is clean and the lotuses are beautiful. One morning, some butterflies and dragonflies are flying over the pool.

Butterflies: Hello!

Dragonflies: Hi!

Mothers: Be careful! Have a good day! Goodbye!

Butterflies & Dragonflies: Bye, Mom!

(Two butterflies and two dragonflies are flying around and playing. At the corner, some little tadpoles are sleeping.)

Tadpole 1: Listen! Listen! So noisy! Let's go and see.

Tadpole 2: Ok, Wow! A new world! How nice!

Butterflies & Dragonflies: Good morning.

Tadpoles: Good morning. Who are you?

Butterflies: We're butterflies.

Dragonflies: We're dragonflies. Who are you?

Tadpoles: We're little tadpoles. Let's be friends.

Butterflies & Dragonflies: All right! Let's sing and dance.

Tadpoles: OK!

Scene 2

Narrators: Tadpoles, butterflies and dragonflies are singing and dancing. And then butterflies' mother and dragonflies' mother are coming.

Mothers: My darling!

Butterflies & Dragonflies: Mummy! Mummy! These are little tadpoles, our new friends.

Mothers: Nice to meet you.

Tadpoles: Nice to meet you.

Mothers: Darling, are you hungry?

Butterflies & Dragonflies: Yes, yes, we are hungry.

Mothers: Let's go home!

Butterflies & Dragonflies: Ok. Goodbye, little tadpoles.
Tadpoles: Bye!

Scene 3

Narrator: The little tadpoles are swimming in the pool. They're sad now.
Tadpole 2: Where's our mummy?
Tadpole 1: Don't cry. Don't cry. Let's go and look for her.
(The fish comes)
Tadpoles: Mummy! Mummy!
Fish: Good morning, little tadpoles.
Tadpole 2: Good morning. Madam. Are you our Mummy?
Fish: No, I'm not.
Tadpole 1: Where's our Mummy?
Fish: Sorry, I don't know.
(The duck comes)
Duck: Good morning, little tadpoles.
Tadpole 1: Good morning. Madam. Are you our Mummy?
Duck: No, I'm not.
Tadpole 2: Where's our Mummy?
Duck: Your mummy has four legs. You can go there and look for her.
(The Tortoise comes)
Tortoise: Good morning, little tadpoles.
Tadpole 2: Good morning. Madam. Are you our Mummy?
Tortoise: No, I'm not your Mummy. Your mummy is green. She's over there.
(The fog comes)
Tadpoles: Mummy! Mummy!
Frog: Here I am! Here I am!
Tadpoles: Mummy! Mummy! We miss you.

Frog: Honey, I miss you, too. Let's swim together, honey.
Tadpoles: We love you, Mummy. Let's go.

（师生改编剧本）

Words and Expressions

butterfly ['bʌtəflaɪ] *n.* 蝴蝶
dragonfly ['drægənflaɪ] *n.* 蜻蜓
tadpole ['tædpəʊl] *n.* 蝌蚪
frog [frɒg] *n.* 青蛙
pool [puːl] *n.* 池塘
clean [kliːn] *adj.* 干净的
lotus ['ləʊtəs] *n.* 莲花
fly [flaɪ] *v.* 飞
corner ['kɔːnə(r)] *n.* 拐角
noisy ['nɔɪzi] *adj.* 喧闹的
sad [sæd] *adj.* 悲伤的
leg [leg] *n.* 腿
tortoise ['tɔːtəs] *n.* 龟
together [tə'geðə(r)] *adv.* 一起

look for 寻找
be careful 小心
nice to meet you 见到你很高兴
go home 回家
here I am 我在这儿

Listening Practice

I. Bingo game

Work in groups, one student read about the script of *The Little Tadpoles Looking for Their Mother*, other students listen carefully, when they hear the adjective from the script, say "Bingo", and write the word in the form quickly, and then he/she wins. And take turns, and change the words into Verbs, Nouns, etc.

words	adjective	verbs	nouns	prepositions	adverbs	conjunctions
student 1						
student 2						
student 3						
student 4						
student 5						

II. Dictation

Listen to the passage three times and supply the missing information.

One beautiful morning, some ___1___ and ___2___ are flying over the ___3___. Some little ___4___ are sleeping at the ___5___. They soon become very good friends, and they are singing and dancing. When butterflies' mother and dragonflies' mother come, the little tadpoles are ___6___ because they don't know where their mother is. They decide to ___7___ their mummy. Duck tells them their mummy has four ___8___. Tortoise tells them their mummy is ___9___. Finally, they find their mummy, ___10___.

Reading Practice

I. Read and choose

1. Which of the following statement is True?

A. Tadpoles are happy because they don't miss their mummy.

B. Butterflies and tadpoles are flying over the pool.

C. Duck is tadpoles' mother.

D. Tadpoles are very happy because finally they find their mummy.

2. The butterflies and dragonflies are playing over the ______.

A. grass

B. tree

C. river

D. pool

3. Butterflies, ______ and tadpoles are soon becoming good friends.

A. dragonflies

B. duck

C. fish

D. frog

4. Little tadpoles think that _____ is their mummy at first.

A. monkey

B. fish

C. duck

D. tortoise

5. Finally, little tadpoles find their mummy, ______.

A. duck

B. tadpole

C. tortoise

D. frog

II. Read and answer

1. Who are the butterflies and dragonflies? Are they little tadpoles' friends?

2. How do the little tadpoles find their mummy?

3. Where are the little tadpoles sleeping?

4. If you were the little tadpole, what would you do, try to find your mother or just leave it?

5. Who is little tadpoles' mother?

Speaking Practice

I. Role Play

Suppose you were the little tadpoles, would you look for your mummy, or just sing, dance and play? Use the following functional sentences, you have to add your own expressions when it is necessary.

- Hi, we are little tadpoles.
- Will you make a friend with me?
- I like dancing and singing.

- Where are you?
- Bye for now.
- Nice to meet you.
- Bye.

II. Problem-Solving

Think of appropriate lines for the animal in the picture above.

III. Delivery Game

The teacher divides the whole class into four or five groups, queue the students. The teacher writes a long sentence from the script in a piece of paper, just let the first student read and recite it for one minute, and let the student retell the sentence to the second student, the second to the third, when the sentence is delivered to the last student, he/she should write it on the blackboard, and translate it into Chinese. The group which has got great speed and relative accuracy wins.

Translating Practice

I. Translate the sentences into Chinese.

Work in pairs, one student reads the following sentences, and the other translates the sentences into Chinese in spoken way. (Add extra sentences from the scripts if necessary.)

1. One morning, some butterflies and dragonflies are flying over the pool!
2. These are little tadpoles, our new friends.
3. The little tadpoles are swimming in the pool.
4. Your mummy has four legs. You can go there and look for her.
5. Let’s swim together, honey.

II. Translate the sentences into English.

Work in pairs, one student reads the following sentences, and the other translates the sentences into English in spoken way. (Add extra sentences from the scripts if necessary.)

1. 见到你很高兴！
2. 她在那儿。
3. 小心点。
4. 你是谁？
5. 别哭，别哭。

Writing Practice

Write a summary of *The Little Tadpoles Looking for Their Mother* in 50 words.

"Ws" / "Who"	doing what	whom	where	when

Part Five: Language Skills

Grammar

Be 动词的一般现在时的形式

be 动词的一般现在时有三种形式，即 am，is，are。

1. 如果主语是第一人称 I（我），be 动词用 am。

如：

I am a student. 我是一名学生。

I am 还可缩写成 I'm。

如：

I'm David. 我是大卫。

2. 如果主语是 you（你，你们），they （他们，它们，她们）或名词复数（两个以上的人或物），be 动词必须用 are。

如：

Are you a boy? 你是男孩吗？

Tom and Lily are good friends. 汤姆和莉莉是好朋友。

They are at home. 他们在家。

are 与主语还可缩写。

如：

We are= We're， They are =They're， You are = You're。are 与 not 可缩写成 aren't。

如：

They aren't students. 他们不是学生。

但是 am 与 not 不能缩写。

3. 如果主语是单数名词、不可数名词或单数第三人称代词（he, she, it），be 动词用 is。

如：

My mother is a cook. 我的妈妈是一名厨师。

He is a student. 他是一名学生。

is 也可与主语缩写。

如：

He is = He's, My mother is = My mother's 等。

但是 This is 不可缩写，而 is 与 not 可缩写成 isn't。

如：

This isn't a book. 这不是一本书。

以下是人称代词与 be 动词搭配的表格及缩写形式。

I	am	I'm
He	is	He's
She		She's
It		It's
We	are	We're
You		You're
They		They're

Exercises

I. Complete the sentences and passage.

A. Complete each of the following sentences with am, is, are.

1. I _____ a student.

A. is B. am C. be D. are

2. You ____ a doctor.

A. is B. am C. be D. are

3. It_____ a car.

A. is B. am C. be D. are

4. They ____ cars.

A. is B. am C. be D. are

5. ____ your mother in China?

A. Is B. Am C. Be D. Are

6. _____ your friends in New York?

A. Is B. Am C. Be D. Are

7. These _____ buses.

A. is B. am C. be D. are

8. Those _____oranges.

A. is B. am C. be D. are

9. Here ______ some flowers for you.

A. is B. am C. be D. are

10. My parents _______very busy every day.

A. is B. am C. be D. are

11. He _______ at school.

A. is B. am C. be D. are

12. Jane and Tom _______ my friends.

A. is B. am C. be D. are

13. They _______ from China.

A. is B. am C. be D. are

14. How old ______ you?

A. is B. am C. be D. are

15. Which dog _____ yours?

A. is B. am C. be D. are

16. I _____OK. And you?

A. is B. am C. be D. are

17. ______ they excited when he heard the news?

A. Is B. Am C. Be D. Are

18. ______ there a Chinese school in New York?

A. Is B. Am C. Be D. Are

19. The dog ______ tall and fat.

A. is B. am C. be D. are

20. The man with big eyes _____ a teacher.

A. is B. am C. be D. are

B. Complete the following passage with am, is, are.

I ___1___ a girl. My name ___2___ Mary. I ___3___ in Class 2, Grade 7. I ___4___ 12 years old. Here ___5___ my family photo. Look! These ___6___ my parents and those ___7___ my grandparents. This boy ___8___ my brother. He ___9___ 15 years old now. That is my cat, Mimi. It __10__ very lovely.

II. Translation Practice

A. Translate the following sentences into English.

1. 我是一个老师。

____

2. 我是一名学生。

____

3. 这支笔是我的。

____

4. 我的名字叫玛丽。

____

5. 我们大家都在这儿。

____

B. Translate the following sentences into Chinese.

1. The girl is Jack’s friend.

____

2. Is your brother in the classroom?

____

3. He is my English teacher.

____

4. My sister’s name is Lucy.

____

5. It is sunny today.

____

Unit Four
Trust

Part One: Phonics

Part Two: Dialogue

Part Three: Text

Part Four: Play — The Wolf and the Seven Little Goats

Part Five: Language Skills

Part One: Phonics

A. 长音“a”——字母组合“ai”和“ay”

1. 拼读发音方式。

字母组合“ai”和“ay”都是长音，都发字母“a”的字母音。其发音方法如下：舌头位置由低向高滑动，先发字母“e”的拼读短音，之后，下颚迅速向上合拢。口形由字母“e”的拼读短音迅速向字母“i”的拼读短音滑动，中间要停顿。包含这个发音的单词如 rain，tail，day，way，pay，play 等。

2. 听一听，学一学字母组合“ai”和“ay”的拼读发音。

(1) mail jail pail paint entertain grain straight tailor

(2) play say may again brain stay jay clay tray sway

3. 仔细听，然后做句子一口气快读练习。

(1) Daisy had a very busy day on Monday.

(2) We wait to buy some bait in the rain.

(3) Kay had to wait for Jay at the bay.

(4) May will stay with Kay all day in the hay.

4. 听一听下列的韵律英语，并熟练朗读。

In the Rain

In the rain,
Ran fast in the rain,

The train ran fast in the rain!
Who will take the train
In the rain?

Going Home Rhyme

Now our day is done,
We've all had lots of fun.
Tomorrow is another day,
And we'll come back to play.

Ray and Jay

Ray and Jay sit in jail all day.
They raided a mail train on its way to Spain.
Ray was afraid that the raid would fail and they wouldn't get paid.
They waited in vain and suffered great pain when they were sent straight to jail without bail.
Jay was a sailor before the raid, now he's a tailor sewing mailbags in jail.

B. 长音“e”——字母组合“ea”和“ee”

1. 拼读发音方式。

字母组合“ea”和“ee”都是长音，都发字母“e”的字母音。发音方法如下：舌头靠近下齿，舌头前部抬高，但是不接触到下齿，唇形扁，接近合上。嘴角向两侧拉伸，像是在微笑。包含这个发音的单词如 eat，meat，tree 等。

2. 听一听，学一学字母组合“ea”和“ee”的拼读发音。

(1) read eagle cream heat team leaf beast beach treat jean

(2) jeep coffee feet beef seed bee cheek feed sneeze teeth

3. 仔细听，然后做句子一口气快读练习。

(1) Eating cream on the beach is my dream.

(2) The leaves on the trees rustle in the breeze.

(3) The queen eats cheese and green sweets.

(4) Feel free to meet my three teenagers.

4. 听一听下列的韵律英语，并熟练朗读。

A Sailor

A sailor went to
Sea, sea, sea,
To see what he could
See, see, see.
But all that he could
See, see, see,
Was the bottom of the deep blue
Sea, sea, sea.

Dreaming

Dreaming of meat and something to eat.
Lying on beaches in tropical heat.
Treating each other to fresh cream and peaches.
Feasting and dreaming on far eastern beaches.

Jeepers Creeers

Jeepers, creepers, where did you get those peepers?
Jeepers, creepers, where did you get those eyes?

This Little Pig

This little pig went to market;
This little pig stayed at home;
This little pig had a roast beef;
This little pig had none;
And this little pig cried,
" Wee, wee, wee, wee, wee!"
All the way home.

C. 长音“i”——字母组合“ie”和“y”

1. 拼读发音方式。

字母组合“ie”和“y”都是长音，都发字母“i”的字母音。发音方法如下：舌头靠近下齿，舌头前部抬高，但是不接触到下齿，唇形扁，接近合上。嘴角向两侧拉伸，像是在微笑。包含这个发音的单词如 lie，die，why，cry 等。

2. 听一听，学一学字母组合“ie”和“y”的拼读发音。

(1) pie die lie

(2) shy sky fly type try

3. 仔细听，然后做句子一口气快读练习。

(1) He tried the pie but he denies he is on a diet.

(2) He knew if he didn't comply he would die.

(3) The typist cried for the coming typhoon.

(4) She tried to fly her kite in the sky.

4. 听一听下列的韵律英语，并熟练朗读。

She cried because he lied,
She said he never tried.
He said he didn't lie,
And now he wants to try, but she said love has died,
Only she complied.

There is pie in my eye.
Will I cry?
Will I die?
Though I am shy.
I will not lie.
It might cause a sty,
But I deny that I will die or cry
From the pie in my eye.

Part Two: Dialogue

Dialgoue 1

Jenny: Are you feeling any better?

Mary: Yes, I'm recovering.

Jenny: Get well soon.

Mary: One month later I will be as strong as a bull.

Jenny: I'm glad to hear that.

Mary: Thanks for your kindness.

Words and Expressions

recover [rɪ'kʌvə(r)] *v.* 恢复

bull ['bʊl] *n.* 公牛

kindness ['kaɪndnəs] *n.* 好意

Decide whether the following statements are True (T) or False (F).

(　　) 1. Mary is ill.

(　　) 2. Mary is getting better.

(　　) 3. Mary will be a bull one month later.

(　　) 4. Jenny is worried about Mary.

(　　) 5. Mary is happy that Jenny is getting better.

Dialogue 2

Jenny: You sound kind of sick.

Susan: I'm under the weather.

Jenny: What's troubling you?

Susan: I think I'm sick from the climbing yesterday.

Jenny: You must be away from exercises for a long time.

Susan: You're right. It's a torture for me.

Jenny: That's too much for illness.

Susan: I haven't been feeling well, but I don't know what's wrong with me.

Jenny: It seems like office workers are prone to suffer from bad health nowadays.

Susan: Yeah, many people break down these days due to working stress.

Jenny: I suggest you go to see a doctor.

Susan: I will go tomorrow.

Words and Expressions

trouble ['trʌb(ə)l] *v.* 折磨

climb [klaɪm] *v.* 爬

exercise ['eksəsaɪz] *n.* 运动

torture ['tɔːtʃə(r)] *n.* 折磨

prone [prəʊn] *adj.* 有……倾向的

nowadays ['naʊədeɪz] *adv.* 现今

suggest [sə'dʒest] *v.* 建议

under the weather 身体不适

for a long time 很长时间

suffer from 患……病

break down 毁掉

working stress 工作压力

Decide whether the following statements are True (T) or False (F).

( ) 1. Susan is in good health.

( ) 2. Susan got ill from the climbing yesterday.

( ) 3. Susan needs exercises.

( ) 4. Susan is under too much working stress.

( ) 5. Susan hates to see doctor.

Dialogue 3

Jenny: Susan, you look so fat.

Susan: Not only fat, but also tired.

Jenny: What's your weight?

Susan: 150 pounds.

Jenny: Put yourself on a diet, otherwise you will be too fat.

Susan: I can't bear eating less.

Jenny: That doesn't mean to eat less necessarily.
Susan: So what do you mean by diet?
Jenny: That means you should eat foods containing less fat.
Susan: I just can't bear that. I have a meat tooth.
Jenny: So you may work out regularly.
Susan: What exercise may I take part in?
Jenny: At the beginning, you may jog. Jogging is an easy fat-consuming exercise.
Susan: How long should I jog?
Jenny: You may jog two miles first, and then run longer and longer.
Susan: Well, tell me how you keep fit.
Jenny: Swimming and playing tennis.
Susan: Pretty good!
Jenny: Sports can make us strong and healthy.

Words and Expressions

weight [weɪt] *n.* 重量
bear [beə(r)] *v.* 忍受
necessarily [ˌnesə'serəli] *adv.* 必要地
contain [kən'teɪn] *v.* 包含
jog [dʒɒg] *v.* 慢跑
fat-consuming 脂肪消耗
work out 锻炼
on a diet 遵守饮食特别规定的

Decide whether the following statements are True (T) or False (F).

(   ) 1. Susan is not only fat, but also tried.
(   ) 2. Susan should put herself on a diet.
(   ) 3. Diet means you should eat less.
(   ) 4. Jogging is an easy fat-consuming exercise.
(   ) 5. Sports can make us strong and healthy, so we should go swimming and play tennis regularly.

Part Three: Text

I am a Chinese student. My name is Xiao Ping. I am brave.

He is a British boy. His name is John. He is smart.

She is a French girl. Her name is Irina. She is beautiful.

You are a Greek policewoman. You are special.

Michael is an American singer. He is famous.

We are Korean young men. We are happy and hard-working.

They are Japanese singers. They are pretty and popular.

They are German engineers. They are intelligent and diligent.

Words and Expressions

student ['stjuːd(ə)nt] *n.* 学生

Eg. 1. He is an outstanding student.

他是一个杰出的学生。

2. I am not your best student, but you are my best teacher.

我并非是您最出众的学生，但您是我最好的老师。

strong [strɒŋ] *adj.* 强壮的；坚固的，结实的

Eg. 1. This chair is not very strong.

这把椅子不太结实。

2. We are strong!

我们是强大的！

smart [smɑːt] *adj.* 聪明的

Eg. 1. Monkeys are very smart animals.

猴子是很聪明的动物。

2. He is a smart kid.

他是一个聪明的孩子。

policewoman [pə'liːswʊmən] *n.* 女警察

Eg. 1. Is that policewoman short or tall?

那个女警察是矮还是高？

2. Is she a policewoman?

她是一个警察吗？

special ['speʃ(ə)l] *adj.* 特别的

Eg. 1. Greece is a special case.

希腊是一个特例。

2. Janelle and Billy held a special birthday party for Max on Sunday.

詹妮尔和比利在上周日为马克斯举办了一场别开生面的生日宴会。

singer ['sɪŋə(r)] *n.* 歌手

Eg. 1. He is a handsome and fashionable singer!

他是时尚帅气歌手！

2. I know she is a good singer.

我知道她是一个很不错的歌手。

famous ['feɪməs] *adj.* 著名的

Eg. 1. She was a good teacher and a famous writer.

她既是一位优秀教师，又是一位著名的作家。

2. Lanzhou is famous for beef noodles.

兰州以牛肉面闻名。

hardworking ['hɑːd,wɜːkɪŋ] *adj.* 努力工作的

Eg. 1. Are they just more hardworking?

他们只是更不辞辛苦？

2. You are a good hardworking man.

你是一个刻苦工作的好人。

pretty ['priti] *adj.* 漂亮的

Eg. 1. Her daughter is now a pretty girl of 18.

她女儿现在一个 18 岁的美少女了。

2. She engages everyone with her pretty girlish ways.

她以漂亮的少女风度迷住了大家。

engineer [endʒɪ'nɪə] *n.* 工程师

Eg. 1. He hopes to be an engineer.

他希望做一名工程设计人员。

2. I work as an engineer.

我是一名工程师。

intelligent [ɪn'telɪdʒ(ə)nt] *adj.* 聪明的

Eg. 1. All human beings are much more intelligent than animals.

所有的人都比动物聪明得多。

2. He is a very intelligent boy.

他是一个很聪明的孩子。

diligent ['dɪlɪdʒ(ə)nt] *adj.* 勤勉的

Eg. 1. He is both wise and diligent, so he makes good in everything.

他既聪明又勤勉，所以每件事他都做得很好。

2. Henry is the most diligent student in our class.

亨利是我们班上最用功的学生。

Chinese [tʃaɪ'niːz] *adj.* 中国的

British ['brɪtɪʃ] *adj.* 英国的

French [frentʃ] *adj.* 法国的

Greek [griːk] *adj.* 希腊的

American [ə'merɪkən] *adj.* 美国的

Korean [kə'riən] *adj.* 韩国的

Japanese [ˌdʒæpə'ni:z] *adj.* 日本的

German ['dʒɜːmən] *adj.* 德国的

Language Focus

I. Make a sentence with the words given below.

1. am / a / i / doctor
   busy / am / i
2. she / a / is /teacher
   is / she / caring
3. is / he / a /policeman
   he / brave / is
4. are / they / singers
   they / friendly / are
5. we / students / are
   are / cheerful / we

II. Translating

Put Chinese into English.

1. 他是一个学生。 他很友好。
2. 她是一个护士。 她很耐心。
3. 我们是教师。 我们很快乐。
4. 他们是工程师。 他们很忙。
5. 你们是老板。 你们很累。

Put English into Chinese.

1. I am a friendly woman.
2. He is a handsome boy.
3. It is an ugly duck.
4. We are brave men.
5. He is a diligent student.

III. Reading Comprehension

Choose the best answer to each of the following questions or incomplete sentences.

There are some new students in my class this term. John is from Tokyo. He speaks Japanese very well. Mike comes from New York. He is twelve years old. Kathy's mother-town is Paris. David lives in Toronto. He is now in our city with his parents. And the tallest girl, Vicky is from Brazil. She likes soccer very much. The other forty students are all Chinese. They get on well with each other.

1. John is from ______.

A. China

B. Japan

C. Japanese

D. the USA

2. Where does Mike come from? ______

A. He is from England.

B. He is from France.

C. He is from the USA.

D. He is from Japan.

3. Which is NOT right? ______

A. David is a Canadian.

B. David's parents are in Canada now.

C. David and his parents are all in China now.

D. David can speak English and French very well.

4. Vicky ______.

A. likes soccer

B. is from Argentina

C. is short

D. doesn't like China

5. There are ______ students in our class.

A. forty

B. forty-three

C. forty-four

D. forty-five

Part Four: Play

The Wolf and the Seven Little Goats

Characters:

Wolf 狼

Mother Goat 羊妈妈

Goat 小羊

Scene 1

Mother Goat: I'm going out. You boys and girls. Don't open the door.

Seven Little Goats: Yes, Mum.

Goat 1: Come back soon, mum, we will miss you.

Mother Goat: Ok, I will be back soon. Please lock the door, my babies.

Seven Little Goats: Ok, Mum. See you later. Bye!

Wolf: Mother Goat is out, I will go to visit the little goats. Hahaha…

Scene 2

Wolf: Come on, children. This is your mother. Open the door.

Seven Little Goats: Oh! No. Your voice is strange. Our mum's voice is very beautiful.

Goat 1: You are not our mum.

Goat 2: Don't open the door.

Goat 3: You are a wolf.

Seven Little Goats: Go away!

Wolf: Oh, they are very clever, en… I have to think something else.

Scene 3

Wolf: Haha, I have a good idea. Let me have a try.

Wolf: Come on, children. This is your mother. Open the door.

Seven Little Goats: Please show your foot.

Goat 4: My mother's foot is white.

Goat 5: Your foot is yellow.

Goat 6: Don't open the door.

Seven Little Goats: You are a wolf.

Wolf: En… I have to think another way.

Scene 4

Wolf: Wow, little goats, my delicious food, I am coming again.

Wolf: Come on, children. This is your mother. Open the door.

Goat 7: This is mother's voice.

Goat 1: Please show your foot.

Goat 2: The foot is white.

Seven Little Goats: Let's open the door.

Wolf: Haha, I am a wolf.

Seven Little Goats: Help! Help!

Scene 5

Mother Goat: Oh! What's the matter! My babies! Where are my children? Where are you? Where are you?

Goat 7: Mommy, I am here!
Mother Goat: Oh, my baby!
Goat 7: The wolf comes and eats us.
Mother Goat: Oh! No! Bad Wolf! I will kill you!
Mother Goat: Here is the wolf. Give me the knife. I will kill you!
Seven Little Goats: Mommy…

（师生改编剧本）

Words and Expressions

goat [gəʊt] *n.* 羊
lock [lɒk] *v.* 锁
child [tʃaɪld] *n.* 孩子
voice [vɔɪs] *n.* 声音
strange [streɪndʒ] *adj.* 奇怪的
something ['sʌmθɪŋ] *pron.* 某事
else [els] *adv.* 其他
foot [fʊt] *n.* 脚
white [waɪt] *n.* 白色
yellow ['jeləʊ] *n.* 黄色
another [ə'nʌðə(r)] *adj.* 另一，另外的
kill [kɪl] *v.* 杀
knife [naɪf] *n.* 刀

go out　出去
open the door　开门
see you later　再见
go away　走开
have a try　试一试

Listening Practice

I. Bingo game

Work in groups, one student read about the script of *The Wolf and the Seven Little Goats*, other students listen carefully, when they hear the adjective from the script, say "Bingo", and write the word in the form quickly, and then he/she wins. And take turns, and change the words into Verbs, Nouns, etc.

words / students	adjective	verbs	nouns	prepositions	adverbs	conjunctions
student 1						
student 2						
student 3						
student 4						
student 5						

II. Dictation

Listen to the passage three times and supply the missing information.

One day, Mother goat is ___1___ and leaves her boys and girls at home. Mother goat asks her children to ___2___ the door. A wolf is very happy to see her out and plans to ___3___ the little goats. He knocks the door for the first time and asks the little goats to open it. The little goats think his ___4___ is very ___5___. For the second time, the wolf changes his voice and asks the little goats to open the door. But the little goats are very ___6___, and ask the wolf to show his ___7___. But, for the third time, the goats ___8___ the door for the wolf. Unfortunately, the wolf eats them and goes to sleep. Mother goat gets home and ___9___ the wolf with the sharp ___10___. All the little goats are rescued.

Reading Practice

I. Read and choose

1. Which of the following statement is True?

A. Mother goat asks little goats to open the door when someone is knocking it.

B. All the little goats are eaten by the wolf.

C. The wolf is killed by the little goats.

D. Mother goat saves all the little goats' lives.

2. _______ visits little goats.

A. A wolf

B. A tiger

C. A lion

D. A bear

3. What color is the wolf's foot?

A. white

B. yellow

C. brown

D. black

4. How many little goats have been eaten by the wolf?

A. seven

B. six

C. five

D. four

5. Mother Goat kills the wolf by _______.

A. gun

B. stick

C. knife

D. axe

II. Read and answer

1. Who is the wolf? Is he the little goats' friend?
2. Why does the wolf ask the little goat to open the door?
3. Where does the Mother goat go?
4. If you were one of the little goats, would you open the door for the wolf?
5. What is the wolf killed by?

Speaking Practice

I. Role Play

Suppose you were one of the little goats, would you go for help, or hide behind the door when the wolf is going to eat you? Use the following functional sentences, you have to add your own expressions when it is necessary.

- Help, help.
- Bad wolf
- Keep quiet.
- Shut up!

II. Problem-Solving

Think of appropriate lines for the animal in the picture above.

III. Delivery Game

The teacher divides the whole class into four or five groups, queue the students. The teacher writes a long sentence from the script in a piece of paper, just let the first student read and recite it for one minute, and let the student retell the sentence to the second student, the second to the third, when the sentence is delivered to the last student, he/she should write it on the blackboard, and translate it into Chinese. The group which has got great speed and relative accuracy wins.

Translating Practice

I. Translate the sentences into Chinese.

Work in pairs, one student reads the following sentences, and the other translates the sentences into Chinese in spoken way. (Add extra sentences from the scripts if necessary.)

1. Mother goat is out, I will go to visit the little goats.
2. Your voice is strange.
3. Please show your foot.

4. Wow, little goats, my delicious food.
5. Give me the knife, I will kill you!

II. Translate the sentences into English.

Work in pairs, one student reads the following sentences, and the other translates the sentences into English in spoken way. (Add extra sentences from the scripts if necessary.)

1. 不要开门！
2. 救命，救命呀。
3. 让我试一试。
4. 妈妈，我在这儿！
5. 走开！

Writing Practice

Write a summary of *The Wolf and the Seven Little Goats* in 50 words.

"Ws" / "Who"	doing what	whom	where	when

Part Five: Language Skills

Grammar

A. Be 动词的否定和疑问

总的规则：be 动词后加 not

如：He is Tom. → He is not Tom.

I am lily. → I am not lily.

They are students. → They are not students.

It is a dog. → It is not a dog.

❖ 注意简写形式：

I am not	(am not 不能简写)	I'm not
He/She/It is not	He/She/It isn't	He/She/It's not
We/You/They are not	We/You/They aren't	We/You/They're not
This is not	This isn't	(this is 不能简写)

B. 含 be 动词的陈述句变一般疑问句

I. 变一般疑问句的规则

He is Tom. → Is he Tom?

② be 动词提前。

③ 首字母大写，原来的首字母改成小写。

④ 句号改成问号。

⑤ 改用升调。

如：This is a book. → Is this a book?

She is very nice. → Is she very nice?

It is his bag. → Is it his bag?

They are good friends. → Are they good friends?

注意①：I am…或 We are…变成 Are you…?

如：I am Jack. → Are you Jack?

We are Chinese. → Are you Chinese?

注意②：my 或 our 变成 your

如：This is my mother. → Is this your mother?

These are our bags. → Are these your bags?

II. 一般疑问句的肯定回答与否定回答

1. 主语一致

如：—Is he Tom?

—Yes, he is. / No, he isn't.

—Are they good friends?

—Yes, they are. / No, they aren't.

注意①：问句用 you，回答改用 I 或 We

如：—Are you Jack?

—Yes, I am. / No, I'm not.

—Are you Chinese?

—Yes, we are. / No, we aren't.

注意②：问句用 this/that 或 these/those，回答改用 it 或 they

Is this your book?　Yes, it is. / No, it isn't.

Are those your books?　Yes, they are. / No, they aren't.

2. 主语替换

①主语是单数女性，用 she 代替

如：—Is your mother a doctor?

—Yes, she is. / No, she isn't.

②主语是单数男性，用 he 代替

如：—Is your father a doctor?

—Yes, he is. / No, he isn't.

③主语是单数事物，用 it 代替

如：—Is your book on the desk?

—Yes, it is. / No, it isn't.

④主语是复数人或物，用 they 代替

如：—Are the boys from America?

—Yes, they are. / No, they aren't.

—Are these books Jack's?

—Yes, they are. / No, they aren't.

Exercises

A. Multiple Choice

1. ______she Lily's mother?

A. Be B. Am C. Is D. are

2. I ______ sorry.

A. / B. am C. are D. is

3. ______ this my ball?

A. Is B. Are C. Am D. Be

4. You ______ a smart boy.

A. are　　B. is　　C. am　　D. be

5. What_______this?

A. is　　B. are　　C. be　　D. /

6. ____Helen a student?

A. Be　　B. Am　　C. Is　　D. Are

7. Those _____oranges.

A. is　　B. are　　C. am　　D. /

8. How old _____you?

A. be　　B. am　　C. is　　D. are

9. Where _____ her father?

A. are　　B. is　　C. am　　D. /

10. The two cups of milk _____ for me.

A. isn't　　B. aren't　　C. be not　　D. is

11. Emma and Kathy ____ my students.

A. are　　B. is　　C. am　　D. is not

12. Your books ____ not good.

A. is　　B. are　　C. be　　D. is not

13. He ___ a boy.

A. be　　B. am　　C. is　　D. aren't

14. It ___ my dog.

A. isn't　　B. aren't　　C. be　　D. are

15. Whose glasses ______ they?

A. are　　B. is　　C. am　　D. isn't

16. _______ there any students in the classroom?

A. Is　　B. Are　　C. Am　　D. isn't

17. —Is she your classmate?

—_________

A. Yes, she is.　　B. No, she is.　　C. Yes, he is.　　D. No, he isn't.

18. —Are those your friends?

—___________

A. Yes, they is. B. No, they are not. C. Yes, he is. D. No, they isn't.

19. How _______ your father?

A. is B. are C. be D. /

20. —Is the library next to the dinning room?

—___________

A. Yes, they are. B. No, it isn't. C. Yes, it isn't. D. No, it is.

B. Complete each of the following sentences with a proper word.

1. She _______ my sister. (表否定)
2. These _______ my books.
3. _____ this Emma's eraser?
4. _____ they your parents?
5. I _____ Jane.
6. They ______ my classmates. (表否定)
7. How old _______ you?
8. There _____ many students in our class.
9. How _____ your grandpa?
10. Where ______ you from?

C. Change the following sentences

I. Change the following affirmative sentences containing Be verbs into general question sentences.

1. She's from Japan.

____

2. Those are his parents.

____

3. There are many countries in the world.

____

4. Dogs are very cute.

____

5. Her favourite food is hot dog.

____

II. Imitate the model sentences and change the following sentences into negative and interrogative sentences.

Eg. That is a book.

否定句：That is not a book.

疑问句：Is that a book?

回答：Yes, it is. / No, it isn't.

1. This is a coat.

否定句：________________________________

疑问句：________________________________?

回答：________________________________

2. I am a student.

否定句：________________________________

疑问句：________________________________?

回答：________________________________

3. You are a star.

否定句：________________________________

疑问句：________________________________?

回答：________________________________

4. These are apples.

否定句：________________________________

疑问句：________________________________?

回答：________________________________

5. That is a tree.

否定句：________________________________

疑问句：________________________________?

回答：________________________________

Unit Five
Trying Everything

Part One: Phonics

A. 长音“o”—— 字母组合“oa”和“oe”

1. 拼读发音方式。

字母组合“oa”和“oe”都是长音，都发字母“o”的字母音。其发音方法如下：舌端离开下齿，舌头平展放松，唇形扁平、放松；然后，下颚稍微向上抬起，自然地向字母组合“oo”的拼读短音滑动，但是还不到字母组合“oo”的拼读短音，中间不要停顿。包含这个发音的单词如 boat，coat，toe 等。

2. 听一听，学一学字母组合“oa”和“oe”的拼读发音。

(1) road coal soap toast cloak coach goat roast

(2) Joe woe roe sloe oboe

3. 仔细听，然后做句子一口气快读练习。

(1) You want some toast, and I want some roast.

(2) Joey buys potatoes and tomatoes.

4. 听一听，并熟练朗读。

Load some coal onto the boat.
She always moans if I loan her coat.
Float the boat across the moat.
The toad has a croaky throat.

Take the coach to the coast.

Joe goes on tip toes he has many foes.
Joe has a woe about the volcanoes.

Be careful when you hoe,
You might hurt your toe.

B. 长音“u”——字母组合“ue”和“ew”

1. 拼读发音方式。

字母组合“ue”和“ew”的发音是长音，第一种读音为字母“u”的字母音，如单词 fuel，issue，few，new 等；字母组合“ue”和“ew”的第二种发音为 long oo，同“moon”中“oo”的发音，如单词 flew，Jew，blue，clue 等。

2. 听一听，学一学字母组合“ue”和“ew”的拼读发音。

(1) few　new　value　tissue　cue　due　dew　stew

(2) drew　threw　flew　shrewd　crew　screw　jewel

3. 仔细听，然后做句子一口气快读练习。

(1) The Jew flew over the sky.

(2) Joey buys potatoes and tomatoes.

4. 听一听，并熟练朗读。

Sue speaks fluent French.
Blue, tissue paper flowers were glued to the door.
The wind blew and dried up the morning dew.
There are few good newspaper stories.

Part Two: Dialogue

Dialogue 1

Susan: Your sister is wonderful, Jenny.

Jenny: Yes, she is. She is very pretty, too.

Susan: Is she very tall?

Jenny: Yes, she is. She has long arms and long fingers.

Susan: You are not tall. Is your father tall?

Jenny: No, he is short. My mother is short. I'm short, too.

Words and Expressions

wonderful ['wʌndəf(ə)l] *adj*. 极好的，精彩的

tall [tɔːl] *adj*. 高的

finger ['fɪŋɡə(r)] *n*. 手指

short [ʃɔːt] *adj*. 短的，矮的

Decide whether the following statements are True (T) or False (F).

(　　) 1. Susan's sister is wonderful.

(　　) 2. Susan's sister is tall.

(　　) 3. Jenny is tall.

(　　) 4. Jenny's father is tall.

(　　) 5. Jenny's mother is short.

Dialogue 2

Susan: What does Lucy look like?

Jenny: She has big blue eyes and blonde hair. Her eyes are very beautiful.

Susan: She must be a beauty. The eyes are the window to one's heart.

Jenny: Yes, she's also lovely.

Susan: From her appearance, I could guess she is from America.

Jenny: You're right!

Susan: How do you know that?

Jenny: Lucy and I are in the same class.

Words and Expressions

blonde [blɒnd] *adj*. 亚麻色的

beautiful ['bjuːtɪf(ə)l] *adj*. 美丽的

window ['wɪndəʊ] *n*. 窗户

lovely ['lʌvli] *adj*. 可爱的

appearance [ə'pɪrəns] *n*. 外貌

Decide whether the following statements are True (T) or False (F).

( ) 1. Lucy has big blue eyes and brown hair.

( ) 2. Lucy is pretty.

( ) 3. Lucy is lovely.

( ) 4. Jenny is from America.

( ) 5. Jenny and Lucy are not in the same class.

Dialogue 3

Susan: Tom, your sister is very beautiful. Is your brother handsome?

Tom: We are all handsome.

Susan: Do you see that large woman? The one with brown hair.

Tom: She has a very nice face. But she is very thin.

Words and Expressions

handsome ['hænsəm] *adj*. 英俊的

woman ['wʊmən] *n*. 妇女；女性

thin [θɪn] *adj*. 薄的；瘦的

Decide whether the following statements are True (T) or False (F).

( ) 1. Tom's sister is very beautiful.

( ) 2. Tom's brother is handsome.

( ) 3. Tom is not handsome.

( ) 4. The large woman has blonde hair.

( ) 5. The large woman has beautiful face.

Dialogue 4

Susan: Jenny, I like your granddaughter very much, she looks so cute.

Jenny: Yeah, she is a beautiful girl.

Susan: Her eyes especially entice me. She got a pair of fascinating blue eyes.

Jenny: Yep, they look just like her mother's eyes.

Words and Expressions

granddaughter ['ɡrændɔːtə(r)] *n*. 孙女；外孙女

especially [ɪ'speʃəli] *adv*. 特别

cute [kjuːt] *adj.* 可爱的

entice [ɪn'taɪs] *v.* 吸引

fascinating ['fæsɪneɪtɪŋ] *adj.* 迷人的

Decide whether the following statements are True (T) or False (F).

(　　) 1. Jenny's granddaughter is lovely.

(　　) 2. Jenny's granddaughter is beautiful.

(　　) 3. Susan got a pair of fascinating blue eyes.

(　　) 4. Jenny's mother got a pair of fascinating blue eyes.

(　　) 5. Jenny's granddaughter's eyes look like her mother's.

Part Three: Text

Are you Japanese?　No, we are not.　We are Chinese.

Are your friends Chinese, too?　No, they are not. They are Japanese.

Are you university students?　Yes, we are.

Are you from Australia?　No, I am not.　I am from Canada.

Is your wife from Canada, too?　No, she isn't.　She is from America.

Are you journalists?　Yes, we are.

Is she a Uygur?　No, she isn't.　She is Kazak.

Is her colleague Kazak, too?　Yes, she is.

Are they University teachers from Northwest Minzu University?

Yes, they are.

Is he a doctor?　No, he isn't.　He is an engineer.

Is he from Yunnan?　Yes, he is.　He is Tujia.

He is polite and easygoing.

Are they tourists?　Yes, they are.

Where are they from?　They are from Northwest part of China.

They are from Qinghai province.

Are they pop singers?　Yes, they are.

Where are they from?　They are from Switzerland.

They are so cool and fashionable.

Words and Expressions

university [ˌjuːnɪ'vɜːsətɪ] *n.* 大学；综合性大学

Eg. 1. She teaches in a university.

她在一所大学任教。

2. I like this university.

我喜欢这所大学。

Australia [ɒ'streɪlɪə] *n.* 澳大利亚

Eg. 1. She moved to Australia.

她移民到澳大利亚了。

2. Australia is a beautiful country.
澳大利亚是一个美丽的国家。

Canada ['kænədə] *n.* 加拿大

Eg. 1. He has lived in Canada for more than twenty years.
他在加拿大已经住了二十多年了。
2. When did you get back from Canada?
你什么时候从加拿大回来的？

America [ə'merɪkə] *n.* 美洲（包括北美洲和南美洲）；美国

Eg. 1. I may go to America.
我也许去美国。
2. He is in America.
他在美国。

journalist ['dʒɜːnəlɪst] *n.* 新闻工作者；报人

Eg. 1. I am a journalist, but I am also Canadian.
我是一名记者，但我也是一位加拿大人。
2. The journalist spent an hour on the tour.
新闻记者在观光上花了一个小时。

colleague ['kɒliːg] *n.* 同事，同僚

Eg. 1. He has told me about the new colleague.
他已经向我告知新同事的情况。
2. I'd like you to meet my colleague.
我想让你认识一下我的同事。

polite [pə'laɪt] *adj.* 有礼貌的，客气的

Eg. 1. He is very polite to people.
他既是一位优秀教师，又是一位著名的作家。
2. Students are polite.
学生们很有礼貌。

easygoing [ˌiːzi'gəʊɪŋ] *adj.* 逍遥自在的；脾气随和的

Eg. 1. His brother is quite easygoing.
他的兄弟好相处。
2. They are loyal and easygoing.
他们诚实和随和。

tourist ['tʊərɪst] *n.* 旅行者，观光客

Eg. 1. Are you a tourist, or a traveller?

你是一个旅行者，还是一个旅游者？

2. We live in a tourist town.

我们住在一个旅游城市里。

Switzerland ['swɪtsələnd] *n.* 瑞士（欧洲国家）

Eg. 1. I did not need to go to Switzerland.

我不必去瑞士。

2. Switzerland is a small country.

瑞士是一个小国家。

fashionable ['fæʃ(ə)nəb(ə)l] *adj.* 流行的；时髦的

Eg. 1. They are very fashionable.

它们都非常流行。

2. Some people want to buy it because it is fashionable.

一些人因为它流行想买。

Language Focus

I. Make a sentence with the words given below.

1. you / are / China / from/ ?

yes / am / i

2. is / a / pupil /she / ?

is / she / yes

3. is / he / a /taxi-driver / ?

he / no / is / not. is / a / he / worker

4. are / they / Canada / from / ?

they / no / are / not. are / they / Russia / from

5. they / doctors / are / ?

are / yes / they

II. Translating

Put Chinese into English.

1. 她是家庭主妇吗？ 不，她是一个医生。

2. 她是医生吗？ 是的，她是一个年青的医生。

3. 他来自日本吗？ 是的，他是一个日本人。

4. 他们是教师吗，是的，他们很严肃。

5. 他们是歌手吗？是的，他们很时尚。

Put English into Chinese.

1. Is she an artist? Yes, she is. She is very popular.

2. Is he a dancer? No, he isn't. He is a model.

3. Are they scientists? Yes, they are. They are intelligent and hardworking.

4. Are they from America? Yes, they are.

5. Are you a good student? Yes, I am. I am kind, easygoing and hardworking.

III. Reading Comprehension

Choose the best answer to each of the following questions or incomplete sentences.

Alan is an English boy. Now he studies in Shanghai Yucai Middle School. He is in Grade Seven. He has a dog. It's black and white. The dog's very clever. Alan likes it very much. Its favorite food is bone(骨头). Every day when Alan gets home, the dog meets him in front of the house.

Alan's friend, Jenny is an American girl. She is in Shanghai, too. They are in the same grade, but in different classes. She has a pet panda. It's also a black and white, but it's not a real panda. It's a toy. The panda is very clean. Jenny often washes it in water. Where is the panda now? Oh, it's sleeping with Jenny. Every night it sleeps with Jenny.

1. Where is Alan from?

A. England.

B. America.

C. Canada.

D. The USA.

2. What's Alan's pet dog's favorite food?

A. Fish.

B. Meat.

C. Chicken.

D. Bone.

3. What grade is Jenny in?

A. Six.

B. Seven.

C. Eight.

D. Nine.

4. What does the dog do when Alan gets home from school?

A. It sleeps with him.

B. It meets him in front of the house.

C. It runs with him.

D. It likes him.

5. What animal is black and white according to the passage(根据文章)?

A. Cat.

B. Dog.

C. Panda.

D. Panda and dog.

Part Four: Play

The Little Horse Crosses the River

Characters:
Little Horse 小马
Mother Horse 马妈妈
Uncle Cow 牛大叔
Brother Squirrel 松鼠弟弟

Scene 1

(At horses' home)

Little Horse: Mummy, I'm as tall as you. I grow up now. Let me carry the bag for you.

Mother Horse: My dear! I'm glad you say that. Yes, you have grown old and tall, and can help me now.

Little Horse: Yes, mummy! Let me carry the bag for you, please!

Mother Horse: Ok, my baby! Take this bag of rice to your Uncle Donkey, will you?

Little Horse: Yes, Mummy! Where does Uncle Donkey live?

Mother Horse: He lives on the other side of the river.

Little Horse: Mummy, I'll get back soon. Bye-bye.

Mother Horse: Bye-bye! Take care!

Scene 2

(By the river)

Cow: Hi, Little Horse, where are you going?

Little Horse: Oh, Uncle Cow, I have to go to Uncle Donkey's house.

Cow: Uncle Donkey's house is on the other side of the river.

Little Horse: Yes, yes! How can I go over the river? Is there a bridge near here?

Cow: No, my child! There is not any! If you want to go to his house, you have to cross the river.

Little Horse: Go cross the river? It is so dangerous.

Cow: No, it is not!

Little Horse: Is the river deep?

Cow: No, it isn't deep. I just came back from the other side, and the water only reaches my calf.

Little Horse: Thanks, Uncle Cow! I'll cross the river right away.

Squirrel: Stop, stop! The river is so deep that one of my fellows had been swept.

Little Horse: Really! It's so scared! It's so lucky not to wade!

Cow: It's not deep! Little Horse, you can wade across the river.

Squirrel: No, no! It's very deep! You can't wade across the river. You will get drowned.

Little Horse: But the river is deep or not? Shall I go on or go back? I'd better go home and ask my mum.

Cow & Squirrel: Yes. You'd better ask your mum.

Scene 3

(At horses' home)

Little Horse: Mummy, mummy! Uncle Cow said that the river was not deep, and I could wade across the river. But Brother Squirrel said that it was very deep, and I couldn't wade across the river. What should I do?

Mother Horse: My child, both Uncle Cow and Brother Squirrel are right in their own way.

Little Horse: Why? Tell me, tell me!

Mother Horse: Uncle Cow's body is big, so he said the river was not deep. Brother Squirrel's body is small, so he said the river was deep.

Little Horse: Oh, I see!

Mother Horse: You should think everything over by yourself.

Little Horse: Ok, mum! I should try it myself.

Mother Horse: Yes, my little boy!

Scene 4

(By the river)

Little Horse: Yes, mummy is right! I should try it myself!

Cow: Go! Little Horse, it is not deep!

Squirrel: Stop, stop! It is dangerous!

Little Horse: Uncle Cow and Brother Squirrel, I should try it myself!

Cow & Squirrel: Ok, good luck!

Little Horse: Haha, in fact, it is not difficult to wade across the river.

Mother Horse: My dear, no matter what happened, we should think it over and try it ourselves.

Little Horse: Yes, mummy!

（师生改编剧本）

Words and Expressions

carry ['kæri] *v.* 驮，搬运

glad [glæd] *adj.* 高兴的

donkey ['dɒŋki] *n.* 驴

bridge [brɪdʒ] *n.* 桥

near [nɪə(r)] *prep.* 近

cross [krɒs] *v.* 横穿过

dangerous ['deɪndʒərəs] *adj.* 危险的

deep [diːp] *adj.* 深的

reach [riːtʃ] *v.* 达到

calf [kɑːf] *n.* 小腿

fellow ['feləʊ] *n.* 家伙

sweep [swiːp] *n.* (风、浪等)刮，吹，冲

really ['riːəli] *adv.* 真的!（表语气）

scared [skeəd] *adj.* 害怕的

wade [weɪd] *v.* 涉水

across [ə'krɒs] *prep.* 穿过

drown [draʊn] *v.* 淹死，溺死

everything ['evriθɪŋ] *pron.* 每件事物

difficult ['dɪfikəlt] *adj.* 困难的

grow up 长大

on the other side 另一边

right away 立刻，马上

had better 最好

in one's own way 自己的方式

good luck 好运

in fact 事实上

no matter what happened 无论发生什么

Listening Practice

I. Bingo game

Work in groups, one student read about the script of *The Little Horse Crosses the River*, other students listen carefully, when they hear the adjective from the script, say "Bingo", and write the word in the form quickly, and then he/she wins. And take turns, and change the words into Verbs, Nouns, etc.

words	adjective	verbs	nouns	prepositions	adverbs	conjunctions
student 1						
student 2						
student 3						
student 4						
student 5						

II. Dictation

Listen to the passage three times and supply the missing information.

Little Horse thinks he is old ___1___ to help his mother. So, Mother Horse asks her son to take a bag of ___2___ to Uncle Donkey. But, Uncle Donkey's house is ___3___ of the river. Uncle Cow thinks the river is not deep, and the water only reaches his ___4___. But Brother Squirrel believes the river is very ___5___, and Little Horse will get ___6___. Little Horse doesn't know what he should do, go on or ___7___? So he goes back home to ask his mother. Mother Horse says both Uncle Cow and Brother Squirrel are right ___8___ because Uncle Cow's body is very big and Brother Squirrel's body is small. Little Horse is very happy because he wants to try it ___9___. ___10___, it is not difficult to wade across the river. And no matter what happened, we should think it over and try it ourselves.

Reading Practice

I. Read and choose

1. Which of the following statement is True?

A. The little horse will carry a bag of rice to Uncle Monkey.

B. Mother horse gets angry because little horse wants to do his mother a favor.

C. Uncle Monkey's house is on the other side of the river.

D. Little horse listens to his mother's words and crosses the river safely.

2. ________ thinks the river is not deep.

A. Uncle Cow

B. Uncle Donkey

C. Brother Squirrel

D. Mother Horse

3. Brother Squirrel thinks the river is very ______.

A. safe

B. funny

C. beautiful

D. dangerous

4. Whose advice do you think is correct?

A. Uncle Cow

B. Uncle Donkey

C. Brother Squirrel

D. Mother Horse

5. Little Horse is very _____ because finally he crosses river safely.

A. happy

B. sad

C. arrogant

D. ambitious

II. Read and answer

1. Who are Uncle Cow and Brother Squirrel? Are they Little Horse's friends?
2. Why does Little Horse go back home and ask his mummy?
3. Where does Little Horse go?
4. If you were Little Horse, would you listen to Uncle Cow and Brother Squirrel's advice?
5. What does Little Horse carry to Uncle Donkey?

Speaking Practice

I. Role Play

Suppose you were the Little Horse, what would do you when you have to cross the river? Use the following functional sentences, you have to add your own expressions when it is necessary.

- Oh, it is dangerous.
- Is it deep or not?
- What should I do?
- Help me!
- Haha, it is easy!
- The river is not deep.
- So long.

II. Problem-Solving

Think of appropriate lines for the animals in the picture above.

III. Delivery Game

The teacher divides the whole class into four or five groups, queue the students. The teacher writes a long sentence from the script in a piece of paper, just let the first student read and recite it for one minute, and let the student retell the sentence to the second student, the second to the third, when the sentence is delivered to the last student, he/she should write it on the blackboard, and translate it into Chinese. The group which has got great speed and relative accuracy wins.

Translating Practice

I. Translate the sentences into Chinese.

Work in pairs, one student reads the following sentences, and the other translates the sentences into Chinese in spoken way. (Add extra sentences from the scripts if necessary.)

1. Take this bag of rice to your Uncle Donkey, will you?
2. Uncle Donkey's house is on the other side of the river.
3. I just came back from the other side, and the water only reaches my calf.
4. The river is so deep that one of my fellows had been swept.
5. Both Uncle Cow and Brother Squirrel are right in their own way.

II. Translate the sentences into English.

Work in pairs, one student reads the following sentences, and the other translates the sentences into English in spoken way. (Add extra sentences from the scripts if necessary.)

1. 妈妈，我和你一样高了。
2. 这儿附近有桥吗？
3. 你最好去问问你妈妈。
4. 我现在就过河。
5. 我应该自己试一试！

Writing Practice

Write a summary of *The Little Horse Crosses the River* in 50 words.

"Ws" / "Who"	doing what	whom	where	when

Part Five: Language Skills

Grammar

人称代词和物主代词

I. 英语中代词分为人称代词和物主代词具体如下表：

		第 一 人 称		第 二 人称		第 三 人 称			
		单数	复数	单数	复数	单 数			复数
人称代词	主 格	I（我）	we（我们）	you（你）	you（你们）	he（他）	she（她）	it（它）	they（他们）
	宾 格	me（我）	us（我们）	you（你）	you（你们）	him（他）	her（她）	it（它）	them（他们）
物主代词	形容词性	my（我的）	our（我们的）	your（你的）	your（你们的）	his（他的）	her（她的）	its（它的）	their（他们的）
	名词性	mine（我的）	ours（我们的）	yours（你的）	yours（你们的）	his（他的）	hers（她的	its（它的）	theirs（他们的）

A. 人称代词分为主格和宾格

1）主格作主语。

如：I am a girl.

我是个女孩。

You are a boy.

你是个男孩

2）宾格作宾语，放在动词或介词之后。

如：I like her.

我喜欢她

Do you know him?

你认识他吗？

Could you help me?

你能帮助我吗？

B. 物主代词分为形容词性的物主代词和名词性的物主代词

形容词性物主代词相当于形容词，在句中只能用作定语，后面必须跟名词。

名词性的物主代词相当于一个名词，必须单独使用，后面不能再跟名词。

如：1. Your room is big, mine is small. (mine=my room)

2. This is not your pen. Yours is on the desk. (yours=your pen)

3. Your classroom is over there, ours is right here. (ours=our classroom)

4. Her coat is black. His is white. Mine is blue. (his=his coat, mine=my coat)

注意：

人称代词主格常用 who、宾格用 whom 提问；物主代词常用 whose 提问.

如：I like storybooks.

Who likes storybooks? (对主格 I 的提问）

This is your bike.

Whose bike is this? (对物主代词 your 的提问）

The umbrella is yours.

Whose umbrella is it? (对物主代词 yours 的提问）

Exercises

A. Mutiple Choice

1. Anna, please give _____ the glasses. I want to read the book.

A. you B. me C. him D. Her

2. She is a student, and _________ name is Julia.

A. its B. her C. hers D.his

3. _______ are his brothers.

A. This B. That C. Those D. It

4. —What's_____ name?

— _______ is Mary.

A. her, Her name B. hers, She name

C. she, Shes name D. his, Hers name

5. This is ______ dormitory. Where is _____?

A. our, them B. us, they C. our, theirs D. ours, theirs

6. Could you help ________ with ________ English, please?

A. I, my B. me, me C. me, my D. my, I

7. — Whose book is it?

— It's _____.

A. you B. mine C. him D. your

8. Are these ______ desks?

A. you B. us C. they D. their

9. My uncle bought a new bike for ________.

A. theirs B. they C. me D. I

10. Who gave ______ the letter? Was _____ Mr. Black?

A. you, it B. you, he C. your, it D. your, that

11. I go to school with some friends of _______.

A. us B. our C. mine D. my

12. Thanks for writing e-mails to ________.

A. he B. my C. me D. I

13. You lost your book. You may have _______.

A. me B. my C. mine D. myself

14. This is not ______ English book, ______ is over there.

A. me, yours B. my, us C. your, mine D. your, yours

15. _________like Chinese food.

A. They B. Their C. Them D. Theirs

16. Between you and ________, he is not a real friend.

A. me B. I C. he D. his

17. — Here's a letter for you, Mike!

— Oh, ________ is from my father.

A. he B. it C. she D. it's

18. Where is ________ books?

A. me B. I C. my D. mine

19. Here ________ are!

A. it B. she C. you D. my

20. These are your books, Linda. Put ________ in your desk, please.

A. it B. they C. them D. you

B. Fill in the blanks with the correct form of the pronoun given.

1. The teachers are very kind to _____. (we)

2. —Is this______ watch? (you)

 —No, it's not ______. It's ______. (I / she)

3. She is a friend of ______. (I)

4. That's very kind of ______. (you)

5. Thank ______for ______help. (you)

6. _____ bike is broken. What about ______? (I / you)

7. What's this? ______is a cat. (it)

8. ______name is Peter. (it)

9. He's _______English teacher. (they)

10. Those books are _______. (they)

C. Make a question about the underlined part.

1. This is <u>our</u> teacher.

____

2. <u>She</u> teaches us English.

____

3. That's <u>her</u> book.

____

4. The pencil box is <u>hers</u>.

____

5. <u>We</u> are students.

____

6. The red cap is <u>mine</u>.

____

7. <u>You</u> are my best friend.

____

8. These are <u>our</u> photos.

____

9. Are those <u>your</u> toys?

____

10. I am a student of <u>his</u>.

____

Unit Six
Self-protection

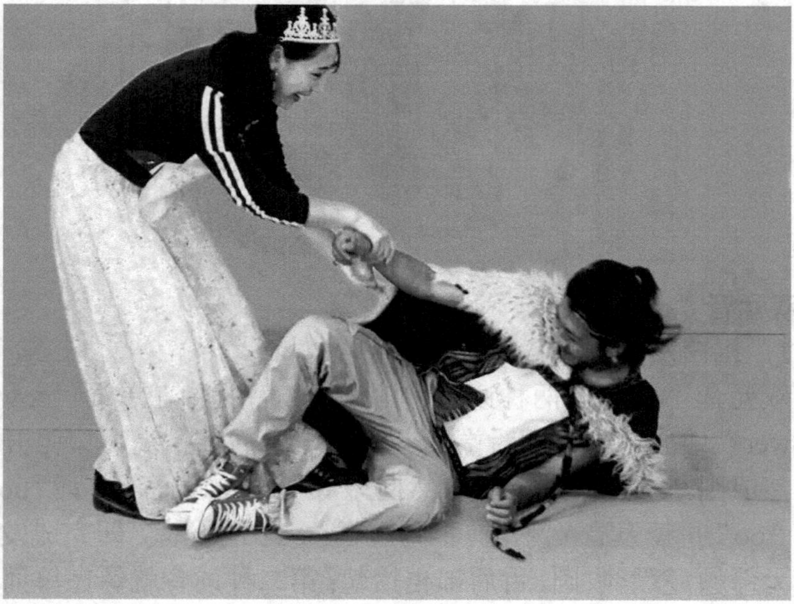

Part One: Phonics
Part Two: Dialogue
Part Three: Text
Part Four: Play—Little Red Riding Hood
Part Five: Language Skills

Part One: Phonics

A. 双元音“ow”

1．拼读发音方式。

双元音“ow”有两种读音：第一种读音就像在单词“cow”和“power”中的读音，即舌端离开下齿，舌后部抬高，口张开，唇形自然成圆，之后，唇收起，自然向短音“oo”的发音（单词“book”中的“oo”拼读发音）滑动，不到短音“oo”的发音，即完成发音，中间无停顿，双唇收圆，舌后部稍抬起；第二种读音就像在单词“low”和“throw”中的读音，即舌端离开下齿，舌平且放松，张口即发生，之后，下颚稍稍向上抬起，自然向短音“oo”的发音滑动，(即单词“book”中“oo”的拼读发音），不到短音“oo”即完成发音，中间无停顿，双唇由扁平收圆。

2. 听一听，学一学字母组合“ow”的拼读发音。

(1) towel powder shower crown frown wow

(2) show grow crow narrow snow tomorrow flow

3. 仔细听，然后做句子一口气快读练习。

(1) Look at the clown! He is wearing a crown.

(2) Howard wants to borrow a tow rope to get out in the snow.

4. 听一听，并熟练朗读。

How did the owl come down from the tower?

Wow! Can you image a cow who really can bow?

Down, down, down!

Town, town, town!

Down to the town.

B. 双元音“ou”

1. 拼读发音方式

双元音“ou”有三种读音：一种读音像在单词“out”和“shout”中的读音一样，另一种读音像在单词“four”和“pour”中的读音一样，而第三种读音像在单词“would”和“could”中的读音一样。

2. 听一听，学一学字母组合“ou”的拼读发音。

(1) out shout mouth south proud house hour mountain

(2) four bought court source gourd pour gourmet

(3) would could soup roulette toucan coupon

3. 仔细听，然后做句子一口气快读练习。

(1) He was proud of shouting for an hour in the mountain.

(2) The gourmet bought four gourds.

(3) Louise has a toucan who likes soup.

(4) The mountain tours are form north to south, and the tours last for about four days.

4. 听一听下列的韵律英语，并熟练朗读。

Walking Is Fun

Walking around is so much fun.
We can go real slow,
Or hurry and run.
We can jump up and down
Like a kangaroo.
I'm having so much fun.
How about you?

We found a thousand round houses abound the town.
We found a mouse in our house.

C. 双元音“oy”“oi”

1. 拼读发音方式。

字母组合“oy”和“oi”是双元音，其发音方法如下：舌头位置由低向高动，先发字母“o”的拼读短音，下颚迅速向上合拢，并迅速向字母“i”的拼读短音滑动，不到字母“i”的拼读短音，中间不要停顿。包含这个拼读发音的单词如 toy，oil 等。

2. 听一听，学一学字母组合“oy”和“oi”的拼读发音。

(1) toy boy joy royal employ soy Troy enjoy loyal

(2) oil point noise choice voice coin moisture

3. 仔细听，然后做句子一口气快读练习。

(1) Troy wants his loyal customers to enjoy his oysters and soy sauce.

(2) Joy gets annoyed with boy’s toys.

(3) This medicine is the best choice for your aching joints.

(4) He appointed Roy to buy some oil.

4.听一听下列的韵律英语，并熟练朗读。

The spoiled boy lost his toy
And made a lot of noise.

Rub on ointment,
Make an appointment,
Beak a joint,
Make a point,
Boil some water,
Spoil your daughter,
Hear a voice,
Let’s rejoice!

D. 复合元音“aw”“au”

1. 拼读发音方式。

字母组合“aw”和“au”是复合元音，其发音方法如下：舌头离开下齿；舌头后部抬高，唇形较圆，往前突出，声带要振动。包含这个拼读音的单词如 draw，straw，caught，taught 等。

2. 听一听，学一学字母组合“aw”和“au”的拼读发音。

(1) jaw paw jig-saw fawn yawn awesome claw

(2) author daughter fault autumn August automatic autograph

3. 仔细听，然后做句子一口气快读练习。

(1) I saw Paul who was yawning.

(2) Tiger's paws are huge with very sharp claws.

(3) The author's daughter was born in autumn.

(4) Pau's daughter Pauline works in Austria.

4. 听一听，并熟练朗读。

(1) Tall Paul ate some awful corn sauce.

(2) The lion yawns and then crawls slowly towards a fawn feeding in the straw.

(3) Last August Paul caught Claudia and Pauline at an automatic vending machine.

E. 字母组合“oo”的长音和短音

1. 拼读发音方式。

字母组合“oo”有长音和短音，其短音发音方法如下：舌头后部要抬高，舌身收缩，舌尖离开下齿；双唇自然收圆，并略往前突出，肌肉略放松；牙床开得较大，大约 1/3；声带要振动；发音短促。包含这个音的单词如 look，good，cook 等。

其长音发音方法如下：舌头后部要抬高，身收缩，舌尖离开下齿；双唇尽量收的小且圆，并往前突出，口腔肌肉保持紧张，声带要振动；发音拉长。包含这个音的单词如 food，cool 等。

2.听一听，学一学字母组合“oo”的短音和长音。

“oo”的短音 stood took foot look cookie wood hood

“oo”的长音 moon root goose tooth mood mushroom

scooter　zoo

3. 仔细听，然后做句子一口气快读练习。

“oo”的短音

(1) His wife looks good and cooks well.

(2) He took a book to have a look.

“oo”的长音

(1) The goose in the zoo is in the mood.

(2) The burglar stole the purse of the burly girl with curly hair.

4. 听一听，并熟练朗读。

(1) The boy with the hooded jacket stood on his foot.

(2) He book a bullet from the wooden box, put it in the gun and shot the woman.

(3) Jools will soon move to Troon and he needs more room.

Part Two: Dialogue

Dialogue 1

William: Do you have any hobbies? What is it or what are they?

John: I'm interested in watching TV or other relaxing games.

William: How do you spend your spare time?

John: I usually read or do some sports.

William: I often sing.

John: Singing can make one relaxed.

Words and Expressions

hobby ['hɒbi] *n.* 嗜好；业余爱好

relaxing [rɪ'læksɪŋ] *adj.* 令人轻松的

games ['ɡeɪmz] *n.* 游戏

be interested in 对……感兴趣

spare time 业余时间

Decide whether the following statements are True (T) or False (F).

(　) 1. John is interested in watching TV and other relaxing games.

(　) 2.William often spends his spare time in reading.

( ) 3. John often spends his spare time in reading and doing some sports.

( ) 4. John likes singing songs.

( ) 5. They are talking about their jobs.

Dialogue 2

William: Hi, John. Where will you go?

John: I will go to the gym to play basketball.

William: You always play basketball. Do you like it very much?

John: Yes, I like it very much.

Words and Expressions

gym [dʒɪm] *n.* 健身房

play basketball 打篮球

very much 非常

Decide whether the following statements are True (T) or False (F).

( ) 1. John is going to play basketball.

( ) 2. John is going to play baseball on the playground.

( ) 3. John does not like playing basketball.

( ) 4. John likes playing soccer.

( ) 5. William wants to play basketball with John.

Dialogue 3

William: What kind of books are you interested in?

John: My favorite books are those about detectives.

William: Well, those books are really good. I like them too. Do you think you are introverted or extroverted?

John: In fact, I wouldn't call myself extroverted. Sometimes I enjoy being by myself very much. But other times, I like sharing activities with others too, especially during these last few years.

Words and Expressions

favorite ['feɪvərɪt] *adj.* 最喜爱的

detective [dɪ'tektɪv] *n.* 侦探

introverted ['ɪntrəvɜːtɪd] *adj.* 性格内向的

extroverted ['ekstrəvɜːtɪd] *adj.* 性格外向的

Decide whether the following statements are True (T) or False (F).

(　　) 1. John's favorite books are those about detectives.

(　　) 2. William doesn't like books about detectives.

(　　) 3. John is an introverted person.

(　　) 4. John enjoys being by himself very much.

(　　) 5. William likes sharing activities with others.

Dialogue 4

William: What kind of sports do you like?

John: I like almost all sports, and I enjoy both playing and watching. I especially like tennis and mountain climbing.

William: What kind of personality do you think you have?

John: Well, I approach things very enthusiastically, I think, and I don't like to leave anything half-done. It makes me nervous. I can't concentrate on anything else until the first thing is finished.

Words and Expressions

tennis ['tenɪs] *n.* 网球

personality [ˌpɜːsə'næləti] *n.* 个性

approach [ə'prəʊtʃ] *v.* 接近

enthusiastically [ɪnˌθjuːzi'æstɪkli] *adv.* 热心地

nervous ['nɜːvəs] *adj.* 神经的；紧张不安的

concentrate ['kɑns(ə)ntreɪt] *v.* 全神贯注；聚集

mountain climbing 爬山

half-done 半完成的

Decide whether the following statements are True (T) or False (F).

(　　) 1. John likes watching sports.

(　　) 2. Tennis and mountain climbing are John's favorite sports.

(　　) 3. John feels nervous if he doesn't finish something.

(　　) 4. John is a sensitive person.

( ) 5. John doesn't like to leave anything half-done.

Part Three: Text

Who is this young man? He is our teacher. He is easygoing.

Who is this pretty girl? She is a policewoman. She is brave.

Who is that serious man? He is our manager. He is strict with us.

Who are those women? They are scientists. They are very demanding.

What are their jobs? They are taxi-drivers. They are very busy.

What are their jobs? They are herdsmen. They are outgoing.

What is his job? He is a dentist. He is very happy.

What is her job? She is a nurse. She is caring and patient.

Words and Expressions

teacher ['tiːtʃə(r)] *n.* 教师；导师

Eg. 1. She is a teacher of music.

她是一位音乐教师。

2. She was a good teacher.

她是一位优秀教师。

brave [breɪv] *adj*. 勇敢的

Eg. 1. He's a brave man.

他是一个勇敢的人。

2. She was a very, very brave girl.

她是一个非常非常勇敢的姑娘。

serious ['sɪəriəs] *adj*. 严肃的；认真的

Eg. 1. I'm not kidding, I'm serious.

我没开玩笑，我是认真的。

2. They all nod their heads, looking rather serious.

他们都点着头，看起来有点严肃。

manager ['mænɪdʒə(r)] *n*. 经理；管理人员

Eg. 1. He ended up as general manager of the company.

他最后成了这家公司的总经理。

2. I will convey the information to the manager.

我将把这个消息通知经理。

strict [strɪkt] *adj*. 严格的；绝对的

Eg. 1. While he loves his students，he is very strict with them.

虽然他爱他的学生，可是他对他们很严格。

2. All products have to pass strict inspection before they go out.

所有产品出厂前必须要经过严格检查。

scientist ['saɪəntɪst] *n*. 科学家

Eg. 1. When I was young I dreamed of becoming a scientist.

我年轻时渴望成为一名科学家。

2. He was not a scientist at all.

他并不能算是一个科学家。

demanding [dɪ'mɑːndɪŋ] *adj.* 苛求的；要求高的

Eg. 1. They are arrogant and demanding.

他们傲慢苛刻。

2. You have a demanding boss.

你有一位要求甚高的老板。

driver ['draɪvə(r)] *n.* 驾驶员

Eg. 1. A careless driver is a danger to the public.

粗心的驾驶员对于公众来说是一种危险。

2. Are you a good driver?

你是一个好的驾驶员？

busy ['bɪzi] *adj.* 忙碌的；热闹的

Eg. 1. she's as busy as before.

她还是像以前一样忙碌。

2. I can't do it now because I am busy.

因为我正忙着，现在不能做此事。

herdsman ['hɜːdzmən] *n.* 牧人

Eg. 1. The herdsman is very young.

这个牧人很年轻。

2. The herdsman falls in love with a pretty girl.

这个牧人爱上了一个漂亮女孩。

outgoing ['aʊtgəʊɪŋ] *adj.* 对人友好的，开朗的

Eg. 1. Soldiers tend to be young males, and they are often outgoing.

士兵们多是年轻的男人，他们通常是外向的。

2. Outgoing people usually have many friends.

外向的人通常有很多朋友。

dentist ['dentɪst] *n.* 牙科医生

Eg. 1. I have gone to the dentist to extract the bad tooth.

我已到牙科医生那里把坏牙拔掉了。

2. You should see your dentist at least once a year.

你应该每年至少见一次你的牙医。

caring ['keərɪŋ] *adj*. 有同情心的；表示或感到关怀或关心的

Eg. 1. You are always so caring for all the people.

你总是对所有人的事都那么关心。

2. Sharing is caring!

分享即是关心！

patient ['peɪʃ(ə)nt] *adj*. 有耐心的，能容忍的

Eg. 1. We must be patient with children.

我们对孩子要有耐心。

2. Teachers should be patient with students.

教师对学生应该耐心。

Language Focus

I. Make a sentence with the words given below.

1. they / are / who / ?
   are / they / employees / our
2. she / who / is / ?
   is / she / boss / your
3. is / he / who / ?
   he / is / singer / a
4. are / their / jobs / what / ?
   they / barbers / are /
5. is / her / job / what / ?
   she / an / is / actress

II. Translating

Put Chinese into English.

1. 她是谁？ 她是一名护士。
2. 他们是谁？ 他们是教师。
3. 她们是谁？ 她们是我们的朋友。
4. 他的工作是什么？ 他的工作是工程师。
5. 她的工作是什么？ 她是艺术家。

Put English into Chinese.

1. Who are they? They are university teachers.
2. Who is he? He is a university student. He is diligent.
3. Who is she? She is my friend's wife.
4. What is her job? She is an airhostess. She is pretty and kind.

5. What are their jobs? They are policemen. They are tall and strong.

III. Reading Comprehension

Choose the best answer to each of the following questions or incomplete sentences.

Mr. Wang is our English teacher. He is more than(多于)fifty years old. He is tall and thin with black hair. He has a big nose and small eyes. He always wears a pair of glasses. He often wears a dark blue jacket and black pants. He is strict (严格的)at his work, but he is kind to us. He teaches English well. He often makes us laugh in his class. We all think English is very interesting. We all like him very much, too.

1. How old is Mr. Wang?

A. 50.

B. 45.

C. More than 50.

D. 55.

2. What does Mr. Wang look like?

A. Tall

B. Short

C. Nice

D. Fat

3. What does he often wear?

A. A watch

B. A pair of glasses

C. A hat

D. A pair of shoes

4. What color is his jacket?

A. Black

B. Green

C. Red

D. Blue

5. How do the students think of Mr. Wang?

A. He is interesting.

B. He is kind.

C. He teaches English.

D. He is funny.

Part Four: Play

Little Red Riding Hood

Characters:

Little Red Riding Hood　　小红帽

Mum　妈妈

Wolf　　狼

Six Ducks　六只小鸭子

Grandma　祖母

Hunter　　猎人

Scene 1

(In Little Red Riding Hood's house)

Little Red Riding Hood: Hi, mummy, what are you doing?

Mum: Grandma is ill. Here are some apples and bananas for her. Take them to her, will you?

Little Red Riding Hood: Ok!

Mum: Be good. Be careful.

Little Red Riding Hood: Yes, mummy! Goodbye, mummy.

Mum: Bye-bye. Darling!

Scene 2

(On the way to grandma's house)

Little Red Riding Hood: Wow! Flowers, how beautiful! One flower, two flowers, three flowers.

Wolf: I am a wolf. I am hungry. Here is a Little Red Riding Hood. Hi, Little Red Riding Hood. Where are you going?

Little Red Riding Hood: To grandma's house. She is ill.

Wolf: I'll eat grandma first. But… Hey, look! Six little baby ducks are dancing.

(Little Red Riding Hood starts dancing with baby ducks, and the wolf is hiding behind a tree.)

Little Red Riding Hood: Hello! Baby ducks, how are you?

Six Ducks: We're fine. Thank you. Where are you going?

Little Red Riding Hood: To grandma's house! Oh, I must go, bye.

Six Ducks: Goodbye.

Scene 3

(In grandma's house)

Wolf: I am very hungry now. Where is grandma's house? Aha, it's here. Bang, bang, bang.

Grandma: Who is it?

Wolf: It's me. Little Red Riding Hood.

Grandma: Come in, come in.

Wolf: Haha, Grandma! I'll eat you!

Wolf: Yummy! I'll sleep.

Little Red Riding Hood: Grandma, grandma.

Wolf: Who is it?

Little Red Riding Hood: It's me. Little Red Riding Hood. What a strange noise!

Wolf: Come in, come in.

Little Red Riding Hood: Oh! What big ears!

Wolf: I can listen to your sweet voice.

Little Red Riding Hood: Wow! What big eyes!

Wolf: I can see your pretty face.

Little Red Riding Hood: Oh! What a big hand!

Wolf: I can hug you.

Little Red Riding Hood: Look! What a big mouth!

Wolf: I can eat you!

Little Red Riding Hood: Oh! No! No!

Wolf: It's delicious. I will go to sleep again. I like sleeping.

Hunter: Where is the wolf? Look! A door. The wolf is sleeping. Oh, what a big stomach! Grandma and Little Red Riding Hood are inside. I must be hurry. Look! Scissors. Cut, cut, cut!

Little Red Riding Hood & Grandma: Thank you!

Hunter: Grandma, give me some needles and thread. Little Red Riding Hood, give me some stones.

Little Red Riding Hood: One stone, two stones, three stones. Put them into the wolf's stomach.

Grandma: I'll thread it.

Hunter: Wake up!

Wolf: Oh, my stomach is so heavy!

Hunter: You big bad wolf, raise your arms.

Wolf: Help! Don't shot me!

Hunter: Bang, bang. Haha, the bad wolf is dead.

Little Red Riding Hood & Grandma: Thank you, hunter.

Hunter: You're welcome.

（师生改编剧本）

Words and Expressions

riding hood ['raɪdɪŋ] [hʊd] *n.* 骑风帽

darling ['dɑːlɪŋ] *n.* 亲爱的

hide [haɪd] *v.* 隐藏

behind [bɪ'haɪnd] *prep.* 在……后面

sleep [sliːp] *v.* 睡觉

noise [nɔɪz] *n.* 噪声

ear [ɪə(r)] *n.* 耳朵

sweet [swiːt] *adj.* 甜的

eye [aɪ] *n.* 眼睛

face [feɪs] *n.* 脸

hand [hænd] *n.* 手

hug [hʌg] *v.* 拥抱

mouth [[maʊθ]] *n.* 嘴

stomach ['stʌmək] *n.* 胃

inside [ˌɪn'saɪd] *prep.* 在……里面

hurry ['hʌri] *n.* 匆忙

needle ['niːd(ə)l] *n.* 针

thread [θred] *n.* 线

heavy ['hevi] *adj.* 重的

raise [reɪz] *v.* 举起

shot [ʃɒt] *v.* 射击

dead [ded] *adj.* 无生命的

come in 进来

listen to　　听
You're welcome　不客气！

Listening Practice

I. Bingo game

Work in groups, one student read about the script of *Little Red Riding Hood*, other students listen carefully, when they hear the adjective from the script, say "Bingo", and write the word in the form quickly, and then he/she wins. And take turns, and change the words into Verbs, Nouns, etc.

words	adjective	verbs	nouns	prepositions	adverbs	conjunctions
student 1						
student 2						
student 3						
student 4						
student 5						

II. Dictation

Listen to the passage three times and supply the missing information.

One day, Little Red Riding Hood's mother asks her to take some fruits to her __1__because she is __2__. On the way to grandma's house, Little Red Riding Hood talks to a __3__. This bad wolf is __4__so he wants to eat both Little Red Riding Hood and grandma as dinner. The wolf comes to grandma's house and eats grandma, and then he pretends to be grandma and eats __5__. A __6__ comes by and hears the very strange __7__ that the wolf makes. He goes into the grandma's house and sees the wolf is __8__, and both Little Red Riding Hood and grandma are in the wolf's __9__. Finally, the hunter cuts the wolf's stomach and saves their__10__.

Reading Practice

I. Read and choose

1. Which of the following statement is True?

A. Little Red Riding Hood plays with six chickens on the way to grandma's house.

B. The wolf eats grandma only.

C. The hunter saves Little Red Riding Hood's life only.

D. The hunter puts some stones in the wolf's stomach.

2. Little Red Riding Hood tells the wolf she is going to ________ house.

A. grandma's

B. hunter's

C. mother's

D. her own

3. Little Red Riding Hood dances with ______ on the way to grandma's house.

A. six ducks

B. wolf

C. hunter

D. flowers

4. Who do you think saves their lives?

A. hunter

B. wolf

C. grandma

D. mummy

5. The hunter cuts the wolf's stomach by _____.

A. needles

B. thread

C. gun

D. scissors

II. Read and answer

1. Who was the wolf? Is he Little Red Riding Hood's friend?
2. Why does Little Red Riding Hood go to grandma's house?
3. Where does Little Red Riding Hood go?
4. If you were Little Red Riding Hood, what would you do, play with six ducks or go to grandma's house directly?
5. What does the hunter put into the wolf's stomach?

Speaking Practice

I. Role Play

Suppose you were Little Red Riding Hood, would you play with six ducks or go to grandma's house directly? Use the following functional sentences, you have to add your own expressions when it is necessary.

- Hi, I'm Little Red Riding Hood.
- Will you make a friend with me?
- I like dancing.
- No, thanks. But I have to go home right now.
- Listen to me, otherwise I will eat you!
- Bye for now.
- So long.

II. Problem-Solving

Think of appropriate lines for the animal in the picture above.

III. Delivery Game

The teacher divides the whole class into four or five groups, queue the students. The teacher writes a long sentence from the script in a piece of paper, just let the first student read and recite it for one minute, and let the student retell the sentence to the second student, the second to the third, when the sentence is delivered to the last student, he/she should write it on the blackboard, and translate it into Chinese. The group which has got great speed and relative accuracy wins.

Translating Practice

I. Translate the sentences into Chinese.

Work in pairs, one student reads the following sentences, and the other translates the sentences into Chinese in spoken way. (Add extra sentences from the scripts if necessary.)

1. Here are some apples and bananas for her. Take them to her, will you?
2. Little Red Riding Hood starts dancing with baby ducks, and the wolf is hiding behind a tree.
3. Grandma, give me some needles and thread. Little Red Riding Hood, give me some stones.
4. My stomach is so heavy!
5. You big bad wolf, raise your arms.

II. Translate the sentences into English.

Work in pairs, one student reads the following sentences, and the other translates the sentences into English in spoken way. (Add extra sentences from the scripts if necessary.)

1. 妈妈，你在干什么呢？
2. 你去哪儿？
3. 她生病了。
4. 狼正在睡觉。
5. 我必须快点。

Writing Practice

Write a summary of *Little Red Riding Hood* in 50 words.

"Ws" / "Who"	doing what	whom	where	when

Part Five: Language Skills

Grammar

A. 名词所有格

名词所有格的构成：

名词所有格表示这一名词与他人、他物的所属关系。

例如：Xiao Lin's sister 小林的姐姐

名词所有格有以下表达方式：

名词词尾加's 的所有格

1. 一般情况在名词后加's。 例如：

That girl's bike is over there. 女孩的自行车在那边。

2. 在以 s 结尾的名词（包括以 s 结尾的复数名词）后面，只加'。如果复数名词不是以 s 结尾的，末尾也要加's。例如：

(1) Today is September 10th, Teachers' Day. 今天是九月十日，教师节。

(2) Children's Day is coming. 儿童节马上就要到了。

3. 表示词组内的并列名词各自的所有关系时，须在各个名词后加's；如果一个东西为两个人或者两个以上的人共同拥有，只在最后一个名词后面加's。例如：

(1) They are John's and Kate's rooms. 这是约翰和凯特的房间。（指他们两人分别的房间）

(2) He is Lily and Lucy's teacher. 他是莉莉和露西的老师。（指他们两人共同的老师）

4. 表示某人的家、店铺等的所有格，一般可以省略它后面所修饰的名词。例如：

My father and I will have dinner at the Johnson's (home). 我爸爸和我将要去约翰逊的家吃晚饭。

We will have our hair cut at the barber's (shop) tomorrow afternoon. 明天下午我们要去理发店理发。

5. 有些指时间、距离、国家、城镇等的名词，也可以加's 构成所有格。例如：

There is something important in today's newspaper. 今天的报纸上有一些重要的东西。

It's about ten minutes' walk from school to our home every day. 每天从学校到我们家步行大约需要十分钟。

6. 英语名词所有格修饰的词，如果前面已经提到过，后面则可以省略，以防止重复，例如：

This is not Dick's pen, but is Jack's. 这不是迪克的笔，但是是杰克的。

B. 用名词所有格表示处所

肉铺叫 a butcher's ['butʃə] shop，但通常略写为 a butcher's。类似情况下的 shop, house, office 都可以省略：

a tailor's ['teilə]裁缝铺、a barber's ['bɑ:bə]理发店、a doctor's 诊所、my sister's 我姐姐的家、stationer's ['steɪʃənə]文具店、Tony's 托尼

的家。

C. 由 of 短语构成的所有格

1. 表示“无生命的名词”一般与 of 构成短语，表示所有关系。例如：There is a river on the other side of the road. 在公路的另一边有一条河。

2. 有时我们用名词 + of +名词所有格构成双重所有格的形式。例如：This is a photo of Mr Brown’s. 这是一张布朗先生的照片。

Exercises

A. Mutliple Choice

1. Room 210 on the third floor is the _____ office. I know some of them.

A. doctors B. doctor’s C. doctors’ D. doctors’s

2. The room is _______. They are twins.

A. Tom and Mike’s B. Tom’s and Mike’s

C. Tom’s and Mike D. Tom and Mike

3. Excuse me, where is the______?

A. men’s room B. mens’ room

C. men’s rooms D. men rooms

4. On the wall there is a_______.

A. China’s map B. map of China

C. China map D. Chinese map

5. This is ______ friend.

A. May’s brother B. May’s brother’s

C. May’s brother of D. May brother’s

6. The woman dressed in blue is ______ mother.

A. Mary’s and Alice’s B. Mary and Alice’s

C. Mary’s and Alice D. Marys and Alices

7. It is _______ between the two cities.

A. three hours drive B. three hour’s drive

C. three hours’s drivers D. three hours’ drive

8. The post card is sent by ____.

A. a friend of my father B. a friend of my father's

C. my father friend D. my father friend's

9. This is _______ room. The twin sisters like it very much.

A. Lucy's and Lily's B. Lucy's and Lily

C. Lucy and Lily's D. Lucy and Lily

10. This is my dress. That one is ______.

A. Mary B. Mary's C. sister D. mother

11. —How's Joy's skirt?

—Her skirt is more beautiful than ________.

A. her sister's and Kate B. her sister and Kate

C. her sister and Kate's D. her sister's and Kate's

12. In ______ time, those mountains will be covered with trees, too.

A. few years B. a few years' C. a few year D. a few year's

13. We will have a ___________holiday after the work.

A. two month B. two–month C. two month's D. two–months

14. Did you hear the ___________report?

A. policemen B. policemen's C. policemens' D. policemens

15. It's about __________walk from my home.

A. five minute B. ten minutes' C. ten minute's D. ten minutes

16. This is my dress. That one is ______________.

A. Mary B. Mary's C. my mother D. my mothers

17. Every morning Jack takes a ________ to his school.

A. 20 minutes walk B. 20 minute's walk

C. 20-minutes walk D. 20-minute walk

18. Where is ___________ sweater? I can't see it.

A. mine B. us C. my D. we

19. __________ mothers prepare them a great a party.

A. Peter and Anne B. Peter's and Anne's

C. Peter's and Anne D. Peter and Anne's

20. The room on the right is ________.

A. her B. she C. Lucy's D. Lucy

B. Complete each of the following sentences with a proper word.

1. The watch is our________ (teacher).
2. Those boys are my good _______ (friend).
3. What's his________________ (brother) names?
4. _______ (Tom) bicycle is new. He likes riding it.
5. _______ (who) doll is this? It's _______ (Linda).
6. _______ (who) footballs are these? They are_______ (Tim and John).
7. ___________ (Tim and John) bedroom is very big and clean.
8. Are these _______ (Jim) black shoes?
9. The _______ (students) coats are very nice.
10. These _______ (girl) kites are flying very high.

C. Translate the sentences into English.

1. __________________________(李明的父母)work in a big hospital.
2. This is ________________________________(我妹妹的书).
3. _________________________________(他们的卧室) are very nice.
4. ______________________________(王丽和王明的父亲) is a doctor.
5. Is this ________________________________(你的好朋友的钢笔)?
6. They are ______________________________(Peter 和 Sam 的老师).
7. ____________________________(教师节) is on September 10th.
8. ____________________________(学生们的桌椅) are very new.
9. We are very happy on ________________(儿童节).
10. He is in ______________________(老师的办公室) now.

Unit Seven
Diligence

Part One: Phonics
Part Two: Dialogue
Part Three: Text
Part Four: Play — The Three Little Pigs
Part Five: Language Skills

Part One: Phonics

A. R—controlled Vowels "ar" 带有"r"的元音"ar"

1. 拼读发音方式。

字母"r"是一个具有神奇魔力的字母，它能控制和改变出现在它前面的元音的拼读发音。当一个元音字母后面有字母"r"时，字母组合具有特殊的发音，如元音字母"a"后面有字母"r"时，组成字母组合"ar"。其拼读发音就像在单词 car，hard 等中的发音一样。

2. 听一听，学一学字母组合"ar"的拼读发音。

car bar charm shark garlic marble garden jar park arm

3. 仔细听，然后做句子一口气快读练习。

(1) There's a large car park at the end of the garden.

(2) The dog barked so hard when I ran through the yard..

4. 听一听下面的韵律英语，并熟练朗读。

Why did the dog bark?
While running through the park?
Was it because it was so dark?

B. R—controlled Vowels "or" 带有"r"的元音"or"

1. 拼读发音方式。

元音字母"o"后面有字母"r"时，组成字母组合"or"，其拼读发音就像在单词 for, storm 中的发音一样。

2. 听一听，学一学字母组合"or"的拼读发音。

corn for storm corner fort horse pork torch port

3. 仔细听，然后做句子一口气快读练习。

(1) Ford is a lord and he plays with his sword.

(2) Can you go to the record shop and order me some orchestral organ music?

4. 听一听下面的韵律英语，并熟练朗读。

A tiny, tiny horn
Hides in the corn,
During a big, big storm.

Would you use a fork
to eat juicy, juicy pork?

Far way to the north,
There was a very big storm!

C. R—controlled Vowels "er" 带有"r"的元音"er"

1. 拼读发音方式。

元音字母"e"后面有字母"r"时，组成字母组合"er"，其拼读发音就像在单词 sister，mother 等中的发音一样。

2. 听一听，学一学字母组合"er"的拼读发音。

father brother letter hunter weather painter river teacher perch

3. 仔细听，然后做句子一口气快读练习。

(1) A farmer and a teacher are riding on a scooter.

(2) Robert crossed over the river when the weather is better in September.

4. 听一听下面的韵律英语，并熟练朗读。

Brother and sister are writing a letter.
They hope the weather will soon get better.
Mother's a baker, a maker of batter.
Father, a teacher is now getting fatter.
Sister gathers her books together.
Brother puts on his shoes of leather.
Yesterday mother buttered some kippers.
Father ws tried and put on his slippers.

D. R—controlled Vowels "ir" 带有 "r" 的元音 "ir"

1. 拼读发音方式。

元音字母 "i" 后面有字母 "r" 时，组成字母组合 "ir"，其拼读发音就像在单词 bird, firm 等中的发音一样。

2. 听一听，学一学字母组合 "ir" 的拼读发音。

shirt skirt circle girl firm stir swirl Sir fir

3. 仔细听，然后做句子一口气快读练习。

(1) Happy birthday! Kirk! You are thirty third now.

(2) The girl's skirt is dirty and she put on her brother's shirt.

4. 听一听下面的韵律英语，并熟练朗读。

Brown bear, brown bear,
Have you seen a fir?
Yes, sir! Yes, sir!
Not far away from here.

The girl in a pink skirt
Likes to twirl her skirt.

E. R—controlled Vowels “ur” 带有“r”的元音“ur”

1. 拼读发音方式。

元音字母“u”后面有字母“r”时，组成字母组合“ur”，其拼读发音就像在单词 nurse，turkey 等中的发音一样。

2. 听一听，学一学字母组合“ur”的拼读发音。

fur church turtle purse burglar curtain curly furniture burly

3. 仔细听，然后做句子一口气快读练习。

(1) The turtle hided in the furniture of the church.

(2) The burglar stole the purse of the burly girl with curly hair.

4. 听一听下面的韵律英语，并熟练朗读。

Can you see the turkey
Turn into a purple turtle?

This furry, furry purse
Belongs to a very nice nurse.

What a magic fur purse!
The nurse turns
And the purse burns.

Part Two: Dialogue

Dialogue 1

William: How many courses do you have this semester?

John: Eight altogether.

William: How are they proportioned?

John: Six are compulsory, two optional.

Words and Expressions

semester [sɪ'mestə(r)] *n.* 学期

proportion [prə'pɔːʃn] *n.* 占比

compulsory [kəm'pʌlsəri] *adj*. 必修的

optional ['ɒpʃənl] *adj*. 选修的

Decide whether the following statements are True (T) or False (F).

(　　) 1. A semester means a one-month student life.

(　　) 2. John has six courses altogether.

(　　) 3. John has six compulsory courses.

(　　) 4. John has to study at least eight courses in this semester.

(　　) 5. John needn't study two optional courses.

Dialogue 2

Mum: Study hard, otherwise you will fail.

John: Yes, Mum.

Mum: Don't render me lip-service, you'd better stay at home tonight.

John: But it's Sunday, isn't it?

Words and Expressions

render lip-service 耍嘴皮子

Decide whether the following statements are True (T) or False (F).

(　　) 1. Mum asks her son to study hard.

(　　) 2. John is going out tonight.

(　　) 3. Mum asks John to stay at home tonight.

(　　) 4. John goes out every night.

(　　) 5. Mum is very angry with John.

Dialogue 3

Tom: Hi. Fancy meeting you here! Where are you heading now?

William: Hello, Tom. I'm going to the library to look for some reference books.

Tom: Oh, really? So coincidence! Me too.

William: Tom, how about your essay? Have you finished it already?

Tom: No, it's hard for me to complete it in a short time. I know little about Cloning.

William: The same to me. You know our major is little related to Cloning.

Tom: Well, at present the best way for us is to look for reference materials.

William: Good idea. Let's go to the library together.

Words and Expressions

head [hed] *v.* 出发

coincidence [kəʊ'ɪnsɪdəns] *n.* 巧合

essay ['eseɪ] *n.* 论文

reference book 参考书

at present 目前

Decide whether the following statements are True (T) or False (F).

(   ) 1. William is going to a lecture.

(   ) 2. Tom is going to the library for some reference books.

(   ) 3. Tom has finished his essay because it is so easy.

(   ) 4. William and Tom know little about cloning.

(   ) 5. They study same subjects.

Dialogue 4

Tom: There were so many courses that I don't know which one is fit for me.

William: You just select the one you're interested in.

Tom: Oh, I want to enroll in the course.

William: Which one? The enjoyment of the movie?

Tom: Yes, I heard that we can watch many films in this class.

Words and Expressions

select [sɪ'lekt] *v.* 选择

enroll [ɪn'rəʊl] *v.* 注册

be fit for 适合

Decide whether the following statements are True (T) or False (F).

(   ) 1. Tom doesn't know which course is fit for him.

(   ) 2. William suggests Tom to select the one he is interested in.

(   ) 3. Tom is interested in the enjoyment of the movie.

(   ) 4. Tom selects this course because he loves movie.

(   ) 5. There are many theatres in the university.

Part Three: Text

There are four students in our dormitory. They are happy.

There is a laptop on my table. The laptop is expensive.

There are four mobile phones on the shelf. The mobile phones are smart.

There is a refrigerator in my kitchen. The refrigerator is clean.

There is a spoon in the cup. The spoon is small.

There are 26,000 students in our university. The students are diligent.

There are 56 ethnic groups including the Hans in China. They are harmonious.

There are about 800 universities in China. They are open.

Words and Expressions

dormitory ['dɔːmətri] *n.* 宿舍，学生宿舍

Eg. 1. Let us have a look at these students' classes and dormitory life.

让我们来看看这些学生的课程和宿舍生活。

2. Walking along, I came to the students' dormitory.

走着走着，我来到了学生宿舍。

laptop ['læptɒp] *n.* 膝上型轻便电脑，笔记本电脑

Eg. 1. What do you think of this laptop?

你觉得这种笔记本电脑怎么样？

2. Whatever laptop you decide to buy, buy it wisely.

无论你决定买什么笔记本，明智地买它。

expensive [ɪk'spensɪv] *adj.* 昂贵的

Eg. 1. He lived in an expensive house.

他住在一幢昂贵的房子里。

2. These are usually very expensive.

这些通常非常昂贵。

mobile ['məʊbaɪl] *adj.* 可移动的

Eg. 1. And in this mobile world, you have to carry it along with you.

他最后成了这家公司的总经理。

2. Could we use that in mobile phones?

我们能在手机中使用那个吗？

shelf [ʃelf] *n.* 架子

Eg. 1. A book tumbled off the shelf.

一本书从架子上掉了下来。

2. Put it here on this shelf.

放在这儿这个架子上。

refrigerator [rɪ'frɪdʒəreɪtə(r)] *n.* 冰箱，冷藏库

Eg. 1. Take the beef out of the refrigerator to defrost.

把牛肉从冰箱里拿出来解冻。

2. You have to lock the refrigerator.

你必须把冰箱锁起来。

spoon [spu:n] *n.* 匙，勺子

Eg. 1. She feeds the baby with a spoon.

她用汤匙喂婴儿。

2. She stirred her coffee with a spoon.

她用汤匙搅拌咖啡。

ethnic ['eθnɪk] *adj.* 种族的；民族的

Eg. 1. We can't be certain that these findings apply to other ethnic groups.

我们不能肯定，这些发现能不能适用于其他种族的人。

2. How many ethnic groups are there in China?

中国有多少个民族？

harmonious [hɑːˈməʊniəs] *adj.* 和谐的，和睦的

Eg. 1. They blend into a harmonious piece of music.

它们混合在一起，能成为音乐中和谐的部分。

2. Honesty, which is the traditional virtue of the Chinese people, can make our life easier and more harmonious.

诚信是中华民族的传统美德，讲诚信可以使我们的生活变得更加容易和和谐。

mobile phone 手机

Eg. 1. He bought a new mobile phone.

他买了一个新手机。

2. The mobile phone is cool.

这个手机很酷。

Language Focus

I. Make a sentence with the words given below.

1. there / people / four / are / my / in / family

   are / we / happy

2. is / there / on / sofa / the / a / bag

   is / it / big

3. is / there / umbrella / an / on / floor / the

   it / is / colorful

4. are / there / books / some / the / on / shelf

   they / interesting / are

5. is / there / cup / a / the / on / desk

   it / pink / is /

II. Translating

Put Chinese into English.

1. 桌子上有两块手表。它们是新的。

2. 这个班里有五名学生。他们很无聊。
3. 铅笔盒里有三支铅笔和两支钢笔。
4. 这个房间里有一台电视机。
5. 这个桌子上有一台电脑。

Put English into Chinese.

1. There are many children on the playground. They are playing soccer.
2. There are two horses and three cows on the grassland.
3. There is a dog on the top of the car. It is cute.
4. There is a guitar in the room.
5. There are two whiteboards in the classroom.

III. Reading Comprehension

Choose the best answer to each of the following questions or incomplete sentences.

This is a park (公园) . There are many flowers in it. Some are red. Some are yellow. There is a river in the park, too. There are some boats in the river. The boats are very small.

It is Sunday. There are many people in the park. Some are walking. Some are playing games. Some old men are sitting under the big tree. Look at these students! They are singing and dancing near the river. Their teacher is playing with them. They are very happy (高兴) .

1. This is a ______.

A. classroom　B. park　C. school　D. bedroom

2. There is a ______ in the park.

A. map　B. picture　C. hill　D. river

3. There are some ______ in the river.

A. boats　B. cats　C. birds　D. buses

4. Some old men are ______ under the big tree.

A. walking　B. dancing　C. sitting　D. singing

5. ______ are very happy.

A. The old men　B. The students

C. Their teacher　D. All the people in the park

Part Four: Play

The Three Little Pigs

Characters:
Aside 旁白
Tom 猪老大
John 猪老二
Harry 猪小弟
Mother Pig 猪妈妈
Wolf 狼

Scene 1

Aside: Once upon a time, a mother pig and her three children lived in a village. Tom and John were brother pigs, and Harry was the youngest one.

Tom: We are the lazy boys, we like eating and sleeping.

John: Yes, yes! We are the lazy boys. We eat and sleep all day and all night.

Harry: I like working, I help my mum to do the housework.

Aside: One day, the mother pig called the three boys together.

Mother Pig: You've grown up, my dear children. It's time for you to make your own houses. Goodbye, little boys. Build your houses and live on your own. Be careful of the wolf.

Three boys: Yes, mum. Goodbye. We will look after ourselves.

Scene 2

Harry: Tom, what are you doing? Why are you picking up those leaves?

Tom: I'm building a house with them.

Harry: But leaves aren't strong enough.

Tom: But it is easy to use.

Harry: John, what are you doing? Why are you picking up those sticks?

John: I'm building a house with them.

Harry: But sticks aren't strong enough.

Tom: Yes, I know. But it is easy.

Tom&John: What are you doing, Harry?

Harry: I'm building a house with bricks.

Tom&John: Bricks! That's too hard.

Harry: I know, but bricks are strong.

Tom&John: How stupid he is! Hahaha… Look, our beautiful houses are done! Let's have a nap.

Harry: Look at my house! It's very strong. The wolf won't get in easily.

Scene 3

Aside: Now the three pigs were living in their own houses. A big bad wolf came for the three little pigs.

Wolf: Little pig, open the door, let me in.

Tom: No…No…

Wolf: Let me in, or I'll huff and I'll puff and I'll blow your house down!

Tom: No… I am scared.

Wolf: This is very easy. Leaves aren't strong.

Aside: The wolf blew the house away in no time. Of course, Tom ran to John's house.

Wolf: Little pig, let me in.

John&Tom: No, we'll never let you in.

Wolf: Well, you can't keep me out of door!

John&Tom: No…

Wolf: This is very easy. Sticks aren't strong.

Aside: The wolf bumped the house. It soon fall down. Tom and John ran to Harry's house.

John&Tom: Help! Help!

Wolf: Stop, you two pigs.

John&Tom: Open the door, Harry. The wolf is coming. Let us in.

Harry: Come in, please. Don't worry. My house is strong.

Wolf: Where did they go? Oh, they are here. Little pigs. Little pigs. Open the door!

Three Pigs: No. No. Go away. You bad wolf.

Wolf: I'll blow it down.

Aside: The wolf blew and blew. But the house was very strong.

Wolf: I'll hit it. Oh!

Harry: Let's boil the water.

Tom&John: OK!

Wolf: Oh, Oh! It's hot. It's hot.

Three Pigs: Oh yeah! The wolf is dead. The wolf is dead.

Aside: Since then, Tom and John worked hard with Harry. They worked and played together.

（师生改编剧本）

Words and Expressions

village ['vɪlɪdʒ] *n.* 村庄
young [jʌŋ] *adj.* 年轻的
lazy ['leɪzɪ] *adj.* 懒惰的
work [wɜːk] *v.* 工作
help [help] *v.* 帮助
housework ['haʊswɜːk] *n.* 家务事
own [əʊn] *adj.* 自己的
build [bɪld] *v.* 建造
ourselves [aʊə'selvz] *pron.* 我们自己
leaf [liːf] *n.* 叶子
easy ['iːzɪ] *adj.* 容易的
stick [stɪk] *n.* 棍子
brick [brɪk] *n.* 砖
nap [næp] *n.* 小睡，打盹儿
huff [hʌf] *v.* 吹气
puff [pʌf] *v.*（从口中）喷出
blow [bləʊ] *v.* 吹
bump[bʌmp] *v.* 碰，撞
boil [bɒɪl] *v.* 煮沸

once upon a time　很久以前
live on one's own　独自生活
look after　照顾
pick up　捡起，拾起
in no time　立刻
fell down　倒塌
since then　从此以后
work hard　努力工作

Listening Practice

I. Bingo game

Work in groups, one student read about the script of *The Three Little Pigs*, other students listen carefully, when they hear the adjective from the script, say "Bingo", and write the word in the form quickly, and then he/she wins. And take turns, and change the words into Verbs, Nouns, etc.

words	adjective	verbs	nouns	prepositions	adverbs	conjunctions
student 1						
student 2						
student 3						
student 4						
student 5						

II. Dictation

Listen to the passage three times and supply the missing information.

___1___, a mother pig and her three children lived in a ___2___. One day, the mother pig told three little pigs that they should make their ___3___ houses. Tom and John were very ___4___. Tom made a house by ___5___ and Harry made a house by ___6___. Both houses are very unsafe. However, Harry made a very strong house by ___7___. One day, a wolf came and he ___8___down Tom's and John's houses easily. So they ran to Harry's house and hid in it. They ___9___ water and ___10___ the wolf.

Reading Practice

I. Read and choose

1. Which of the following statement is True?

A. Harry is the oldest pig.

B. Tom is the youngest one.

C. A mother pig and her two children lived in a city.

D. Harry likes working and helps her mother to do the housework.

2. Tom built his house by ______.

A. leaves

B. bricks

C. steel

D. sticks

3. Wolf came to ______'s house firstly?

A. Tom

B. Mother pig

C. Harry

D. John

4. Whose house is the strongest one?

A. Tom

B. Harry

C. John

D. Mother pig

5. Finally, Tom and John become ________ boys.

A. lazy

B. hard-working

C. strong

D. kind

II. Read and answer

1. Who was Harry? Is he Tom and John's eldest brother?
2. Why did mother pig ask three pigs to live on their own?
3. Where did the mother pig and her three children live?
4. If you were a little pig, what kind of house would you like to build?
5. How did three pigs kill the wolf?

Speaking Practice

I. Role Play

Suppose you were Harry, what would you do to kill the wolf? Use the following functional sentences, you have to add your own expressions when it is necessary.

- Hi, I'm a wolf.
- Open the door, otherwise I will kill you.
- I like eating delicious pig.

- Who is it?
- Give me the …
- The bad wolf is dead.
- Remember me!
- So long.

II. Problem-Solving

Think of appropriate lines for the houses in the picture above.

III. Delivery Game

The teacher divides the whole class into four or five groups, queue the students. The teacher writes a long sentence from the script in a piece of paper, just let the first student read and recite it for one minute, and let the student retell the sentence to the second student, the second to the third, when the sentence is delivered to the last student, he/she should write it on the blackboard, and translate it into Chinese. The group which has got great speed and relative accuracy wins.

Translating Practice

I. Translate the sentences into Chinese.

Work in pairs, one student reads the following sentences, and the other translates the sentences into Chinese in spoken way. (Add extra sentences from the scripts if necessary.)

1. Once upon a time, a mother pig and her three children lived in a village.
2. Now the three pigs were living in their own houses.
3. Let me in, or I'll huff and I'll puff and I'll blow your house down!
4. The wolf blew the house away in no time.
5. The wolf bumped the house. It soon fall down.

II. Translate the sentences into English.

Work in pairs, one student reads the following sentences, and the other translates the sentences into English in spoken way. (Add extra sentences from the scripts if necessary.)

1. 我害怕！
2. 你干吗呢？
3. 我们吃了睡，睡了吃。
4. 是时候去盖属于你们自己的房子了。
5. 我们烧些水吧。

Writing Practice

Write a summary of *The Three Little Pigs* in 50 words.

"Ws" / "Who"	doing what	whom	where	when

Part Five: Language Skills

Grammar

特殊疑问句

以特殊疑问词开头,对句中某一成分提问的句子叫特殊疑问句。 常用的疑问词有：what，who，whose，which，when，where，how，why。我们把疑问词分为三类：

疑问代词	what（什么） who（谁,做主语） which（哪个,在一定范围内） whose（谁的）whom（谁,做宾语）
疑问形容词	What(什么） which（哪个） whose（谁的,指附属关系）
疑问副词	when（何时,询问时间） where（何地,询问地点） why（为什么,询问原因） how（如何,询问手段、方式、工具以及程度）

A. 疑问代词的用法

1. what 引导的疑问句

此类疑问句可以对主语、表语和宾语提问。

What's in the room? 屋子里有什么？（对主语提问）

What do you like? 你喜欢什么？（对宾语提问 ）

What is this? 这是什么？（对表语提问）

What day is today? 今天星期几？（对表语提问）

2.who，whose，which 引导的疑问句

此类疑问句可以对主语、表语、宾语提问。

Who closed the window? 谁关的窗户？（对主语提问）

Who is she? 她是谁？（对表语提问）

Whose banana is this? 这是谁的香蕉？(对定语提问)

Which is Tom's? 哪个是汤姆的？ (对主语提问)

Which do you like? 你喜欢哪个？(对宾语提问）

B. 疑问形容词的用法

1. what, which, whose 后面跟上名词时，这三个疑问词起形容词作用。

What color do you like? 你喜欢什么颜色？（对宾语提问）

Which book do you read? 你读哪本书？（对宾语提问）

Whose bike is this? 这是谁的自行车？（对表语提问）

C. 疑问副词的用法

疑问副词在句中做状语，所以它们不可能对主语提问。

1. when 引导的疑问句表时间

When will you come back? 你何时回来？

When were you born? 你什么时候出生的？

2. where 引导的疑问句询问地点

Where do you live? 你住在哪儿？

Where are you going? 你准备去什么地方？

3. why 引导的疑问句询问原因

Why do you come here? 你为什么来这儿？

Why don't you go to school? 你为什么不上学？

Why are you late? 你为什么迟到了？

4. how 引导的疑问句询问方式、方法、手段及天气状况、身体状况等，how 还可以用来询问长短、宽窄、高低、多少等。

How do you go to the airport? 你怎么去机场？

How is the weather today? 今天天气怎么样？

How are you? 你好吗？

How is your mother? 你母亲好吗?

How old are you? 你多大了？

How many students are there? 那里有多少学生？

Exercises

A. Mutliple Choice

1. ________many oranges do you want?

A. Where B. How C. When D. Why

2. —________did you come back?

— I came back last Friday.

A. When B. Which C. What D. Where

3. —________ are you?

— I am fine, thank you.

A. What B. Where C. How D. Why

4. — _______ color do you like?

— Pink.

A. How　　B. Why　　C. Which　　D. What

5. —_______ T-shirt is it?

— It's Betty's.

A. What　　B. Why　　C. Whose　　D. Where

6. —_______ did you go last night?

— I went to the cinema.

A. Where　　B. Which　　C. When　　D. What

7. —_______ is your name?

— I'm Ellen.

A. What　　B. Why　　C. Whose　　D. Where

8. —______ one do you like?

— I like black one.

A. Who　　B. How　　C. Which　　D. What

9. —_______ is Xiaoming's mother?

— Xiaoming's mother is a nurse.

A. What　　B. Which　　C. When　　D. Where

10. —_______ books are those ?

— They are theirs.

A. Where　　B. Which　　C. Whose　　D. Who

11. —_____ is that boy?

— He is my brother.

A. Where　　B. Which　　C. Whose　　D. Who

12. —_____ are you from?

— I'm from Gansu province.

A. Where　　B. When　　C. Why　　D. Who

13. —_____ do you go to school?

— I go to school from Monday to Friday.

A. Where　　B. Which　　C. When　　D. What

14. — _____ do you live?

— I live in campus.

A. Where B. Which C. What D. Who

15. ______ many pencils do you have?

A. What B. How C. Where D. Whose

16. — ______ dormitory is this?

— This is mine.

A. What B. Whose C. Where D. How

17. —______ are you late?

— I got stuck in a traffic jam.

A. What B. Why C. Where D. How

18. —_____ do you like to drink?

—I'd like a cup of tea.

A. What B. Which C. Why D. How

19. —______ is the police station?

— It's over there.

A. When B. Whose C. Where D. How

20. —______ is the weather today?

— It's cloudy

A. How B. Which C. Where D.When

B. Fill in the blank with their Chinese meaning.

1. What colour ( ) 2. What time ( ) 3. What day ( )
4. How old ( ) 5. How many ( ) 6. How much ( )
7. How tall ( ) 8. How long ( ) 9. How often ( )
10. How soon ( ) 11.How far ( ) 12. How high ( )

C. Make a question about the underlining part by using Who, What, When, Where, How many and How.

1. She is <u>my sister.</u>

____

2. They are <u>in the classroom.</u>

____

3. I often go swimming <u>on Sunday</u>.

____

4. I live in <u>Changjiang road</u>.

____

5. Lily likes to play with <u>Sally</u>.

____

6. The rulers are <u>in the pencil-box</u>.

____

7. I'm late because of <u>the traffic jam</u>.

____

8. I have <u>10</u> brothers.

____

9. That is <u>a fish</u>.

____

10. I go to school <u>by bus</u>.

____

Unit Eight
Inner Strength

Part One: Phonics

Part Two: Dialogue

Part Three: Text

Part Four: Play—The Tiger and the Fox

Part Five: Language Skills

Part One: Phonics

A. B b and P p Sounds

1. 拼读发音方式。

字母“b”和“p”都有字母音和拼读音，字母音就是在字母“ABCDE…LMNOPQ…”中的读音，而它们的拼读音是这样的：/b/和/p/，是一对爆破音。发这两个音时都是双紧闭、屏住气，然后突然放开，使气流冲出口腔，气流送出时，形成爆破。不同的是，发前者时声带有振动，发后者时声带不振动。无论字母“b”和“p”在单词的首或尾，它们的拼读音都是相同的，如 big，bad，boy，book，butter，boat，bee，cab，pat，park，peach，pet，stop，sheep，lip，tip。

2. 发音规则。

字母 **B b**

(1) 辅音字母 b 在单词中一般发/b/，如 best，about，globe，back。

(2) 字母 b 在词尾是-mb 和-bt 的组合中不发音，如 climb，debt。

字母 **P p**

(1) 辅音字母 p 在单词中一般发/p/，如 people，past，top，appear。

(2) 辅音字母 p 有时不发音，如 receipt，psychology。

3. 听一听，学一学字母“b”和字母“p”的拼读发音。

含有字母“**b**”的拼读音

(1) bee ball big cab box tub bear bag bed
b-ee b-all b-ig c-ab b-ox t-ub b-ear b-ag b-ed

(2) busy as a bee brown bread and butter Big Ben be an early bird

含有字母“**p**”拼读音

(1) pack park pull paper cap pig party popcorn
p-a-ck p-ar-k p-u-ll p-a-per c-ap p-ig p-ar-t-y p-op-c-or-n

(2) as easy as pie pig in a poke a plate of porridge a pack of peanuts

4. 仔细听，然后做句子一口气快读练习。

含有字母“**b**”拼读音

(1) Practice makes perfect.

(2) We must help the poor.

(3) Did Peter pass the exam?

(4) Please book a room for Paul.

含有字母“**p**”拼读音

(1) Barking dogs do not bite.

(2) This bank was robbed by a mob.

(3) Bob is absent because of backache.

(4) Ben’s bike was broken by a bad guy.

5. 听一听下列的韵律英语，并熟练朗读。

Blue Bird, Blue Bird.
What do you say?
I say Bb b,
Blue, Blue Bird!

There lived a bear, also a boar.
The bear could not bear the boar.
The boar thought the bear a bore.

B. D d and T t Sounds

1. 拼读发音方式。

字母“d”和“t”都有字母音和拼读音，字母音就是在字母“ABCDE…OPQRST…”中的读音，而它们的拼读音是这样的：

/d/和/t/，是一对爆破音。发这两个音时都是舌尖紧贴上齿沿、屏住气，然后突然放开，使气流冲出口腔。气流送出时，形成爆破。不同的是，发前者时声带有振动，发后者时声带不振动。

2. 发音规则。

字母 **D d**

(1) 字母 d 在一般情况下发/d/，如 dark，mud，pride。

(2) 动词过去式-ed 结尾，前面是清辅音时发/t/，如 helped，walked。

前面是浊辅音时发/d/，如 rubbed，hugged。

前面是/d/和/t/时发/id/，如 needed，started。

字母 **T t**

字母 t 一般发/t/，如 teach，heart，meeting，letter。

3. 听一听，学一学字母“d”和字母“t”的拼读发音。

含有字母“d”拼读音

(1) dot　dog　duck　spider　cloud　wind　spade　bird
d-ot　d-og　d-u-ck　s-p-i-d-er　cl-ou-d　w-in-d　s-p-a-d-e　b-ir-d
diamond
d-i-a-m-o-n-d

(2) dad did the job　a red deer　study hard　don’t do it　day in and day out

含有字母“t”拼读音

(1) turtle　towel　tiger　tent　tomato　tube　tunnel
t-ur-t-l-e　t-ow-e-l　t-i-g-er　t-en-t　t-o-m-a-t-o　t-u-b-e　t-u-n-n-e-l
tall　ticket
t-all　t-i-ck-e-t

(2) take a trip　take a bite　take a back seat　take the heat　teacher’s pet

(3) 10,222　ten thousand, two hundred and twenty two

(4) 22,222　twenty two thousand, two hundred and twenty two

4. 仔细听，然后做句子一口气快读练习。

含有字母“d”拼读音

(1) Don't depend on anybody.

(2) Daddy is in the bed.

(3) I'm glad you did that.

(4) My daughter likes bread instead of rice.

含有字母“t”拼读音

(1) Ted is taller than Tom.

(2) Not at all.

(3) Don't waste time.

(4) Let me have a rest.

5. 听一听下列的韵律英语，并熟练朗读。

Dolly Duck, Dolly Duck.
What do you say?
I say Dd d,
Dolly, Dolly Duck!

Two times four is eight.
But ten to two is late.
Ten times ten is not the time.
But ten past ten is fine.

C. F f and V v Sounds

1. 拼读发音方式。

字母“f”和“v”都有字母音和拼读音，字母音就是在字母“CDEF…UVWX…”中的读音，而它们的拼读音是这样的：/f/和/v/，是一对摩擦音。发这两个音时都是上齿轻触下唇，气流从唇齿间的缝隙通过，形成摩擦音。不同的是发前者时声带不振动，发后者时声带振动。

2. 发音规则。

字母 **F f**

(1) 字母 f 发/f/，如 first，after，half。

(2) 个别情况发/v/，如 of。

字母 **V v**

字母 v 发/v/，如 visit，live，heavy。

3. 听一听，学一学字母“f”和字母“v”的拼读发音。

含有字母“f”拼读音

(1) van fan full fast flag film food fog flu fly fun

v-an f-an f-u-ll f-a-st fl-ag f-i-l-m f-oo-d f-o-g fl-u fl-y f-u-n

(2) fast food first sight fresh fish fifty five lives face to face feel free fine your feet

含有字母“v”拼读音

(1) very violin vain vase vacuum beaver

v-e-r-y v-i-o-l-in v-ai-n v-a-s-e v-a-c-uu-m b-ea-v-er

David river

D-a-v-i-d r-i-v-er

(2) very well very good violin Valentine's Day velvet glove

David's vase

4. 仔细听，然后做句子一口气快读练习。

含有字母“f”拼读音

(1) Fortunately, Frank's father fixed the phones.

(2) When it's fall, there is a fine field of wheat.

(3) My French friends flew here from France last Friday.

(4) The butterfly flied from a flower to a flower.

含有字母“v”拼读音

(1) He has a valuable valley villa.

(2) Van is a kind of vehicle.

(3) Victor only eats vegetables.

(4) His voice varies with the tune of the violin.

5. 听一听下列的韵律英语，并熟练朗读。

Funny Fish, Funny Fish.
What do you say?
I say Ff f,
Funny, Funny Fish.

Van, van, van.
A very big van.

Vv says v v.
Van van van.

Vitamin A and Vitamin C,
Vitamin tablets for you and for me.

Part Two: Dialogue

Dialogue 1

William: Do you like your neighbors?

Tom: Yes, I lived in a comfortable environment. It's peaceful!

William: Fortunately!

Tom: We can help him when someone needs help.

William: Just like a warm family.

Tom: That's true.

Decide whether the following statements are True (T) or False (F).

( ) 1. Tom likes his living environment.

( ) 2. William dislike his neighbors.

( ) 3. Tom will help his neighbors when someone needs help.

( ) 4. Tom likes his family.

( ) 5. William wants to live with Tom.

Dialogue 2

William: Look at my home town. The streets are very wide.

Tom: It's beautiful.

William: It changed a lot. There used to have many temples, but now they became school, net-club, shopping center and so on.

Tom: Great!

Decide whether the following statements are True (T) or False (F).

( ) 1. William's home town is very beautiful.

( ) 2. The street are very narrow.

(   ) 3. There used to have many hospitals in William's hometown.

(   ) 4. Now there are many temples in the street.

(   ) 5. William's hometowm has been changed a lot.

Dialogue 3

William: I live in a bit of a rough neighborhood. It's just down the street from all the nightclubs. You probably don't want to walk around after dark.

Tom: It can't be that bad.

William: I wish it wasn't, but there is actually a lot of crime around here.

Tom: Really? I never would have guessed.

William: I will move to a safe community next week.

Tom: A wise decision!

Words and Expressions

rough [rʌf] *adj*. 乱的

nightclub ['naɪtklʌb] *n*. 夜总会

actually ['æktʃuəli] *adv*. 实际上

crime [kraɪm] *n*. 犯罪活动

walk around 四处走走

Decide whether the following statements are True (T) or False (F).

(   ) 1. William's living environment is very poor.

(   ) 2. There are lots of nightclubs near William's house.

(   ) 3. At night, it's very safe for William to go out.

(   ) 4. There is a lot of crime around here.

(   ) 5. William has no plan to move.

Dialogue 4

William: I think the biggest environment problem in our country is air pollution.

Tom: Yes, I agree.

William: We have reduced emission of air pollutants in recent years, but cars are still a major source of them.

Tom: The problem is now on a truly global scale. I don't believe that any single country can do anything about it.

William: I think you're right. Environment pollution demands a global response.

Words and Expressions

pollution [pə'luːʃn] *n.* 污染

emission [ɪ'mɪʃn] *n.* 散发

major ['meɪdʒə(r)] *adj.* 主要的

pollutant [pə'luːtənt] *n.* 污染物

scale [skeɪl] *n.* 规模

demand [dɪ'mɑːnd] *n.* 需求

response [rɪ'spɒns] *n.* 反应

Decide whether the following statements are True (T) or False (F).

(　　) 1. William thinks the biggest environment problem in the world is air pollution.

(　　) 2. Smoking is a major source of air pollution.

(　　) 3. Recently emission of air pollutants has been reduced a lot.

(　　) 4. Environment pollution is a big issue.

(　　) 5. We mustn't drive a car in our daily life.

Part Three: Text

Are there many cars on the street?

Yes, there are. There are many new cars on the street.

Are there many people singing and dancing in the park?

No, there aren't. It is raining now.

Are there foreign students in the university?

Yes, there are. The foreign students are from America, Canada and Russia.

Is there any river in this city?

Yes, there is. The Yellow River is flowing through the city.

Is there any famous local dish in Lanzhou?

Yes, there is. Beef Noodle of Lanzhou is well known in China.

Is there a book on the table?

No, there isn't. There are two teapots on the table.

Words and Expressions

street [striːt] *n.* 街道

Eg. 1. We must make a turn at the next street.

我们必须在下一个街口掉转车头。

2. The street is clean and wide.

这个街道又干净又宽。

sing [sɪŋ] *vi.* 唱歌；歌颂

Eg. 1. You sing well.

你唱得很好。

2. We can sing.

我们能唱歌。

dance [dɑːns] *vt.* 跳舞；使跳跃

Eg. 1. Will you dance with me?

你愿意和我跳舞吗?

2. I like to dance.

我喜欢跳舞。

rain [reɪn] *v.* 下雨；降雨

Eg. 1. It is raining heavily.

正在下大雨。

2. It almost rains every day in this summer.

这个夏天几乎每天都下雨。

foreign ['fɒrɪn] *adj.* 外国的；外交的

Eg. 1. The foreign students studying in Beijing come from all parts of the world.

在北京学习的外国留学生来自世界各地。

He is learning two foreign languages.

他在学习两种外国语。

Russia ['rʌʃə] *n.* 俄罗斯

Eg. 1. How do you feel about Russia?

你们觉得俄罗斯怎么样？

2. They come from Russia.

他们是俄罗斯人。

river ['rɪvə] *n.* 河；江

Eg. 1. They were swimming in the river.

他们在河中游泳。

2. It is a deep river.

这是一条很深的河。

city ['sɪtɪ] *n.* 城市，都市

Eg. 1. The city is quite strange to me.

这个城市对我来说很陌生。

2. Shanghai is an internationalized city in China.

上海是中国的一座国际化都市。

flow [fləʊ] *v.* 流动，涌流

Eg. 1. Rivers flow into the sea.

江河流入海中。

2. You flow. You accept.

你流动。你接受。

local ['ləʊk(ə)l] *adj.* 地方性的；乡土的

Eg. 1. You can find these books in any local bookstore.

你在当地的任意一所书店都能找到此类书。

2. Every evening the local people walk around the park.

每天晚上，当地居民常在这个公园里散步。

dish [dɪʃ] *n.* 盘；餐

Eg. 1. This dish tastes good.

这盘菜的滋味不错。

2. The dish smells good.

这道菜闻起来很好。

teapot ['tiːpɒt] *n.* 茶壶

Eg. 1. She threw the teapot at him.

她将茶壶向他掷去。

2. I want to buy a teapot.

我想买个茶壶。

beef noodle 牛肉面

Eg. 1. Which beef noodle shop will we go to today?

我们今天要去吃哪一家牛肉面？

2. There are two bowls of beef noodle on the table.

桌子上有两碗牛肉面。

Language Focus

I. Make a sentence with the words given below.

1. there / are / some / in / refrigerator / eggs / the / ?

there / are / yes

2. are / some / notebooks / there / the / in / library / ?

there / no / are / not

3. are / there / people / many / the / in / park / ?

yes / there / are

4. are / there / cars / the / on / street / ?

there / yes / are

5. is / there / cat / a / the / tree / in / ?

there / not / is / no

II. Translating

Put Chinese into English.

1. 桌子上有一把尺子吗？是的，桌子上有一把尺子。
2. 房间里有人吗？没有。
3. 床上有两个玩具吗？是的，床上有两个玩具。
4. 这条街上有两家超市吗？是的，这里有两家超市。
5. 他的包里有太阳镜吗 ？是的，他的包里有太阳镜。

Put English into Chinese.

1. Are there two beautiful girls on the street? Yes, there are. They are waiting for their friends.
2. Are there any toilet in the restaurant? Yes, there is one toilet in the corner.
3. Is there a library in the university? Of course, there are two libraries in the university.
4. Are there any labs in the university? There are more than ten labs in the university.
5. Is there any primary school in this community? Yes, there is one primary school and one high school in this community.

III. Reading Comprehension

Choose the best answer to each of the following questions or incomplete sentences.

It's Sunday. There are many people in the bus. And an old man is looking here and there. He wants to find an empty seat (空座位). Then he finds one. He goes to it. A small bag is on the seat. And a young man is sitting beside (在……旁边) it.

"Is this seat empty?" asks the old man.

"No, it's for a woman. She goes to buy some bananas." says the young man.

"Well." says the old man, "Let me sit here please. When she comes back, I will (将) leave here."

The bus starts (开动).

"She doesn't come, but her bag is here. Let me give her the bag." Then the old man throws the bag out of the bus window.

The young man jumps up and shouts: "Don't throw! It's my bag!"

1. The old man wants to find an empty seat ________.

A. in the room B. in the bus C. beside the driver D. in a car

2. The old man finds an empty seat. He goes there and finds there is ______on it.

A. a man B. a woman C. a bag D. a coat

3. The young man says the seat is for ______.

A. a man B. a woman C. a boy D. a girl

4. The bus starts. The old man_____.

A. asks the woman to sit on the seat

B. takes the bag to the woman

C. throws the bag to the young man

D. throws the bag out of the window

5. Whose bag is it?

A. The old man B. The woman C. The young man D. A pretty girl

Part Four: Play

The Tiger and the Fox

Characters:

Aside 旁白

Tiger 老虎

Fox 狐狸

Bear 熊

Frog 青蛙

Rabbit 兔子

Scene 1

Aside: One day, in a forest a fox ran into a tiger, which made the tiger very angry.

Tiger: I'm a great tiger. I am very strong. I am very brave. I'm the king of the forest. But now, I'm very hungry. I must find something to eat at once. Ah, a fox! Haha, a great meal.

Fox: Oh, my God! A tiger! What should I do?

Tiger: I'd like to eat you, my baby fox! Haha…

Fox: Yes, yes, you should eat me, but you know what?

Tiger: What? Tell me quickly!

Fox: Yes, you have the name of "King of the forest", but I'm the king of the forest in real!

Tiger: What? How dare you say that?

Fox: Yes, I'm the king of the forest.

Tiger: Impossible.

Fox: Do you know that all the animals in the forest are scared of me?

Tiger: Scared of you, a fox?

Fox: Yes, so if you want to eat me, I will let you die right now.

Tiger: What are you talking about? Are you crazy?

Fox: If you don't believe me, just follow me and see who the king of the forest is.

Tiger: Ok, Let's go!

Scene 2

Fox: Hello, bear! Hello, frog! Hello, rabbit.

Bear & Frog & Rabbit: Hello! Oh, my God! A tiger! Run!

Fox: Tiger, now you see, they are so frightened of me! They all run away!

Tiger: Yes, you are right! It's true! I'm so sorry! You are the king of the forest.

Fox: Will you still eat me?

Tiger: No, My king! I will go!

Fox: Go! Go away!

Tiger: Fox is the king of the forest! Fox is the king of the forest!

（师生改编剧本）

Words and Expressions

meal [miːl] *n.* 一餐，一顿饭

quickly ['kwɪklɪ] *adv.* 迅速地

dare [deə] *v.* 胆敢

at once 立刻，马上

be scared of 害怕

be frightened of 对……感到恐惧

run away 跑开

Listening Practice

I. Bingo game

Work in groups, one student reads about the script of *The Tiger and The Fox*, other students listen carefully, when they hear the adjective from the script, say "Bingo", and write the word in the form quickly, and then he/she wins. And take turns, and change the words into Verbs, Nouns, etc..

words	adjective	verbs	nouns	prepositions	adverbs	conjunctions
student 1						
student 2						
student 3						
student 4						
student 5						

II. Dictation

Listen to the passage three times and supply the missing information.

One day, in a ____1____, a fox ran into a ____2____, which made the tiger very ____3____. The tiger was very ____4____, so he wanted to eat the fox ____5____. But the fox told the tiger that he is the king of the forest, and all the animals in the forest were ____6____ of him. The tiger thought the fox was ____7____. The fox asked the tiger to go around the forest with him and see who the king of the forest is. They walked ____8____ in the forest, and all small animals ____9____. Finally, the fox became the ____10____ of the forest.

Reading Practice

I. Read and choose

1. Which of the following statement is True?

A. A fox ran into a bear one day.

B. The fox are frightened of the tiger.

C. The tiger ate the fox.

D. The fox is very clever, and cheats the tiger.

2. At the beginning of the story, the tiger thinks the fox is ________.

A. crazy

B. honest

C. lovely

D. cute

3. Who is the real king of the forest?

A. fox

B. tiger

C. bear

D. lion

4. All small animals ran away when they saw _______.

A. fox

B. bear

C. rabbit

D. tiger

5. At the end of the story, who became the king of the forest?

A. tiger

B. lion

C. bear

D. fox

II. Read and answer

1. Were the fox and the tiger good friends?
2. Why did the tiger want to eat the fox?
3. Where did the tiger and the fox live?
4. If you were the fox, what would you do to save your own life?
5. What does this story tell us?

Speaking Practice

I. Role Play

Suppose you were the fox, what would you do to save your own life from the tiger? Use the following functional sentences, you have to add your own expressions when it is necessary.

- Hi, I'm a fox.
- Will you make a friend with me?
- I admire you very much.
- Listen to me, otherwise I will eat you!
- Bye for now.
- Remember me!
- Help! Help! Help me!
- I am your best friend – fox!

II. Problem-Solving

Think of appropriate lines for the animals in the picture above.

III. Delivery Game

The teacher divides the whole class into four or five groups, queue the students. The teacher writes a long sentence from the script in a piece of paper, just let the first student read and recite it for one minute, and let the student retell the sentence to the second student, the second to the third, when the sentence is delivered to the last student, he/she should write it on the blackboard, and translate it into Chinese. The group which has got great speed and relative accuracy wins.

Translating Practice

I. Translate the sentences into Chinese.

Work in pairs, one student reads the following sentences, and the other translates the sentences into Chinese in spoken way. (Add extra sentences from the scripts if necessary.)

1. I must find something to eat at once.
2. Yes, yes, you should eat me, but you know what?
3. You have the name of "King of the forest", but I'm the king of the forest in real!
4. Do you know that all the animals in the forest are scared of me?
5. Tiger, now you see, they are so frightened of me!

II. Translate the sentences into English.

Work in pairs, one student reads the following sentences, and the other translates the sentences into English in spoken way. (Add extra sentences from the scripts if necessary.)

1. 我是一只大老虎。我又壮又勇敢。
2. 我是森林之王。
3. 快点告诉我。
4. 你怎敢如此说？
5. 你在说什么？疯了吗？

Writing Practice

Write a summary of *The Tiger and the Fox* in 50 words.

"Ws" / "Who"	doing what	whom	where	when

Part Five: Language Skills

Grammar

There be 句型

there be 句型，表示“有”，表示某处存在某（物）人。基本结构为“There be +某物（某人）+某地（某时）”。常见的结构有以下两种：

1. There is +单数名词（不可数名词）+介词短语，如：

There is a ruler on the desk.

书桌上有一把尺子。

There is some water in the bottle.

瓶子里有一些水。（水是不可数名词）

2. There are +复数名词+介词短语，如：

There are three apples on the tree.

树上有三个苹果。

There are some bananas on the desk.

桌子上有一些香蕉。

3. There is +不可数名词+地点状语（即使有 some 也是单数）

Notes：There is some+不可数名词，There are some+可数名词复数，如：

There is some water in the bottle.

瓶子里有一些水。（水是不可数名词）

There are some students in the classroom.

Notes：如果“be”后的主语是由 and 连接的两个或两个以上的名词，那么 be 的形式要遵循“**就近**”的原则。也就是说，“be”的形式是由与它最近的那个名词来决定的。若那个名词是单数或不可数名词，要用 is，是复数名词就用 are，如：

1. There is a teacher and some students in the classroom.
2. There are some students and a teacher in the classroom.

Exercises

I. Multiple Choice

1. There are_____ pens in my pencil box.

A. a B. one C. some D. an

2. There is _____ big bed in my bedroom.

A. a B. some C. an D.two

3. There are _____ new books in my bag.

A. a B. one C. two D. an

4. There is _____ ruler on the desk.

A. a B. an C. the D. some

5. There is______cap on the desk.

A. one B. an C. the D. three

6. There are ______ pencil boxes in the book bag.

A. one B. an C. three D. the

7. There are_____ pencils in my pencil box.

A. one B.an C. some D.the

8. There is _______ book in his hand.

A. a B. not C. some D. an

9. There ________ a pencil, a pencil-box and two books on the table.

A. is B. are C. no D. not

10. There _______ two chairs, one bed and one desk in the bedroom.

A. is B. Are C. have D. are

11. There are _____ days in a week.

A. two B. five C. seven D. Four

12. There are _______ dwarfs in *Snow White*.

A. five B. seven C. eight D. nine

13. Be careful! There are some _____ on the floor.

A. kids B. water C. box D. milks

14. There _____ so many people at today's meeting.

A. is B. have C. are D. a

15. Oh，there is _____ apple on the three.

A. a B. an C. some D. the

16. There is ______ rocking chair in my bedroom.

A. a B. an C. five D. the

17. There are _____ new books for you.

A. a B. an C. two D. the

18. There is _______ pencil-box on the desk.

A. a B. an C. some D. two

19. There ________ a glass of water on the table.

A. is B. are C. be D. are not

20. There _____ a lot of meat on the plate.

A. is B. are C. some D. be

II. Complete each of the following sentences with a proper demonstrative pronoun

1. 学校图书馆有各种各样的书。

_______________ all kinds of books __________________________.

2. 墙上有一些风筝。

There _________some kites on the wall.

3. 桌子上有一本书和两支钢笔。

There ___________ a book and two pens on the desk.

4. 钱包里有些钱。

There ____________ some money in the purse.

5. 我的书包里有一些照片。

_________________ some pictures in my bag.

6. 我们学校有许多班。

There ____________ many ___________ in our school.

7. 树上有一只鸟。

There ___________ bird in the tree.

8. 教室里有许多学生。

There __________ many students in the classroom.

9. 我们学校里有三栋楼，还有一个漂亮的花园。

There _________ three buildings and a beautiful garden in our school.

10. 树上有很多苹果。

There ________________ on the tree.

II. Translating Practice

A. Put Chinese into English.

1. 桌子上有些香蕉。
2. 动物园里有些老虎。
3. 书桌上有一张纸。
4. 教室里有一块黑板。
5. 客厅里有一台电视机。

B. Put English into Chinese.

1. There is a bottle of milk in the refrigerator.
2. There is a football under the chair.
3. There is a bar of chocolate on the table.
4. There is a schoolbag on the sofa.
5. There is an eraser in the pencilcase.

Unit Nine
Love

Part One: Phonics

A. 字母 H h

1. 拼读发音方式。

字母“h”有字母音和拼读音，字母音就是在字母“HIGKL…”中的读音，而它的拼读音是这样的：发音送气，气流溢出口腔，气流摩擦两条声带间的缝隙成音，但是声带不振动。包括这个拼读发音的单词如 hop（单足跳），horse，house，home 等。

2. 发音规则。

(1) 辅音字母 h 在单词中一般发 /h/，如：have，hair。

(2) 字母 h 有时不发声，如 heir，honest。

3. 听一听，学一学字母“h”的拼读发音。

(1) heat　hand　happy　holly　hen　hat　hut

h-ea-t　h-an-d　h-a-pp-y　h-o-lly　h-en　h-at　h-ut

(2) hand in hand　heavy heart　happy hunting　hungry as a horse　happy Halloween

4. 仔细听，然后做句子一口气快读练习。

(1) He had to help her.

(2) The house has been half done.

(3) Her husband is a hard-hearted man.

(4) It’s very hot, so the horseman decides to give the horses a bath.

5. 听一听下列的韵律英语，并熟练朗读。

Honey Hen, Honey Hen.
Honey, Honey Hen.
Hh says h h.
Honey, Honey Hen.

Henry has a high street home he hardly ever habits.
He has to hire a hotel room; his house is full of rabbits.
Henry couldn't help himself, his situation hopeless.
Now Harry doesn't have a home, the rabbits made him homeless.

B. 字母 L l

1. 拼读发音方式。

字母“l”有字母音和拼读音，字母音就是在字母“LMNOP…”中的读音，而它的拼读音是这样的：舌尖和上颚前端紧贴近，双唇略张大一些，气流从舌头两侧流出，声带振动。包括这个拼读发音的单词如 love，late 等。

2. 发音规则。

(1) 字母 l 通常发 / l/，如 list，kill，clay，apple 等。

(2) 字母 l 在字母组合 alf，alk，alm，ould 等中往往不发音，如 half，talk，walk，calm，could，should 等。

但此音在单词中，发音方式有以下几种变体：

(1) 位于词首元音前时，舌伸向口腔最前部，形成“清晰”/i/，如 lesson；

(2) 位于词尾元音后时，舌尖与舌叶位于后齿龈形成“模糊” /i/，如 bull；

(3) 与清爆破音形成辅音群时清音化，如 place；

(4) 在软腭音前时，舌位稍后移，如 milk；

(5) l 与 e 组合作结尾音时，有时可以和前面的辅音构成自成音节，如 little。

3. 听一听，学一学字母“l”的拼读发音。

(1) log leg lion leaf lamb list lake lullaby

l-og l-eg l-o-i-n l-ea-f l-a-mb l-i-st l-a-k-e l-u-l-l-a-b-y

land

l-a-nd

(2) last laugh level best a love letter lock and load

a lost lamb lemons and limes Leo the lion letter of the law

4. 仔细听，然后做句子一口气快读练习。

字母“l”在元音前

(1) Lilly is eleven.

(2) The little girl won at last.

(3) There are few leaves left on the low willow.

(4) Liz’s face is like a red apple.

字母“l”在元音后

(1) He pulled through that fearful illness.

(2) Heal the dying people all over the world, please.

(3) This loyal man needs to add oil to his car.

(4) You will see the seagulls in a while.

5. 听一听，并熟练朗读。

Lazy Lion

Lazy Lion, Lazy Lion.
What do you say?
I say Ll, l.
Lazy, Lazy Lion.

Lose

Lose your way (get lost)
Lose your keys (cannot find)
Lose your cool (get angry)
Lose your face (lose your respect)
Lose your head (become confused)
Lose touch (no longer have contact with someone)

Lose it (lose control)

C. 字母 M m

1. 拼读发音方式。

字母"m"有字母音和拼读音，字母音就是在字母"LMNOP…"中的读音，而它的拼读音是这样的：闭上双唇，软腭下垂，气流从鼻腔流出，声带振动。包括这个声音的单词如 mud，mother，map，man，sum，ham，number 等。

2. 发音规则。

字母 m 通常发/m /，如 make，seem，harmful 等。

3. 听一听，学一学字母"m"的拼读发音。

(1) maze map mail mile musk mug meat
m-a-z-e m-ap m-ai-l m-i-l-e m-u-s-k m-ug m-ea-t
milk mop marble
m-i-l-k m-op m-ar-b-l-e

(2) Mickey Mouse make more money make a meal
made in America more and more make me mad
too much meat Muslim men magical music

4. 仔细听，然后做句子一口气快读练习。

(1) My name is Mike.
(2) The milk man is murmuring.
(3) He made coffee every morning.
(4) My mother is beautiful but emotional.

5. 听一听下列的韵律英语，并熟练朗读。

Miss Mouse, Mouse
Lives in this house, house.
Mm says m, m.
Miss Mouse, Mouse.

When I saw the team
I wanted to scream.

My uncle always chews his gum
to the beat of the drum.

I scream, you scream,
we all scream for ice cream.

D. 字母 N n

1. 拼读发音方式。

字母“n”有字母音和拼读音，字母音就是在字母“LMNOP…”中的读音，而它的拼读音是这样的：舌尖紧贴上齿龈，软腭声带振动。包括这个声音的单词如：nut，name，night，note，nest 等。

2. 发音规则。

字母 n 通常发/n/，如 nose，ban，banana，clean。

3. 听一听，学一学字母“n”的拼读发音。

(1) nest noodles nail ninety nod neck nut nap
n-e-st n-oo-d-l-e-s n-ai-l n-i-n-e-t-y n-od n-e-ck n-ut n-ap

(2) next nurse neck and neck new numbers niece and nephew
new napkins November the nineteenth a nail on the wall

4. 仔细听，然后做句子一口气快读练习。

(1) Nancy is nine and Norman is nineteen.

(2) Nancy never eats noodles and Norman never eats nuts.

(3) Ann announced the train was arriving next.

(4) She is learning another language.

5. 听一听下列的韵律英语，并熟练朗读。

No, No, No.
Noboday knows.
Nn says n, n.
No, No, No.

Nina never knew her new neighbor Nero Knew her.

Canners can can what they can can
but cannot can things can't be canned.

Ann sent Andy ten hens
and Andy sent Ann ten pens.

Part Two: Dialogue

Dialogue 1

Tom: I think I have fallen in love with her.

William: Oh, really? Who is the lucky girl?

Tom: Lucy, who sits next to me in the classroom.

William: Does she love you?

Tom: I'm not sure. But at least she doesn't hate me.

William: Good luck, boy. I wish you will be lovers.

Tom: Thank you very much.

Words and Expressions

lucky ['lʌki] *adj*. 幸运的

hate [heɪt] *v*. 憎恨

fall in love 坠入爱河；爱上某人

Decide whether the following statements are True (T) or False (F).

(　) 1. Tom falls in love with Lily.

(　) 2. Tom and Lucy are classmates.

(　) 3. Lucy doesn't like Tom.

(　) 4. William loves Lucy.

(　) 5. William doesn't want them to be lovers.

Dialogue 2

Kate: Do you love me?

Tom: Yes, so much.

Kate: Really? I love you, too! But I don't understand why you say like this.

Tom: Sometimes I'm very boring. I don't know what I should do. I only know that I love you, so much.

Kate: You really care about our relationship. But please take it easy!

Words and Expressions

understand [ʌndə'stænd] *v.* 理解

boring ['bɔrɪŋ] *adj.* 无聊的；令人厌烦的

relationship [rɪ'leʃən'ʃɪp] *n.* 关系；关联

take it easy 从容

Decide whether the following statements are True (T) or False (F).

(　　) 1. Kate wondered if Tom loved her.

(　　) 2. Tom doesn't love Kate anymore.

(　　) 3. Tom cares about the relationship with Kate.

(　　) 4. Tom is a foolish guy.

(　　) 5. This is a dialogue between two lovers.

Dialogue 3

Jane: Where did you go last weekend?

Tom: I went on an urgent business last Friday and forgot to tell you.

Jane: I had planned how we were going to spend our weekend. I waited for you until midnight.

Tom: I'm sorry. It was my fault. Would you please forgive me?

Jane: You're away too far.

Tom: Sorry, I will tell you my schedule from now on.

Words and Expressions

weekend ['wikend] *n.* 周末

business ['bɪznɪs] *n.* 商业；生意

urgent ['ɜːdʒənt] *adj.* 紧急的

fault [fɔlt] *n.* 错误

forgive [fə'gɪv] *v.* 原谅

schedule ['ʃedju:l] *n.* 时间表

be away too far 太过分了

Decide whether the following statements are True (T) or False (F).

(　　) 1.Tom went on an urgent business last weekend.

(　　) 2. Jane spent her weekend with Tom last week.

(　　) 3. Jane was angry with Tom because he didn't bring her flowers.

(　　) 4. Jane was glad that Tom admitted his fault.

(　　) 5. Jane is Tom's teacher.

Dialogue 4

William: Within you I lose myself, without you I find myself waiting to be lost again.

Mary: You look like a poet now.

William: At the touch of love everyone becomes a poet.

Mary: Really?

William: Look into my eyes, you will see what you mean to me.

Words and Expressions

poet ['poət] *n.* 诗人

touch [tʌtʃ] *v.* 接触

mean [miːn] *v.* 意味

Decide whether the following statements are True (T) or False (F).

(　　) 1. William lost his way.

(　　) 2. William is a poet.

(　　) 3. William and Mary are lovers.

(　　) 4. William loves Mary very much.

(　　) 5. William falls in love with Mary.

Part Three: Text

How many universities are there in the city?

There are about twenty universities in our city.

How many people are there in your family?

There are four people in my family, my parents, my sister and I.

How many mountains are there in this region?

There are two mountains in this region.

How many hospitals are there in this community?

There are five hospitals in this community.

How many scissors are there in the box?

There are six scissors in the box. They are sharp.

How many supermarkets are there in this area?

There are two big supermarkets in this area. They are convenient.

Words and Expressions

twenty ['twentɪ] *n.* 二十

Eg. 1. The seller said I look like twenty in this dress.

售货员说我穿这条裙子看起来像二十岁。

2. He is twenty, she is eighteen.

他二十岁，她十八岁。

family ['fæməlɪ] *n.* 家庭；亲属

Eg. 1. He comes from a very rich family.

他出身于一个富裕家庭。

2. He is very happy with his family.

他和家人在一起很幸福。

parent ['peər(ə)nt] *n.* 父亲（或母亲）；父母亲

Eg. 1. You know your parents.

你了解你的父母。

2. All parents love their children.

所有的父母都爱他们的孩子。

sister ['sɪstə] *n.* 姐妹

Eg. 1. My sister gave me a bag.

姐姐送我一个包。

2. He likes her as much as he likes his sister.

他很喜欢她，同喜欢他的姐妹一样。

mountain ['maʊntən] *n.* 山

Eg. 1. He was the first to top the mountain peak.

他是第一个登上这座山峰的人。

2. The mountain lies between two counties.

这座山介于两县之间。

region ['riːdʒ(ə)n] *n.* 地区

Eg. 1. The sky is blue in this region.

这个地区的天是蓝的。

2. It is a peaceful region.

这是和平地区。

hospital ['hɒspɪt(ə)l] *n.* 医院

Eg. 1. The hospital has five hundred beds.

这所医院有五百张病床。

2. This is the biggest hospital in Lanzhou.

这是兰州最大的医院。

community [kə'mju:nətɪ] *n.* 社区

Eg. 1. You should teach all to others in your community.

你应该把你所知道的教给你所在社区的其他人。

2. The new hospital will benefit the entire community.

新医院将有益于整个社区。

scissors ['sɪzəz] *n.* 剪刀

Eg. 1. She got her little kid scissors.

她拿来了她的儿童小剪刀。

2. My scissors are made of steel.

我的剪刀由钢铁构成。

box [bɒks] *n*. 箱，盒子

Eg. 1. Put the box here.

把箱子放在这里。

2. We need some kind of box.

我们也的确需要某种盒子。

sharp [ʃɑːp] *adj*. 锋利的；刺耳的

Eg. 1. I have a sharp knife in my hand now.

现在我手中有一把锋利的刀子。

2. His teeth are sharp. The lion is not afraid.

它的牙齿是锋利的。这狮子不害怕。

supermarket ['suːpəmɑːkɪt; 'sjuː-] *n*. 超级市场

Eg. 1. You are in a supermarket with your parents.

你与你的父母在一家超级市场。

2. This supermarket is so big. I like shopping here.

这家超市如此大。我喜欢在这里购物。

convenient [kən'viːnɪənt] *adj*. 方便的

Eg. 1. It's not convenient to talk here.

这里谈话不方便。

2. You can give me a call if you are convenient.

你可以在你方便的时候给我打电话。

Language Focus

I. Make a sentence with the words given below.

1. many / how / there / are / books / the / on / desk / ?

are / there / books / four / the / on / desk

2. how / many / chairs / there / are / the / in / room / ?

are / there / chairs / six / room / the / in

3. are / there / how / many / computers / the / lab / in / ?

there / twenty / are / the / in / lab / computers

4. are / there / shoes / many / how / the / on / floor / ?

there / eight / are / shoes / floor / on / the

5. how / students / many / in / the / are / there / classroom / ?

there / are / students / nine / classroom / the / in

II. Translating

Put Chinese into English.

1. 你们班有多少男生？ 我们班有十五个男生。
2. 桌子上有多少支铅笔？ 桌子上有八支铅笔。
3. 这个房子里有多少房间？ 这个房子有五个房间。
4. 这个花园里有多少棵树？ 这个花园里有三棵树。
5. 这个房间里有几条狗？ 这个房间里有六条狗。

Put English into Chinese.

1. How many swimming pools in this city? There are about ten swimming pools in this city.
2. How many hotels are there on this street? There are two hotels on this street.
3. How many post offices are there in this community? There are two post offices in this community.
4. How many cars are there in this parking lot? There are about two hundred cars in the parking lot.
5. How many schools are there in this city? There are about eighty schools in this city.

III. Reading Comprehension

Choose the best answer to each of the following questions or incomplete sentences.

There are four seasons(季节) in a year. March, April and May make the spring season. June, July and August make the summer season. September, October and November make the autumn season. December, January and February make the winter season.

Near the North Pole(北极) there are two seasons: winter and summer. The winter nights are long. For more than two months you can't see the sun, even at noon. The summer days are long. For more than two months the sun never sets and there is no night.

In the tropics(热带地区) there are also two seasons: a rainy season and a dry season.

1. How many seasons are there in a year? _____

A. two　　B. three　　C. four　　D. one

2. October is _____.

A. spring　　B. summer　　C. autumn　　D. winter

3. How many seasons are there near the North Pole?

A. two　　B. three　　C. four　　D. one

4. Near the North Pole, the summer days are _____.

A. short　　B. hot　　C. cold　　D. long

5. How many seasons are there in the tropics? _____

A. one　　B. two　　C. three　　D. four

Part Four: Play

The Gifts

Characters:

Aside 旁白
Della 德拉
Jim 吉姆
Madam 理发店老板娘
Sir 钟表店老板

Scene 1

Aside: Tomorrow will be Christmas. But Della feels very sad because she has no money to buy a present for her husband, Jim. She has only one dollar and eighty-seven cents. They have only 20 dollars a week, it doesn't leave much for saving.

Della: Life is so hard for me. Though I saved money for many months, I still have only one dollar and eighty-seven cents. How sad…

Jim: Life is so hard for me. I want to buy Della a Christmas present, but I don't have money. How sad…

Aside: In fact, Della and Jim have two possessions in which they both take very great pride. One is Jim's gold watch, which has been his father's and his grandfather's. The other is Della's long beautiful hair.

Della: I…I…I have to have my hair cut and sold it. In that way I can get some money. Oh… I can buy a beautiful present for Jim.

Scene 2

(At the shop – "Madam Sofronie. We Buy Hair Goods of All Kinds")

Della: Will you buy my hair?

Madam: Yes, I buy all kinds of hair. Sit down, please. Take your hat off and let me have a look. Oh, very beautiful. Very good! Twenty dollars, Ok?

Della: Madam, I need money! Please, give me some more! How about thirty dollars?

Madam: You've got really beautiful hair. Twenty-five dollars! Deal?

Della: All right. But I need cash now. Please give it to me quickly.

Madam: Here you are. Twenty-five dollars.

Della: Thank you! Bye-bye.

Scene 3

(At the shop – "Golden Watch")

Jim: Sir, look at my watch. Is it nice? I want to sell it. Will you buy it?

Sir: Oh, what a beautiful gold watch. Oh, very nice. Forty dollars, ok?

Jim: All right. Thank you, sir.

Scene 4

Aside: Della spent two hours in the streets. Then she stopped at a gold shop and bought a gold watch chain. Now, Della is at home.

Della: Oh, what a beautiful gold watch chain. I think it must match Jim's watch. When he sees it he must be very happy.

(Suddenly the door opened and in came Jim.)

Jim: You—?

Della: Jim. Don't look at me that way. I had my hair cut off and sold it because I couldn't have lived through Christmas without giving you a present. Jim, it will grow quickly. You don't mind, do you? I just have to do it. My hair grows very fast, you know. Say "Merry Christmas". Jim, and let's be happy.

Jim: You've cut off your hair?

Della: I've cut if off and sold it. I tell you — sold and gone. Jim, It's Christmas Eve, be good to me.

Jim: But, look! I bought this comb for you. It's a Christmas present for you.

（师生改编剧本）

Words and Expressions

tomorrow [tə'mɒrəʊ] *n.* 明天
Christmas ['krɪsməs] *n.* 圣诞节
because [bɪ'kɒz] *conj.* 因为
present ['preznt] *n.* 礼物
husband ['hʌzbənd] *n.* 丈夫
dollar ['dɒlə] *n.* 美元
cent [sent] *n.* 分
leave [liːv] *v.* 留下
saving ['seɪvɪŋ] *n.* 存款
though [ðəʊ] *conj.* 尽管
month [mʌnθ] *n.* 月
possession [pə'zeʃ(ə)n] *n.* 所有物
pride [praɪd] *n.* 自豪
grandfather ['græn(d)fɑːðə] *n.* 祖父
chain [tʃeɪn] *n.* 链
match [mætʃ] *n.* 匹配
without [wɪ'ðaʊt] *prep.* 没有
eve [iːv] *n.* 前夕
comb [kəʊm] *n.* 梳子
sit down 坐下
take…off 脱下，摘下
have a look 看一看
don't mind 不介意
Merry Christmas 圣诞快乐

Listening Practice

I. Bingo game

Work in groups, one student reads about the script of *The Gifts*, other students listen carefully, when they hear the adjective from the script, say "Bingo", and write the word in the form quickly, and then he/she wins. And take turns, and change the words into Verbs, Nouns, etc..

words	adjective	verbs	nouns	prepositions	adverbs	conjunctions
student 1						
student 2						
student 3						
student 4						
student 5						

II. Dictation

Listen to the passage three times and supply the missing information.

Christmas is coming, but Della feels very ___1___ because she has no money to buy a ___2___ for her husband, Jim. They have only 20 dollars a week, it doesn't ___3___ much for ___4___. In fact, Della and Jim have two ___5___ in which they both take very great pride. One is Jim's gold ___6___. The other is Della's long beautiful ___7___. Della sells her beautiful hair to buy a gold watch ___8___for Jim, but Jim does the same. He sells his gold watch to buy a___9___for his wife. Although they both sell their most precious thing, but they know they ___10___ each other deeply.

Reading Practice

I. Read and choose

1. Which of the following statement is True? ________

A. They want to but a present to each other for New Year.

B. Della has a very beautiful gold ring.

C. The couple love each other deeply.

D. Della and Jim are pride of each other.

2. Della sold her long beautiful hair for ________.

A. twenty dollars

B. twenty-five dollars

C. thirty dollars

D. forty dollars

3. Jim got his gold watch from his _______.
A. father and grandfather
B. mother
C. uncle
D. grandmother
4. Della bought a ______ for her husband.
A. gold watch chain
B. gold watch
C. comb
D. gold ring
5. The couple were very ______ for the present they bought for each other.
A. sad
B. satisfied
C. unhappy
D. sorry

II. Read and answer

1. Who is Madam? Is she Della's friend?
2. Why did Della sell her hair?
3. Where did Della go to sell her hair?
4. If you were Jim, would you sell your gold watch for your wife's present?
5. What did Jim buy for his wife?

Speaking Practice

I. Role Play

Suppose you were Jim, what would you buy for your wife as Christmas present? Use the following functional sentences, you have to add your own expressions when it is necessary.

- Hi, darling, Merry Christmas.
- I have a present for you.
- I love you.
- Do you like it?
- Thank you, my darling.
- You're welcome.

• Have a nice day!

II. Problem-Solving

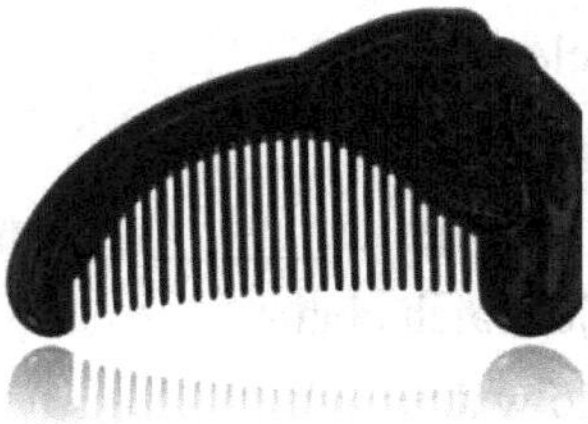

Think of appropriate lines for the gold watch and comb in the pictures above.

III. Delivery Game

The teacher divides the whole class into four or five groups, queue the students. The teacher writes a long sentence from the script in a piece of paper, just let the first student read and recite it for one minute, and let the student retell the sentence to the second student, the second to the third, when the sentence is delivered to the last student, he/she should write it on the blackboard, and translate it into Chinese. The group which has got great speed and relative accuracy wins.

Translating Practice

I. Translate the sentences into Chinese.

Work in pairs, one student reads the following sentences, and the other translates the sentences into Chinese in spoken way. (Add extra sentences from the scripts if necessary.)

1. But Della feels very sad because she has no money to buy a present for her husband!
2. In fact, Della and Jim have two possessions in which they both take very great pride.
3. Then she shopped at a gold shop and bought a gold watch chain.
4. I had my hair cut off and sold it because I couldn't have lived through Christmas without giving you a present.
5. It's Christmas Eve, be good to me.

II. Translate the sentences into English.

Work in pairs, one student reads the following sentences, and the other translates the sentences into English in spoken way. (Add extra sentences from the scripts if necessary.)

1. 生活太艰难了！
2. 夫人，我需要钱！请多给我些。
3. 哇，好漂亮的金表。
4. 这是给你的圣诞礼物。
5. 圣诞快乐。

Writing Practice

Write a summary of *The Gifts* in 50 words.

"Ws" / "Who"	doing what	whom	where	when

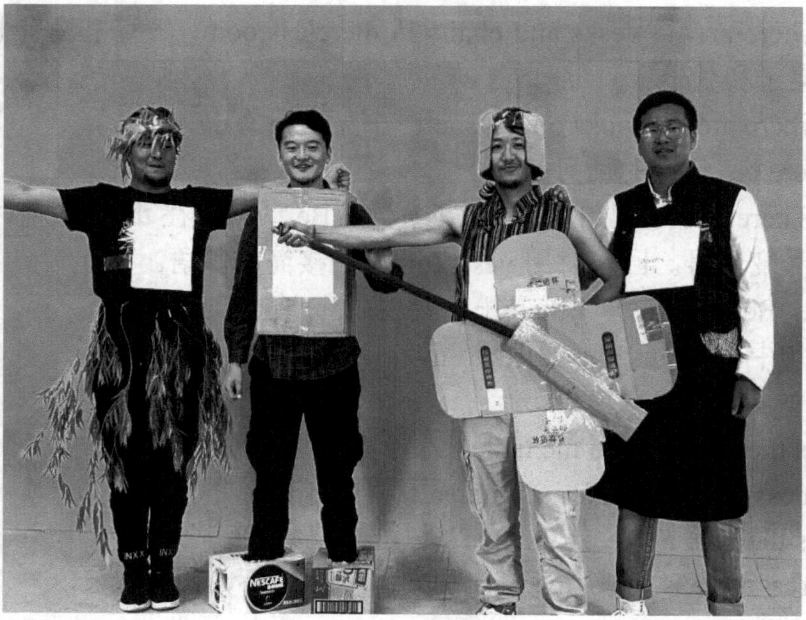

Part Five: Language Skills

Grammar

There be 句型的否定句和疑问句

1. There be 句型的否定句

There be 句型的否定句有两种构成方式：

一种是将否定词 not 放在 be 之后。There＋be（is/are）＋not＋某物/某人＋地点/时间。

注意：There＋be（is/are)＋some 只用于肯定句表示“一些”，当否定句中表示“许多”的时候，可用 many 修饰可数名词，用 much 修饰不可数名词。

如：

There is not a bed in the room. 房间里没有床。

There are not any people in the classroom. 教室里没有任何人。

There are not apples on the apple-tree. 苹果树上没有苹果。

There are not people at home. 家里没有人。

另一种是在主语前加上不定代词“no”。

如：

There is no water in the bottle. 瓶子里没有水。

There are no desks and chairs in the classroom. 教室里没有很多桌子和凳子。

There are no books on the shelf. 书架上没有书。

2. There be 句型的疑问句

在“There is/are...”的疑问句中，要把 Be 动词放在 there 之前，并将句号变问号。回答时用 yes 或 no，后接简单答语。

句式：Be（Is/Are）＋there＋某物/某人＋地点/时间？

疑问句中出现的 some 要改成 any。

如：

Is there a lamp on the table? 桌子上有台灯吗？

Yes，there is. / No，there isn't. 是，有。/ 不，没有。

Is there an apple on the tree? 树上有苹果吗？

Yes, there is. / No, there isn't. 是，有。/ 不，没有。

Are there five books on the desk? 桌子上有五本书吗？

Yes, there are. / No, there aren't. 是，有。/ 不，没有。

Is there any water in the bottle? 瓶子里有水吗？

Yes, there is. / No, there isn't. 是，有。/ 不，没有。

Exercises

I. Multiple Choice

1. — Are there any maps on the wall?

— __________

A. There are some. B. Yes, there is.

C. Yes, there is one. D. No, there are.

2. — There aren't ___ trees near the house.

— There is only one.

A. any B. some C. many D. much

3. How many ____ are there in the picture?

A. woman B. women C. boy D. milk

4. There ____ two bowls of rice on the table.

A. is B. have C. has D. are

5. — Are there _____ houses near the river?

— Yes, there are______.

A. some, some B. any, some C. any, any D. some, any

6. There ______ any rice in the bowl.

A. are B. is C. isn't D. aren't

7. There_____ not _____ milk in the cup on the table.

A. are, many B. are, much C. is, many D. is, much

8. There is some milk in the bottle, _____?

A. isn't there B. aren't there C. isn't it D. are there

9. There isn't _______water in the glass. Let's go and get some.

A. many B. lots C. any D. some

10. — There _______a lot of meat on the plate. Would you like some?

— Just a little, please.

A. is B. are C. am D. be

11. —_______is in the house?

— There is an old woman in the house.

A. What　B. Whose　C. Who　D.Which

12. ______ there any sheep on the hill?

A. Is　B. Are　C. Be　D. Am

13. There _____ a pair of jeans on the bed.

A. be　B. is　C. are　D. am

14. There ____ a bottle of juice and some fruits in the fridge.

A. be　B. is　C. am　D. are

15. There ____ any desks or chairs in the room.

A. is　B. are　C. isn’t　D. aren’t

16. There are some _____ in the glass.

A. milks　B. water　C. nuts　D. waters

17. There ____ two cups of tea on the table.

A. are　B. is　C. am　D. Is

18. _____ any flowers on both sides of the street?

A. Is there　B. Are there　C. There are　D. Isn’t there

19.______ there a radio on your desk?

A. Are　B. Be　C. Am　D. Is

20. There is some ______ on the plate.

A. apple　B. bread　C. banana　D. sandwich

II. Complete each of the following sentences with a proper word.

1. There _______ any beautiful photos on the desk. (否定句)
2. There are four ______ (苹果) in the box.
3. There is a dog in the _______ (花园).
4. There is a bed in the _______ (卧室).
5. There are two ______ (学生) in the classroom.
6. _______ four apples on the tree?
7. There are five birds ________(树上).
8. There are five children playing ________ (客厅里).
9. There is _______ (一只蝴蝶) in the garden.

10. There's _____ (一把尺子) in the pencil box.

III. Translating Practice

A. Translate the following sentences into English.

1. 桌子上有一本书和两只铅笔。

____.

2. 汤姆的铅笔盒里有两只钢笔。

____.

3. 树上有苹果吗？

____?

4. 在瓶子里有一些水。

____.

5. 桌子上有个球吗?

____?

B. Translate the following sentences into Chinese.

1. Are there any rabbits in the garden?

____?

2. There are two desks and four chairs in the teachers' office.

____.

3. Is there any fish in the water?

____?

4. There are not any people in the classroom.

____.

5. Are there five books on the desk?

____?

Glossary

Unit One　Friendship

Dialogue

New Words

quite [kwaɪt]	*adv.*	非常
spend [spend]	*v.*	度过；花（时间）
holiday ['hɒlədeɪ]	*n.*	节日
sightseeing ['saɪtsiːɪŋ]	*n.*	观光
pretty ['prɪti]	*adv.*	相当
immediately [ɪ'miːdiətli]	*adv.*	立即
show [ʃəʊ]	*v.*	展示
sight [saɪt]	*n.*	景象
introduce [ˌɪntrə'djuːs]	*v.*	介绍
enjoy [ɪn'dʒɔɪ]	*v.*	喜欢
speak [spiːk]	*v.*	讲
feel [fiːl]	*v.*	感觉
promise ['prɒmɪs]	*v.*	许诺
expect [ɪk'spekt]	*v.*	期望

Phrases and Expressions

take care of	照顾

Text

New Words

greeting ['griːtɪŋ]	*n.*	问候
gift [gɪft]	*n.*	礼物

traditional [trə'dɪʃ(ə)n(ə)l]	*adj.*	传统的
costume [kɒstjuːm]	*n.*	服装
painting ['peɪntɪŋ]	*n.*	绘画
musical ['mjuːzɪk(ə)l]	*adj.*	音乐的
instrument ['ɪnstrʊm(ə)nt]	*n.*	仪器

Play

New Words

hungry ['hʌŋgrɪ]	*adj.*	饥饿的
lion ['laɪən]	*n.*	狮子
little ['lɪt(ə)l]	*adj.*	小的
rabbit ['ræbɪt]	*n.*	兔子
bear [beə]	*n.*	熊
squirrel ['skwɪr(ə)l]	*n.*	松鼠
monkey ['mʌŋkɪ]	*n.*	猴子
roar [rɔː]	*v.*	吼叫，咆哮
king [kɪŋ]	*n.*	国王
forest ['fɒrɪst]	*n.*	森林
enough [ɪ'nʌf]	*adv.*	足够地
follow ['fɒləʊ]	*v.*	跟随
rush [rʌʃ]	*v.*	冲
small [smɔːl]	*adj.*	小的
animal ['ænɪm(ə)l]	*n.*	动物
bite [baɪt]	*v.*	咬
teeth [tiːθ]	*n.*	牙齿
carrot ['kærət]	*n.*	胡萝卜
please [pliːz]	*v.*	请
anyway ['enɪweɪ]	*adv.*	不管怎样
welcome ['welkəm]	*v.*	欢迎
porridge ['pɒrɪdʒ]	*n.*	麦片粥

peanut ['piːnʌt]	*n.*	花生
peach [piːtʃ]	*n.*	桃子
grass [grɑːs]	*n.*	草地
delicious [dɪ'lɪʃəs]	*adj.*	美味的

Unit Two　Gratitude

Dialogue

New Words

public ['pʌblɪk]	*adj.*	公共的
phone [fəʊn]	*n.*	电话
long-distance [lɒŋ 'dɪstəns]	*adj.*	[通信]长途的
call [kɔ:l]	*v.*	打电话
timer ['taɪmə(r)]	*n.*	计时器
start [stɑ:t]	*v.*	开始
automatically [ˌɔ:tə'mætɪklɪ]	*adv.*	自动地
dial ['daɪəl]	*v.*	打电话，拨电话号码
company ['kʌmpəni]	*n.*	公司
customer ['kʌstəmə(r)]	*n.*	顾客，客户
service ['sɜ:vɪs]	*n.*	服务
available [ə'veɪləbl]	*adj.*	可获得的；可使用的
tonight [tə'naɪt]	*n.*	今晚
overtime ['əʊvətaɪm]	*n.*	超出的时间
project ['prɒdʒekt]	*n.*	项目，工程
log [lɒg]	*v.*	把…载入正式记录
book [bʊk]	*v.*	预订
relax [rɪ'læks]	*v.*	轻松
wrong [rɒŋ]	*n.*	故障，错误
zero ['zɪərəʊ]	*n.*	（数字）零
outside [ˌaʊt'saɪd]	*n.*	外面
shot [ʃɒt]	*n.*	尝试，努力

Phrases and Expressions

customer service manager	客户经理
take a message	捎个口信

Text

New Words

yurt [jʊət; jɜːt]	*n.*	（游牧地区用兽皮或毛毯所盖的）圆顶帐篷
portable ['pɔːtəb(ə)l]	*adj.*	便携式的
preserved [prɪ'zɜːvd]	*adj.*	保藏的；腌制的
grassland ['grɑːslænd]	*n.*	草原
Mongolia [mɔŋ'gəuliə]	*n.*	蒙古

Play

New Words

fisherman ['fɪʃəmən]	*n.*	渔夫
goldfish ['gəʊl(d)fɪʃ]	*n.*	金鱼
narrator [nə'reɪtə]	*n.*	叙述者
once [wʌns]	*adv.*	曾经
ugly ['ʌglɪ]	*adj.*	丑的
wife [waɪf]	*n.*	妻子
poor [pɔː(r)]	*adj.*	贫穷的
catch [kætʃ]	*v.*	抓住
reward [rɪ'wɔːd]	*n.*	报答
worry ['wʌrɪ]	*v.*	担心
become [bɪ'kʌm]	*v.*	成为，变得
angry ['æŋgrɪ]	*adj.*	生气地，愤怒的
foolish ['fuːlɪʃ]	*adj.*	愚蠢的
hut [hʌt]	*n.*	小屋
cottage ['kɒtɪdʒ]	*n.*	村舍
beach [biːtʃ]	*n.*	海滩

anymore [enɪ'mɔː]	*adv.*	不再
stupid ['stjuːpɪd]	*adj.*	愚蠢的
queen [kwiːn]	*n.*	女王
servant ['sɜːv(ə)nt]	*n.*	仆人
impossible [ɪm'pɒsɪb(ə)l]	*adj.*	不可能的

Phrases and Expressions

go back	回去
go down to	延续至
What's the matter?	怎么了？
become tired of	变得厌倦
look at	看
get tired of	疲倦
swim away	游开
come back	回来

Unit Three Growing up

Dialogue

New Word

careful ['keəfl]	*adj.*	仔细的，小心的
foggy ['fɒgi]	*adj.*	有雾的，雾气朦胧的
sunny ['sʌni]	*adj.*	和煦的，照到阳光的
heavily ['hevɪli]	*adv.*	大量地
umbrella [ʌm'brelə]	*n.*	雨伞
crop [krɒp]	*n.*	农作物，庄稼
smell [smel]	*v.*	嗅，闻
weather ['weðə(r)]	*n.*	天气，气象
turn [tɜ:n]	*v.*	使变为
warm [wɔ:m]	*adj.*	暖和的，温暖的
wear [weə(r)]	*v.*	穿着，戴着
thick [θɪk]	*adj.*	厚的

camera ['kæmərə]	*n.*	照相机，摄影机
photo ['fəʊtəʊ]	*n.*	照片，相片
flower ['flaʊə(r)]	*n.*	花
brilliant ['brɪliənt]	*adj.*	才华横溢的，明亮的
invite [ɪn'vaɪt]	*v.*	邀请
join [dʒɔɪn]	*v.*	加入，参加
excellent ['eksələnt]	*adj.*	优秀的，太好了
exactly [ɪg'zæktli]	*adv.*	恰恰，确切地，精确地
gate [geɪt]	*n.*	门

Phrases and Expressions

be good for	对……有好处
have a walk	散步

Text

New Words

palace ['pælɪs]	*n.*	宫殿
emperor ['empərə(r)]	*n.*	皇帝
people ['piːp(ə)l]	*n.*	人，人类
terrific [tə'rɪfɪk]	*adj.*	极好的
elegant ['elɪg(ə)nt]	*adj.*	优雅的
popular ['pɒpjʊlə]	*adj.*	受欢迎的

Play

New Words

butterfly ['bʌtəflaɪ]	*n.*	蝴蝶
dragonfly ['drægənflaɪ]	*n.*	蜻蜓
tadpole ['tædpəʊl]	*n.*	蝌蚪
frog [frɒg]	*n.*	青蛙
pool [puːl]	*n.*	池塘
clean [kliːn]	*adj.*	干净的

lotus ['ləʊtəs]	*n.*	莲花
fly [flaɪ]	*v.*	飞
corner ['kɔːnə]	*n.*	拐角
noisy ['nɔɪzɪ]	*adj.*	喧闹的
sad [sæd]	*adj.*	悲伤的
leg [leg]	*n.*	腿
tortoise ['tɔːtəs]	*n.*	龟
together [tə'geðə]	*adv.*	一起

Phrases and Expressions

look for	寻找
be careful	小心
nice to meet you	见到你很高兴
go home	回家
here I am	我在这儿

Unit Four　Trust

Dialogue

New Word

recover [rɪ'kʌvə(r)]	*v.*	恢复
bull [bʊl]	*n.*	公牛
kindness ['kaɪndnəs]	*n.*	好意
trouble ['trʌbl]	*v.*	折磨
climb [klaɪm]	*v.*	爬
execise ['eksəsaɪz]	*n.*	运动
torture ['tɔːtʃə(r)]	*n.*	折磨
prone [prəʊn]	*adj.*	有……倾向的
nowadays ['naʊədeɪz]	*adv.*	现今
suggest [sə'dʒest]	*v.*	建议
weight [weɪt]	*n.*	重量

bear [beə(r)]	*v.*	忍受
necessarily [ˌnesə'serəli]	*adv.*	必要地
contain [kən'teɪn]	*v.*	包含
jog [dʒɒg]	*v.*	慢跑

Phrases and Expressions

under the weather	身体不适
for a long time	很长时间
suffer from	患……病
break down	毁掉
working stress	工作压力
fat-consuming	脂肪消耗
work out	锻炼
on a diet	遵守饮食特别规定的

Text

New Words

student ['stjuːd(ə)nt]	*n.*	学生
strong [strɒŋ]	*adj.*	强壮的
smart [smɑːt]	*adj.*	聪明的
policewoman [pə'liːswʊmən]	*n.*	女警察
special ['speʃ(ə)l]	*adj.*	特别的
singer ['sɪŋə(r)]	*n.*	歌手
famous ['feɪməs]	*adj.*	著名的
hardworking ['hɑːd,wɜːkɪŋ]	*adj.*	努力工作的
pretty ['priti]	*adj.*	漂亮的
engineer [endʒɪ'nɪə]	*n.*	工程师
intelligent [ɪn'telɪdʒ(ə)nt]	*adj.*	聪明的
diligent ['dɪlɪdʒ(ə)nt]	*adj.*	勤勉的
Chinese [tʃaɪ'niːz]	*adj.*	中国的
British ['brɪtɪʃ]	*adj.*	英国的

French [frentʃ]	*adj.*	法国的
Greek [gri:k]	*adj.*	希腊的
American [ə'merɪkən]	*adj.*	美国的
Korean [kə'riən]	*adj.*	韩国的
Japanese [ˌdʒæpə'ni:z]	*adj.*	日本的
German ['dʒɜːmən]	*adj.*	德国的

Play

New Words

goat [gəʊt]	*n.*	羊
lock [lɒk]	*v.*	锁
child [tʃaɪld]	*n.*	孩子
voice [vɒɪs]	*n.*	声音
strange [streɪndʒ]	*adj.*	奇怪的
something ['sʌmθɪŋ]	*pron.*	某事
else [els]	*adv.*	其他
foot [fʊt]	*n.*	脚
white [waɪt]	*n.*	白色
yellow ['jeləʊ]	*n.*	黄色
another [ə'nʌðə]	*adj.*	另一，另外的
kill [kɪl]	*v.*	杀
knife [naɪf]	*n.*	刀

Phrases and Expressions

go out	出去
open the door	开门
see you later	再见
go away	走开
have a try	试一试

Unit Five　Trying Everything

Dialogue

New Word

wonderful ['wʌndɚfəl]	*adj.*	极好的，精彩的
tall [tɔːl]	*adj.*	高的
finger ['fɪŋgɚ]	*n.*	手指
short [ʃɔːt]	*adj.*	短的，矮的
blonde [blɑnd]	*adj.*	亚麻色的
beautiful ['bjuːtɪfl]	*adj.*	美丽的
window ['wɪndəʊ]	*n.*	窗户
lovely ['lʌvlɪ]	*adj.*	可爱的
appearance [ə'pɪrəns]	*n.*	外貌
handsome ['hænsəm]	*adj.*	英俊的
woman ['wʊmən]	*n.*	妇女；女性
thin [θɪn]	*adj.*	薄的；瘦的
granddaughter ['grændɔtɚ]	*n.*	孙女；外孙女
especially [ɪ'spɛʃlɪ]	*adv.*	特别
cute [kjʊt]	*adj.*	可爱的
entice [ɪn'taɪs]	*v.*	吸引
fascinating ['fæsɪnetɪŋ]	*adj.*	迷人的

Text

New Words

university [juːnɪ'vɜːsɪtɪ]	*n.*	大学；综合性大学
Australia [ɒ'streɪlɪə]	*n.*	澳大利亚
Canada ['kænədə]	*n.*	加拿大
America [ə'merɪkə]	*n.*	美洲（包括北美和南美洲）；美国
journalist ['dʒɜːnəlɪst]	*n.*	新闻工作者；报人
colleague ['kɒliːg]	*n.*	同事，同僚

polite [pə'laɪt]	*adj.*	有礼貌的，客气的
easygoing ['izɪ,goɪŋ]	*adj.*	逍遥自在的；脾气随和的
tourist ['tʊərɪst]	*n.*	旅行者，观光客
Switzerland ['swɪtsələnd]	*n.*	瑞士（欧洲国家）
fashionable ['fæʃ(ə)nəb(ə)l]	*adj.*	流行的；时髦的

Play

New Words

carry ['kærɪ]	*v.*	驮，搬运
glad [glæd]	*adj.*	高兴的
donkey ['dɒŋkɪ]	*n.*	驴
bridge [brɪdʒ]	*n.*	桥
near [nɪə]	*prep.*	近
cross [krɒs]	*v.*	横穿过
dangerous ['deɪndʒərəs]	*adj.*	危险的
deep [diːp]	*adj.*	深的
reach [riːtʃ]	*v.*	达到
calf [kɑːf]	*n.*	小腿
fellow ['feləʊ]	*n.*	家伙
sweep [swiːp]	*n.*	（风、浪等）刮，吹，冲
really ['rɪəlɪ]	*adv.*	真的!（表语气）
scared [skeəd]	*adj.*	害怕的
wade [weɪd]	*v.*	涉水
across [ə'krɒs]	*prep.*	穿过
drown [draʊn]	*v.*	淹死，溺死
everything ['evrɪθɪŋ]	*pron.*	每件事物
difficult ['dɪfɪkəlt]	*adj.*	困难的

Phrases and Expressions

grow up	长大
on the other side	另一边
right away	立刻，马上

had better		最好
in one's own way		自己的方式
good luck		好运
in fact		事实上
no matter what happened		无论发生什么

Unit Six Self-protection

Dialogue

New Word

hobby ['hɒbi]	*n.*	嗜好；业余爱好
relaxing [rɪ'læksɪŋ]	*adj.*	令人轻松的
games ['ɡeɪmz]	*n.*	游戏
gym [dʒɪm]	*n.*	健身房
favorite ['fevərɪt]	*adj.*	最喜爱的
detective [dɪ'tɛktɪv]	*n.*	侦探
introverted ['ɪntrəvɝtɪd]	*adj.*	内向的
extroverted ['ɛkstro'vɝtɪd]	*adj.*	性格外向的
tennis ['tenɪs]	*n.*	网球
personality [pɝsə'næləti]	*n.*	个性
approach [ə'prəʊtʃ]	*v.*	接近
enthusiastically [in,θju:zi'æstikəli]	*adv.*	热心地
nervous ['nɝvəs]	*adj.*	神经的；紧张不安的
concentrate ['kɑnsn'tret]	*v.*	全神贯注；聚集

Phrases and Expressions

be interested in		对……感兴趣
spare time		业余时间
play basketball		打篮球
very much		非常
mountain climbing		爬山
half-done		半完成的

Text

New Words

teacher ['tiːtʃə]	*n.*	教师；导师
brave [breɪv]	*adj.*	勇敢的
serious ['sɪərɪəs]	*adj.*	严肃的；认真的
manager ['mænɪdʒə]	*n.*	经理；管理人员
strict [strɪkt]	*adj.*	严格的；绝对的
scientist ['saɪəntɪst]	*n.*	科学家
demanding [dɪ'mɑːndɪŋ]	*adj.*	苛求的；要求高的
driver ['draɪvə]	*n.*	驾驶员
busy ['bɪzɪ]	*adj.*	忙碌的；热闹的
herdsman ['hɜːdzmən]	*n.*	牧人
outgoing ['aʊtgəʊɪŋ]	*adj.*	对人友好的，开朗的
dentist ['dentɪst]	*n.*	牙科医生
caring ['keərɪŋ]	*adj.*	有同情心的；表示或感到关怀或关心的
patient ['peɪʃ(ə)nt]	*adj.*	有耐心的，能容忍的

Play

New Words

riding hood ['raɪdɪŋ] [hʊd]	*n.*	骑风帽
darling ['dɑːlɪŋ]	*n.*	亲爱的
hide [haɪd]	*v.*	隐藏
behind [bɪ'haɪnd]	*prep.*	在……后面
sleep [sliːp]	*v.*	睡觉
noise [nɔɪz]	*n.*	噪声
ear [ɪə]	*n.*	耳朵
sweet [swiːt]	*adj.*	甜的
eye [aɪ]	*n.*	眼睛
face [feɪs]	*n.*	脸

hand [hænd]	*n.*	手
hug [hʌg]	*v.*	拥抱
mouth [[maʊθ]]	*n.*	嘴
stomach ['stʌmək]	*n.*	胃
inside [ɪn'saɪd]	*prep.*	在……里面
hurry ['hʌrɪ]	*n.*	匆忙
needle ['niːd(ə)l]	*n.*	针
thread [θred]	*n.*	线
heavy ['hevɪ]	*adj.*	重的
raise [reɪz]	*v.*	举起
shot [ʃɒt]	*v.*	射击
dead [ded]	*adj.*	无生命的

Phrases and Expressions

come in	进来
listen to	听
You're welcome	不客气！

Unit Seven Diligence

Dialogue

New Word

semester [sɪ'mestə(r)]	*n.*	学期
proportion [prə'pɔːʃn]	*n.*	占比
compulsory [kəm'pʌlsəri]	*adj.*	必修的
optional ['ɒpʃənl]	*adj.*	选修的
head [hed]	*v.*	出发
coincidence [kəʊ'ɪnsɪdəns]	*n.*	巧合
essay ['eseɪ]	*n.*	论文
select [sɪ'lekt]	*v.*	选择
enroll [ɪn'rəʊl]	*v.*	注册

Phrases and Expressions

render lip-service	耍嘴皮子
reference book	参考书
at present	目前
be fit for	适合

Text

New Words

dormitory ['dɔːmətri]	*n.*	宿舍，学生宿舍
laptop ['læptɒp]	*n.*	膝上型轻便电脑，笔记本电脑
expensive [ɪk'spensɪv]	*adj.*	昂贵的
mobile ['məʊbaɪl]	*adj.*	可移动的
shelf [ʃelf]	*n.*	架子
refrigerator [rɪ'frɪdʒəreɪtə(r)]	*n.*	冰箱，冷藏库
spoon [spuːn]	*n.*	匙，勺子
ethnic ['eθnɪk]	*adj.*	种族的
harmonious [hɑː'məʊniəs]	*adj.*	和谐的，和睦的

Phrases and Expressions

mobile phone	手机

Play

New Words

village ['vɪlɪdʒ]	*n.*	村庄
young [jʌŋ]	*adj.*	年轻的
lazy ['leɪzɪ]	*adj.*	懒惰的
work [wɜːk]	*v.*	工作
help [help]	*v.*	帮助
housework ['haʊswɜːk]	*n.*	家务事
own [əʊn]	*adj.*	自己的
build [bɪld]	*v.*	建造
ourselves [aʊə'selvz]	*pron.*	我们自己

leaf [liːf]	*n.*	叶子
easy ['iːzɪ]	*adj.*	容易的
stick [stɪk]	*n.*	棍子
brick [brɪk]	*n.*	砖
nap [næp]	*n.*	小睡，打盹儿
huff [hʌf]	*v.*	吹气
puff [pʌf]	*v.*	（从口中）喷出
blow [bləʊ]	*v.*	吹
bump[bʌmp]	*v.*	碰，撞
boil [bɒɪl]	*v.*	煮沸

Phrases and Expressions

once upon a time	很久以前
live on one's own	独自生活
look after	照顾
pick up	捡起，拾起
in no time	立刻
fell down	倒塌
since then	从此以后
work hard	努力工作

Unit Eight　Inner Strength

Dialogue

New Word

rough [rʌf]	*adj.*	乱的
nightclub ['naɪtklʌb]	*n.*	夜总会
actually ['æktʃuəli]	*adv.*	实际上
crime [kraɪm]	*n.*	犯罪活动
pollution [pə'luːʃn]	*n.*	污染
emission [ɪ'mɪʃn]	*n.*	散发
major ['meɪdʒə(r)]	*adj.*	主要的

pollutant [pə'luːtənt]	*n.*	污染物
scale [skeɪl]	*n.*	规模
demand [dɪ'mɑːnd]	*n.*	需求
response [rɪ'spɒns]	*n.*	反应

Phrases and Expressions

walk around	四处走走

Text

New Words

street [striːt]	*n.*	街道
sing [sɪŋ]	*v.*	唱歌；歌颂
dance [dɑːns]	*v.*	跳舞；使跳跃
rain [reɪn]	*v.*	下雨；降雨
foreign ['fɒrɪn]	*adj.*	外国的；外交的
Russia ['rʌʃə]	*n.*	俄罗斯
river ['rɪvə]	*n.*	河；江
city ['sɪtɪ]	*n.*	城市，都市
flow [fləʊ]	*v.*	流动，涌流
local ['ləʊk(ə)l]	*adj.*	地方性的；乡土的
dish [dɪʃ]	*n.*	盘；餐
teapot ['tiːpɒt]	*n.*	茶壶

Phrases and Expressions

beef noodle	牛肉面

Play

New Words

meal [miːl]	*n.*	一餐，一顿饭
quickly ['kwɪklɪ]	*adv.*	迅速地
dare [deə]	*v.*	胆敢

Phrases and Expressions

at once	立刻，马上

be scared of		害怕
be frightened of		对……感到恐惧
run away		跑开

Unit Nine Love

Dialogue

New Word

lucky ['lʌki]	*adj.*	幸运的
hate [heɪt]	*v.*	憎恨
understand [ʌndə'stænd]	*v.*	理解
boring ['bɔrɪŋ]	*adj.*	无聊的；令人厌烦的
relationship [rɪ'leʃən'ʃɪp]	*n.*	关系；关联
weekend ['wikend]	*n.*	周末
business ['bɪznɪs]	*n.*	商业；生意
urgent ['ɜːdʒənt]	*adj.*	紧急的
fault [fɔlt]	*n.*	错误
forgive [fə'gɪv]	*v.*	原谅
schedule ['ʃedjuːl]	*n.*	时间表
poet ['poət]	*n.*	诗人
touch [tʌtʃ]	*v.*	接触
mean [miːn]	*v.*	意味

Phrases and Expressions

take it easy		从容
fall in love		坠入爱河；爱上某人
be away too far		太过分了

Text

New Words

twenty ['twentɪ]	*n.*	二十
family ['fæməlɪ]	*n.*	家庭；亲属
parent ['peər(ə)nt]	*n.*	父亲（或母亲）；父母亲

sister ['sɪstə]	*n.*	姐妹
mountain ['maʊntən]	*n.*	山
region ['riːdʒ(ə)n]	*n.*	地区
hospital ['hɒspɪt(ə)l]	*n.*	医院
community [kə'mjuːnətɪ]	*n.*	社区
scissors ['sɪzəz]	*n.*	剪刀
box [bɒks]	*n.*	箱，盒子
sharp [ʃɑːp]	*adj.*	锋利的；刺耳的
supermarket ['suːpəmɑːkɪt; 'sjuː-]	*n.*	超级市场
convenient [kən'viːnɪənt]	*adj.*	方便的

Play

New Words

tomorrow [tə'mɒrəʊ]	*n.*	明天
Christmas ['krɪsməs]	*n.*	圣诞节
because [bɪ'kɒz]	*conj.*	因为
present ['preznt]	*n.*	礼物
husband ['hʌzbənd]	*n.*	丈夫
dollar ['dɒlə]	*n.*	美元
cent [sent]	*n.*	分
leave [liːv]	*v.*	留下
saving ['seɪvɪŋ]	*n.*	存款
though [ðəʊ]	*conj.*	尽管
month [mʌnθ]	*n.*	月
possession [pə'zeʃ(ə)n]	*n.*	所有物
pride [praɪd]	*n.*	自豪
grandfather ['græn(d)fɑːðə]	*n.*	祖父
chain [tʃeɪn]	*n.*	链
match [mætʃ]	*n.*	匹配
without [wɪ'ðaʊt]	*prep.*	没有
eve [iːv]	*n.*	前夕
comb [kəʊm]	*n.*	梳子

Phrases and Expressions

sit down	坐下
take…off	脱下，摘下
have a look	看一看
don’t mind	不介意
Merry Christmas	圣诞快乐

大学英语情境式教学教材

第一册答案

Unit One Friendship

Part Two: Dialogue

Dialogue 1

1. T 2. F 3. F 4. T 5. F

Dialogue 2

1. T 2. T 3. T 4. F 5. T

Dialogue 3

1. F 2. T 3. F 4. F 5. T

Dialogue 4

1. T 2. F 3. F 4. T 5. T

Part Three: Text

Language Focus

I. Make a sentence with the words given below.

1. This is a book.
2. This is a red bag.
3. That is a yellow table.
4. That student is a Chinese.
5. It is a beautiful box.

II. Translating

Put Chinese into English.

1. This is a table.
2. That is a chair.
3. This room is very big.
4. This is a cute dog.
5. It is a cat.

Put English into Chinese.

1. 这位是我同学，他很勤奋。
2. 这位是我男朋友，他很友善。
3. 那是一场很棒的生日宴会。
4. 这是一个有着许多花的美丽花园。
5. 它是座大城市，有很多高楼大厦。

III. Reading Comprehension

Choose the best answer to each of the following questions or incomplete sentences.

1. C　2. A　3. D　4. D　5.D

Part Four: Play

Listening Practice

I. Bingo game

Omitted

II. Dictation

Listen to the passage three times and supply the missing information.

1. king　2. forest　3. rush　4. animals　5. bite
6. teeth　7. carrots　8. porridge　9. peaches　10. apple

Reading Practice

I. Read and choose

1. D　2. C　3. C　4. A　5. A

II. Read and answer

Omitted

Speaking Practice

I. Role Play

Omitted

II. Problem-Solving

Omitted

III. Delivery Game

Omitted

Translating Practice

I. Translate the sentences into Chinese.

1. 吼!吼！我是只狮子，森林之王。没有人比我更强壮！吼!吼！
2. 去，自己找食物去。
3. 冲向小动物，用你锋利的牙齿咬它们。去，现在就去做。
4. 你想要点胡萝卜吗？
5. 桃子是最好吃的食物。

II. Translate the sentences into English.

1. Be brave.
2. I'm hungry.
3. Follow me!
4. Thank you !
5. I don't like it.

Writing Practice

Omitted

Part Five: Language Skills

Exercises

A. Multiple Choice

1. C　2. D　3. C　4. C　5. A　6. A　7. D　8. C　9. D　10. B

11. C　12. B　13. A　14. B　15. C　16. B　17. B　18. B　19. B　20. D

B. Complete each of the following sentences with a proper demonstrative pronoun.

1.this, that　2. these　3.these, These　4. this, This　5. this, that, It

6.those　7. this　8. that　9.This, he　10. Those

C. Translating Practice

I. Translate the sentences into English.

1. This is my ruler.
2. That is your book.
3. These are my pencils.
4. This is my good friend, Helen.
5. It's a lovely day.

II. Translate the sentences into Chinese.

1. 这是一个橘子。
2. 这些是自行车。
3. 这些是黄色杯子。
4. 这是只狐狸。
5. 那些是练习册。

Unit Two Gratitude

Part Two: Dialogue

Dialogue 1

1. T 2. F 3. T 4. F 5. F

Dialogue 2

1. T 2. T 3. F 4. T 5. F

Dialogue 3

1. T 2. F 3. T 4. T 5. F

Dialogue 4

1. T 2. F 3. T 4. T 5. T

Part Three: Text

Language Focus

I. Make a sentence with the words given below.

1. Is this a big car?

2. Is that a white bird?
3. Is that a tall boy?
4. Is that a long river?
5. Is it a colorful bird?

II. Translating

Put Chinese into English.

1. Is this a computer? Yes, it is.
2. Is that a Japanese girl? No, she isn't. She is a Chinese girl.
3. Is this a big school? Yes, it is.
4. Is that a beautiful picture? Yes, it is.
5. Is that a novel? No, it isn't. It is a magazine.

Put English into Chinese.

1. 这是那座著名的塔吗？是的。
2. 那是一条河吗？不是的，是一个湖。
3. 这是本很难理解的书吗？不是的，很容易理解。
4. 它是有很多房间的大房子吗？是的。
5. 那是长城，世界奇迹之一。

III. Reading Comprehension

Choose the best answer to each of the following questions or incomplete sentences.

1. D　2. C　3. B　4. B　5. B

Part Four: Play

Listening Practice

I. Bingo game

Omitted

II. Dictation

Listen to the passage three times and supply the missing information.

1. fisherman	2. ugly	3. caught	4. reward	5. angry
6. cottage	7. tired	8. palace	9. queen	10. angry

Reading Practice

I. Read and choose

1. A 2. B 3. A 4. A 5. D

II. Read and answer

Omitted

Speaking Practice

I. Role Play

Omitted

II. Problem-Solving

Omitted

III. Delivery Game

Omitted

Translating Practice

I. Translate the sentences into Chinese.

1. 一天，渔夫抓住了一条金鱼。
2. 回到海边去，告诉金鱼，我要一个小屋。
3. 但是几天后，渔夫的老婆厌倦了它。
4. 我想成为女王。让金鱼来做我的仆人。
5. 渔夫等呀等，但是金鱼再也没有回来。

II. Translate the sentences into English.

1. This time, the fish got angry.
2. Where are you?
3. I don't like it.
4. You are stupid.
5. Don't worry.

Writing Practice

Omitted

Part Five: Language Skills

Exercises

A. Multiple Choice

1. D　2. A　3. C　4. D　5. C　6. B　7. D　8. A　9. A　10. D

11. C　12. B　13. A　14. C　15. A　16. D　17. B　18. B　19. D　20. C

B. Complete each of the following sentences with a proper word.

1. an　2. are　3. Those　4. is　5. is

6. this　7. pencils　8. This　9. Is　10. are

C. Translating Practice

I. Translate the sentences into English.

1. What is that?

2. What are these?

3. Are those broccoli?

4. Are these your exercise books?

5. — What is this?

— It is Lucy's kite.

II. Translate the sentences into Chinese.

1. — 这些是你的书吗？ — 是的。

2. — 那些是熊吗？ —不，不是的。

3. — 这个在英语里是什么？ — 是玩具。

4. — 那些在英语里是什么？ — 是玫瑰花。

5. — 这是你的伞吗？ — 不是的。

Unit Three　Growing Up

Part Two: Dialogue

Dialogue 1

1. F　2. F　3. T　4. T　5. T

Dialogue 2

1. F 2. F 3. T 4. F 5. F

Dialogue 3

1. T 2. T 3. F 4. F 5. T

Dialogue 4

1. F 2. F 3. T 4. T 5. F

Part Three: Text

Language Focus

I. Make a sentence with the words given below.

1. Is it an interesting story? Yes, it is.
2. What is it? It is a boring book.
3. What is that? That is a tall tree.
4. What is it? It is a long rope.
5. Is it a restaurant? No, it isn't. It is a hotel.

II. Translating

Put Chinese into English.

1. What is this? This is an interesting book.
2. What is that? That is a chair.
3. Is this a bank? Yes, it is.
4. Is that the tallest building in the city? Yes, it is.
5. Is that your mother? No, she isn't. She is my aunt, my mother's sister.

Put English into Chinese.

1. 那是什么？那是一个彩色的风筝。
2. 它是这个国家唯一的河流吗？是的。
3. 那边的建筑是什么？埃菲尔铁塔。
4. 这是什么？灯。
5. 那是什么？小船。

III. Reading Comprehension

Choose the best answer to each of the following questions or incomplete sentences.

1. A 2. B 3. B 4. A 5. C

Part Four: Play

Listening Practice

I. Bingo game

Omitted

II. Dictation

Listen to the passage three times and supply the missing information.

1. butterflies	2. dragonflies	3. pool	4. tadpoles	5. corner
6. sad	7. look for	8. legs	9. green	10. frog

Reading Practice

I. Read and choose

1. D 2. D 3. A 4. B 5. D

II. Read and answer

Omitted

Speaking Practice

I. Role Play

Omitted

II. Problem-Solving

Omitted

III. Delivery Game

Omitted

Translating Practice

I. Translate the sentences into Chinese.

1. 一天早上，蝴蝶和小蜻蜓在池塘上飞来飞去。
2. 这是小蝌蚪，我们的新朋友。
3. 小蝌蚪在池塘里游泳。
4. 你们的妈妈有四条腿。你们可以去那边找她。
5. 亲爱的，让我们一起游泳吧。

II. Translate the sentences into English.

1. Nice to meet you!

2. She is over there.

3. Be careful.

4. Who are you?

5. Don't cry, don't cry.

Writing Practice

Omitted

Part Five: Language Skills

Exercises

I. Complete the sentences and passage.

A. Complete each of the following sentences with am,is,are.

1. B 2. D 3. A 4. D 5. A 6. D 7. D 8. D 9. D 10. D

11. A 12. D 13. D 14. D 15. A 16. B 17. D 18. A 19. A 20. A

B. Complete the following passage with am,is,are.

1. am 2. is 3. am 4. am 5. is

6. are 7. are 8. is 9. is 10. is

II. Translating Practice

A. Translate the sentences into English.

1. I am a teacher.

2. I am a student.

3. This pen is mine.

4. My name is Mary.

5. We are all here.

B. Translate the sentences into Chinese.

1. 这个女孩是杰克的朋友。

2. 你哥哥在教室吗？

3. 他是我的英语老师。

4. 我妹妹叫露丝。

5. 今天天气晴朗。

Unit Four Trust

Part Two: Dialogue

Dialogue 1

1. T　2. T　3. F　4. T　5. F

Dialogue 2

1. F　2. T　3. T　4. T　5. F

Dialogue 3

1. T　2. T　3. F　4. T　5. T

Part Three: Text

Language Focus

I. Make a sentence with the words given below.

1. I am a doctor.　I am busy.
2. She is a teacher.　She is caring.
3. He is a policeman.　He is brave.
4. They are singers.　They are friendly.
5. We are students.　We are cheerful.

II. Translating

Put Chinese into English.

1. He is a student. He is friendly.
2. She is a nurse. She is patient.
3. We are teachers. We are happy.
4. They are engineers. They are busy.
5. You are bosses. You are tired.

Put English into Chinese.

1. 我是一个友好的女人。
2. 他是一个英俊的男孩。
3. 它是一只丑鸭子。
4. 我们是勇敢的男人。

5. 他是一个勤奋的学生。

III. Reading Comprehension

Choose the best answer to each of the following questions or incomplete sentences.

1. B 2. C 3. B 4. A 5. D

Part Four: Play

Listening Practice

I. Bingo game

Omitted

II. Dictation

Listen to the passage three times and supply the missing information.

1. going out	2. lock	3. visit	4. voice	5. stranger
6. clever	7. foot	8. open	9. kills	10. knife

Reading Practice

I. Read and choose

1. D 2. A 3. B 4. B 5. C

II. Read and answer

Omitted

Speaking Practice

I. Role Play

Omitted

II. Problem-Solving

Omitted

III. Delivery Game

Omitted

Translating Practice

I. Translate the sentences into Chinese.

1. 羊妈妈出门了，我要去拜访这些小羊羔。

2. 你的声音好奇怪。
3. 请给我们看看你的脚。
4. 哇哦，小羊羔，我的美餐。
5. 给我刀，我要杀了你。

II. Translate the sentences into English.

1. Don't open the door.
2. Help, help.
3. Let me have a try.
4. Mommy, I am here.
5. Go away!

Writing Practice

Omitted

Part Five: Language Skills

Exercises

A. Multiple Choice

1. C	2. B	3. A	4. A	5. A	6. C	7. B	8. D	9. B	10. B
11. A	12. B	13. C	14. A	15. A	16. B	17. A	18. B	19. A	20. B

B. Complete each of the following sentences with a proper word.

1.isn't	2. are	3. Is	4. Are	5. am
6. aren't	7. are	8. are	9. is	10. are

C. Change the following sentences

I. Change the following affirmative sentences containing Be verbs into general question sentences.

1. Is she from Japan?
2. Are those his parents?
3. Are there many countries in the world?
4. Are dogs very cute?
5. Is her favorite food hot dog?

II. Imitate the model sentences and change the following sentences into negative and interrogative sentences.

1. This is not a coat.

   Is this a coat?

   Yes, it is. / No, it isn't.

2. I am not a student.

   Are you a student?

   Yes, I am. / No, I am not.

3. You are not a star.

   Are you a star?

   Yes, I am. / No, I am not.

4. These are not apples.

   Are these apples?

   Yes, these are. / No, these are not.

5. That is not a tree.

   Is that a tree?

   Yes, it is. / No, it is not.

Unit Five　Trying Everything

Part Two: Dialogue

Dialogue 1

1. F　2. F　3. F　4. F　5. T

Dialogue 2

1. F　2. T　3. T　4. F　5. F

Dialogue 3

1. T　2. T　3. F　4. F　5. T

Dialogue 4

1. T　2. T　3. F　4. F　5. T

Part Three: Text

Language Focus

I. Make a sentence with the words given below.

1. Are you from China? Yes, I am.
2. Is she a pupil? Yes, she is.
3. Is he a taxi-driver? No, he is not. He is a worker.
4. Are they from Canada? No, they are not. they are from Russia.
5. Are they doctors? Yes, they are.

II. Translating

Put Chinese into English.

1. Is she a housewife? No, she is not. She is a doctor.
2. Is she a doctor? Yes, she is a young doctor.
3. Is he from Japan? Yes, he is a Japanese.
4. Are they teachers? Yes, they are very serious.
5. Are they singers? Yes, they are fashionable.

Put English into Chinese.

1. 她是一位艺术家吗？是的，她是。她很著名。
2. 他是位舞者吗？不，他不是。他是位模特。
3. 他们是科学家吗？是的，他们是。他们很有智慧并且刻苦。
4. 他们来自美国吗？是的。
5. 你是好学生吗？是的。我和善、外向并且努力。

III. Reading Comprehension

Choose the best answer to each of the following questions or incomplete sentences.

1. A　2. D　3. B　4. B　5. B

Part Four: Play

Listening Practice

I. Bingo game

Omitted

II. Dictation

Listen to the passage three times and supply the missing information.

1. enough 2. rice 3. on the other side 4. calf 5. deep
6. drowned 7. go back 8. in their own way 9. himself 10. In fact

Reading Practice

III. Read and choose

1. D 2. A 3. D 4. D 5. A

IV. Read and answer

Omitted

Speaking Practice

I. Role Play

Omitted

II. Problem-Solving

Omitted

III. Delivery Game

Omitted

Translating Practice

I. Translate the sentences into Chinese.

1. 把这袋米送给你的驴叔叔，好吗？
2. 驴叔叔的房子在河的另一边。
3. 我刚刚从河对岸过来，河水只到我的小腿。
4. 河水太深了，我的一个同伴被冲走了。
5. 牛大叔和松鼠老弟站在自己的立场上，都是正确的。

II. Translate the sentences into English.

1. Mum, I am as tall as you.
2. Is there a bridge near here?
3. You'd better ask your mum.
4. I'll cross the river right away.

5. I should try it myself!

Writing Practice

Omitted

Part Five: Language Skills

Exercises

A. Multiple Choice

1. B 2. B 3. C 4. A 5. C 6. C 7. B 8. D 9. C 10. A

11. C 12. C 13. C 14. D 15. A 16. C 17. B 18. C 19. C 20. C

B. Fill in the blanks with the correct form of the pronoun given.

1. us 2. your, mine, hers 3. mine 4. you 5. you, your

6. My, yours 7. It 8. Its 9. their 10. theirs

C. Make a question about the underlined part.

1. Whose teacher is this?
2. Who teaches us English?
3. Whose book is that?
4. Whose is the pencil box?
5. Who are students?
6. Whose is the red cap?
7. Who are your best friend?
8. Whose photos are these?
9. Whose toys are those?
10. Whose student are you?

Unit Six Self-protection

Part Two: Dialogue

Dialogue 1

1. T 2. F 3. T 4. F 5. F

Dialogue 2

1. T 2. F 3. F 4. F 5. F

Dialogue 3

1. T 2. F 3. F 4. T 5. F

Dialogue 4

1. T 2. T 3. T 4. F 5. T

Part Three: Text

Language Focus

I. Make a sentence with the words given below.

1. Who are they?	They are our employees.
2. Who is she?	She is your boss.
3. Who is he?	He is a singer.
4. What are they jobs?	They are barbers.
5. What is her job?	She is an actress.

II. Translating

Put Chinese into English.

1. Who is she?	She is a nurse.
2. Who are they?	They are teachers.
3. Who are they?	They are our friends.
4. What is his job?	He is an engineer.
5. What is her job?	She is an artist.

Put English into Chinese.

1. 他们是谁？	他们是大学教师。
2. 他是谁？	他是一名大学生。他非常勤奋。
3. 她是谁？	她是我朋友的妻子。
4. 她的工作是什么？	她是名空姐。她漂亮又和善。
5. 他们的工作是什么？	他们是警察。他们又高又壮。

III. Reading Comprehension

Choose the best answer to each of the following questions or incomplete sentences.

1. C 2. A 3. B 4. D 5. B

Part Four: Play

Listening Practice

I. Bingo game

Omitted

II. Dictation

Listen to the passage three times and supply the missing information.

1. grandmother 2. ill 3. wolf 4. hungry 5. Little Red Riding Hood
6. hunter 7. noise 8. sleeping 9. stomach 10. lives

Reading Practice

I. Read and choose

1. D 2. A 3. A 4. A 5. D

II. Read and answer

Omitted

Speaking Practice

I. Role Play

Omitted

II. Problem-Solving

Omitted

III. Delivery Game

Omitted

Translating Practice

I. Translate the sentences into Chinese.

1. 这是给她的苹果和香蕉。你能把它们送到她那儿去吗？
2. 小红帽开始和小鸭子跳舞，一只狼藏在树后。
3. 奶奶，给我些针线。小红帽，给我拿些石头来。
4. 我的胃好重！

5. 大坏狼，举起手来。

II. Translate the sentences into English.

1. Mummy, what are you doing?
2. Where are you going?
3. She is ill.
4. The wolf is sleeping.
5. I must be hurry.

Writing Practice

Omitted

Part Five: Language Skills

Exercises

A. Multiple Choice

1. C 2. B 3. A 4. B 5. B 6. B 7. D 8. B 9. C 10. B

11. D 12. B 13. B 14. B 15. B 16. B 17. D 18. C 19. B 20. C

B. Complete each of the following sentences with a proper word.

1. teacher's 2. friends 3. brother's 4. Tom's 5. Whose, Linda's

6. Whose, Tim's and John's 7. Tim and John's 8. Jim's 9. students'

10. girls'

C. Translate the following sentences into English

1. Li Ming's parents'
2. my sister's book
3. Their bedrooms
4. Wang Li and Wang Ming's father
5. your best friend's pen
6. Peter and Sam's teachers
7. Teachers' Day
8. Students' chairs and desks
9. Children's Day
10. teachers' office

Unit Seven Diligence

Part Two: Dialogue

Dialogue 1

1. F 2. F 3. T 4. T 5. F

Dialogue 2

1. T 2. T 3. T 4. F 5. F

Dialogue 3

1. F 2. T 3. F 4. T 5. F

Dialogue 4

1. T 2. T 3. T 4. F 5. F

Part Three: Text

Language Focus

I. Make a sentence with the words given below.

1. There are four people in my family. We are happy.
2. There is a bag on the sofa. It is big.
3. There is an umbrella on the floor. It is colorful.
4. There are some books on the shelf. They are interesting.
5. There is a cup on the desk. It is pink.

II. Translating

Put Chinese into English.

1. There are two watches on the desk. They are new.
2. There are five students in the class. They are boring.
3. There are three pencils and two pens in the pencil-box.
4. There is a TV machine in the room.
5. There is a computer on the desk.

Put English into Chinese.

1. 操场上有许多孩子。他们正在踢足球。
2. 草地上有两匹马和三头牛。
3. 车顶上有一只狗。它很可爱。
4. 房间里有一把吉他。
5. 教室里有两块白板。

III. Reading Comprehension

Choose the best answer to each of the following questions or incomplete sentences.

1. B　2. D　3. A　4. C　5. D

Part Four: Play

Listening Practice

I. Bingo game

Omitted

II. Dictation

Listen to the passage three times and supply the missing information.

1. Once upon a time	2. village	3. own	4. lazy	5. leaves
6. sticks	7. bricks	8. blew	9. boiled	10. killed

Reading Practice

I. Read and choose

1. D　2. A　3. A　4. B　5. B

II. Read and answer

Omitted

Speaking Practice

I. Role Play

Omitted

II. Problem-Solving

Omitted

III. Delivery Game

Omitted

Translating Practice

I. Translate the sentences into Chinese.

1. 从前，一只猪妈妈和它的三个孩子住在村庄里。
2. 现在，三只小猪住在它们自己的房子里。
3. 让我进来，不然我就吹，再吹，一直吹，直到把你们的房子吹倒！
4. 狼立马就把房子吹跑了。
5. 狼猛吹房子。很快它就倒了。

II. Translate the sentences into English.

1. I am scared.
2. What are you doing?
3. We eat and sleep all day and all night.
4. It's time for you to make your own houses.
5. Let's boil the water.

Writing Practice

Omitted

Part Five: Language Skills

Exercises

A. Multiple Choice

1. B　2. A　3. C　4. D　5. C　6. A　7. A　8. C　9. A　10. C

11. D　12. A　13. C　14. A　15. B　16. B　17. B　18. A　19. C　20. A

B. Fill in the blank with their Chinese meaning.

1.什么颜色　2. 什么时间　3. 哪天　4. 多大　5. 多少（可数）

6. 多少（不可数）7. 多高　8. 多久　9. 多长时间一次　10. 多快

11. 多远　12. 多高

C. Make a question about the underlining part by using Who, What, When, Where, How many and How.

1. Who is she?
2. Where are they?
3. When do you often go swimming?
4. Where do you live?
5. Who does Lily like to play with?
6. Where are the rulers?
7. Why are you late?
8. How many brothers do you have?
9. What is that?
10. How do you go to school?

Unit Eight Inner Strength

Part Two: Dialogue

Dialogue 1

1. T 2. F 3. T 4. F 5. F

Dialogue 2

1. T 2. F 3. F 4. F 5. T

Dialogue 3

1. T 2. T 3. F 4. T 5. F

Dialogue 4

1. F 2. F 3. T 4. T 5. F

Part Three: Text

Language Focus

I. Make a sentence with the words given below.

1. Are there some eggs in the refrigerator? Yes, there are.

2. Are there some notebooks in the library? No, there are not.
3. Are there many people in the park? Yes, there are.
4. Are there cars on the street? Yes, there are.
5. Is there a cat on the tree? No, there is not.

II. Translating

Put Chinese into English.

1. Is there a ruler on the desk? Yes, there is.
2. Are there any people in the room? No, there are not.
3. Are there two toys on the bed? Yes, there are.
4. Are there two supermarkets in the street? Yes, there are.
5. Is there a pair of sunglasses in his bag? Yes, there is.

Put English into Chinese.

1. 街上有两个漂亮女孩吗？ 是的， 她们正在等她们的朋友。
2. 餐馆里有厕所吗？ 是的，拐弯处有一个厕所。
3. 大学里有图书馆吗？ 当然，有两个图书馆呢。
4. 大学里有实验室吗？ 有不止十个实验室。
5. 社区里有小学吗？ 是的，社区里有一所小学和一所中学。

III. Reading Comprehension

Choose the best answer to each of the following questions or incomplete sentences.

1. B 2. C 3. B 4. D 5. C

Part Four: Play

Listening Practice

I. Bingo game

Omitted

II. Dictation

Listen to the passage three times and supply the missing information.

1. forest	2. tiger	3. angry	4. strong	5. at once
6. scared	7. crazy	8. around	9. ran away	10. king

Reading Practice

I. Read and choose

1. D 2. A 3. B 4. D 5. D

II. Read and answer

Omitted

Speaking Practice

I. Role Play

Omitted

II. Problem-Solving

Omitted

III. Delivery Game

Omitted

Translating Practice

I. Translate the sentences into Chinese.

1. 我要立刻找点吃的。
2. 是的，是的，你应该吃了我，但是你知道什么吗？
3. 你有“森林之王”的美称，但是我才是真正的森林之王。
4. 你知道森林里的小动物都怕我吗？
5. 老虎，你看，它们都很怕我！

II. Translate the sentences into English.

1. I'm a great tiger. I am very strong. I am very brave.
2. I'm the king of the forest.
3. Tell me quickly.
4. How dare you say that?
5. What are you talking about? Are you crazy?

Writing Practice

Omitted

Part Five: Language Skills

Exercises

A　Multiple Choice

1. C　2. A　3. C　4. A　5. A　6. C　7. C　8. A　9. A　10. D

11. C　12. B　13. A　14. C　15. B　16. A　17. C　18. A　19. A　20. A

B. Complete each of the following sentences with a proper demonstrative pronoun.

1. There are, in the university's library　2. are　3. is

4. is　5. There are　6. are, classes　7. is a

8. are　9. are　10. are many apples

III. Translating Practice

A. Translate the following sentences into English.

1. There are some bananas on the table.
2. There are some tigers in the zoo.
3. There is a piece of paper on the desk.
4. There is a blackboard in the classroom.
5. There is a TV machine in the living room.

B. Translate the following sentences into Chinese.

1. 冰箱里有一瓶牛奶。
2. 椅子下有一个足球。
3. 桌子上有一块巧克力。
4. 沙发上有一个书包。
5. 铅笔盒里有一块橡皮。

Unit Nine　Love

Part Two: Dialogue

Dialogue 1

1. F　2. T　3. F　4. F　5. F

Dialogue 2

1. T 2. F 3. T 4. F 5. T

Dialogue 3

1. T 2. F 3. F 4. F 5. F

Dialogue 4

1. F 2. F 3. T 4. T 5. T

Part Three: Text

Language Focus

I. Make a sentence with the words given below.

1. How many books are there on the desk? There are four books on the desk.
2. How many chairs are there in the room? There are six chairs in the room.
3. How many computers are there in the lab? There are twenty computers in the lab.
4. How many shoes are there on the floor? There are eight shoes on the floor.
5. How many students are there in the classroom? There are nine students in the classroom.

II. Translating

Put Chinese into English.

1. How many boys are there in your class? There are fifteen boys in your class.
2. How many pencils are there on the desk? There are eight pencils on the desk.
3. How many rooms are there in the house? There are five rooms in the house.
4. How many trees are there in the garden? There are three trees in the garden.
5. How many dogs are there in the room? There are six dogs in the room.

Put English into Chinese.

1. 城市里有几个游泳池？ 城市里有十个游泳池.
2. 街上有几个宾馆？ 街上有两个宾馆。
3. 社区有几个邮局？ 社区有两个邮局。
4. 停车场上有几辆汽车？ 停车场上大约有两百辆汽车。
5. 城市里有几所学校？ 城市里大约有八所学校。

III. Reading Comprehension

Choose the best answer to each of the following questions or incomplete sentences.

1. C 2. C 3. A 4. D 5. B

Part Four: Play

Listening Practice

I. Bingo game

Omitted

II. Dictation

Listen to the passage three times and supply the missing information.

1. sad 2. present 3. leave 4. living 5. possessions

6. watch 7. hair 8. chain 9. comb 10. love

Reading Practice

I. Read and choose

1. C 2. B 3. A 4. A 5. B

II. Read and answer

Omitted

Speaking Practice

I. Role Play

Omitted

II. Problem-Solving

Omitted

III. Delivery Game

Omitted

Translating Practice

I. Translate the sentences into Chinese.

1. 但是德拉非常悲伤，因为她没钱给她的丈夫买份礼物。
2. 实际上，德拉和蒂姆拥有两件非常让他们骄傲的东西。

3. 然后，她在一家金店购物，买了一条金表带。
4. 我把头发剪掉，卖了，因为圣诞节不给你礼物，我简直活不下去了。
5. 今天是圣诞节前夜，对我好点。

II. Translate the sentences into English.

1. Life is so hard for me!
2. Madam, I need money! Please, give me some more!
3. What a beautiful gold watch.
4. It's a Christmas present for you.
5. Merry Christmas.

Writing Practice

Omitted

Part Five: Language Skills

Exercises

I. Multiple Choice

1. C 2. C 3. B 4. D 5. B 6. C 7. D 8. A 9. C 10. A
11. C 12. A 13. B 14. B 15. D 16. C 17. A 18. B 19. D 20. B

II. Complete each of the following sentences with a proper word.

1. are not 2. apples 3. garden 4. Bedroom 5. students
6. Are there 7. on the tree 8. in the living room 9. a butterfly 10. A ruler

III. Translating Practice

A. Translate the following sentences into English.

1. There is a book and two pencils on the desk.
2. There are two pens in Tom's pencil case.
3. Are there any apples on the tree?
4. There is some water in the glass.
5. Is there a ball on the table?

B. Translate the following sentences into Chinese.

1. 花园里有兔子吗？

2. 教师办公室里有两张桌子和四把椅子。
3. 水里有鱼吗？
4. 教室里没有人。
5. 书桌上有五本书吗？

大学英语
情境式教学教材

（全二册）

下 册

马纳琴　原　媛　主　编
杨晓娅　梁玉娟　副主编

中国社会科学出版社

Content II

Unit One
Honesty

Part One: Phonetic Knowledge

Part Two: Dialogue

Part Three: Text

Part Four: Play：The Emperor’s New Clothes (I)

Part Five: Language Skills

Part One: Phonetic knowledge

A. 字母 R r

1. 拼读发音方式。

字母“r”有字母音和拼读音，字母音就是在字母“RST…”中的读音。而它的拼读音是这样的：卷起舌尖，靠近上齿龈后部，向后面的硬腭弯曲，双唇噘起，气流经过，并和舌面及上齿龈后面摩擦成音，声带振动。包括这个拼读音的单词如 road，rice， very，carry 等。

2. 发音规则。

字母 r 通常发 / r /，如 Rest，rain，free。

3. 听一听，学一学字母“r”的拼读发音。

(1) rat rug rod race room rain rose rabbit river red
r-at r-ug r-od r-a-c-e r-oo-m r-ai-n r-o-se r-a-bb-it r-i-v-er r-ed

(2) a red red rose rock and roll as green as grass
break fresh ground rather correct

4. 仔细听，然后做句子一口气快读练习。

(1) All roads lead to Rome.

(2) Rose is in red today.

(3) If you always rest, your brain well rust.

(4) Reed is riding a red horse.

5. 听一听下列的韵律英语，并熟练朗读。

Rainbow Rabbit,
Run, run, run.
Rr says r, r.
Run! Rabbit, run!

Run rabbit, run rabbit run, run, run.
Here comes the farmer with his gun, gun, gun.
He won't cry without his rabbit pie.
So run rabbit, run rabbit, run, run, run.

B. 字母 W w

1. 拼读发音方式。

字母“w”有字母音和拼读音，字母音就是在字母“WXYZ…”中的读音。而它的拼读音是这样的：舌头后部向软腭抬起，双唇收圆且小，并向前突出，声带振动。包括这个拼读发音的单词如 want，wash，watch，swap 等。

2. 发音规则。

(1) 字母 w 一般情况下发 / w /，如 west，sweat，between。

(2) 有时不发声，如 wrong，sword，answer。

(3) 字母组合 wh 在字母 a，e，i，y 前发 /w/，如 what，where，which，why；在 o 之前发 /h/，如 who，whole。

3. 听一听，学一学字母“w”的拼读发音。

(1) wet wall win wind was word worry
w-et w-all w-in w-i-n-d w-a-s w-or-d w-or-r-y

(2) world wide web warm weather wonderful world
wax works a windy winter's day

4. 仔细听，然后做句子一口气快读练习。

(1) He always waits for me after work.

(2) We are going to sell wheel chairs.

(3) They painted the wall white.

(4) Wait a while and see what's going.

5. 听一听下列的韵律英语，并熟练朗读。

Where is the witch?
Where is the witch?
Ww says w, w.
Witch, witch, witch.

If two witches watched two watches,
Which witch would watch which watch?
Which wristwatch is a Swiss wristwatch?

I wish to wish the wish you wish to wish,
but if you wish the wish the witch wishes,
I won't wish the wish you wish to wish.

C. 字母 Z z

1. 拼读发音方式。

字母"z"有字母音和拼读音，字母音就是在字母"WXYZ…"中的读音。而它的拼读音是这样的：舌尖靠近下齿龈，气流从下齿龈和舌尖之间的缝隙流出，发音不送气，舌尖和下齿龈摩擦成音，声带振动。包括这个拼读音的单词如：zag，zoo，zero，zip 等。

2. 发音规则。

字母 z 通常发 / z /，如 amaze，zone。

3. 听一听，学一学字母"z"的拼读发音。

(1) zebra　zero　zigzag　zoom　zoo　zipper　zip
z-e-br-a　z-e-r-o　z-ig-z-ag　z-oo-m　z-oo　z-i-pp-er　z-ip

(2) zip zippers　cozy clothes　a zebra in the zoo　analyze news
examine her disease　seize the crazy man

4. 仔细听，然后做句子一口气快读练习。

(1) Jez likes to play Zombie games.

(2) Liz is very crazy.

(3) Elizabeth does not like the exam.

(4) Alexander deserves a praise.

5. 听一听下列的韵律英语，并熟练朗读。

Zebra, Zebra.
How do you do!
Zz says z, z.
Zoo, Zoo, Zoo!

This is a zither(齐特琴),
Is this a zither?
This is Zoe's sister's zither.

Jez wears a fez and his chest has a wheeze.
He is lazy and he's crazy and his nose can sneeze.
He's a wizard in a blizzard.
And he'll sizzle in the drizzle,
But he's puzzled by the hazard in the maze.

Part Two: Dialogue

Dialogue 1

Jane: What would you like today?

Mary: Is there anything to recommend?

Jane: Would you like to try the one-pound super hot and spicy hamburger?

Mary: Uh, I don't think so, I'd probably have heartburn for a week after downing that monster.

Jane: Then what do you want?

Mary: I think I'll just order a hamburger with some mustard and lettuce.

Jane: How about something to drink?

Mary: A coke, please.

Jane: Will this be for here or to go?

Mary: Oh, to go.

Jane: En, Ok. Your total comes to ten ninety.

Mary: Okay. Here is the money.

Words and Expressions

recommend [rekə'mend] *v.* 推荐

spicy ['spaɪsɪ] *adj.* 辣的

hamburger ['hæmbɜ:gə] *n.* 汉堡包

probably ['prɒbəblɪ] *adv.* 很可能

heartburn ['hɑːtbɜːn] *n.* 胃灼热

monster ['mɒnstə] *n.* 残忍的东西

mustard ['mʌstəd] *n.* 芥末

lettuce ['letɪs] *n.* 生菜

Decide whether the following statements are True (T) or False (F).

1. [ ] The waitress recommends a very cheap hamburger meal.
2. [ ] Mary orders a hamburger with some mustard and lettuce.
3. [ ] Mary orders a cup of coffee.
4. [ ] Mary spends over 10 pounds totally.
5. [ ] Mary eats in the restaurant.

Dialogue 2

Jane: Hello is this the Sunshine Restaurant?

Mary: Yes, it is. May I help you?

Jane: Could I reserve a table for Sunday May 11th at six thirty p.m.?

Mary: Certainly. For how many people, please?

Jane: For three people. We would like a quiet table, please.
Mary: Of course, would you like a table in the main restaurant or in a private room?
Jane: The main restaurant will be fine.
Mary: We will take care of that. May I have your name, please?
Jane: This is Tribbiani.
Mary: Can you spell that, please?
Jane: Tribbiani. T-R-I-B-B-I-A-N-I.
Mary: Thank you Mrs. Tribbiani. We look forward to seeing you.
Jane: See you Sunday.
Mary: Good bye.

Words and Expressions

reserve [rɪ'zɜːv] *v.* 预约
certainly ['sɜːt(ə)nli] *adv.* 当然
private ['praɪvɪt] *adj.* 私人的
look forward to 期待

Decide whether the following statements are True (T) or False (F).

1. [ ] Jane books a table for five people.
2. [ ] Jane will have her lunch on May 11th.
3. [ ] Jane likes a table in a quiet private room.
4. [ ] Jane's given name is Tribbiani.
5. [ ] Mary is a receptionist in a restaurant.

Dialogue 3

Jane: Good evening, this is Kevin Mutton House.
Mary: Hello. I'd like to make a reservation.
Jane: At what time can we expect you?
Mary: Thursday evening, say, around six thirty.
Jane: How many in your party?
Mary: There will be six of us.

Jane: Smoking or non-smoking?

Mary: Oh I don't think about that. Smoking, I guess.

Jane: May I have your name and telephone number, please?

Mary: Sure, it's Geller and my number is 52527334.

Jane: Ok, Mrs. Geller. That's a party of six for Thursday evening at 6:30. Is that correct?

Mary: That's right. Thank you. Goodbye.

Words and Expressions

reservation [rezə'veɪʃ(ə)n] *n.* 预约

expect [ɪk'spekt] v. 期待

correct [kə'rekt] *adj.* 正确的

Decide whether the following statements are True (T) or False (F).

1. [ ] Mary books two tables in Jane Mutton House.
2. [ ] Mary will have her dinner at 5 p.m.
3. [ ] Mary asks for non-smoking area.
4. [ ] Mary's booking number is 52527334.
5. [ ] There are five people having dinner together.

Dialogue 4

Jane: Good evening. How many people do you have?

Mary: Three. We have two adults and a kid.

Jane: Would you like buffet or regular dinner specials?

Mary: We'd like to try your buffet. How much do you charge for each?

Jane: $15 for each adult; $12 for kids.

Mary: OK, Should I pay first?

Jane: No, we will bring the bill to you later.

Mary: I see. Should I pay extra for soft drinks?

Jane: No, but we do charge for alcoholic drinks.

Mary: Okay, where can we get the food?

Jane: Please go to the tables over there.

Mary: After I finished these, can I go back for more?
Jane: Sure, as long as your stomach is happy.
Mary: Great.

Words and Expressions

buffet ['bʊfeɪ] *n.* 自助餐
regular ['regjʊlə] *adj.* 定期的
special ['speʃ(ə)l] *n.* 特色菜
charge [tʃɑːdʒ] *v.* 收费
alcoholic [ælkə'hɒlɪk] *adj.* 含酒精的
stomach ['stʌmək] *n.* 胃

Decide whether the following statements are True (T) or False (F).

1. [ ] There are three people having buffet together.
2. [ ] They like to try regular dinner specials.
3. [ ] The price is the same for everyone.
4. [ ] Mary has to pay before the meal.
5. [ ] Mary also should pay for soft drinks.

Part Three: Text

Mongolian yurt has a round appearance.

He has a very stressful job.

He has a degree in music and he can play any style of music.

The young man has two cows and five horses.

John has a business in his city.

We have some money in the bank.

They have fantastic and diverse websites.

They have different approaches to gardening.

They have different needs and rights.

Words and Expressions

yurt [jʊət; jɜːt] *n.*（游牧地区用兽皮或毛毯所盖的）圆顶帐篷

Eg. 1. He lived in a yurt in a friend's garden.

他曾经住在朋友家花园的帐篷里。

2.Yurt is a traditional Mongolian dwelling house.

蒙古包是蒙古的传统民居。

round [raʊnd] *adj.* 圆的

Eg. 1. Jamie's eyes grew round with delight.

杰米高兴得瞪圆了眼睛。

2.This is a big round table.

这是一张大圆桌。

appearance [ə'pɪər(ə)ns] *n.* 外貌，外观

Eg. 1. You should not judge by appearances.

你不该以貌取人。

2. She's the kind of woman who takes pride in her appearance.

她是那种对自己的外貌感到自豪的女人。

stressful ['stresfəl] *adj.* 紧张的；有压力的

Eg. 1. Because I have a terrible job and it's very stressful.

因为我有一份烦心的工作，压力特别大。

2. High up there, stressful and low pay.

地位很高，压力大，但收入很少。

degree [dɪ'griː] *n.* 学位

Eg. 1. He went down without taking a degree.

他大学毕业没有获得学位。

2. This degree will qualify you for teaching.

这个学位将使你有资格当教师。

style [staɪl] *n.* 风格；时尚

Eg. 1. The very style of the book fascinates.

这本书的风格本身就令人着迷。

2. She has a style of her own in everything.

她在各方面都有自己的独特风格。

fantastic [fæn'tæstɪk] *adj.* 极好的，不可思议的

Eg. 1. You look fantastic!

你看上去棒极了！

2. It's a fantastic place, really beautiful!

这真是个好地方，漂亮极了！

website ['websaɪt] *n.* 网站（全球资讯网的主机站）

Eg. 1. My website is only for new customers.

我的网站只是为了新客户。

2. There are many shopping websites.

这里有许多购物网站。

approach [ə'prəʊtʃ] *n.* 方法；途径

Eg. 1. Which approach should you use?

您应当使用哪种方法？

2. So I went with the other approach.

所以我找了其他的方法。

Language Focus

I. Make a sentence with the words given below.

1. has / very good / a / he / job.
2. two cows / five horses / I / have / and.
3. city / Batu / his / factory / has a / in.
4. different / they / to / gardening / have / approaches.
5. has / no / in / pocket / she / money / her.

II. Translating

Put Chinese into English.

1. 我有一支新的钢笔。
2. 他们有很多钱。
3. 晚餐我有鱼吃。
4. 她有一辆旧车。
5. 他没有主意。

Put English into Chinese.

1. He has lunch at home every day.
2. They have an English lesson every day.
3. We have some apples.
4. she has blue eyes.
5. Lucy has a twin sister.

III. Reading Comprehension

Choose the best answer to each of the following questions or incomplete sentences.

Everybody has a home. People have homes. Animals have homes. People live in many kinds of houses. Animals have different kinds of homes, too.

Some animals live in holes (洞) under the ground. The woodchuck (土拨鼠) lives under the ground. His home has two doors. If any animal comes into one door, the woodchuck goes out through the other. Some animals live in holes in trees. Some squirrels (松鼠) build nests (窝) high in trees. Most of the birds live in nests in trees. But hawks (鹰) build their nests high in the mountains (山).

1. The story is about _____.

A. the homes of some people

B. some people

C. some animals

D. the homes of some animals

2. _____ live under the ground.

A. All the animals

B. the woodchucks

C. some squirrels

D. Most of the birds

3. How many doors are there in the woodchuck's house? _____

A. One

B. Two

C. Three.

D. None.

4. Hawks build their homes _____.

A. in the river

B. in the field

C. under the ground

D. high on the mountains

5. People live in _____.

A. holes

B. trees

C. different kinds of houses

D. Mountains

Part Four: Play

The Emperor's New Clothes (I)

Characters:
Narrator 旁白
Cheater A 骗子 A
Cheater B 骗子 B
Emperor 国王
Chamberlain 大臣
Waiter 男侍者
Waitress 女侍者

Narrator: Long ago and far away, there lived an emperor. This emperor was very vain and could think about nothing but his clothes. He had wardrobes and cupboards full of clothes. He changed his clothes from time to time.

News of the emperor spread to distant kingdoms and finally came to the ears of two very shady characters.

Scene 1

Cheater A (they asked themselves): Could we? Could we fool the emperor who loves his new clothes?

Cheater B: Let's try.

Narrator: They left their homes and travelled to the emperor's country and applied to see the emperor.

Cheater A: Dear chancellor, we have something very special to show the emperor.

Minster: That's what everyone says.

Cheater A: Ah, but this is magical. We have invented new clothes by using a very special material and secret method.

Waiter: The Chamberlain has arrived!

Waitress: His Majesty is in his dressing room! Please follow me.

Chamberlain: Your Majesty, two weavers want to show you something magical.

Emperor: Something magical? Oh, I love new things, order the two weavers to come here at once!

Chamberlain: Come on in.

Cheaters: Your majesty!

Emperor: What special skills do you have?

Cheater A: We come to be at your service from the far east. We can weave the most beautiful cloth.

Cheater B: The colors and patterns are very fine.

Cheater A: It feels like silk but is as warm as wool.

Cheater B: It is as light as air, a most wonderful fabric.

Emperor: So why you say your cloth are magical?

Cheater A: Oh! Your majesty! It is gold, silver and rainbow colored, all at the same time. And people who are stupid cannot see them.

Emperor: There is a grand parade in the city in two weeks' time, I need a new outfit for it. Can one be ready in time?

Cheater A: Oh yes, your Majesty. But there is a problem. The cloth is very expensive to make.

Emperor: It doesn't matter. Money is not an issue. I must have an outfit. Just see the Chamberlain and he'll sort it out. Make it here in the palace.

Scene 2

Narrator: Several days passed.

Emperor: Chamberlain, go to the weavers and see how the clothes is processing. The parade is only a week now.

Chamberlain: Yes, Your majesty.

(Chamberlain goes to see the two weavers, knocking at the door)

Cheater A: Enter! (Very exciting)

Chamberlain: The Emperor has sent me to check on the progress of the clothes. (Staring at the weavers)

Cheater A: Is it not beautiful? See the luster, feel the softness!

Cheater B: Oh, wise Chamberlain, now you can see why it is magical. Only the truly clever and brilliant can see the cloth. Most people would see an empty loom, but a clever man like you will see our wonderful cloth.

Chamberlain: Um, (don't know what to say) oh, my god! Am I foolish? Am I unqualified? I would not let others know it! (Talking to himself)

Cheater A: Are you satisfied?

Chamberlain: Of course. It is quite marvelous. The colors, the shimmer of the gold and silver threads. Marvelous.

Cheater A: Oh, you are so wise.

Narrator: The Emperor was very impatient and couldn't wait for the Chamberlain to return. After ten minutes of pacing up and down, he went to the weavers' room, followed by half of his court.

(They go into the weavers' room)

Emperor: Why?

Chamberlain: Your Majesty, a wise man such as you can surely see the colors and sheen of this magical cloth.

Emperor: Oh, my god! Am I foolish? Am I unqualified? I would not let others know about it! (Talking to himself) Of course I can, it's beautiful. Simply enchanting. When can my outfit be made? When can it be sent to the royal tailors!

Cheater B: Your Majesty, we would be delighted to make your outfit for you. There is no need to trouble your hard-working tailor. It is such a difficult fabric to cut and sew. We will make the suit.

Emperor: Very well.

Cheater A: Is it not beautiful? Of course, only the wise and very clever person can see the beauty of the cloth. Look at the colors, feel the weight. (Talking to others)

Others: Of course!

Narrator: The weavers muttered and discussed at the emperor's fittings, stitching here, cutting there until at last the suit was made.

Narrator: The following day was the day of the parade.

Words and Expressions

emperor ['empərə(r)] *n.* 皇帝，君主

Eg. 1. The daughter of an emperor does not worry about finding a husband.

皇帝的女儿不愁嫁。

2. The emperor had unlimited power.

皇帝权力无限。

vain [veɪn] *adj.*自负的

Eg. 1. She's too vain to wear glasses.

她太爱虚荣，不肯戴眼镜。

2.I think he is shallow, vain and untrustworthy.

我认为他浅薄虚荣，不可信任。

spread [spred] *vt.& vi.*（使）传播；（使）散布

Eg. 1.The good news spreads to the whole class.

好消息传遍了全班。

2.The disease spreads easily.

这种疾病容易传播。

shady ['ʃeɪdɪ] *adj.* 阴暗的；名声不好的

Eg. 1.Now at least she can choose her customers, and reject any who seem too shady.

至少现在她可以选择自己的客人，拒绝任何看上去可疑的人。

2. I think there must be something very shady about this contract.

我觉得这张合同里面一定有什么猫腻儿。

fool [fu:l] *vt.* 愚弄，欺骗

Eg. 1.Don't be fooled by his appearance

别被他的外表欺骗了。

2.They tried to fool you into coming after us.

他们想要骗你来追踪我们。

weave [wi:v] *vt.* 编织；编排

Eg. 1. She then had the idea to weave it.

之后，她有了编织蚕丝的想法。

2. They used leaves to weave a boat.

他们用树叶编织小船。

parade [pə'reɪd] *n.*游行；检阅

Eg. 1. He had them on parade at six o'clock in the morning.

他让他们早晨 6 点列队接受检阅。

2. The following day was the day of the parade.

第二天便是游行的日子。

marvelous ['mɑːvɪləs] *adj*.不可思议的；非凡的

Eg. 1. “Isn’t this marvelous?” she said.

“这是不是太不可思议了？”她说。

2.It seems to me a most marvelous book.

这本书我觉得奥妙之至。

impatient [ɪm'peɪʃnt] *adj*.不耐烦的；热切的

Eg. 1. I'd been waiting for twenty minutes and I was getting impatient.

我等了二十分钟，有点不耐烦了。

2.Try not to be too impatient with her.

尽量别对她没耐心。

long ago 从前

far away 遥远

pace up and down 走来走去；徘徊

dressing room 更衣室；化妆室

from time to time 时不时，经常

Listening Practice

I. Bingo game

Work in groups, one student read about the script of *Emperor’s New Clothes*, other students listen carefully, when they hear an adjective from the script, say “Bingo”, and write the word in the form quickly, and then he/she wins. And take turns, and change the words into Verbs, Nouns, etc.

words	adjective	verbs	nouns	prepositions	adverbs	conjunctions
student 1						
student 2						
student 3						
student 4						
student 5						

II. Dictation

Listen to the passage three times and supply the missing information.

Long ago and far away, there lived an ___1___. This Emperor was very___2___ and could think about nothing but his___3___. He had wardrobes and cupboards full of clothes. He changed his clothes___4___. News of the Emperor spread to distant kingdoms and finally came to the ears of two very ___5___characters. They tried to fool the emperor. They ___6___their homes and travelled to the Emperor's country and applied to see the Emperor. Several days passed. The Emperor was very impatient and couldn't wait for the Chamberlain to ___7___. After ten minutes of pacing up and down, he went to the weavers' room, ___8___ by half of his court. The weavers muttered and ___9___at the Emperor's fittings, stitching here, cutting there until at last the suit was made. The following day was the day of the ___10___.

Reading Practice

A. Read and choose

1.Which of the following statement is True?______

A. This Emperor was very vain and could think about nothing but his clothes.

A. This Emperor was not interested in beautiful clothes.

C. This Emperor had few clothes in his wardrobes and cupboards.

D. This Emperor invited two weaver to make new clothes for him .

2.Two cheaters tried to ______the Emperor.

A. Kill

B. fool

C. expect

D. love

3.Two cheaters told the emperor that people who are ______ cannot see the magical clothes.

A. clever

B. shy

C. stupid

D. polite

4. The Emperor was very____ and couldn't wait for the Chamberlain to return.

A. angry

B. sad

C. happy

D. impatient

5. Who can see the magical clothes?

A. The Emperor cannot see the magical clothes at all.

B. The Chamberlain can really see the magical clothes.

C. The weavers can see the magical clothes.

D. Nobody

B. Read and answer

1. Who is the emperor? What does he like?
2. Why do two cheaters try to fool the emperor?
3. Can you imagine this magical and beautiful clothes said by two cheaters?
4. If you were the cheaters, what would you say to the emperor when he came to see the magical clothes?
5. What does the Emperor and Chamberlain see when they come into the weaver's room?

Speaking Practice

I. Role Play

Suppose you were one of the weavers, what will happen when the emperor came to see the new clothes? Use the following functional sentences, you must add your own expressions when it is necessary.

- Oh, my god! Am I foolish? Am I unqualified? What did you see?
- Of course, I can, it's beautiful.
- Is it not beautiful? only the wise and very clever can see the magical cloth.
- Your Majesty, a wise man can see the magical cloth.
- I would not let others know about it!
- Look at the colors, feel the weight.
- But I really can see nothing.
- It is quite marvelous.

II. Problem-Solving

Think of appropriate lines for the emperor in the picture above.

Translating Practice

I. Translate the sentences into Chinese.

Work in pairs, one student reads the following sentences, and the other translates the sentences into Chinese in spoken way. (Add extra sentences from the scripts if necessary.)

1. Long ago and far away, there lived an Emperor.
2. He changed his clothes from time to time.
3. We have invented a new cloth by using a very special material and secret method.
4. After ten minutes of pacing up and down, the emperor went to the weavers' room, followed by half of his court.
5. Look at the colors, feel the weight.

II. Translate the sentences into English.

Work in pairs, one student reads the following sentences, and the other translates the sentences into English in spoken way. (Add extra sentences from the scripts if necessary.)

1. 这个国王很自负，心里只想着他的衣服。
2. 我们能否愚弄一下这个爱衣服的国王呢？
3. 我们已经发明了一种使用特殊材料和秘密方法制作的新衣服。

4. 国王派我来检查衣服制作的进展情况。
5. 没必要再麻烦您勤劳地裁缝了。

III. Delivery Game

The teacher divides the whole class into four or five groups, queuing the students. The teacher writes a long sentence from the script in a piece of paper, just let the first student read and recite it for one minute, and let the student retell the sentence to the second student, the second to the third, when the sentence is delivered to the last student, he/she should write it on the blackboard, and translate it into Chinese. The group which has got great speed and relative accuracy wins.

Writing Practice

Write a summary of *Emperor's New Cloth* in 100 words.

"Ws" / "Who"	doing what	whom	where	when

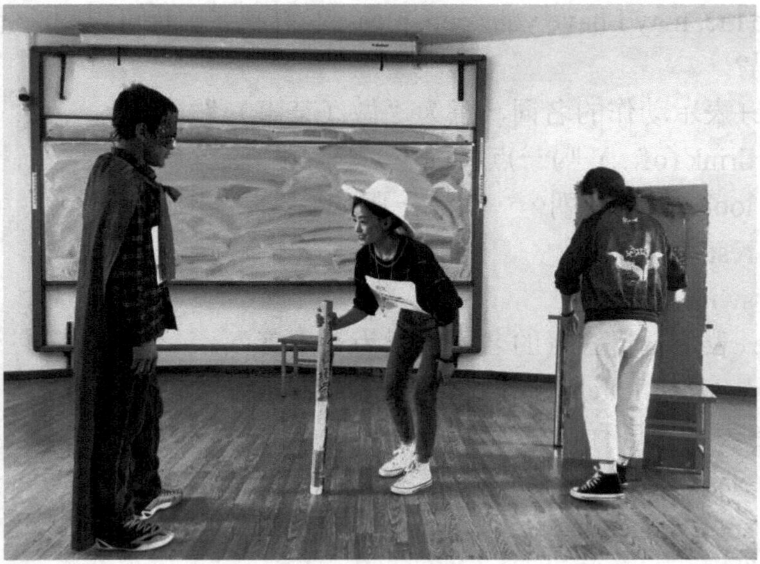

Part Five: Language Skills

Grammar

have/ has 的用法（I）

（1）谓语动词 have 表示“有”，有两种形式：have 和 has，前者用于第一人称、第二人称和第三人称复数，has 用于第三人称单数或单数名词。

例如：I have a pear and he has two bananas. 我有一个梨，他有两个香蕉。

You have a new English teacher. 你们有了一个新的英语老师。

She has two big eyes. 她有一双大眼睛。

（2）have、has 的用法。

①have/has 作“有”讲，强调“所属关系”。其主语一般是人，有时也可以是物。

They have many new books. 他们有许多新书。

She has a lot of pretty skirts. 她有很多漂亮的裙子。

This desk has four legs. 这张桌子有四条腿。

②have 可以作“买”讲。

I want to have a kilo of oranges. 我想买一公斤橘子。

May I have a new bike? 我可以买个新自行车吗?

③have 作“用、使用”讲。

Excuse me, may I have your pen, please? 打扰了，我可以用一下你的钢笔吗?

④have+表示动作的名词，意为“做（某事）”。

have a drink (of…) 喝一点（……）

have a look (at…)（朝……）看一眼

have a rest 休息一下

have a swim 游泳

⑤have+表示一日三餐的名词，意为“用餐”。

have breakfast/ lunch / supper、dinner 吃早饭/午饭/晚饭。

⑥have 表示“进行、举行”。

have a class（学生）上课

have a sports meeting 开运动会

have a party 举行聚会
⑦have+表示疾病的名词，有时也用 have got。
have a bad cold 患重感冒
have (got) a cough 咳嗽
have(got) a headache 头痛
⑧have+表示一段时间的名词，表示“经历；度过”。
have a good time 度过快乐的时光，玩得愉快
have a good summer holiday 度过愉快的暑假

（3）have/ has 句型与 there be 句型的比较：两者都表示“有”，但用法不同。前者表示所属关系，即表示“某人或某物有什么”，而后者表示存在，表示“某地有什么”。

I have new books. 我有一些新书。
There are a lot of pretty skirts in the shop. 商店里有很多漂亮的裙子。

Exercises

I. Fill in the blanks with “ have, has ”

1. I ____ a dog.
2. She ____ beautiful hair.
3. We ____ a big house.
4. We ____ a happy family.
5. The cat ____ a short tail.
6. You ____ a good teacher.
7. Dogs ____ two ears.
8. Girls ____ many skirts.
9. My mother _____ many dresses.
10. Lily ____ a barbie doll.

II. Correct the Mistakes.

1. The dog have a long tail. (   )
2. His father and mother has a son. (   )
3. The U.K's flag have stars and stripes. (   )
4. Tom have a big truck. (   )

5. Beijing have the Palace Museum.　(　　)

III. Translating Practice.

Translate the following into English.

1. 他有很多好朋友。
2. 我们有一些漂亮的花。
3. 晚上我们吃什么？
4. 小明有点头疼。
5. 我可以买个新书包吗？

Translate the following into Chinese.

1. I have a new computer.
2. I have breakfast everyday.
3. Everybody has two hands.
4. We will have a birthday party tonight.
5. They have English class everyday.

Unit Two
Truth

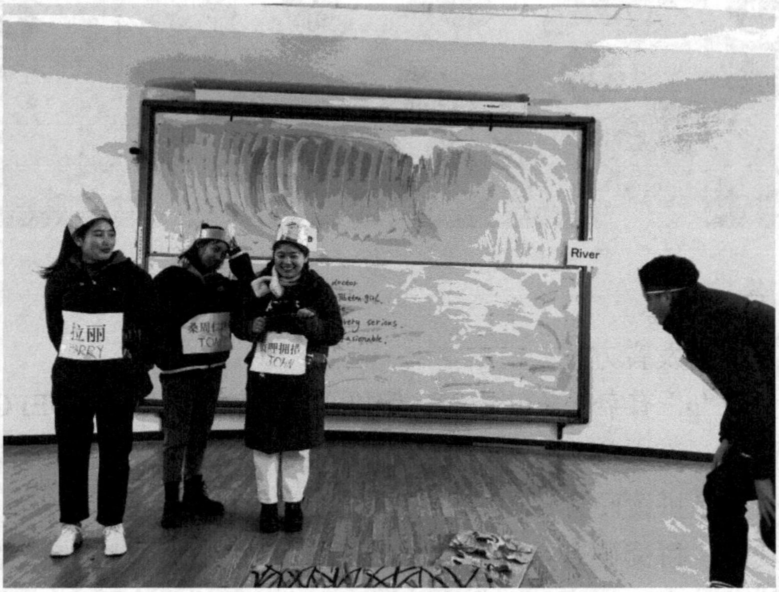

Part One: Phonetic Knowledge

Part Two: Dialogue

Part Three: Text

Part Four: Play：The Emperor’s New Clothes (2)

Part Five: Language Skills

Part One: Phonetic Knowledge

一、字母 G g

1. 拼读发音方式。

字母“g”有字母音和拼读音，字母音就是在字母“ABCDEFG…”中的读音。而它的拼读音与字母音不同。字母“g”的拼读音有两种：一种是拼读硬音，另一种是拼读软音。

其中，**拼读硬音**是这样的：舌后部紧贴软腭，然后突然离开，气流从舌后部和软腭之间冲出，发出爆破音。发音不送气，声带振动。硬音“g”常常在字母“a”“o”“u”前面。包括这个拼读发音的单词如 gold，gift，goose（鹅），gun 等。

拼读软音是这样的：舌尖顶在上齿龈后部分，先不发音，然后舌尖立即离开上齿龈，双唇略向前突出，并稍稍收成圆形，气流从舌尖和硬腭及上齿龈之间的缝隙流出，发出破擦音。“软音 g”常常在字母“e，i，y”前面。包括这个拼读发音的单词如 giant，gentleman，Germany，gigantic（巨大的），gypsy（吉卜赛人）等。

2. 发音规则。

（1）字母 g 元音字母 a，o，u 前，在辅音字母前及在词尾时发 / g /，叫硬 g，如 god，glad，hug，bag。

（2）字母 g 在字母 e，i，y 前发/ dʒ /，叫软 g。如 pigeon，gist，但有例外，如 girl，begin，gift。

3. 听一听，学一学字母“g”的拼读发音。

拼读硬音“g”

(1) gold gift egg dragon dog goat gas glad go gum
g-o-l-d g-i-f-t e-gg d-r-a-g-o-n d-og g-oa-t g-a-s
g-l-ad g-o g-um

(2) green grass give the gril a gift as good as gold a graceful girl

拼读软音“g”

(1) gentle gym gypsy giant huge village bridge cage germ
gen-t-l-e g-y-m g-y-p-s-y g-i-an-t h-u-g-e v-i-ll-a-g-e
br-idge c-a-ge g-e-m

(2) a giant gentleman a dangerous bridge a huge cage
a great magician

4. 仔细听，然后做句子一口气快读练习。

拼读硬音“g”

(1) A group of gorillas are eating grapes in the trees.

(2) Dogs and dragons are playing on the green grassland.

拼读软音“g”

(1) A gentle gentlemen built a huge bridge in the village.

(2) This gypsy was kept in a huge cage and he regarded the cage as his gym.

5. 听一听下列的韵律英语，并熟练朗读。

Giant, giant magician,
Giant, giant magician.
Gg says g, g.
Giant, giant magician.

gaggle 一群
gorilla 大猩猩
golden 金色的
giraffe 长颈鹿
geese 鹅（复数）
grease 油膏
grape 葡萄
sunshine 阳光
glittering 闪耀的

A gaggle of geese, a gun full of grease,
A group of gorillas, eating grapes in the trees,
Golden sunshine and green, green grass,
Giant giraffes and glittering glass.

二、字母 J j

1. 拼读发音方式。

字母“j”有字母音和拼读音，字母音就是在字母“HIJK…”中的读音。而它的拼读音是这样的：舌尖顶在上齿龈后部分，先不发音，然后舌尖立即离开上齿龈，双唇略向前突出，并稍稍收成圆形，气流从舌尖和硬腭及上齿龈之间的缝隙流出，发出擦音。包括这个拼读发音的单词如 Jeep，jelly，jellybean 等。

2. 发音规则。

字母“j”通常发 / dʒ /，如 just，jest，July。

3. 听一听，学一学字母“j”的拼读发音。

(1) jacket jam jar jet jig jingle job joy jug junk
j-a-ck-e-t j-am j-ar j-et j-ig j-i-n-g-l-e j-ob
j-oy j-ug j-un-k

(2) jingle bells Jame’s juice jugglers juggle jellyfish on the jetty
Jack in the jeep a jar of jelly beans junk food

4. 仔细听，然后做句子一口气快读练习。

(1) James lost his job just now.

(2) Do you like Jack's Jazz music?

(3) Jim jogs in the jungle.

(4) A gentle judge judges justly.

5. 听一听下列韵律英语，并熟练朗读。

Jumpy Jack, Jumpy Jack.

Jump, jump, jump.

Jj says j, j.

Jumpy, Jumpy, Jack.

James the jailer changed jail's chairs and chained the chairs to the jail.

Jane jellyfish jumps the waves.

Part Two: Dialogue

Dialogue 1

Bob: I spent the whole night counting sheep last night.

Mary: You may be too excited to sleep.

Bob: Yeah. Susan promised to go out for a bike ride today with me.

Mary: But it is raining now.

Bob: I know what you want to say. The damned weather is really ruining everything.

Mary: There is always a second chance for everything.

Bob: Are you free this weekend, Mary?

Mary: Yes. What's up?

Bob: Let's go out in some woods this Sunday.

Mary: It's just what I'd love to. We have worked a week. Just two of us.

Bob: I thought that the whole family could go together.

Mary: I'm afraid that the kids can't. Linda is going on a trip this weekend with her friends.

Bob: What about Jane?

Mary: She is busy with her study.

Bob: Oh, I hope that they could enjoy themselves.

Mary: They probably would.

Bob: Then, we'll go, just two of us.

Words and Expressions

count [kaʊnt] *v.* 计数

promise ['prɒmɪs] *v.* 许诺

damned [dæmd] *adj.* 糟糕的

ruin ['ruːɪn] *v.* 毁灭

Decide whether the following statements are True (T) or False (F).

1. [ ] Bob didn't sleep well last night.
2. [ ] Bob is going out for a walk.
3. [ ] The weather is very good for riding bicycles.
4. [ ] The kids will be very busy at the weekend.
5. [ ] Linda will be busy with her study.

Dialogue 2

Mary: I'm going to work with my father at the store the summer. How about you?

Jane: I'm going to camp. I've not gone to camp for four summers.

Mary: I've never gone to camp. What do you do there?

Jane: We do many things. In the morning, we go swimming and boating. In the afternoon, we play basketball or tennis. We sit around a campfire at night. We sing or tell stories.

Mary: That sounds wonderful.

Jane: I have planned to camp in the mountain this summer vacation. That will be wonderful, right?

Mary: I'm afraid that bad weather will set your holiday plans back by a week.

Jane: That's too bad. I wondered what I can do for fun indoors.

Mary: You can still keep on working.

Jane: Working? I'd rather not.

Mary: I'm afraid it's too cold.

Jane: Don't worry. We can make campfire to get warm.

Words and Expressions

store [stɔː] *n.* 商店

camp [kæmp] *n.* 露营

wonderful ['wʌndə(r)fl] *adj.* 极好的

vacation [və'keɪʃn] *n.* 假期

indoor ['ɪndɔː] *adj.* 户内的

Decide whether the following statements are True (T) or False (F).

1. [ ] Mary is going to work with her father at a factory this summer.
2. [ ] Mary has been to camp many times.
3. [ ] Jane is going to camp because she has not gone to camp for four summers.
4. [ ] They usually go swimming and boating in the afternoon.
5. [ ] Jane has planned to camp in the mountain area this summer vacation.

Dialogue 3

Receptionist: Good afternoon, sir! Welcome to Sunshine Hotel! May I help you?

Peter: Yes. I'd like to have a double room with bath.

Receptionist: Have you made a reservation?

Peter: Yes, a few days ago, under the name of Peter Brown.

Receptionist: OK, let me check, …Mr. Brown, a double room with bath and television for three nights, right?

Peter: Right.

Receptionist: Well, you are put in Room 806. Would you please fill in the registration form and sign your name at the end?

Peter: Yes. … Here you are. By the way, would you please give me a wake-up call at six thirty tomorrow morning?

Receptionist: Certainly, sir. Let me check all the details: Room 806, three nights, and a morning call at 6:30 tomorrow. Is that all?

Peter: Yes.

Receptionist: Here is your key card, sir. The room attendant will lead you to your room.

Words and Expressions

receptionist [rɪ'sepʃ(ə)nɪst] *n.* 接待员

registration [redʒɪ'streɪʃ(ə)n] *n.* 登记

sign [saɪn] *v.* 签名

wake-up call 电话叫醒服务

room attendant 客房服务员

Decide whether the following statements are True (T) or False (F).

1. [ ] Peter is going to visit Sunshine Hotel so he is making a

reservation.

2. [ ] Peter reserves a twin room with bath and television.
3. [ ] Peter booked this room a few days ago under the name of his.
4. [ ] Peter asks a morning wake-up call service.
5. [ ] The receptionist leads Peter and his family to his room.

Dialogue 4

Receptionist: Good morning, sir. Can I help you?

Peter: Yes, I'm leaving today. Can I have my bill settled?

Receptionist: Of course, sir. May I have your name?

Peter: My name is Peter Brown, and my room number is 806.

Receptionist: Just a second, please. Mr. Brown, here is your bill. Please check.

Peter: I'm sorry. I suppose there is a mistake indeed. I only stayed here for three nights, not four.

Receptionist: Just a second, please. I'll check it. … I'm sorry, Mr. Brown, this is a miscalculation. So, the fee in total should be $180.

Peter: Now you're right. Could I pay with a credit card?

Receptionist: What kind of card do you have?

Peter: Visa.

Receptionist: That's acceptable. …Okay, here are your bill and receipt. Thank you, sir. Hope you have enjoyed your stay at our hotel.

Peter: Certainly, I have. Thank you.

Receptionist: You're welcome. Goodbye.

Words and Expressions

miscalculation [ˌmɪskælkjə'leʃən] *n.* 误算

fee [fiː] *n.* 费用

acceptable [ək'septəb(ə)l] *adj.* 可接受的

bill [bɪl] *n.* 账单

receipt [rɪ'siːt] *n.* 收据

credit card 信用卡

Decide whether the following statements are True (T) or False (F).

1. [ ] Peter is checking out.
2. [ ] Peter is asking for his bill.
3. [ ] There is a mistake in his bill. He stays in Sunshine Hotel for three nights, not four.
4. [ ] The receptionist miscalculates Peter's bill and makes apologies.
5. [ ] Peter pays his bill with his debit card.

Part Three: Text

Do you have any books on grassland protection?

No, I haven't. I think Gesang has.

Does she have a mobile phone?

Yes, she has. She has two mobile phones.

Does he have a car?

Yes, he has. He has a blue car.

Do you have a laptop?

Yes, I have. Can I borrow it? Sure, no problem.

Do you have any brothers or sisters?

No, I haven't. I am the only child of my family.

Do you have a garden or any pets?

I do not have a garden, but I have some pets.

Do you have any advice for the writers?

No, I haven't. I think their writing is pretty good.

Do you have any formal education in your field?

Yes, I have. I have a graduate degree in my field.

Words and Expressions

protection [prə'tekʃ(ə)n] *n*. 保护；防卫

Eg. 1. Every citizen may claim the protection of the law.

每个公民都可以要求受到法律的保护。

2. You don't have much protection.

你并没有什么保护措施。

mobile ['məʊbaɪl] *adj*. 可移动的

Eg. 1. Give me a call on my mobile phone.

给我的手机打个电话。

2. Have you got my mobile phone number?

你有我的手机号码吗？

laptop ['læptɒp] *n.* 膝上型轻便电脑，笔记本电脑

Eg. 1. What do you think of this laptop?

你觉得这种笔记本电脑怎么样？

2. I will travel with my laptop.

我要带着我的笔记本电脑旅行。

advice [əd'vaɪs] *n.* 建议；忠告

Eg. 1. Now you can give me some advice.

现在你可以给我一些忠告。

2. At last they yield to our advice.

他们终于听从了我们的劝告。

formal ['fɔː m(ə)l] *adj.* 正式的

Eg. 1. A formal agreement between the countries.

两国间的正式协议。

2. I shall get up carefully; the party is very formal.

我会精心打扮的，这个聚会很正式。

education [ˌedʒʊ'keɪʃn] *n.* 教育

Eg. 1. All parents want a good education for their children.

所有父母都希望孩子接受良好教育。

2. She had no formal education.

她没受过正规教育。

field [fiːld] *n.* 领域，田野

Eg. 1. They will scope out another new field.

他们还将要开拓一个新的领域。

2. Beautiful field is a picture itself.

美丽的田野是天然的画幅。

graduate ['grædʒʊət] *n.* 研究生；毕业生

Eg. 1. He's a graduate in philosophy.

他哲学专业毕业。

2. A graduate of Edinburgh University.

爱丁堡大学的毕业生。

degree [dɪ'griː] *n.* 等级；学位

Eg. 1. He went down without taking a degree.

他大学毕业没有获得学位。

2. This degree will qualify you for teaching.

这个学位将使你有资格当教师。

Language Focus

I. Make a sentence with the words given below.

1. have / do / any / you / books
2. you / advice / me / have / do / any / for
3. do / brothers / sisters / have / or / you /any
4. their / bikes / think / are / very / I / beautiful
5. book/ am /very / interested / I / this/ in

II. Translating

Put Chinese into English.

1. 我弟弟有一个新的铅笔盒。
2. 你有移动电话吗？
3. 玛丽有兄弟姐妹吗？
4. 我们今天有英语课吗？
5. 他有任何意见么？

Put English into Chinese.

1. Do you have something to eat?
2. Do you have any books on history?
3. Do you have any friends in Singapore?
4. Does she have blue eyes?
5. Does she have a computer?

III. Reading Comprehension

Choose the best answer to each of the following questions or incomplete sentences.

Do you need friends? I'm sure your answer is "Yes, of course. Everybody does!" You need friends when you play and when you work.

If you have friends, you will feel happy. If you have no friends, you will feel lonely .

Do you know how to make friends? There is only one good way—You make friends by being friendly.

A friendly person is interested in other people. He is always helpful. If you want to make friends with a new classmate, you can talk with him, and tell him about the other classmates in your class and try your best to be helpful to him.

1. We need friends _____.

A. because we must play with them

B. Because we must work with them

C. when we play and when we work

D. when we talk with them

2. If we want to make friends, we should _____.

A. be politely to them

B. be friendly to them.

C. be afraid of them

D. when we talk with them.

3. A friendly person is _________ other people.

A. interested in

B. worried about

C. surprised at

D. like them

4. If we want to make friends with a new classmate, ______.

A. we can talk with them

B. we must try to help him

C. we can tell him about the other classmates in our class

D. A、B and C

5. Which of the following is true?

A. No one needs friends.

B. Everyone needs friends.

C. Only classmates need friends.

D. Someone needs friends.

Part Four: Play

The Emperor's New Clothes (II)

Characters:

Emperor	国王
Chamberlain	大臣
Cheater A	骗子 A
Cheater B	骗子 B
Waiter	男侍者
Waitress	女侍者
Narrator	旁白
Audience	观众

Scene 3

Emperor: How about those new clothes?

Chamberlain: It will be finished soon!

Waiter: Here come the weavers!

Emperor: Let them in!

Cheaters: Your Majesty! Here are your clothes!

Cheater A: These are the trousers.

Cheater B: This is the coat.

Chamberlain: Only see, your majesty, is it nice?

Others: Wow, look, what a design! What beautiful colors!

Emperor: Beautiful!

Cheaters: Thanks, your majesty!

Chamberlain: Hurry up, put on your new clothes, please, your majesty!

Emperor: Ok! Ok!

Emperor: Am I not the handsomest man in my marvelous suit? (Talking to his waitress) Just look at the tiny stitches and the lacework. Truly marvelous.

Waitress: Undoubtedly, sir. There is no outfit on earth to equal this one.

Narrator: The Emperor was dressed in his new suit and ready for the parade. News of his amazing outfit had reached the people of the town and all wanted to see him. There were people crowded along the sides of the streets.

Chamberlain: The parade now begins!

Audience A: It's said that only the truly clever and brilliant can see the cloth. Most people would see an empty loom, but a clever man will see the wonderful cloth.

Audience B: Oh, really? What a suit!

Little Boy: What suit? The emperor has nothing on!

Audience C: Oh, God, listen! A child says he has nothing on!

Audience D: It's true! No clothes! The emperor is naked!

Audience E: But he has nothing on!

Emperor: Am I? Oh, no! But the parade must go on!

Words and Expressions

design [dɪ'zaɪn] *v. n.* 设计；图案

Eg. 1.We may be able to design a course to suit your needs.

我们或许可以专门设计一门课程，以满足你的需求。

2.They drew up the design for the house in a week.

他们在一周内就画出了房子的图样。

undoubtedly [ʌn'daʊtɪdlɪ] *adv.*无疑；毋庸置疑地

Eg. 1. This is undoubtedly correct.

这显然是正确的。

2.They had undoubtedly made progress in six years.

毫无疑问, 他们在 6 年间取得了进展。

outfit['aʊtfɪt] *n.*一套服装

Eg. 1.She was wearing an expensive new outfit.

她穿着一身昂贵的新衣裳。

2.She was wearing a beautiful outfit.

她穿着漂亮的一套衣服。

equal ['i:kwəl] *vt.*等于；比得上

Eg. 1.There is no outfit on earth to equal this one.

世界上再没有什么衣服和这件相比。

2.My handwriting equals yours.

我的书法和你的一样好。

tiny ['taɪni] *adj.*极小的，微小的

Eg. 1.The living room is tiny.

起居室非常小。

2.Though she was tiny, she had a very loud voice.

她虽然个头小，嗓音却非常洪亮。

stitches [s'tɪtʃɪz] *n.*（缝纫或编织中的）一针（stitch 的名词复数）；缝法

Eg. 1.Her mother counted the stitches on her knitting needles.

她母亲数了数编织针上的针数。

2.The design can be worked in cross stitch.

这个图案可以用十字针法绣出来。

lacework ['leɪswɜ:k] *n.*网状物，花边

Eg. 1.Just look at the tiny stitches and the lacework.

就看看这针法和花边吧。

2.This suit has beautiful lacework.

这件衣服的花边很漂亮。

brilliant ['brɪliənt] *adj.*才华横溢的；明亮的

Eg. 1.What a brilliant idea!

真是个绝妙的主意！

2.She had a brilliant mind.

她头脑聪明。

loom [lu:m] *n.*织布机

Eg. 1.The shuttle flies back and forth on the loom.

织布机上梭子来回地飞动。

2.This is an empty loom.

这是一个空织布机。

naked ['neɪkɪd] *adj.*裸体的，裸露的

Eg. 1.The children ran naked through the garden.

孩子们光着身子跑过花园。

2.Those two little mice were naked and blind.

那两只小老鼠还没长毛，眼睛也尚未睁开。

Your Majesty	陛下
hurry up	赶快
put on	穿上
go on	继续
look at	看着
be dressed in	穿着……
has nothing on	什么都没穿

Listening Practice

I. Bingo game

Work in groups, one student read about the script of *Emperor's New Cloth*, other students listen carefully, when they hear the adjective from the script, say

"Bingo", and write the word in the form quickly, and then he/she wins. And take turns, and change the words into Verbs, Nouns, etc.

words	adjective	verbs	nouns	prepositions	adverbs	conjunctions
student 1						
student 2						
student 3						
student 4						
student 5						

II. Dictation

Listen to the passage three times and supply the missing information.

The emperor waited and waited. He asked the chamberlain whether his magical clothes was ready. Finally two ___1___took the clothes to the emperor. The chamberlain and two weavers spoke ___2___of the clothes. They helped the emperor ___3___the coat and trousers. The emperor was ___4___in his new suit and ready for the___5___. News of his amazing outfit had reached the people of the town and all wanted to see him. There were people ___6___along the sides of the streets. Then the parade began. The audiences praised the emperor's clothes. A little ___7___asked what suit the Emperor was on but he had ___8___on! The other ___9___said it was true! No clothes! The emperor was naked! The emperor was so surprised and asked himself that he was really ___10___? Oh, no! But the parade must go on!

Reading Practice

I. Read and choose

1. Which of the following statement is True?_____

A. The Emperor brought his new clothes from the weaver's room by himself.

B. The chamberlain helped the weavers make the new clothes for the emperor.

C. The weavers brought the new clothes for the emperor.

D. The weavers did not finish the new clothes.

2. Which of the following word is not used to describe the new clothes?_____

A. beautiful

B. marvelous

C. amazing

D. ugly

3. The Emperor was dressed in his new suit and ready for the_____.

A. parade

B. branches

C. trunk

D. root

4. According to two cheaters, only_______ people can't see these magical clothes.

A. clever

B. stupid

C. smart

D. angry

5. When the parade begins, only a little kid thinks the emperor is _____.

A. hardsome

B. cool

C. sad

D. naked

II. Read and answer

1. Did the Emperor wait for a long time for his new clothes?
2. What did two weavers say about the new clothes?
3. Why did almost all of people say these new clothes were beautiful?
4. Who didn't think the emperor was having clothes on? Why?
5. What did the emperor say to himself finally?

Speaking Practice

I. Role Play

Suppose you were the little boy, when you saw the parade is on and the emperor was walking on the street, what would you say? What would the emperor respond? Use the following functional sentences, and you must add your own expressions when it is necessary.

- Oh, is he the emperor?
- Is his new clothes beautiful?
- What are they talking about?
- Oh, where is the new clothes?
- My god, what happened to my new clothes?
- But I can't see any clothes.
- He has nothing on.
- Oh, no! but the parade must go on!

II. Problem-Solving

Think of appropriate lines for these three people in the picture above.

Translating Practice

I. Translate the sentences into Chinese.

Work in pairs, one student reads the following sentences, and the other translates the sentences into Chinese in spoken way. (Add extra sentences from the scripts if necessary.)

1. Wow, look, what a design! What beautiful colors!
2. Hurry up, put on your new clothes, please, your majesty!

3. Am I not the handsomest man in my marvelous suit?

4. News of his amazing outfit had reached the people of the town and all wanted to see him.

5. Oh, God, listen! A child says he has nothing on!

II. Translate the sentences into English.

Work in pairs, one student reads the following sentences, and the other translates the sentences into English in spoken way. (Add extra sentences from the scripts if necessary.)

1. 新衣服马上就做好了。
2. 陛下，这是您的新衣服！
3. 据说只有真正聪明的人才会看见这件衣服。
4. 很多人拥挤在街道两边。
5. 这是真的！没穿衣服！国王是裸体的！

III. Delivery Game

The teacher divides the whole class into four or five groups, queuing the students. The teacher writes a long sentence from the script in a piece of paper, just let the first student read and recite it for one minute, and let the student retell the sentence to the second student, the second to the third, when the sentence is delivered to the last student, he/she should write it on the blackboard, and translate it into Chinese. The group which has got great speed and relative accuracy wins.

Writing Practice

Write a summary of *Emperor's New Clothes* in 100 words.

"Ws" / "Who"	doing what	whom	where	when

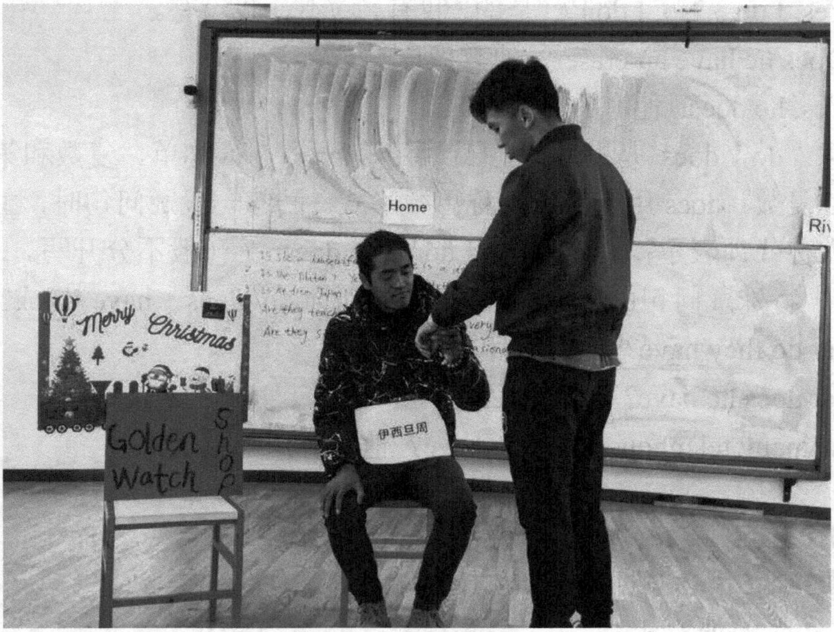

Part Five: Language Skills
Grammar

have/ / has 的用法（II）

（1）否定句：

主语+don’t（doesn’t）+have +…

例如：

We don’t have any water here. 我们这儿没有水。

This wall doesn’t have a window in it. 这面墙上没有一扇窗户。

She does not have a sister. 她没有姐姐。

We don’t have any classes on Saturday. 我们星期六没有课。

（2）一般疑问句：

Do (Does)+主语+have+…?

肯定回答：Yes, 主语+do（does）。

否定回答：No, 主语+don’t（doesn’t）。例如：

—Do you have a ruler? 你有尺子吗?

—Yes, I do. / No, I don't. 是的，我有。 /不，我没有。
—Does he have an eraser? 他有橡皮吗?
—Yes, he does. 他有的。

注意：do，does 是助动词，do 用于第一、二人称单、复数和第三人称复数；does 用于第三人称单数形式。回答一般疑问句时，主语用人称代词表示；否定回答中 don't 或 doesn't 一般不分开写。

（3）特殊疑问句由特殊疑问词 + 助动词 do/ does + have 构成。

What do they have? 他们有什么?
What does he have? 他有什么?
How many telephones do they have? 他们有几部电话?

Exercises

I. Fill in the blanks with "don't, doesn't".

1. I______ have a cat.
2. He ______have dogs.
3. She______ have long hair.
4. We______ have a big house.
5. They______ have a happy family.
6. It ______ have a short tail.
7. You ______ have a good teacher.
8. Elva ______ have a bad temper.
9. Tom ______ have a red pen.
10. My mother______ have a beautiful nose.

II. Sentence pattern transformation.

1. I have a pen.
(1) 否定句 I _____ _______ a pen.
(2) 一般疑问句 _______ _______ _______ a pen?
2. Lucy has a pencil.
(1) 否定句 Lucy _______ _______ a pencil.
(2) 一般疑问句 _______ Lucy _______ a pencil?

3. My mother has a beautiful scarf.

(1) 否定句 My mother _______ _______ a beautiful scarf.

(2) 一般疑问句 _______ your mother _______ a beautiful scarf ?

4. They have a lot of friends.

(1) 否定句 They _______ _______ a lot of friends.

(2) 一般疑问句 _______ they _______ a lot of friends?

5. We have a good teacher.

(1) 否定句 We _______ _______ a good teacher.

(2) 一般疑问句 _______ _______ _______ a good teacher?

III. Translating Practice

Translate the following into English.

1. 我们星期六没有课。
2. 莉莉有玩具小汽车吗？
3. 他有英语书吗？
4. 你早饭吃什么？
5. 瓶子里没有牛奶。

Translate the following into Chinese.

1. Do you have a big house?
2. Does he have an eraser?
3. What do they have?
4. How many telephones do they have?
5. She does not have a sister.

Unit Three
Wisdom

Part One:	Phonetic Knowledge
Part Two:	Dialogue
Part Three:	Text
Part Four:	Play: The Tale of Aladdin(I)
Part Five:	Language Skills

Part One: Phonetic Knowledge

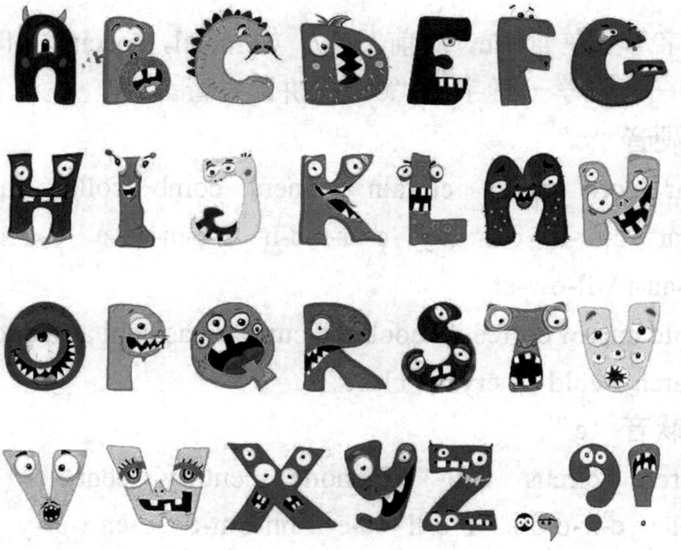

一、字母 C c

1. 拼读发音方式。

字母“c”有字母音和拼读音，字母音就是在字母“ABC…”中的读音。和字母“g”一样，它的拼读音有两种：一种是拼读硬音，另一种是拼读软音。

拼读硬音是这样的：舌后部紧贴软腭，然后突然离开，气流从舌后部和软腭之间冲出，发出爆破音。发音送气，声带不振动。硬音“c”常常在字母“a, o, u”前面。包括这个拼读音的单词如 cat，collar，cook，contest 等。

拼读软音是这样的：舌尖靠近下齿龈，气流从下齿龈和舌尖之间的缝隙流出，发音送气，舌尖和下齿龈摩擦成音。声带不振动。软音“c”常常在字母 “e，i，y”前面。包括这个声音的单词如 city，cent，cite，ice 等。

2. 发音规则。

（1）字母 c 在元音字母 a，o，u 前、在词尾以及在组合 cl 中发 /

k /，如 cat，class。

（2）字母 c 在元音字母 e，i(y)前发/ s /，叫软 c，如 cell，cite，cycle。

（3）字母 c 在 ia，ie，io 前发/ ʃ /，如 racial，special，efficient。

3. 听一听，学一学字母“c”的拼读发音。

拼读硬音“c”

(1) car corn candy curtain camera comb collar cauliflower

c-ar c-or-n c-an-d-y c-ur-t-ai-n c-e-m-e-r-a c-o-mb c-o-ll-ar c-au-l-i-fl-ow-er

(2) cold cup of coffee cook the curry as cool as a cucumber catch a cold crystal clear

拼读软音“c”

(1) circle circus cell cellphone century cent

c-ir-cle c-ir-c-u-s c-e-ll c-e-ll-ph-o-n-e c-en-t-ur-y c-en-t

(2) a service center Princess and Prince cold as ice

rats and mice a nice city space for peace

4. 仔细听，然后做句子一口气快读练习。

拼读硬音“c”

(1) Care cares his cat.

(2) Callum drinks a cup of coffee and drives his car to work.

拼读软音“c”

(1) Children ride on bicycles and tricycles.

(2) We cycle to the city on bicycles and motorcycles.

5. 听一听下列的韵律英语，并熟练朗读。

Candy Cat, Candy Cat.

What do you say?

I say Cc c,

Candy, Candy Cat.

Keep clean socks in a clean sock stack.

Keep clean stockings in a clean stocking stack.

cider 苹果酒 **cereal** 谷物

celery 芹菜 **cylinder** 圆筒容器

cellar 酒窖

Cecil makes cider in the city centre.

Cecil's cider is made from cereals and celery.

Cecil makes his cider in cement cylinders.

Cecil keeps the cider in his cellar.

Cecil's family have been making cider in the city for over half a century.

二、字母 K k

1. 拼读发音方式。

字母“k”有字母音和拼读音，字母音就是在字母“HIJK…”中的读音。而它的拼读音是这样的：舌后部紧贴软腭，然后突然离开，气流从舌后部和软腭之间冲出，发出爆破音。发音送气，声带不振动。包括这个拼读发音的单词如 talk，king，kite，junk 等。

2. 发音规则。

字母“k”通常发 / k /，如 kiss，book，joke。

3. 听一听，学一学字母“k”的拼读发音。

(1) kart kitten kiwi king kebab keeper Korean kangaroo Kungfu kitchen

k-ar-t k-i-tt-e-n k-i-w-i k-i-n-g k-e-b-a-b k-ee-p-er K-o-r-ea-n k-an-g-a-r-oo K-u-n-g f-u k-i-t-ch-e-n

(2) Ku Klux Klan kids in the kindergarten Ken kisses kangaroo kill the king

4. 仔细听，然后做句子一口气快读练习。

(1) Keiser is talking with a Korean who can play Kungfu.

(2) Kenny Kangaroo kicks a ball.

(3) Katy cooks king size kebabs with tomato ketchup in the kitchen.

(4) Katy keeps the kitchen clean.

5. 听一听下列的韵律英语，并熟练朗读。

Kick, kick, kick!
Kangaroos kick.
Kk says k, k.
Kick, kick, kick!

Derck took a book to the park.
Derck likes to drink Kiwi juice.
Derek got a mark on the back of his book.

Part Two: Dialogue

Dialogue 1

Peter: I heard you've got a good job. How are you doing?

Mary: Yes, but I can't do it well.

Peter: Why?

Mary: My knowledge is poor; many things I don't know.

Peter: You must continue to receive education.

Mary: Yes, but I have no time. Can you give me some advice?

Peter: I think you can try education on the internet.

Mary: How to study on the internet?

Peter: You may attend university on the internet. You can listen to lessons and ask questions. The teacher will answer you on the internet. It seems the same as you do at school.

Mary: That's great. I'll have a try.

Peter: Good luck!

Words and Expressions

knowledge ['nɒlɪdʒ] *n.* 知识

continue [kən'tɪnjuː] *v.* 继续

Decide whether the following statements are True (T) or False (F).

1. [ ] Mary got a very good job but she can't handle it.
2. [ ] Peter suggests Mary to get further education.
3. [ ] Mary is too busy to receive any education.
4. [ ] Peter thinks online education is very good for Mary.
5. [ ] Mary can't ask any question on the internet because the teacher is too busy to answer the students' questions.

Dialogue 2

Mary: I have some news for you. I'm going to have dinner with Michael, the boy whom I met online several months ago.

Peter: Really? Be cautious.

Mary: I will. Please don't be so fussy. I didn't know him yesterday.

Peter: I know, but you'd better take further cautions. Did you give out your personal information?

Mary: Of course not. Anyway, I revealed only some because I kind of began to trust him.

Peter: Remember to date in public places and not to let him escort your home.

Mary: Yes, I will remember. Any more advice?

Peter: Use your common sense.

Mary: Ok, thanks! I'll call you later.

Words and Expressions

online [ɒn'laɪn] *adv.* 在线的

several ['sevrəl] *adj.* 几个的
cautious ['kɔːʃəs] *adj.* 谨慎的
fussy ['fʌsɪ] *adj.* 大惊小怪的
further ['fɜːðə] *adj.* 更进一步的
caution ['kɔːʃ(ə)n] *n.* 小心
personal ['pɜːs(ə)n(ə)l] *adj.*个人的
reveal [rɪ'viːl] *v.* 透露
escort ['eskɔːt] *v.* 护送
common sense 常识

Decide whether the following statements are True (T) or False (F).

1. [ ] Mary is going to meet her boyfriend.
2. [ ] Peter thinks it is very dangerous to meet a boy whom Mary actually is not familiar with.
3. [ ] Peter asks Mary not give out her personal information.
4. [ ] Mary denies Peter's advice because she begins to trust the boy.
5. [ ] Peter worries about Mary.

Dialogue 3

Reception: Hello, Miss. What can I do for you this afternoon?
Mary: I need a haircut. But you seem so busy today.
Reception: Yes, it is busy today. We usually have a lot more clients on the weekend. Would you like to take a seat and wait for a while, please?
Mary: OK. But how long will I have to wait? Is it going to be more than thirty minutes?
Reception: It should be around that. If you'd like, please feel free to read the magazines while you wait.
Mary: Thank you.
(Twenty minutes later)

Reception: Sorry to keep you waiting, Miss. Our hairdresser, Mr. Lee, he's just finishing with a client in a moment or two. Will you have a shampoo first? I will get a gown for you.

Mary: OK. Thanks.

Words and Expressions

client ['klaɪənt] *n.* 客户

gown [gaʊn] *n.* 长袍

【Notes】

Feel free to do something 常译为请随意，请等等。例如：我能用一下你的电话吗？请随便用。不要客气，请随便提建议。

Decide whether the following statements are True (T) or False (F).

1. [ ] Mary goes to a barber shop.
2. [ ] The barber shop is very busy so Mary has to wait for more than an hour.
3. [ ] Mary is reading the magazines while she waits.
4. [ ] Mary waits for about twenty minutes.
5. [ ] Mary washed her hair at home.

Dialogue 4

Jenny: Excuse me, could you tell me if this is the right bus for Qianmen?

Lisa: No, I'm afraid it isn't.

Jenny: Do you by any chance know what number I should take and where to get it?

Lisa: Well, you can take bus No. 1 at Gongzhufen Stop.

Jenny: I see, but could you tell me how to get to Gongzhufen Stop?

Lisa: Sure. Just go straight till you get to the traffic lights, then turn right and walk until you see the new flyover. The bus stop is on the left-hand side of the bridge. You can't miss it.

Jenny: Mm…do I have to change?

Lisa: No, you don't. The bus stops at Tiananmen Square. That's where you get off. Then you walk across the square. Qianmen is to the south of the square. But it would be much quicker by underground this time of day.

Jenny: Really? Can I take the underground from Gongzhufen?

Lisa: Yes, you can.

Jenny: I see. Thanks very much.

Lisa: You are welcome.

Words and Expressions

flyover ['flaɪəʊvə] *n.* 立交桥

underground [ʌndə'graʊnd] *n.* 地铁

by any chance 碰巧

go straight 直走

traffic lights 红绿灯

get off 下车

Decide whether the following statements are True (T) or False (F).

1. [ ] Jenny is going to Gongzhufen Bus Stop.
2. [ ] Lisa tells Jenny that she should take bus No. 1 to Gongzhufen.
3. [ ] Lisa suggests Jenny to get off at Tiananmen Square.
4. [ ] Qianmen is to the south of the Tiananmen Square.
5. [ ] Taking underground is much quicker than bus at this time of day.

Part Three: Text

How many pets do you have?

I have three pets, two dogs and one cat.

How many computers do you have?

I have two computers. I have one laptop and one desktop computer.

How many brothers and sisters do you have?

I have one brother and two sisters.

How many books do you have?

I have many books.

How many sunglasses does the famous actor have?

She has over three hundred sunglasses. She can wear different sunglasses every day.

How many bags does the pop singer have?

She has about five hundred bags of different colors and different styles.

How many fans does he have?

He has numerous fans. 80% of his fans are young girls.

How many cameras does he have?

He does not have any cameras. He can use mobile phone to take pictures.

Words and Expressions

computer [kəm'pjuːtə] *n.* 计算机，电脑

Eg. 1. I have the latest computer software.

我有最新的计算机软件。

2. The information is stored on computer.

信息储存在电脑里。

desktop ['desktɒp] *n.* 桌面，台式机

Eg. 1. Clean up the desktop a little bit.

先收拾一下桌面。

2. He would not permit anybody to use his desktop.

他不允许任何人使用他的电脑。

sunglasses ['sʌnglɑːsɪz] *n.* 太阳镜

Eg. 1. What do you think of my new sunglasses?

你觉得我的新太阳镜怎么样？

2. What color should I choose for my sunglasses?

我该挑一副什么颜色的太阳镜呢？

famous ['feɪməs] *adj.* 著名的

Eg. 1. Many famous people have stayed in the hotel.

许多名人都曾下榻这家酒店。

2. France is famous for its wine.

法国以其葡萄酒而闻名。

actor ['æktə] *n.* 演员，男演员

Eg. 1. Her son wants to be an actor.

她儿子想当演员。

2. Which actor do you like best?

你最喜欢哪个男演员？

pop [pɒp] *adj.* 流行的；通俗的；热门的

Eg. 1. She talks and thinks nothing but pop music.

除了流行音乐，她什么也不谈，什么也不想。

2. The pop songs she sings are very pleasant.

她唱的流行歌曲怪好听的。

fans [fæns] *n.* 狂热者，粉丝（fan 的复数形式）

Eg. 1. We would be her fans even without these achievements.

即使没有这些成绩我们仍是她的粉丝。

2. Thank you to all my family, friends and fans for all your support.

感谢我所有的家人、朋友和粉丝，谢谢你们的支持。

numerous ['njuːm(ə)rəs] *adj.* 许多的，很多的

Eg. 1. There are numerous reasons for this.

这里有很多方面的原因。

2. I have numerous engagements next week.

下星期我有许多约会。

camera ['kæm(ə)rə] *n.* 照相机；摄影机

Eg. 1. Is this camera new or secondhand?

这架照相机是新的还是旧的?

2. He set the camera up in the dark and waited.

他在夜里架起了照相机，静静地等着。

Language Focus

I. Make a sentence with the words given below.

1. many / books / you/ do / have
2. bags / how / does / Lily / have / many
3. does / he / not / have / any / toys
4. we / many / pictures / have / beautiful
5. has / two / she / good / friends

II. Translating

Put Chinese into English.

1. 这周你们有多少节课？
2. 他有多少本英语书？
3. 他每天学习英语。
4. 玛丽有几个兄弟姐妹？
5. 我没什么可说的了。

Put English into Chinese.

1. How many bikes do you have?
2. She has no confidence in dancing.
3. I have just one question.
4. How many chickens does he have?
5. How many departments do we have?

III. Reading Comprehension

Choose the best answer to each of the following questions or incomplete sentences.

How many different languages are spoken in the world today? There are about 5,000 different languages. Nearly 900 languages are spoken in India.

Chinese is the language spoken by the greatest number of people in the world. But the most widely spoken language in the world is English. Three hundred and thirty million people speak English as the first language. Nearly twice as many-about 650 million people speak it as second or foreign language.

How many words are there in the English language? There are about 490,000 words. Also, there are about 300, 000 words used in science. There are more words in English than many other languages. But most people use no more than 60, 000 words.

1. How many languages are spoken in India? _______

A. Less than 650

B. More than 900

C. Almost 900

D. Only 1

2. Which language is spoken by the most people? _______

A. Chinese

B. English

C. Indian

D. Japanese

3. How many people speak English as the first language? _______

A. 33,000,000

B. 330,000,000

C. 300,000

D. 3,000,000

4. How many English words are used often? _______.

A. 190,000

B. 300,000

C. 60,000

D. 490,000

5. The topic maybe is _______.

A. The languages in the world

B. The words in the world

C. English language

D. The English and Chinese languages

Part Four: Play

The Tale of Aladdin(I)

Characters:

Aside: 旁白

Aladdin: 阿拉丁

Genie: 魔灯神怪

Jasmine: 茉莉公主

Sultan: 茉莉公主的父亲

Scene 1

Aside: Ah, good evening to you, my friend. Welcome to my Land of Mystery! Ok, tell me what you are in need of today! Surely there must be something! What about this? (Hold up a strange item) Or this? (Holds up another item) Or look at this… (Holds the third item) Wait… Don't go… I can see that you are only interested in special things. Why not consider this? (He pulls out the magic lamp) This … this is not an ordinary lamp! It once changed a young man's life. His name was Aladdin. Ok, let's start this story. (He sets the lamp down and exits. Aladdin enters. He is whistling a tune.)

Scene 2

Aladdin: (Notice the lamp) Hey, what's this? Whew… it's so dirty…probably just garbage. (He rubs the lamp clean)

Genie: (Genie appears. Aladdin is astonished.) Who are you that calls me from my lamp?

Aladdin: What?

Genie: Who are you? And why have you called me?

Aladdin: I didn't call. I mean I don't think I did. Ah… I am sorry to disturb… (Genie interrupts)

Genie: What's your name?

Aladdin: A…A…Aladdin. Please don't hurt me.

Genie: (Bows to Aladdin) I am the genie of the lamp, and you are my master. I will obey you. I will do anything you say. So tell me what your command is?

Aladdin: You mean that you live in this lamp and when I rub it you will come out and do whatever I told you!

Genie: (Nods) That is correct!

Aladdin: As-sa.

Genie: I don't understand.

Aladdin: Never mind. Ok first I want to wish for some nice clothes and new shoes… no wait… first I wish that I could leave this place to see the rest of the world…no no no, wait, I wish… Wow, who is that? She is beautiful! (Just then Jasmine enters. She is crying. She sits down. Aladdin makes a sign to the genie to keep quiet and crosses to her) Why are you crying?

Scene 3

Jasmine: Well, wouldn't you?

Aladdin: Wouldn't I what?

Jasmine: Cry if you were me?

Aladdin: Oh, I don't know. I don't think so.

Jasmine: But he has such small mean eyes…

Aladdin: He does? (He looks around)

Jasmine: And he's bald. And just because he is a general in the army. My father says that I have to marry him.

Aladdin: Well, you don't always have to do what your father says.

Jasmine: I do. I do. I do. My father is Sultan… you know he is the king, and if I don't obey… (She makes a cutting sign across her neck)

Aladdin: Wow… I guess being a princess isn't so great after all. There must be something that I can do to help. (Aladdin suddenly has an idea. He looks over at the Genie and at his magic lamp) Hey, I've got an idea! (Suddenly there is the sound of footsteps) What's that?

Jasmine: Oh no, it's my father. I shouldn't be talking with you. If he finds you…(She makes a cutting sign across her neck) Hurry… Hide…Over there… (Aladdin runs and hides. The Sultan enters. Aladdin watches.)

Sultan: I have been looking all over for you. Well, my foolish daughter. Have you thought about my suggestion? You will marry the general, right?

Jasmine: I suppose so, father. What else can I do?

Sultan: Wonderful! A wise decision. There is nothing to cry about. You will have a magnificent ceremony, and we shall have a parade in the streets… a band… music…delicious food… and…Oh, I can't wait any more. (Aladdin interrupts him)

Aladdin: Excuse me, Mr. Sultan, sir…

Sultan: Who is this poor guy?

Aladdin: (Very nervous) Ah… Aladdin, sir. (He bows)

Sultan: What are you doing here? Guards! Guards!

Aladdin: Wait please! I came here to give my honor to you.

Sultan: Your honor. What kind of honor?

Aladdin: I came here to offer a more worthy husband for your daughter, sir.

Sultan: Better than a general? Impossible.

Aladdin: Oh, yes, it is, sir. It is the most amazing man. He is a brave and honorable knight and has mysterious and magical powers.

Sultan: Hmmm… And who is this person that you are speaking of?

Aladdin: This person is me. (Says it weakly) Yes, it is me. (Says it stronger. At first the Sultan frowns, but then he smiles, and then he starts to laugh. Aladdin and Jasmine pretend to laugh with him.)

Sultan: (He finally stops laughing) Guards, take him away!

Aladdin: No, wait! Please sir, listen to me. I am telling the truth… I can prove it!

Sultan: All right then if you want to marry my daughter you must pass a test! There is a dragon that has been killing many of the villagers in my kingdom. Come to my palace before sunset tomorrow with the dragon's head. If you kill him, you can marry my daughter.

Aladdin: (Swallows) Very well, sir. (He bows to the Sultan and winks at Jasmine.)

Jasmine: (The Sultan is dragging her out) Oh, Aladdin you shouldn't have do this!

Words and Expressions

mystery ['mɪstri] *n.*秘密，谜

Eg. 1. He's a lady of mystery.

她是个神秘的女人。

2.The mystery hero immediately alerted police after spotting a bomb.

那个无名英雄发现炸弹后马上报了警。

consider[kən'sɪdə(r)] *vt.* & *vi.*考虑；认为

Eg. 1. We're considering buying a new car.

我们在考虑买一辆新车。

2.He was considering what to do next.

他在考虑下一步怎么办。

ordinary['ɔ:dnri] *adj.*普通的；一般的

Eg. 1. This is an ordinary sort of day.

这是平平常常的一天。

2.I am an ordinary people like you.

我和你一样都是普通人。

astonished [ə'stɒnɪʃt] (astonish 的过去式和过去分词) *adj.*吃惊的

Eg. 1. He was astonished to learn he'd won the competition.

他听说他比赛赢了，感到很惊讶。

2.My parents looked astonished at my news.

我的父母听到我的消息后显得十分惊讶。

rub [rʌb]*vt.*擦，摩擦

Eg. 1. She took off her glasses and rubbed them hard.

她摘下眼镜使劲擦着。

2.Don't rub your eyes.

不要揉你的眼睛。

pretend [prɪ'tend] *vi.*装扮；假装

Eg. 1. He pretended not to notice.

他假装没注意。

2.She didn't love him, though she pretended to.

她并不爱他，虽然她装出爱的样子。

drag [dræg] *vt.* 拖拽；拖地而行

Eg. 1.I dragged the chair over to the window.

我把椅子拖到了窗口那边。

2.They dragged her from her bed.

他们把她从床上拽了起来。

bow [bəʊ] *vi.*弓；鞠躬

Eg. 1. He bowed low to the assembled crowd.

他向集结的人群深深地鞠了一躬。

2.The people all bowed down before the emperor.

所有人都给皇帝鞠躬。

wink [wɪŋk] *vi.*使眼色；递眼色

Eg. 1. He winked at her and she knew he was thinking the same thing that she was.

他冲她眨了眨眼，她便知道他的想法和她一样。

2.Jack winked at his bride-to-be.

杰克向他的准新娘使了个眼色。

Listening Practice

I. Bingo game

Work in groups, one student read about the script of *The Tale of Aladdin*, other students listen carefully, when they hear an adjective from the script, say "Bingo", and write the word in the form quickly, and then he/she wins. And take turns, and change the words into Verbs, Nouns, etc.

words	adjective	verbs	nouns	prepositions	adverbs	conjunctions
student 1						
student 2						
student 3						
student 4						
student 5						

II. Dictation

Listen to the passage three times and supply the missing information.

Aladdin picked up a dirty ___1___and did not know what it was, suddenly Gene___2___. Gene told Aladdin that he lived in the lamp, and Aladdin was his___3___. He asked Aladdin what his ___4___was. Aladdin began to wish that he could leave this place to see the rest of the ___5___. Suddenly Aladdin saw a girl crying and he didn't know who she was? The girl was Jasmine. Jasmine told Aladdin that her father, a king, asked her to marry a general in the army. If she didn't ___6___his father's order, she would be ___7___. While Jasmine did not want to marry the general. While Aladdin told the king he wanted to marry his daughter. Then the king ordered that if Aladdin could kill a ___8___that has been killing many of the villagers in his ___9___, Aladdin would marry his Jasmine. Jasmine ? about that and didn't ___10___.

Reading Practice

Read and choose

1.Which of the following statement is True? ______

A. Aladdin lost his lamp.

B. Gene was the master of the lamp.

C. Aladdin was the master of the lamp.

D. Aladdin invented this lamp.

2. When Aladdin_____the lamp, Gene will come out and do whatever the master told him.

A. rub

B. touch

C. hit

D. smash

3. First Aladdin wanted to wish for some______.

A. money

B. bread

C. books

D. clothes and shoes

4. The king asked Jasmine to marry a _______.

A. general

B. millionaire

C. prince

D. beast

5. Aladdin told the king a person who was the best man to marry his daughter was (a) _____.

A. general

B. prince

C. lion

D. himself

Read and answer

1. Who was Genie?
2. What was Aladdin's wish?
3. Who was Jasmine? Why was she crying?
4. How did Aladdin save and help Jasmine?
5. Would the king marry his daughter to Aladdin?

Speaking Practice

I. Role Play

Suppose you were Aladdin, what would you say when you see Genie coming out from the lamp? Use the following functional sentences, and you have to add your own expressions when it is necessary.

- Hi, nice to see you.
- Who are you?
- Where are you from?
- Well, it sounds good.
- What is your wish?

II. Problem-Solving

Think of appropriate lines for the man in the picture above.

Translating Practice

I. Translate the sentences into Chinese.

Work in pairs, one student reads the following sentences, and the other translates the sentences into Chinese in spoken way. (Add extra sentences from the scripts if necessary.)

1. I will obey you.
2. Wow… I guess being a princess isn't so great after all.
3. You mean that you live in this lamp and when I rub it you will come out and do whatever I told you!
4. There is nothing to cry about.
5. I came here to offer a more worthy husband for your daughter, sir.

II. Translate the sentences into English.

Work in pairs, one student reads the following sentences, and the other translates the sentences into English in spoken way. (Add extra sentences from the scripts if necessary.)

1.好的，首先我的愿望是得到一些上好的衣服和新鞋子。
2.他上下打量着 Genie 和他的魔灯。
3.你考虑了我的建议吗?
4.他是一个勇敢荣耀的骑士，并且有着神秘的魔法。
5.有一条龙已伤害了我王国中许多村民的生命。

III. Delivery Game

The teacher divides the whole class into four or five groups, queuing the students. The teacher writes a long sentence from the script in a piece of paper, just let the first student read and recite it for one minute, and let the student retell the sentence to the second student, the second to the third, when the sentence is delivered to the last student, he/she should write it on the blackboard, and translate it into Chinese. The group which has got great speed and relative accuracy wins.

Writing Practice

Write a summary of The Tale of Aladdin in 100 words.

"Ws" / "Who"	doing what	whom	where	when

Part Five: Language Skills
Grammar

do 和 does 的用法

（1）作为行为动词，跟其他动词一样，如 study，walk，go 等。do 用于主语第一人称、第二人称和第三人称复数形式的句中，does 用于主语第三人称单数的句中。它的意思是“做”，如：We do morning exercise everyday. 我们每天做早操。He does his homework in the evening.他每天晚上做作业。 They do their homework every day .他们每天做作业。

（2）作为助动词，也就是帮助主要动词构成否定和疑问句。do 用于当主语是第一人称、第二人称及第三人称复数时及两个以上的人或者事物。does 用于当主语是第三人称单数或单独的事物时。

①否定句的结构是 do/ does + not，也可以缩写成 don't/ doesn't，并将原句中的实意动词变为原型，如：I don't like him. 我不喜欢他。She doesn't go to school. 她不去上学。He doesn't do his homework in the evening. 他晚上不做作业。

②疑问句的结构是 Do/ Does +主语+谓语动词原型…如：Do you want to be a teacher？你想成为一个老师吗？Do his friends go to park every day？他的朋友们每天都去公园吗？Does Jim get up at seven every day？吉姆每天七点起床吗？What time does he go to school every day？他每天几点钟上学？

Exercises

I. Fill in the blanks with "do, does , don't, doesn't"

1. _____ he watch TV at night? Yes, he _____.
2. ____ you go to school every day? No, I ___.
3. ____ Jack like apples?
4. ____ Tina go swimming on Sunday?
5. ____ they play football? Yes, they _____.
6. ____ we have a good teacher? Yes, we _____.
7. ____ your dog walk in the zoo?
8. ____ I have a big nose? No, you ___.
9. I ___ speak Japanese. ___ you speak Japanese?
10. ____ their mothers go shopping? No, they ____.

II. Sentence pattern transformation.

1. I have a soccer ball.

(1) 否定句 ______________________

(2) 一般疑问句 ______________________?

2. She plays the piano.

(1) 否定句 ______________________.

(2) 一般疑问句 ______________________?

3. My parents like vegetables.

(1) 否定句 ________________________.

(2) 一般疑问句 ________________________?

4. He likes eating eggs for breakfast.

(1) 否定句 ________________________.

(2) 一般疑问句 ________________________?

5. They watch football games on TV.

(1) 否定句 ________________________.

(2) 一般疑问句 ________________________?

III. Translating Practice

Translate the following into English.

1. 你想成为一名医生吗？
2. 他的朋友们每天都去踢球吗？
3. 汤姆来自哪里？
4. 我不住在这儿。
5. 玛丽不喜欢游泳。

Translate the following into Chinese.

1. Do they play football after school?
2. What does he do after school?
3. He doesn’t know my name.
4. Does Tom play computer games?
5. They don’t like ice cream.

Unit Four
Being Yourself

Part One:	Phonetic Knowledge
Part Two:	Dialogue
Part Three:	Text
Part Four:	Play: The Tale of Aladdin(II)
Part Five:	Language Skills

Part One: Phonetic Knowledge

一、字母组合 qu

1. 拼读发音方式。

字母组合“qu”形成一个辅音音丛，发/kw/的音。就是说，先发“k”的音，就像在单词“cap”中的发音一样。而“W”的音，就像在单词“will”中的发音一样。关键在于唇位，为了发“W”音，嘴唇要很圆，上下唇之间要有很小的缝隙，上下唇之间并不接触，然后迅速从“k”音滑动到“W”音，声带振动，气流冲出腔，发成此音。包括此音的单词有 quick，queen，quack，question 等。

2. 发音规则。

字母组合“qu”通常发 / kw /，如 queen，quality。

3. 听一听，学一学字母组合“qu”的拼读发音。

(1) quail earthquake quilt quality quarrel question quiet quick quiz

qu-ai-l　e-a-r-th-qu-a-k-e　qu-i-l-t　qu-a-l-i-t-y qu-a-rr-e-l

qu-e-s-t-i-o-n　qu- i-e-t　qu-i-ck　qu-i-z

(2) quick temper　question time　queen and quack　quality and quantity

a quill pen　quarter final

4. 仔细听，然后做句子一口气快读练习。

(1) The queen queued for a quarter and an hour.

(2) It’s quite quiet in Queensberry.

5. 听一听下列的韵律英语，并熟练朗读。

Quack, quack, Queen Duck.

Quack, quack, quack!

Qq says q, q.

Quack, quack, quack!

二、字母 S s

1. 拼读发音方式。

字母“s”有字母音和拼读音，字母音就是在字母“RST…”中的读音。而它的拼读音是这样的：舌尖靠近下齿龈，气流从下齿龈舌尖之间的缝隙流出，发音送气，舌尖和下齿龈摩擦成音，声带不振动。包括这个拼读音的单词如 some，suck，salt，slim 等。

2. 发音规则。

(1) 字母 s 在词首通常发 / s /，如 spider，sky。

(2) 在两个元音字母之间发/ z /，如 music，prison。

(3) 在词中, s 的后面是清辅音发 / s /，后面是浊辅音发/ z /，如 desk，beast，husband。

(4) 在词尾时，s 前面是清辅音发 / s /，是浊辅音或元音发/ z /，如 books，beds。

3. 听一听，学一学字母“s”的拼读发音。

(1) slide sail salad sand saw seat see seven skirt

s-l-i-d-e s-ai-l s-a-l-a-d s-an-d s-aw s-ea-t s-ee s-e-v-e-n s -k-ir-t

(2) sugar and spice silver spoon slow but safe sweet as sugar salad and sauce

4. 仔细听，然后做句子一口气快读练习。

(1) She shuts her shop at six o’clock sharp.

(2) Susan will be sixteen on the seventeenth of September.

(3) My sister likes south Sweden.

(4) Stop saying like that!

5. 听一听下列的韵律英语，并熟练朗读。

She sells seashells on the seashore,
And shells she sells on the seashore
are all sea shells
I am sure.

Stars like silver in the sky,
Sand on seashores never dry,
Sunshine, snow, the sky and space,
This world is such a special place.

Part Two: Dialogue

Dialogue 1

John: I know it's only been the weekend, but it seems a long time to me. I miss you when we're not together.

Jenny: Me, too.

John: Did you have a good time at home this weekend?

Jenny: No, just the usual. I watched TV, listened to music, and helped my mother with the housework.

John: Sounds like a real ball. I was thinking about it this weekend. Do you know how long we've been going together?

Jenny: About three months.

John: Yeah, three months or so. I want to ask you a question and I hope you will answer it as honestly as you can, OK?

Jenny: Go ahead.

John: What do you think of me?

Jenny: I think you are sincere, enthusiastic, brave…

John: You know I really care about you, don't you? You are the kindest girl I've ever met. You are beautiful, active and considerate. There are times when I feel that a day without you is like a day without sunshine. I love you…

Jenny: I…

Words and Expressions

honestly ['ɒnɪstlɪ] *adv.* 真诚地

sincere [sɪn'sɪə] *adj.* 诚挚的

enthusiastic [ɪn,θjuːzɪ'æstɪk] *adj.* 热情的

brave [breɪv] *adj.* 勇敢的

active ['æktɪv] *adj.* 活跃的

considerate [kən'sɪd(ə)rət] *adj.* 体贴的

go ahead 继续

Decide whether the following statements are True (T) or False (F).

1. [ ] John and Jenny love each other quite deeply.
2. [ ] Jenny made a lot of fun at home last weekend.
3. [ ] John and Jenny have been together for a long time.
4. [ ] Jenny thinks John is handsome and brave.
5. [ ] John loves Jenny in his heart.

Dialogue 2

Mike: I had a great time on our last date.

Phoebe: Me too.

Mike: What are you up to this weekend?

Phoebe: Nothing.

Mike: Would you like to go skating? I was thinking of going out to the lake on Saturday. It's great out there. Would you like to go with me?

Phoebe: I'd love to, but I don't care for skating very much.

Mike: OK. There're a bunch of us going bowling on Sunday. Would you like to go?

Phoebe: I like bowling, but I prefer to be alone with you.

Mike: Would you like to go dancing tonight?

Phoebe: I don't feel like going out tonight; I'm way too tired. I miss you, sweetheart.

Mike: I miss you too. Then tell me where you'd like to go on our next date.

Phoebe: How about the seaside?

Mike: Anything you say, honey.

Phoebe: Are you busy on the 24th?

Mike: The 24th… I have time, but I can't wait that long. I'm dying to see you. Let's make it another time.

Phoebe: Okay.

Words and Expressions

skate [skeɪt] *v.* 滑冰

bunch [bʌn(t)ʃ] *n.* 群

bowl [bəʊl] *v.* 打保龄球

seaside ['siːsaɪd] *n.* 海边

Decide whether the following statements are True (T) or False (F).

1. [ ] They had great fun on their last date.
2. [ ] They both agree to go to the lake on this Saturday.
3. [ ] Phoebe dislikes skating so she is not happy to go to the lake with Mike.
4. [ ] Phoebe likes bowling, but she wants to be alone with Mike.
5. [ ] Finally, Phoebe decides to go dancing with Mike tonight.

Dialogue 3

Susan: I can't stand being with you anymore. I'm sick of your drinking.

John: I swear never to drink again. Just give me another chance, please!

Susan: How many chances have I given you? I've given up on you!

John: You know how hard I've tried to quit. I'd be lost without you. I'll not let you go.

Susan: It's not just for your drinking, but your lacking sense of responsibility.

John: I have to make money to support the family, so I have little time left to share with you.

Susan: Even if I was seriously ill, you couldn't spare a moment.

John: I've told you I happened to be on a more important meeting at that time.

Susan: I just don't trust you any more.

Words and Expressions

stand [stænd] *v.* 忍受

swear [sweə] *v.* 发誓

sense [sens] *n.* 观念

responsibility [rɪˌspɒnsə'bɪlətɪ] *n.* 责任

seriously ['sɪərɪəslɪ] *adv.* 认真地

Decide whether the following statements are True (T) or False (F).

1. [ ] John is an alcoholic.
2. [ ] Susan forgave John many times before.
3. [ ] Susan is very disappointed about John's lacking sense of responsibility.
4. [ ] John is very busy with his work so he has no time to accompany his wife.
5. [ ] Susan doesn't trust John anymore, and she wants to separate

with her husband.

Dialogue 4

Susan: We're through.

Roger: Why?

Susan: Why? Isn't it obvious? First, you impose way too much on me, and I'm tired of it. Second, you stood me up on Valentine's Day.

Roger: I'm really sorry for that, but I've sent you several messages to explain. My mum was seriously ill on that day and I had to look after her.

Susan: But I ended up finding out later that night that you were with another girl at a cafe near your home.

Roger: That girl was my cousin.

Susan: You've got so many cousins. I called you later that night, but you didn't have the guts to answer the phone.

Roger: I didn't take my cell phone with me at that time.

Susan: I don't buy your story.

Roger: I know you can't hear me right now. Please calm down. Anyway, I don't want to part. I'll drop by tomorrow.

Susan: No, don't. I don't want to see you anymore. Don't ever call me again.

Words and Expressions

through [θruː] *adj.* 完结的

obvious ['ɒbvɪəs] *adj.* 明显的

impose [ɪm'pəʊz] *v.* 欺骗

explain [ɪk'spleɪn] *v.* 说明

cousin ['kʌz(ə)n] *n.* 堂（表）兄弟姐妹

gut [gʌt] *n.* 胆量

stand up 放鸽子

drop by 顺便拜访

Decide whether the following statements are True (T) or False (F).

1. [ ] Susan decided to break up with Roger because she has been cheated on.
2. [ ] Susan was stood up on Valentine's Day.
3. [ ] Roger had to look after his mum on Valentine's Day because she was seriously ill.
4. [ ] Susan called Roger on Valentine's Day and found out he was with another girl in a café.
5. [ ] Roger was a sincere boy.

Part Three: Text

Almost all children like to eat hamburger.

They visit their relatives every week.

We play football or volleyball every weekend.

We want to see more progress in your work.

They open their window and clean their house every day.

The boy milk his cow every morning.

She often drinks a cup of coffee and eats cookie at tea time.

She asks students to select one member of their group to read the poem.

He organizes every big party in his class.

He learns Spanish in his spare time.

Words and Expressions

relative ['relətɪv] *n.* 亲属

Eg. 1. Get a relative to look after the children.

找个亲戚来照看这些孩子。

2. He has neither friends nor relatives.

他没有朋友，也没有亲人。

progress ['prəʊgres] *n.* 进步，发展

Eg. 1. She makes good progress.

她取得了显著进步。

2. They made no progress in the heavy snow.

他们在大雪中无法前进。

milk [mɪlk] *vt.* 榨取；挤奶

Eg. 1. Farm workers milk cows by hand.

农场工人们用手给奶牛挤奶。

2. He milks his cows every morning.

他每天早晨挤奶。

cookie ['kʊkɪ] *n.* 饼干；小甜点

Eg. 1. A glass of milk and a cookie.

一杯牛奶和一块小甜饼。

2. A chocolate chip cookie.

带巧克力碎粒的小甜饼。

select [sɪ'lekt] *vt.* 挑选；选拔

Eg. 1. You can select any one of them.

您可以选择他们其中任何一个人。

2. We selected him as our monitor.

我们选他做我们的班长。

poem ['pəʊɪm] *n.* 诗

Eg. 1. His poem is poorly.

他的诗作得不好。

2. A book of love poems.

一本爱情诗集。

organize ['ɔ:gənaɪz] *vt.* 组织

Eg. 1. They will organize a club.

他们将组建一个俱乐部。

2. How do you organize your team?

您是如何组织团队的？

Spanish ['spænɪʃ] *n.* 西班牙语；西班牙人

Eg. 1. How do you know Spanish?

你怎么会说西班牙语？

2. I learn Spanish every day.

我每天学习西班牙语。

spare [speə] *adj.* 多余的

Eg. 1. Have you got any spare boxes?

你有没有多余的盒子？

2. Do you have any spare cash?

你手头有闲钱吗？

Language Focus

I. Make a sentence with the words given below.

1. TV / Daniel / watches/ evening / every
2. day / do / I / every / my / homework
3. go / we / school / to / morning / every
4. John / from / Canada / comes
5. student / is / She / good / a

II. Translating

Put Chinese into English.

1. 我们都喜欢游泳。
2. 牧民每天给奶牛挤奶。
3. 他每天学习英语。
4. 他们通常利用业余时间学绘画。
5. 我们经常在课后去操场踢球。

Put English into Chinese.

1. Lily eats tomatoes for dinner.

2. I get up at six every day.

3. She plays sports every day.

4. The earth goes around the sun.

5. Her mother teaches English at a middle school.

III. Reading Comprehension

Choose the best answer to each of the following questions or incomplete sentences.

Mr. Lewis was a dance teacher. He was a nice man and always had a lot of students. One year he moved to a new town, and was soon teaching many students in the dance school there, but he decided to move again to a big city. He would have more work there.

When one of his students heard that he was going to leave, she said to him, "The new teacher won't be as good as you are." Mr. Lewis was happy when he heard this, but he said, "Oh no. I'm sure he'll be as good as I am — or even better." The student said, "No. Five teachers have come and gone while I've been here, and each new one was worse than the last."

1. Mr. Lewis was a nice man and he had _______.

A. few students

B. Few students

C. many students

D. No students

2. Why did Mr. Lewis want to move to a big city? _______

A. He hated the small town.

B. He couldn't make a living in the small town.

C. It would be easy for him to have more work in the city.

D. It made him spend more money in the town.

3. The student thought that _______

A. Mr. Lewis was a good teacher

B. Mr. Lewis was the best teacher

C. Mr. Lewis was worse than the last

D. Mr. Lewis would be worse than the last

4. Before Mr. Lewis ______ teachers came to the town to teach dancing.

A. three

B. four

C. five

D. six

5. From the story we can conclude that the student wished _____.

A. to have a better teacher

B. to have a worse teacher

C. to become a dance teacher

D. to see the sixth teacher

Part Four: Play

The Tale of Aladdin (II)

Characters:

Aladdin: 阿拉丁

Genie: 魔灯神怪

Aside: 旁白

Jasmine: 茉莉公主

Sultan: 茉莉公主的父亲

Scene 4

Aladdin: (Rubs lamp. Genie comes to life.) Dear boy, I am glad to see you!

Genie: You look terrible, what happened?

Aladdin: I fell in love.

Genie: Oh, that explains …

Aladdin: You said that you would do anything for me, didn't you?

Genie: Yes. I am your servant.

Aladdin: Excellent. Come with me to the village tonight… and we must defeat a dragon together.

Genie: (Looks a bit scared and surprised) But I thought that you just wanted new shoes?

Aladdin: Come on! We don't have much time! (They run out)

Aside: Aladdin and the Genie went to the village later that night, and what they saw… was a dragon, with long sharp teeth and evil green eyes. (We hear the roar of a dragon.) Oh, my god! Oh, excuse me… now where was I? Ah, yes. The dragon was breathing fire and had a thick cloud of smoke coming from his nose. Aladdin and his magic Genie fought with the dragon. And whom do you think will win? (Waits for audience response) Hmm… well, just watch and see.

Scene 5

Sultan: (Looking at his watch) Well, it seems as if Mr. Aladdin has disappeared. I guess that it must be the end of your foolish friend. Probably dead… (Just then Aladdin enters)

Aladdin: (He is carrying the head of the dragon) Sir, look what I have got. I passed your test.

Sultan:You amazed me, Aladdin. You killed the dragon. I underestimated you. You shall marry my daughter.

Jasmine: Oh, thank you, father. (She runs to embrace him.)

Sultan: Come, come here, you two. We shall plan the wedding feast, my children!

Aladdin: (Bows) Father. (Sultan exits) Oh, I almost forgot I have a present for you. (Aladdin pulls out the lamp.)

Jasmine: It's beautiful, it is more than I ever hoped for.

Aladdin: A wedding present. (Jasmine takes the lamp and gives Aladdin a kiss.)

Words and Expressions

defeat [dɪ'fi:t] *vt.*挫败；击败

Eg. 1.He defeated the champion in three sets.

他三盘击败了冠军。

2.The team defeated their opponents.

这个球队将对手一一击败。

breath [breθ] *n.*呼吸；呼吸力

Eg. 1.I could smell the whisky on his breath.

我能闻到他呼出的威士忌的味道。

2.He took a deep breath, and began to climb the stairs.

他深吸了一口气，然后开始爬楼梯。

amaze [ə'meɪz] *vt.*使大为吃惊，使惊奇

Eg. 1.He amazed us by his knowledge of Welsh history.

他对威尔士的历史知之甚多，让我们惊讶。

2.He always amazes me.

他总能给我惊喜。

underestimate [ˌʌndər'estɪmeɪt] *vt.*低估；看轻

Eg. 1.I think a lot of people still underestimate him.

我觉得很多人仍然低估了他。

2.Don't underestimate people.

别把人看扁了。

evil ['i:vl] *adj.*邪恶的，罪恶的

Eg. 1.She's an evil woman.

她是个邪恶的女人。

2.It is an evil dragon.

这是一条邪恶的龙。

embrace [ɪm'breɪs] *n.*拥抱

Eg. 1.He held her in a warm embrace.

他热烈地拥抱着她。

2.There were tears and embraces as they said goodbye.

他们分别时又是流泪，又是拥抱。

disappear [ˌdɪsə'pɪə(r)] *vi.*不见，消失

Eg. 1.The plane disappeared behind a cloud.

飞机消失在云层里。

2.Lisa watched until the train disappeared from view.

莉萨一直看着火车从视线中消失。

wedding ['wedɪŋ] *n.*婚礼；婚宴

Eg. 1.Have you been invited to their wedding?

他们有没有邀请你参加婚礼？

2.She looked beautiful on her wedding day.

她在自己的婚礼那天看上去很漂亮。

feast [fi:st] *n.*宴会；盛会

Eg. 1.The evening was a real feast for music lovers.

这个晚会真是让音乐爱好者大饱耳福。

2.Lunch was a feast of meat and vegetables, cheese, and fruit, with unlimited wine.

午餐是肉、蔬菜、奶酪和水果的盛宴，还有无限量的葡萄酒。

come to life 苏醒

fight with 和……战斗

pass test 通过考试，通过考验

wedding feast 婚宴

pull out 拉出来

Listening Practice

I. Bingo game

Work in groups, one student read about the script of *The Tale of Aladdin (II)*, other students listen carefully, when they hear an adjective from the script, say "Bingo", and write the word in the form quickly, and then he/she wins. And take turns, and change the words into Verbs, Nouns, etc.

words	adjective	verbs	nouns	prepositions	adverbs	conjunctions
student 1						
student 2						
student 3						
student 4						
student 5						

II. Dictation

Listen to the passage three times and supply the missing information.

In order to ___1___ the evil dragon and win the love, Aladdin asked ___2___ to help him. Aladdin and the Genie went to the ___3___ later that night, and what they saw was a dragon, with long ___4___ teeth and evil green eyes. The dragon was ___5___ fire and had a thick cloud of smoke coming from his nose. Aladdin and his ___6___ Genie fought with the dragon. Meanwhile, The King thought that Aladdin has ___7___. He guessed that Aladdin must be ___8___. At this moment, Aladdin arrived and was carrying the head of the dragon. Aladdin said he passed the ___9___. The king said he underestimated Aladdin and his action ___10___ him. Finally, the king agreed Aladdin would marry his daughter.

Reading Practice

I. Read and choose

1. Which of the following statement is **NOT** True? ______

A. With the help of Genie, Aladdin defeated the dragon.

B. Aladdin failed and died.

C. Aladdin won the love and married the king's daughter.

D. The king agreed to marry his daughter to Aladdin finally.

2. Aladdin asked Genie to help him to ______.

A. fight for the evil dragon

B. give him new clothes and shoes

C. find a beautiful girl

D. give him money

3. The king wanted to have a test and asked Aladdin to ______.

A. build a castle

B. give him a magic lamp

C. bring him delicious food

D. kill an evil dragon

4. Which of the following words are not used to describe the dragon? ______.

A. Long sharp teeth

B. Evil green eyes

C. Breathing fire

D. Kind and happy smile

5. What did Aladdin give to Jasmine as a gift of wedding? A ______

A. ring

B. necklace

C. lamp

D. book

II. Read and answer

1. Who is the Jasmine?

2. Why did Aladdin ask Genie to help him?

3.Why did the king ask Aladdin to kill the dragon?

4. How did Aladdin defeat the dragon?

5. Why did Aladdin win Jasmine's love?

Speaking Practice

I. Role Play

Suppose you were Aladdin and you met Jasmine after defeating the evil dragon, what would the dialogue happen? Use the following functional sentences, and you have to add your own expressions when it is necessary.

- Hi, dear, I am back.
- Oh, my god, everything goes well?
- You did a good job.
- What happened?
- The evil dragon was killed by me.
- You are super hero.
- Please marry me.
- Well, I will.

II. Problem-Solving

Think of appropriate lines for the roles in the picture above.

Translating Practice

I. Translate the sentences into Chinese.

Work in pairs, one student reads the following sentences, and the other translates the sentences into Chinese in spoken way. (Add extra sentences from the scripts if necessary.)

1.You said that you would do anything for me, didn't you?

2.Excellent. Come with me to the village tonight… and we must defeat a dragon together.

3.The dragon was breathing fire and had a thick cloud of smoke coming from his nose.

4.It's beautiful, it is more than I ever hoped for.

5.I guess that it must be the end of your foolish friend.

II. Translate the sentences into English.

Work in pairs, one student reads the following sentences, and the other translates the sentences into English in spoken way. (Add extra sentences from the scripts if necessary.)

1. 亲爱的男孩，很高兴见到你！
2. 你看起来很糟糕，发生什么事了？
3. 快来！我们时间不多了。
4. 我们要计划婚宴了，我的孩子们！
5. 阿拉丁和他的魔法 Genie 向龙开战了。

III. Delivery Game

The teacher divides the whole class into four or five groups, queuing the students. The teacher writes a long sentence from the script in a piece of paper, just let the first student read and recite it for one minute, and let the student retell the sentence to the second student, the second to the third, when the sentence is delivered to the last student, he/she should write it on the blackboard, and translate it into Chinese. The group which has got great speed and relative accuracy wins.

Writing Practice

Write a summary of *The Tale of Aladdin*(II) in 100 words.

"Ws" / "Who"	doing what	whom	where	when

Part Five: Language Skills

Grammar

名词

一、名词的种类

英语名词从形式上进行分类，可以分为专有名词和普通名词两大类。

从意义上划分，英语名词可分为个体名词、集体名词、物质名词和抽象名词四类。

从可数和不可数来看，个体名词可以用数目来计算，称为可数名词。物质名词、抽象名词和专有名词无法用数目来计算，称为不可数名词。集合名词有的可数，有的不可数。

二、名词的数

规则名词的复数形式：

名词的复数形式，一般在单数形式后面加-s 或-es。其构成方法与读音规则具体如下：

（1）规则名词复数。

① 一般情况在词尾加-s。如：map-maps，sea-seas，girl-girls，day-days。

② 以 s，x，ch，sh 结尾的名词后加-es。如：class-classes，box-boxes，watch-watches，dish-dishes。

③ 以-f 或-fe 结尾的词。

直接加-s：如 belief-beliefs，chief-chiefs，proof-proofs，roof-roofs，gulf-gulfs。

变-f 和-fe 为 v 再加-es：如 leaf-leaves，thief-thieves，knife-knives，loaf-loaves，wife-wives。

④ 以辅音字母加 y 结尾的名词，变 y 为 i 加-es：如 party-parties，family-families，story-stories，city-cities。

以元音字母加 y 结尾的名词，或专有名词以 y 结尾的，加-s：如 toy-toys，boy-boys，day-days，ray-rays，Henry-Henrys。

⑤ 以辅音字母加-o 结尾的名词。

一般加-es：如 hero-heroes，Negro-Negroes，potato-potatoes，tomato-tomatoes

不少外来词加-s：如 piano-pianos，photo-photos，auto-autos，kilo-kilos，solo-solos。

两者皆可：如 zero-zeros/zeroes，volcano-volcanoes/ volcanos。

⑥ 以元音字母加-o 结尾的名词加-s：radio-radios，bamboo-bamboos，zoo-zoos。

⑦ 以-th 结尾的名词加-s：如 truth-truths，mouth-mouths，month-

months，path-paths。

（2）不规则名词复数。

英语里有些名词的复数形式是不规则的，现归纳如下：

① 改变名词中的元音字母或其他形式。如：man-men，woman-women，foot-feet，goose-geese，tooth-teeth，mouse-mice。

② 单复数相同。如：sheep，deer，series，fish，species，li，yuan，jin。

③ 只有复数形式。如：ashes，trousers，clothes，thanks，goods，glasses。

④ 一些集体名词总是用作复数。如：people，police，cattle，staff。

⑤ 部分集体名词既可以作单数（整体）也可以作复数（成员）。如：audience，class，family，crowd，couple，group，committee，government，population，crew，team，public，enemy，party。

⑥ 复数形式表示特别含义。如：customs（海关），forces（军队），times（时代），spirits（情绪），drinks（饮料），sands（沙滩)，papers（文件报纸），manners（礼貌），looks（外表），brains（头脑智力），greens（青菜），ruins（废墟）。

⑦ 表示“某国人”复数时加-s。如：Americans，Australians，Germans，Greeks，Swedes，Europeans。

单复数同形 。如：Swiss，Portuguese，Chinese，Japanese。

以-man 或-woman 结尾的改为-men，-women 如：Englishmen，Frenchwomen。

⑧ 合成名词将主体名词变为复数。如：sons-in-law，lookers-on，passers-by，story-tellers，boy friends。

无主体名词时将最后一部分变为复数。如：grown-ups，housewives，stopwatches。

将两部分变为复数。如：women singers，men servants。

Exercises

I. Multiple Choice

1. -Would you like____tea? -No, thanks. I have drunk two____.

A. any, bottles of orange　　B. some, bottles of orange

C. many, bottles of oranges D. few, bottle of oranges

2. He is hungry. Give him ____ to eat.

A. two breads B. two piece of bread

C. two pieces of bread D. two pieces of breads

3. I would like to have____.

A. two glasses of milk B. two glass of milk

C. two glasses of milks D. two glass of milks

4. Can you give me ____?

A. a tea B. some cup of tea

C. a cup tea D. a cup of tea

5. Please give me____paper.

A. one B. a piece C. a D. a piece of

6. John bought____for himself yesterday.

A. two pairs of shoes B. two pair of shoe

B. two pair of shoes D. two pairs shoes

7. We need some more____. Can you go and get some, please?

A. potato B. potatos C. potatoes D. potatoe

8. ____are used for cutting things.

A. Knife B. Knives C. Knifes D. Knies

9. What big____ the tiger has!

A. tooth B. teeth C. tooths D. toothes

10. Please remember to give the horse some tree____.

A. Leafs B. leaves C. leaf D. leave

11. —Can we have some ____? —Yes, please.

A. banana B. oranges C. apple D. pear

12. On the table there are five____.

A. Tomatoes B. piece of tomatoes C. tomatoes D. tomato

13. —How many ____ have you got on your farm? —I've got five.

A. sheeps B. sheep C. pig D. chicken

14. They got much ____ from those new books.

A. ideas B. photos C. information D. stories

15. The blouse is made of ____.

A. a wool B. these wool C. wools D. wool

16. Some ____ came to our school for a visit that day.

A. Germans B. Germen C. Germany D. Germanies

17. A group of____ will visit the museum tomorrow.

A. Hungarian B. Australian C. Japanese D. American

18. This table is made of____.

A. many glass B. glasses C. some glasses D. glass

19. Children should make____ for old people in a bus.

A. room B. a room C. rooms D. one room

20. How many____were there in the street when the accident happened?

A. policeman B. polices C. police D. peoples

II. Write the plural form of the following words.

mouse ( ), man ( ), sheep ( ), tooth ( ), child ( ),

boy ( ), belief ( ), roof ( ), wolf ( ), life ( ),

piano ( ), photo ( ), potato ( ), zero ( ), box ( )

III. Translating Practice

Translate the following into English.

1. 你有多少颗牙齿?
2. 他有三个小孩。
3. 教室里有许多的盒子。
4. 你会弹钢琴吗?
5. 这家餐厅有许多老鼠。

Translate the following into Chinese.

1. He had a few white hairs.
2. 80% of the population in China are peasants.
3. Where are my glasses?
4. Here are some pairs of new shoes.
5. My new pair of trousers is too long.

Unit Five
Love

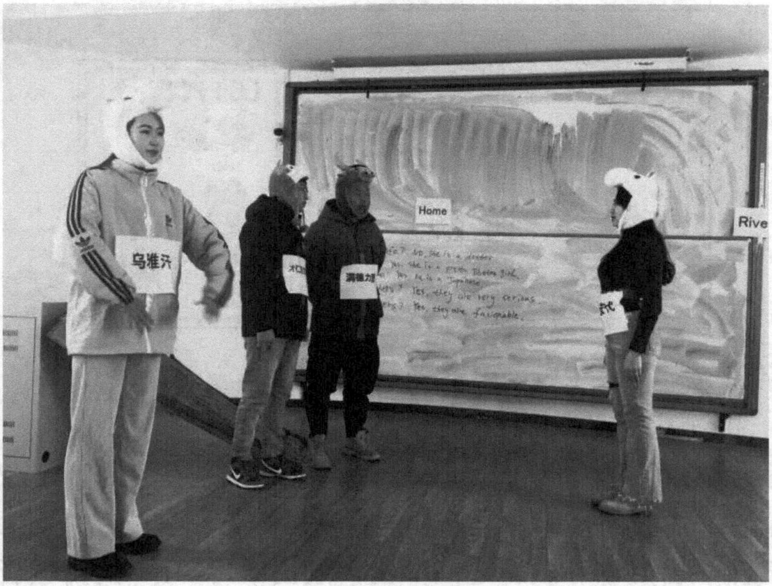

Part One: Phonetic Knowledge

Part Two: Dialogue

Part Three: Text

Part Four: Play :Beauty and the Beast(I)

Part Five: Language Skills

Part One: Phonetic Knowledge

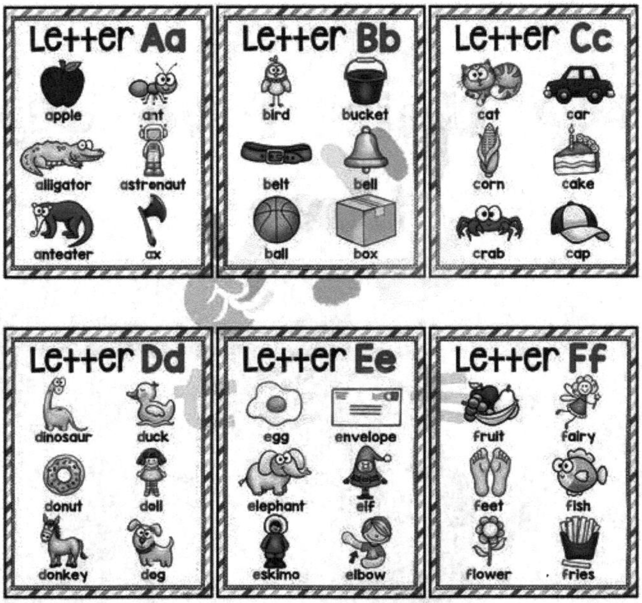

一、字母 X x

1. 拼读发音方式。

字母“x”有字母音和拼读音，字母音就是在字母“XYZ...”中的读音。而它的拼读音是这样的：舌后部紧贴软腭，然后突然离开，气流从舌后部和软腭之间冲出，发出字母“k”的拼读音，随后，向“S”的拼读音滑动。发音送气，声带不振动。包括这个声音的单词如 fix，text，six，box，fox，extra 等。

2. 发音规则。

（1）字母“x”通常发 / ks /，如 exercise，fax。

（2）字母“x”后面是元音且是重读音时发/ gz /，如 exact，exist。

3. 听一听，学一学字母“x”的拼读发音。

(1) Texas box ax ox exit extra exercise x-ray fox
T-e-x-a-s b-ox a-x o-x e-x-it e-x-tr-a e-x-er-c-i-s-e x-r-ay f-ox

(2) an extra examination as strong as ox a fox in a box
farmers' axes

4. 仔细听，然后做句子一口气快读练习。

(1) Maxine is sixteen years old and Rex is sixty six.

(2) A vixen is a female fox.

(3) Alex likes to play saxophone.

(4) Felix fox has a box.

5. 听一听下列的韵律英语，并熟练朗读。

Box, box, box.

Fox, fox, fox.

Xx says x, x.

Ox, ox, ox.

二、字母 Y y

1. 拼读发音方式。

字母“y”有字母音和拼读音，字母音就是在字母“XYZ…”中的读音。而它的拼读音是这样的：舌头前部向软腭抬起，双唇扁平，声带振动。声音一经发出，马上向其后面的元音滑动。包括这个拼读发音的单词如 yellow，yell，yesterday，yogurt（酸奶），yes 等。

2. 发音规则。

（1）字母“y”在词首一般情况下发 / j /，如 yoke，yard，you。

（2）字母“y”在重读开音节中发/ ai /，如 cry，spy。

字母“y”在以“y，yse”结尾的多音节动词中也发/ ai /，如 justify，analyse。

（3）字母“y”在非重读音节中往往发/ i /，如 tiny，factory。

3. 听一听，学一学字母“y”的拼读发音。

(1) yogurt yoga Yahoo yoyo yard Yale
y-o-g-ur-t y-o-g-a Y-a-hoo y-o-y-o y-ar-d Y-a-l-e

(2) yogurt is yummy Yangtze River a yellow yo-yo yell out
yelling young man

4. 仔细听，然后做句子一口气快读练习。

(1) Stop yawning in my class.

(2) She said yes yesterday.

(3) The yellow bird has yelled for many years in the yard of Yale .

(4) Young girls like yoga and yogurt.

5. 听一听下列的韵律英语,并熟练朗读。

Yum, yum, yum.
Yellow, yellow yam.
Yy says y, y.
Yum, yum, yum!

Red yo-yo, yellow yo-yo, red yo-yo, yellow yo-yo
Blue yo-yo, yellow yo-yo, blue yo-yo, yellow yo-yo
Green yo-yo, yellow yo-yo, green yo-yo, yellow yo-yo

Part Two: Dialogue

Dialogue 1

James: Happy New Year, Michelle.

Michelle: Happy New Year, James. Come and enjoy some nice drinks with us, will you?

James: Thank you, I will. What are you up to today?

Michelle: First, I'm going to get ready for the parade. I have a great costume. Then later today, I'm going to church. If you want, I can give you a costume and you can be in the parade too. It will be fun, you should come .

James: Sure, why not? It sounds like fun. Why are you going to church?

Michelle: My father likes to go and I told him I would go with him.

James: What for?

Michelle: Lots of people, especially seniors, like to go to church and attend the evening service.

Words and Expressions

costume [kɒstjuːm] *n.* 服装
church [tʃɜːtʃ] *n.* 教堂
especially [ɪ'speʃəlɪ] *adv.* 特别
senior ['siːnɪə] *n.* 较年长者
evening service 晚礼拜

Decide whether the following statements are True (T) or False (F).

1. [ ] James and Michelle meet on the 1st of January.
2. [ ] Michelle invites James for a drink.
3. [ ] Michelle is going to join the parade, and she has a great clothes for that.
4. [ ] James is going to the church with his father.
5. [ ] The seniors like to go to church for evening service.

Dialogue 2

Li Ping: Happy Thanksgiving Day!
Lisa: Do you have any plans?
Li Ping: Not really, all my friends are going home. It's like Chinese Spring Festival. What are you going to do?
Lisa: If you're interested, you can come with me and my friends to Ada's parents' place. Ada's whole family will be there.
Li Ping: That's very kind. Thanks. I'd love to come.
Lisa: That's wonderful. I'm glad you're coming. We get to see how other families spend their Thanksgiving.
Li Ping: Could you tell me something about it?

Lisa: It's usually a big family get-together. We always have lots of delicious food, like turkey and stuffing, but sometimes we have ham instead. We have yams, corn, carrots and fruit pies or pumpkin pies.
Li Ping: That sounds like a big feast, like what we have at Spring Festival. I'm getting hungry just thinking about it.
Lisa: Me too. I can't wait to see everyone. It should be lots of fun.

Words and Expressions

turkey ['tɜːkɪ] *n.* 火鸡
stuffing ['stʌfɪŋ] *n.* 填充物
ham [hæm] *n.* 火腿
yam [jam] *n.* 甘薯
corn [kɔːn] *n.* 玉米
carrot ['kærət] *n.* 胡萝卜
pumpkin ['pʌmpkɪn] *n.* 南瓜
feast [fiːst] *n.* 盛宴
Thanksgiving Day 感恩节
Chinese Spring Festival 中国春节
get-together 聚会

Decide whether the following statements are True (T) or False (F).

1. [ ] Thanksgiving Day is a western festival, and all the western countries will celebrate it.
2. [ ] Lisa is going back home and celebrates Thanksgiving Day with her family.
3. [ ] Lisa invites Li Ping to her home.
4. [ ] Thanksgiving Day is a big family get-together.
5. [ ] Chinese usually have a big feast at Spring Festival.

Dialogue 3

Tom: Merry Christmas, Lisa.

Lisa: Merry Christmas, Tom.

Tom: What are you doing there on the computer?

Lisa: Come and have a look. I received many beautiful e-cards. They're from my friends all over the world. Christmas wishes for all my friends!

Tom: That's pretty interesting. Did you get one from Helen? The reason why I ask is that I'm looking for her number.

Lisa: Sorry, I don't have it. But I do have her e-mail. Do you want me to send it to you?

Tom: Yeah, that would be great. Thanks.

Lisa: No worries. I'll just forward her card and you can get it from the E-mail. I would really like to talk to her again. I kind of miss her a little these days.

Tom: Thanks a million!

Lisa: My pleasure!

Words and Expressions

forward ['fɔːwəd] *v.* 转寄

Decide whether the following statements are True (T) or False (F).

1. [ ] Tom is watching TV.
2. [ ] Lisa received many beautiful e-cards from her friends from all over the world.
3. [ ] Tom is very interested in Lisa's e-cards.
4. [ ] Tom is asking for Helen's e-mail address.
5. [ ] Lisa tells Tom Helen's phone number.

Dialogue 4

Tom: Here are some flowers, love. Happy Valentine's Day!

Lisa: Those are beautiful! They smell lovely. Thank you.

Tom: This is to let you know that I still love you after all these years. I knew that there would be ups and downs when I married you. But through it all, you've always been my valentine.

Lisa: How sweet! You've always been my love too.

Tom: I don't think I say this enough, but I want to thank you for your kindness and patience. You've always been there for me.

Lisa: I'll do everything for you, love, you know that. Maybe you didn't realize, but you made every day a joyous moment and a happy occasion.

Tom: I'm so glad that we met one another.

Words and Expressions

kindness ['kaɪn(d)nɪs] *n.* 仁慈

patience ['peɪʃ(ə)ns] *n.* 耐心

realize ['rɪəlaɪz] v. 意识到

joyous ['dʒɒɪəs] *adj.* 令人高兴的

occasion [ə'keɪʒ(ə)n] *n.* 时刻

up and down 起起伏伏

Decide whether the following statements are True (T) or False (F).

1. [ ] Today is Children's Day.
2. [ ] Tom is Lisa's husband.
3. [ ] There are many ups and downs since they married.
4. [ ] They love each other deeply.
5. [ ] They have been quite happy together.

Part Three: Text

Do you like to drink orange juice?

No, I don't. I like to drink tomato juice.

Do they know her age?

Yes, they do. It is not a secret.

Does he get up early in the morning?

Yes, he does. He gets up at six every morning.

Does he like his work?

Yes, he does. He is interested in his work.

Does she have a pink case?

No, she doesn't. Her case is blue.

Does she listen to music on weekend?

Yes, she does. She likes to listen to classical music.

Do you read books in your free time?

No, I don't. I am not a good reader.

Do you want to swim this afternoon?

Yes, I do. Can we swim together?

It sounds good. Let's go together.

Words and Expressions

tomato [tə'mɑːtəʊ] *n.* 番茄，西红柿

Eg. 1. I like tomato and Cream Cheese Sandwich.

我喜欢番茄和奶油奶酪三明治。

2. Red tomato goes into the pot.

红色的西红柿进入锅中。

secret ['siːkrɪt] *n.* 秘密；秘诀

Eg. 1. I can't tell you. It's a secret .

我不能告诉你，这是个秘密。

2. Don't worry. Your secret is safe with me.

别担心，我会替你保守秘密。

case [keɪs] *n.* 箱子

Eg. 1. No more clothes will go into this case.

这手提箱再也装不下衣服了。

2. He planted his case on the table.

他把箱子稳稳地放在桌上。

listen ['lɪsn] *vi.* 听，倾听

Eg. 1. We sat around listening to music.

我们围坐着听音乐。

2. Listen, I want you to come with me.

听着，我要你跟我一起去。

classical ['klæsɪk(ə)l] *adj*. 古典的；经典的

Eg. 1. classical music

古典音乐

2. A leading classical violinist.

一名出类拔萃的古典音乐小提琴家。

together [tə'geðə] *adv*. 一起；同时

Eg. 1. They decided to spend more time together.

他们决定要花更多时间在一起。

2. He and my father were at school together.

他和我父亲一起上过学。

sound [saʊnd] *vi*. 听起来

Eg. 1. The whole story sounded very odd.

整个故事听起来很古怪。

2. That sounds a good idea.

那主意听起来很不错。

Language Focus

I. Make a sentence with the words given below.

1. you / do / to / like / orange /drink / juice
2. get / does / he / up / in / the morning/ early
3. do /want / you / to / afternoon / swim / this
4. books / you / read / free / do / your / in / time
5. he / does / work / his / like

II. Translating

Put Chinese into English.

1. 你抽烟吗？
2. 她喜欢这本书吗？
3. 他们每天都去学校吗？
4. 他在周末听音乐吗？

5. 我们早餐吃面包吗？

Put English into Chinese.

1. Do you want to pass CET 4？
2. Do you study English?
3. Do they play football after school?
4. Does he like swimming?
5. Do they often watch TV in dormitory?

III. Reading Comprehension

Choose the best answer to each of the following questions or incomplete sentences.

Pandas' faces look like cats', but their fat bodies and short tails are like bears'. Pandas are very lovely and they are friendly to people. People likes them very much. Most Pandas live in China. The northwestern（西北的）part of Sichuan Province（省）and southern（南方的）part of Gansu Province are their hometowns. Pandas like to climb trees. They usually live in the forests of high mountains, eat bamboo（竹子）and drink spring water.

1. The panda mainly lives in_____.

A. America

B. Shanghai

C. London

D. China

2. _____ is like a cat's.

A. The panda

B. The panda's face

C. The panda's body

D. The panda's tail

3. Where are the pandas' hometowns?

A. Guangdong and Gansu.

B. Sichuan and Suzhou.

C. Gansu and Sichuan

D. Hubei and Sichuan

4. What's the panda's main food? _____

A. Rice.

B. Meat.

C. Bamboo.

D. Grass.

5. Where do the pandas usually live in? _____

A. River

B. Grassland.

C. Forest.

D. Desert.

Part Four: Play

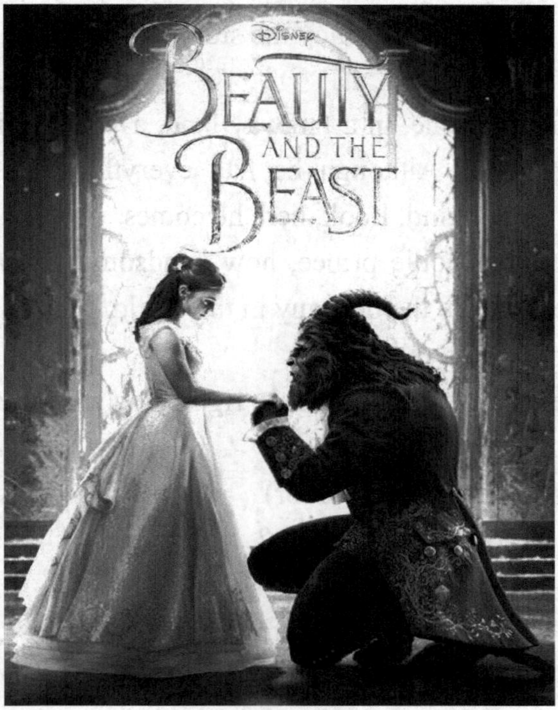

Beauty and the Beast (I)

Characters:

Aside: 旁白

Servant: 仆人

Prince: 王子

Old woman: 老妇人

Fairy: 仙女

Beast: 野兽

Beauty: 美女

Beauty's father: 美女的父亲

Playboy: 花花公子

Aside: Hello, everybody. Today I will tell you a very beautiful love story. I hope you will enjoy the story.

Scene 1

Aside: Once upon a time, in a faraway land, a young prince lived in a shining castle. Although he had everything, he was spoiled, selfish, and unkind. Look, here he comes.

Servant A: Oh, my noble prince, how handsome you are! How rich you are! You are the best guy in the world.

Prince: Oh, am I? You, tell me…

Servant B: Yes, yes! He is absolutely right! You are the best guy in the world.

(Someone knocks at the door)

Prince: Who is knocking at the door?

Servants: Let's have a look.

Old woman: Oh, my honorable prince! It's cold outside and I'm so hungry and sleepy. May I stay overnight at your castle? I will give you this rose in return.

Servants: (whisper) Poor dirty old lady!

Prince: Get out of my castle, you ugly beggar… get out at once!

Servants: Go, go, go away…

Old woman: Don't judge anyone by his appearance, young man! (She becomes a fairy.)

Fairy: There is no love in your heart, young man. As a punishment, you will be transformed into a hideous beast. You must learn how to love others and earn a girl's true love. If you fail, you will be the beast forever.

Prince: No, oh, no… oh my god, I'm so sorry! It's my fault! I promise I will love other people. Please don't, please…

Fairy: It's too late!

(Prince becomes a beast)

Servants: Oh, a beast!

Beast: What happened to me? Why? I don't want to be a beast! Wait, wait…

Beast: Who will fall in love with an ugly beast? Who can help me?

Scene 2

Aside: One day, beauty's father learned that all his ships had been lost in the storm. He was penniless and would have to move to a tiny cottage on the edge of the woods.

Beauty's Father: I'm so sorry, but all my ships had been lost in a storm, we have to move to a tiny cottage on the edge of the woods. My dear daughter, I must go to find another job.

Beauty: Everything will be alright, Daddy.

Beauty's Brother: Where will you go, father? Don't leave us! We don't have any servants and the house is so small.

Beauty's Father: I must go to a faraway place to sign a big business contract. If I succeed we would be rich again and move back to our house.

Beauty's Brother: What? Oh, Dad. If you are successful, please bring us some pretty gifts.

Beauty's Father: What kind of pretty gifts do you want, my dear children?

Beauty's Brother: I want a diamond and a lot of beautiful clothes so the daughter of the king would fall in love with me, my dear father!

Beauty's Father: OK, I will get all those for you. And you, my little darling, what do you want?

Beauty: I want a rose, a red rose. Oh, Daddy, I will miss you!

Beauty's Father: I'll miss you too. But I have to go now.

Beauty's Brother: Goodbye, my dear father, remember to bring me a diamond and beautiful clothes!

Beauty: Goodbye, father. I'll miss you, too. I love you!

Scene 3

Aside: The old man came back with the diamond and beautiful clothes, but there was no rose everywhere. He found he lost his way, and this shining castle appeared in front of him.

Beauty's Father: Woo… I didn't know that this was here, I must be lost! It's so big and beautiful. (Knock at the door) Hello! Is anybody in? Please open the door! Oh, the door was opened. Woo… so many delicious dishes, I'm so hungry right now. The master of this castle must be a kind and warmhearted man. Let me eat something. En? There are so many roses! I shall get one for my little daughter.

Beast: You! How dare you get into my garden!

Beauty's Father: Oh, no…

Beast: How dare you! I have given you food, but you are so greedy! How dare you get into my garden! I will kill you and eat you!

Beauty's Father: No, Please forgive me! I only want a rose for my daughter, I promised her to get one for her. Please don't kill me!

Beast: You have a daughter? Is she pretty?

Beauty's Father: Yes, yes. She is the most beautiful girl in the world. She is like an angle.

Beast: Ok. Then I won't kill you. But you must take your little daughter here. I want to see her!

Beauty's Father: But, but… Oh, I understand.

Beast: If she is not here in three days, I will kill and eat you!

Scene 4

Aside: The old man got home and told his daughter what happened.

Beauty's Father: I am so unlucky! I was caught by a beast when I was picking the rose for you.

Beauty: Oh, no… are you alright, my dearest father!

Beauty's Father: Yeah! I'm ok, but he wants to see you, my little darling!

Beauty: Daddy, I love you! I will go to see the beast! I won't let him kill you!

Beauty's Father: I won't let the beast see you, either! But he is so strong that nobody can beat him!

Beauty's Brother: It's all your fault! Why did you ask for a rose? Do you want to kill Daddy!

Beauty: No, no… I will go to the castle to see the beast. He said if I go there, he won't kill our father!

Beauty's Father: No! My dear! You are my best love! I won't let you go!

Beauty: Oh, don't worry, daddy! I will be fine. I will be back soon. Bye, father!

Beauty's Father: NO!NO!NO!

Beauty's Brother: She must be eaten… hahaha…

Scene 5

Aside: When the Beauty was on her way, she was harassed by a playboy.

Playboy: I am a handsome boy, I like beautiful girls. Hahaha…

Beauty: …

Playboy: Woo… What a beautiful girl! Here is a present for you!

Beauty: I'm sorry, but I don't know you! I don't need your present! I just want to save my father.

Playboy: Don't go! I am a handsome boy and you are a beautiful girl, we are a good match! I need you! I will help you save your father!

Beauty: No, don't touch me!

(The Beast comes on the stage)

Beast: What are you doing? Roar…

Playboy: Ah…(fainted)

Words and Expressions

castle ['kɑ:sl]*n.*城堡

Eg. 1.He grabbed at the opportunity to buy his castle.

他抓住机会买下了他的城堡。

2.The restoration to the castle took a year and cost a lot of money.

修复城堡花了一年时间和大量的钱。

shining ['ʃaɪnɪŋ] *adj.*光亮的；华丽的

Eg. 1.She is a shining example to us all.

她是我们所有人的光辉榜样。

2.Mary is a shining example to me.

玛丽是我的光辉榜样。

handsome ['hænsəm] *adj.*英俊的，健美的

Eg. 1.He's the most handsome man I've ever met.

他是我见过的最俊美的男子。

2.He was aptly described as "tall, dark, and handsome".

他被恰如其分地描述为“高大、黝黑、相貌堂堂”。

absolutely ['æbsəlu:tli] *adv.*绝对地；完全地

Eg. 1.You're absolutely right.

你完全正确。

2.He made it absolutely clear.

他把此事讲得一清二楚。

delicious [dɪ'lɪʃəs] *adj.*美味的，可口的

Eg. 1.Who cooked this? It's delicious.

谁做的？味道好极了。

2.Pecan nuts are delicious both raw and cooked.

美洲山核桃不论生的还是熟的都很好吃。

spoiled[spɔɪld] *adj.*被宠坏的

Eg. 1.The only son had been pampered and spoiled.

这个独子娇生惯养，被宠坏了。

2.The young parents spoiled their only son.

那对年轻的父母惯坏了他们的独生子。

transform [træns'fɔ:m] *vt.*变换；改变

Eg. 1.A witch changed the boy into a mouse.

女巫把那男孩变成了一只老鼠。

2.The leaves on the trees transform colour in the autumn.

树叶在秋天改变颜色。

fail[feɪl] *vt.& vi.*失败，不及格

Eg. 1.Some schools fail to set any homework

有些学校没有布置任何作业。

2.She failed to get into art college.

她未能进入艺术学院。

success [sək'ses] *n.*成功，成就

Eg. 1.What's the secret of your success?

你成功的秘诀是什么？

2.I didn't have much success in finding a job.

我找工作没什么结果。

forgive [fə'gɪv] *vt.& vi.*原谅；饶恕

Eg. 1. I'll never forgive her for what she did.

我绝不会原谅她做的事。

2.I can’t forgive that type of behaviour.

我不能宽恕那种行为。

match [mætʃ] *n.*相配的人（或物）

Eg. 1. Helen's choice of lipstick was a good match for her skin-tone.

海伦选择的唇膏很适合她的肤色。

2.Her nails were painted bright red to match her dress.

她的指甲涂成了大红色，为的是与裙子相配。

Listening Practice

I. Bingo game

Work in groups, one student read about the script of *Beauty and the Beast*（I）, other students listen carefully, when they hear an adjective from the script, say “Bingo”, and write the word in the form quickly, and then he/she wins. And take turns, and change the words into Verbs, Nouns, etc.

words	adjective	verbs	nouns	prepositions	adverbs	conjunctions
student1						
student2						
student3						
student4						
student5						

II. Dictation

Listen to the passage three times and suppty the missing information.

Once upon a time, in a ____1____land, a young prince lived in a shining____2____. Although he had everything, he was ____3____, selfish, and unkind. Look, here he comes. One day, beauty’s father learned that all his ships had been ____4____in the storm. He was penniless and would have to ____5____to a tiny cottage on the edge of the woods. The old man came back with the ____6____and beautiful clothes, but there was no ____7____everywhere. He ____8____he was lost his way, and this shining castle ____9____in front of him. The old man got home and told his daughter what ____10____.

Reading Practice

I. Read and choose

1.Which of the following statement is True?_____

A. The prince wanted to be a beast.

B. The prince turned himself into a beast.

C. The old women was actually a fairy.

D. The prince agreed the old women to stay overnight at his castle.

2. Why the fairy punished the prince to become a beast? Because the prince was_____.

A. kind

B. handsome

C. selfish

D. brave

3. What kind of gift did the beauty want to get from his father? A _____.

A. castle

B. rose

C.garden

D. ship

4. The beast won't kill the beauty's father, if the father bring his _____ to the castle.

A. servant

B. wife

C. son

D. daughter

5. What did the beauty meet when she went to see the prince. A_____.

A. playboy

B. beast

C. farmer

D. lion

II. Read and answer

1.Who is the prince?

2. Why did prince prevent the old woman from getting into his castle?

3. How can the prince turn from the beast to himself?

4. If you were the beauty, what gift do you want to get from her father?

5. When the beauty was harassed by the playboy who appeared?

Speaking Practice

I. Role Play

Suppose you were the beast, when he saw the beauty's father outside the castle, what would you say to her father. Use the following functional sentences, and you have to add your own expressions when it is necessary.

- It's so big and beautiful.
- Hello! Is anybody in?
- How dare you!
- But you must take your little daughter here.
- The master of this castle must be a kind and warmhearted man.
- There are so many roses!
- I will kill you and eat you!
- I only want a rose for my daughter.
- Then I won't kill you.

II. Problem-Solving

Think of appropriate lines for the beauty in the picture above.

Translating Practice

I. Translate the sentences into Chinese.

Work in pairs, one student reads the following sentences, and the other translates the sentences into Chinese in spoken way. (Add extra sentences from the scripts if necessary.)

1. Once upon a time, in a faraway land, a young prince lived in a shining castle.
2. It's cold outside and I'm so hungry and sleepy.
3. Don't judge anyone by his appearance, young man!
4. There is no love in your heart, young man.
5. Who will fell in love with an ugly beast?

II. Translate the sentences into English.

Work in pairs, one student reads the following sentences, and the other translates the sentences into English in spoken way. (Add extra sentences from the scripts if necessary.)

1.谁在敲门?
2.老人回到家告诉了他女儿所发生的事情。
3.当我为你摘玫瑰花时被一个野兽抓住。
4.我是个帅气的男孩，你是一个漂亮的女孩，我们很般配。
5.她是世界上最漂亮的女孩。

III. Delivery Game

The teacher divides the whole class into four or five groups, queuing the students. The teacher writes a long sentence from the script in a piece of paper, just let the first student read and recite it for one minute, and let the student retell the sentence to the second student, the second to the third, when the sentence is delivered to the last student, he/she should write it on the blackboard, and translate it into Chinese. The group which has got great speed and relative accuracy wins.

Writing Practice

Write a summary of *Beauty and the Beast*(I) in 100 words.

"Ws" / "Who"	doing what	whom	where	when

Part Five: Language Skills

Grammar

冠词

冠词作为一种虚词，在英语中只能和名词一起使用。英语冠词分为不定冠词 a/an、定冠词 the 以及零冠词。

一、不定冠词的用法

不定冠词有两个，为 a 和 an。a 用在辅音开头的单词前面，an 用于以元音开头的单词前。例如：a box，an orange。

（1）表示数量“一”“一类人”或“一类东西，事物”。如：

There is a policeman at the door.

门口有个警察。

There is an apple on the table.

桌子上有一个苹果。

This is a student.

这是一个学生。

She is a teacher.

她是个老师。

（2）不定冠词用于头一次出现的单数名词之前。例如：

There is a box in the room. The box is heavy.

房间里有个箱子。这个箱子很重。

（3）不定冠词用于某些固定短语中。例如：

have a try 试一下　take a break 休息一下　have a good day 玩得开心　a great deal of 大量的　in a hurry 匆忙的　catch a cold 感冒

二、定冠词的用法

（1）表示某个或某些特定的人或物。

Tom is the monitor of our class.

汤姆是我们班的班长。

The horse is a useful animal.

马是一种有用的动物。

（2）世界上独一无二的事物。

the sun 太阳　the earth 地球　the world 世界

（3）特指双方都明白的人或物或上文提到过的人或事。

He has a pen and the pen is given by his sister.

他有一支笔是他姐姐给他的。

I am cold, would you please close the door.

我很冷，麻烦把门关上。

（4）用在序数词和最高级前面。

第一 the first　第二 the second　第三 the third

他是我们班最高的。 He is the tallest in our class.

（5）定冠词用于某些名词或者形容词前，表示一类人，一个民族，阶级或阶层。例如：

the Chinese 中国人 the rich 富人

the dead 死者 the deaf 聋人

（6）用在表示乐器的名词前。

He can play the piano/violin/guitar...

他会弹钢琴/拉小提琴/弹吉他......

（7）用在姓氏的复数名词前。

The Greens are watching TV.

格林一家在看电视。

（8）定冠词的其他用法。

用于表示江河海洋山脉沙漠的名词前：the Changjiang River 长江 the Red Sea 红海 the Taiwan Straits 台湾海峡 the Gulf of Mexico 墨西哥湾 the Alps 阿尔卑斯山 the Sahara Desert 撒哈拉沙漠

用于国家名称前：the People's Republic of China 中华人民共和国 the United States 美国

用于公共建筑名前：the National Gallery 国家美术馆 the Military Museum 军事博物馆

用于机关、团体名词前：the State Council 国务院 the Senate 参议院 the House of Representatives 众议院

三、零冠词的用法

名词前既不用不定冠词 a/an，也不用定冠词 the。

（1）表示球类、棋类的运动项目不加冠词。例如：

play football 踢足球 play chess 下象棋

（2）在一日三餐名词前不用冠词。例如：

have breakfast/lunch/supper 吃早饭/午饭/晚饭

（3）州名，国名，人名前不用。

Asia is the largest continent.

亚洲是最大的州。

（4）名词已经有了物主代词、指示代词、不定代词、名词所有格。
She is my sister.
她是我姐姐。
（5）节日、假日、星期几、月份、季节前不用。
Today is Friday.
今天是星期五。
（6）交通工具名词前不用冠词。
by car 坐汽车　　by ship 坐船
by plane 坐飞机　　on foot 步行
（7）泛指概念。
I like music.
我喜欢音乐。
Bananas are yellow.
香蕉是黄色的。

Exercises

I. Multiple Choice

1. There is _______ house in the picture. There is ________old woman near______ house.
A. an；a；the　　B. a；an；the　　C. the；a；an　　D. a；the；an
2. He has already worked for ______ hour.
A. the　　B. an　　C. a　　D. /
3. Alice is fond of playing ______ piano.
A. the　　B. an　　C. a　　D. /
4. He often has ________ egg and some milk for breakfast.
A. /　　B. a　　C. the　　D. an
5. —What's the trouble with Lily?
—She does not go to________ school and stay in _____bed now.
A. a；　/　　B. the；　the　　C. /；　/　　D. /；　a
6. —Do you have _______ dictionary?
—No，but Lucy has ______ new dictionary on the bookshelf.

A. a；the　　B. the；the　　C. the；a　　D. a；a

7. _______ earth is round.

A. A　　B. An　　C. The　　D. /

8. There is _______ "L" in the word "LUCK".

A. a　　B. the　　C. an　　D. /

9. ______ terrible weather we've been having these days!

A. How a　　B. What a　　C. How　　D. What

10. When do you have _____breakfast every day?

A. a　　B. an　　C. the　　D. /

11. —Does Jim have _______ ruler? —Yes，he has _______ .

A. an；some　　B. a；one　　C. a；/　　D. any；one

12. There is _______old bike. _______ old bike is Mr Zhao's.

A. an；The　　B. the；An　　C. a；The　　D. the；The

13. _______ apple a day keeps the doctors away.

A. The　　B. A　　C. An　　D. Two

14. At that time Tom was _______ one-year-old baby.

A. a　　B. an　　C. the　　D. /

15. We can't see _______ sun at _______ night.

A. the；the　　B. the；/　　C. a；/　　D. /；/

16. _______ useful book it is!

A. What an　　B. How a　　C. What a　　D. What

17. _______ Great Wall is _______ longest wall in the world.

A. a　　B. The；the　　C. A；the　　D. The；a

18. They made him _______ king.

A. a　　B. the　　C. an　　D. /

19. His father is _______ English teacher. He works in our school.

A. a　　B. an　　C. the　　D. /

20. Don't play _______ basketball here. It's dangerous.

A. a　　B. an　　C. /　　D. the

II. Fill in the blanks with "/、a、an、the"

1. _______ milk is food. ________ milk in this cup has gone bad.

2. —Do you like playing _____ football? —Yes. But I have only _____ basketball.

3. Do you know _______girl on ________another side of ________ lake?

4. There's ________ ″u″ and ________ ″s″ in ________word ″use″.

5. She says ________animals can't live without ________air.

6. His father, who is ________honest man, is teaching in _______ university.

7. Which is heavier, ________elephant or ________ horse?

8. ________ cold wind was blowing from the north.

9. Xiaomei saw______interesting film last night. _______film was about_______ kind doctor.

10. You can have _________ second try if you fail _______ first time.

III. Translating Practice

Translate the following into English.

1. 昨晚下了一场大雨。

2. 张飞是他们的班长。

3. 她是一位医生。

4. 桌子上有一个苹果。

5. 那边有一个老妇人。

Translate the following into Chinese.

1. We wait here for half an hour.

2. Students often play football after school.

3. They often have supper in a restaurant.

4. The Smiths are talking happily.

5. Pandas live in China.

Unit Six
Inner Beauty

Part One: Phonetic Knowledge
Part Two: Dialogue
Part Three: Text
Part Four: Play: Beauty and the Beast (2)
Part Five: Language Skills

Part One: Phonetic Knowledge

一、辅音字母组合 bl cl fl

1. 拼读发音方式。

辅音混合音“bl”

辅音混合音“bl”的特点是辅音组合。在这个辅音组合里，每个辅音依然保持自身的发音。当拼读的时候，这里的两个辅音一定要连读，即从前面的第一个辅音迅速滑到第二个辅音，中间不能停顿。包含辅音混合音“bl”发音的单词如 blackboard，blocks，blind，bleed 等。

辅音混合音“cl”

辅音混合音“cl”的特点是辅音组合。在这个辅音组合里，每个辅音依然保持自身的发音。当拼读的时候，这里的两个辅音一定要连读，即从前面的第一个辅音迅速滑到第二个辅音，中间不能停顿。包含辅音混合音“cl”发音的单词如 clink，cliff，client 等。

辅音混合音“fl”

辅音混合音“fl”的特点是辅音组合。在这个辅音组合里，每个辅音依然保持自身的发音。当拼读的时候，这里的两个辅音一定要连读，即从前面的第一个辅音迅速滑到第二个辅音，中间不能停顿。包含辅音混合音“fl”发音的单词如 flag，fly，flame，flash，fluid 等。

2. 听一听，学一学下列字母组合的拼读发音。

(1) blade blast blend blouse black blur bloom blonde

(2) cluster club clay clover class clip clock cloud

(3) fluent flea flesh flower flood flue flame flutter

3. 仔细听，然后做句子一口气快读练习。

(1) Blake dyed his blonder hair black.

(2) Blue Bird blamed himself for his blunder.

(3) The clouds are close to the cliff.

(4) My client claims he has climbed the cliff.

(5) Floyd is fluent in French.

(6) Floyd's favorite food is flat fish, sometimes he goes fishing for hours.

二、辅音字母组合 br cr fr

1. 拼读发音方式。

辅音混合音"br"

辅音混合音"br"的特点是辅音组合。在这个辅音组合里，每个辅音依然保持自身的发音。当拼读的时候，这里的两个辅音一定要连读，即从前面的第一个辅音迅速滑到第二个辅音，中间不能停顿。包含辅音混合音"br"发音的单词如 Brandy，bridge，bread，brother 等。

辅音混合音"cr"

辅音混合音"cr"的特点是辅音组合。在这个辅音组合里，每个辅音依然保持自身的发音。当拼读的时候，这里的两个辅音一定要连读，即从前面的第一个辅音迅速滑到第二个辅音，中间不能停顿。包含辅音混合音"cr"发音的单词如 crop，crocodile，creep，crisp，crown 等。

辅音混合音"fr"

辅音混合音"fr"的特点是辅音组合。在这个辅音组合里，每个辅音依然保持自身的发音。当拼读的时候，这里的两个辅音一定要连读，即从前面的第一个辅音迅速滑到第二个辅音，中间不能停顿。包含辅音混合“fr”发音的单词如 frog，free，fresh，freezer，frost 等。

2. 听一听，学一学下列字母组合的拼读发音。

(1) brain brush broom brief breakfast brown brilliant

(2) cream crispy crush credit crazy cracker crystal crook

(3) France fruit frozen fried freedom fridge fragrance

3. 仔细听，然后做句子一口气快读练习。

(1) Bring me a brush and a broom.

(2) The weather is breezy today, but tomorrow will be bright and sunny.

(3) The cream crackers are very crispy and crunchy.

(4) The crowd went crazy and cried.

(5) The frog is free on Friday.

(6) This French likes the fragrance of fresh flowers.

Part Two: Dialogue

Dialogue 1

Jenny: What's up? You sound a little down in the dumps.

Lisa: I quarreled with my roommate last night.

Jenny: Calm down! Shouting won't help.

Lisa: She is really outrageous.

Jenny: What happened?

Lisa: Last night, I took a quick shower and went to bed. I couldn't fall asleep, because Susan was there in the living room, playing her stupid stereo so loud. I kindly told her to turn that down a little bit. She shouted at me.

Jenny: What? She can't do this to you.

Lisa: Well, she did it anyway.

Jenny: What did you do?

Lisa: I shouted it back of course.

Jenny: You won't accomplish anything by hollering at her, right? You are worked up till now. Why not wait until you cool down a bit?

Lisa: What would you do if you were in my shoes?

Jenny: Just stay cool. When you get back home tonight, tell her that you didn't mean to quarrel with her.

Lisa: Okay. Let bygones be bygones.

Jenny: Good.

Words and Expressions

quarrel ['kwɒr(ə)l] *v.* 吵架

outrageous [aʊt'reɪdʒəs] *adj.* 粗暴的

shower ['ʃaʊə] *n.* 淋浴

stereo ['sterɪəʊ] *n.* 立体声系统

accomplish [ə'kʌmplɪʃ] *v.* 完成

holler ['hɒlə] *v.* 大声叫喊

down in the dumps 垂头丧气

cool down 平静下来

let bygones be bygones 既往不咎

Decide whether the following statements are True (T) or False (F).

1. [ ] Lisa quarreled with her roommate Susan this morning.
2. [ ] Lisa shouted it back because she was very angry.
3. [ ] Jenny thought Lisa shouldn't fight back and holler at Susan.
4. [ ] Jenny suggested Lisa cool down and do apologize to Susan.
5. [ ] Lisa thought Jenny was right and listened to her words.

Dialogue 2

Policeman: Good morning, Madam.

Jenny: Good morning, officer. I lost my suitcase this morning. Yeah, I wonder if it was handed in here.

Policeman: Sit down, please. We shall need some details. Can you describe your suitcase?

Jenny: Well, it's a brown leather suitcase.

Policeman: There are several suitcases handed in there that are the same as you described. So any particularities about it?

Jenny: Ah, yes, my initials "J. C." in capital letters are on the handle.

Policeman: I will go and have a look. There is one with "J. C." on the handle. Can you tell me what are in the suitcase?

Jenny: A skirt, a CD player and a necklace.

Policeman: I think the suitcase belongs to you.

Jenny: Thanks a lot.

Policeman: You're welcome.

Words and Expressions

suitcase ['suːtkeɪs] *n.* 手提箱

describe [dɪ'skraɪb] *v.* 描绘

leather ['leðə] *n.* 皮革

particularity [pəˌtɪkjʊ'lærɪtɪ] *n.* 特质

initial [ɪ'nɪʃl] *n.* (名字的) 首字母

handle ['hænd(ə)l] *n.* 把手

hand in 交上

capital letter 大写字母

Decide whether the following statements are True (T) or False (F).

1. [ ] Jenny lost her black leather suitcase.
2. [ ] There are Jenny initials "J.C." in capital letters on the suitcase's handle.
3. [ ] The policeman found Jenny's suitcase.

4. [ ] There is a pair of shoes in Jenny's suitcase.
5. [ ] Finally the policeman gave the suitcase to Jenny.

Dialogue 3

Interviewer: Tell me a little bit about yourself.
Jenny: My name is Jenny and I live in shanghai, I was born in 1980. My major was electrical engineering.
Interviewer: What kind of personality do you think you have?
Jenny: Well, I approach things very enthusiastically, I think, and I don't like to leave things half-done. I'm very organized and extremely capable.
Interviewer: What would you say are your weaknesses and strengths?
Jenny: Well, I'm afraid I'm a poor speaker, however I'm fully aware of this, so I've been studying how to speak in public. I suppose my strengths are that I'm persistent and a fast-learner.
Interviewer: How do you relate to others?
Jenny: I'm very co-operative and have good teamwork spirit.

Words and Expressions

personality [pɜːsə'nælɪtɪ] *n.* 个性
approach [ə'prəʊtʃ] *v.* 着手处理
enthusiastically [in,θju:zi'æstikəli] *adv.* 满腔热情地
organized ['ɔːgəˌnaɪzd] *adj.* 做事有条理的
extremely [ɪk'striːmlɪ] *adv.* 极其
capable ['keɪpəb(ə)l] *adj.* 有才干的
persistent [pə'sɪst(ə)nt] *adj.* 坚持的
co-operative [kəu'ɔpərətiv] *adj.* 合作的
electrical engineering 电机工程
aware of 意识到

Decide whether the following statements are True (T) or False (F).

1. [ ] Jenny is having an interview.
2. [ ] Jenny was an electrical engineering student.
3. [ ] Jenny is very enthusiastic, organized and extremely capable.
4. [ ] Jenny is very good at speaking in public.
5. [ ] Jenny is also co-operative and has good teamwork spirit.

Dialogue 4

Jenny: Do you know how to apply for a visa to the U.S.?

Lisa: Yes. Log on to the website of the United States Embassy in Beijing and fill in the application forms.

Jenny: And then?

Lisa: Then make an appointment by telephone and wait for the interview. Could you tell me why you're going to the U.S.?

Jenny: I'm on a business trip to visit some companies in the U.S. next month.

Lisa: Really? Have you contacted the companies there?

Jenny: Yes. And I'm collecting information about these companies.

Lisa: I heard most of the business visas are approved, so don't worry.

Jenny: I know, but I'm still very nervous.

Lisa: Take it easy! As long as you make full preparations, everything will be OK!

Jenny: I hope so. I will follow your instructions and log on to the website of the United States Embassy in Beijing and fill in the application forms.

Lisa: Yes, that's necessary. Besides, you have to prepare some documents related to your company.

Jenny: OK. Thank you very much.

Words and Expressions

embassy ['embəsɪ] *n.* 大使馆
contact ['kɒntækt] *v.* 联系
approve [ə'pruːv] *v.* 批准
instruction [ɪn'strʌkʃ(ə)n] *n.* 指示
document ['dɒkjʊm(ə)nt] *n.* 文件
log on 登录
take it easy 放轻松
relate to 有关

Decide whether the following statements are True (T) or False (F).

1. [ ] Jenny is going to the U.S. for a holiday.
2. [ ] Lisa suggests that Jenny should go to the United States Embassy directly.
3. [ ] Jenny has contacted the companies to collect information.
4. [ ] Usually most of the business visas are approved.
5. [ ] Jenny should prepare some documents related to her company.

Part Three: Text

When does he do his homework?

He does his homework after supper.

Where do you come from?

I come from Australia.

What does she do at home?

She watches TV at home.

How does he get to the top of the mountain?

He gets there by walking.

How do you learn English so well?

I learn English by reading a lot.

How often do you visit your grandparents?

I visit my grandparents once a week.

Where does she go with her children every weekend?

She goes to park with her children every weekend.

Who interviews the employees every year?

The boss of the company interviews the employees every year.

Words and Expressions

homework ['həʊmwɜːk] *n.* 家庭作业

Eg. 1. Do you do homework every day?

你们每天都做家庭作业吗？

2. Please help me with my homework.

请帮助我做我的家庭作业。

supper ['sʌpə] *n.* 晚餐，晚饭；夜宵

Eg. 1. We had supper in a small Italian place.

我们在一家意大利小餐馆吃了晚饭。

2. Have you eaten supper?

你吃过晚饭了吗？

Australia [ɔ'streljə] *n.* 澳大利亚，大洋洲

Eg. 1. He transplanted his family to Australia.

他把家迁到澳大利亚。

2. He went out to Australia about five years ago.

他大约在五年前移居澳大利亚。

mountain ['maʊntən] *n.* 山；山脉

Eg. 1. The road passes over a steep mountain.

这条路翻越一架陡峭的高山。

2. They swam in a cool mountain stream.

他们在清凉的山间溪流中游泳。

visit ['vɪzɪt] *n.* 访问；参观

Eg. 1. This visit will always remain in my memory.

这次访问将永远留在我的记忆中。

2. My father will visit New York next week.

我父亲下周将要访问纽约。

grandparent ['græn(d)peər(ə)nt] *n.* 祖父母

Eg. 1. My grandparents live in Sussex.

我的祖父母住在萨塞克斯郡。

2. Did you ever live with your grandparents?

你和祖父母一起生活过吗？

interview ['ɪntəˌvjʊ] *v.* 面试；接见

Eg. 1. I'd interviewed him often in the past.

我过去经常采访他。

2. The boss of the company interviews the employees every year.

公司老板每年要面试很多从业人员。

employee [ɪm'plɔɪi;ˌemplɔɪ'i:] *n.* 雇员；从业员工

Eg. 1. The boss dismissed the employee.

老板解雇了那个雇员。

2. He brought around a new employee this afternoon.

他今天下午把一位新雇员带来。

company ['kʌmp(ə)nɪ] *n.* 公司

Eg. 1. Which company do you work for?

你在哪家公司上班？

2. The company was set up just one year ago.

这家公司是一年前刚成立的。

Language Focus

I. Make a sentence with the words given below.

1. does / What / like / she
2. time / does / what / morning / get / up / he / every
3. do / what / know / you
4. do / how / learn / so / English / well / you
5. you / like / what / do / to / drink

II. Translating

Put Chinese into English.

1. 你的爸爸在哪工作？
2. 你弟弟好吗？
3. 她喜欢哪本书？
4. 他的毛衣是什么颜色的？
5. 你什么时候回家？

Put English into Chinese.

1. How do you go to school every day?
2. What can I do for you?
3. Why do you get up so early?
4. What class are you in?
5. Where are you from?

III. Reading Comprehension

Choose the best answer to each of the following questions or incomplete sentences.

Lucy and Lily are twins. They look the same. They are both 1.60 meters tall. They have round faces, big eyes and long hair. They often wear the same clothes. They are in the same class—Class 5. They both get up at six o'clock. After breakfast they walk to school together. But they have some differences. Lucy is lovely and active. She talks a lot. Lily is quiet and gentle（温柔）. She talks a little. Lucy likes fruit but Lily likes meat. Lucy is good at English, and Lily is good at Chinese. They both work hard.

1. Lucy and Lily are________.

A. friends

B. brothers

C. teachers

D. twins

2. Lucy and Lily are________.

A. in the same class

B. thirteen

C. very beautiful

D. very tall

3. From the passage we know that________.

A. they have breakfast before six

B. their home is near school

C. they have big eyes and short hair

D. they like fruit very much

4. Their characters (性格) are________

A. the same

B. quite different

C. very active

D. quiet

5. Which of these is true? ________

A. They are good at English.

B. They go to school by bike.

C. They like the same clothes.

D. They are in Class 6.

Part Four: Play

Beauty and the Beast（II）

Characters:

Beast	野兽
Beauty	美女
Aside	旁白
Prince	王子

Scene 6

Beast: You must be his daughter!

Beauty: Yes, I am.

Beast: Please come with me!

(The Beast takes Beauty to his castle)

Beauty: Woo… It's beautiful!

Beast: This is my home! Do you like it?

Beauty: Yes, it's so nice!

Beast: This is your bedroom. Good night, my beauty.

Beauty: En… And where do you sleep?

Beast: In my room.

Beauty: Oh…

Scene 7

Beauty: There's something sweet and almost kind. But he was mean and he was coarse and unrefined, but now he's dear, and so unsure. I wonder why I didn't see it there before.

Beast: She glanced this way. And when we touched she didn't shudder at my paw. No, it can't be. I'll just ignore. But then she's never looked at me that way before. (to Beauty) Beauty, I have something to show you. But first, you have to close your eyes. It's a surprise!

Beauty: May I open them?

Beast: Alright, alright, now!

Beauty: I can't believe it! I've never seen so many books in my whole life!

Beast: You like it?

Beauty: It's wonderful!

Beast: It's yours!

Beauty: New and a bit alarming. Who'd have ever thought that this could be? True that he's no Prince Charming. But there's something in him that I simply didn't see. (to Beast) Oh, this is one of my favorites! It's "King Arthur" . Have you ever read it?

Beast: No.

Beauty: you don't know what you're missing. I'd love to read this again. Wait… you can read this first.

Beast: No, that's alright!

Beauty: No, really, you read it!

Beast: On, no, you…

Beauty: No, you!

Beast: No! I can't…

Beauty: You never learned to read?

Beast: Only a little ,and long ago.

Beauty: Well, it just so happens that this is the perfect book to read aloud. Come here, sit by me.

Beast: I never knew books could do that.

Beauty: Do what?

Beast: Take me away from this place, make me forget for a little while.

Beauty: Forget?

Beast: Who I … What I am…

Beauty: We have something in common, you know.

Beast: What is that?

Beauty: In the town where I come from, the people think I'm odd…

Beast: You?

Scene 8

Aside: Two weeks later.

Beast: Are you happy living here?

Beauty: Yes, I am. But I miss my dad. I want to see him.

Beast: Now, tell me, do you love me?

Beauty: What?

Beast: Do you love me?

Beauty: Love you? No, but I do like you, a lot.

Beast: Ok, never mind. Ahahah…

Aside: Two hours later.

Beast: You want to see your father, don't you?

Beauty: Yes, I miss him very much.

Beast: Go, just go! Never come back.

Beauty: Thank you. You are the best guy in the world.

Beast: Thanks. But I am nothing, but a beast.

Beauty: Bye.

Scene 9

Aside: One night, the Beauty made a dream. She dreamed the beast had lain in his garden, and he would die very soon.

Beauty: NO!

(Beauty rushed to the castle.)

Beauty: Oh, no. Don't die! Keep alive!

Beast: You are back. Didn't I tell you never come back again? I will die soon. Leave me alone. Leave me…

Beauty: No… I can't leave you here. I… I love you.

Beast: What?

Beauty: I love you, Beast.

Prince: I love you too.

Beauty: Oh, your face... Oh, look at you! You are a prince.

Prince: A fairy transformed me into a beast as punishment. Only a girl's true love could break the spell. You saved my life, my beautiful girl.

Beauty: Oh… I love you!

Words and Expressions

mean [mi:n] *adj.*吝啬的；刻薄的

Eg. 1.Don’t be so mean to your little brother!

别对你弟弟那么刻薄！

2.She's always been mean with money.

她在花钱方面总是非常吝啬。

coarse [kɔ:s] *adj.*粗糙的；粗鄙的；粗野的

Eg. 1.He’s a coarse, foul-mouthed bully.

他是一个粗俗无礼、满嘴脏话的恶棍。

2.She spoke in a quiet voice but used remarkably coarse expressions.

她说话声音很小，但是用了些特别粗俗的字眼儿。

unrefined [ˌʌnrɪ'faɪnd] *adj.* 粗俗的；不文雅的

Eg. 1.He is an unrefined boy.

他是一个粗俗的男孩。

2.After receiving high education, she became an refined girl from an unrefined girl.

经过高等教育，她从一个没有教养的女孩变为一个优雅的女孩。

shudder ['ʃʌdə(r)] *vt.& vi.*战栗；发抖

Eg. 1.Alone in the car, she shuddered with fear.

她一个人待在车里，害怕得直哆嗦。

2.I shuddered at the thought of all the trouble I’d caused.

一想到我闯的祸，我就不寒而栗。

ignore [ɪg'nɔ:(r)] *vt.*忽视，不顾

Eg. 1.I made a suggestion but they chose to ignore it.

我提了个建议，但他们不予理会。

2.We cannot afford to ignore their advice.

我们不能不考虑他们的劝告。

favorite ['feɪvərɪt] *n.*特别喜欢的人（或物）

Eg. 1.She was a favorite with his schoolmasters but not his schoolmates.

学校的老师们很喜欢他，但同学们并不待见他。

2.Chocolate ice-cream is my favorite.

alarming [ə'lɑ:mɪŋ] *adj.*使人害怕的，扰乱人心的

Eg. 1.The disease has spread at an alarming rate.

这种病以惊人的速度传播开来。

2.An alarming film was shown in this theatre.

这家影院上映了一部令人恐慌的电影。

common ['kɒmən] *adj.*普通的；通俗的

Eg. 1.Some birds which were once a common sight are now becoming rare.

有些曾经随处可见的鸟类现在日益稀少。

2.This is a common spelling mistake.

这是常犯的拼写错误。

spell [spel] *n.*咒语，魔法

Eg. 1.They say she died after a witch cast a spell on her.

他们说她是被一个女巫施了魔法后死的。

2.Even sensible Frank had fallen under her spell.

甚至连一向理智的弗兰克都被她迷住了。

Listening Practice

I. Bingo game

Work in groups, one student read about *Beauty and the Beast*(II), other students listen carefully, when they hear an adjective from the script, say "Bingo", and write the word in the form quickly, and then he/she wins. And take turns, and change the words into Verbs, Nouns, etc.

words	adjective	verbs	nouns	prepositions	adverbs	conjunctions
student 1						
student 2						
student 3						
student 4						
student 5						

II. Dictation

Listen to the passage three times and supply the missing information.

After defeating the __1__, the prince took the beauty to his shinning castle. And he gave a room to the beauty. Beauty felt that the beast was __2__and coarse, but now he's dear. At the same time, the beast thought that when they __3__she didn't shudder at his paw. One day the beast brought a gift to the beauty, it was a __4__. They began to read together and they felt that there are something __5__between them. Two weeks later, the beauty __6__her father and the beast agreed to let her go home, and asked her never to come back. One night, the Beauty made a __7__. She dreamed the beast had lain in his garden, and he would__8__ very soon. Beauty didn't want the beast die and she rushed to the castle. The beast asked the beauty to leave him __9__and let her go, but the beauty would like to stay with him. Then the beast told the beauty that a fairy transformed him into a beast as punishment. Only a girl's true__10__ could break the spell. It was the love that saved his life.

Reading Practice

I. Read and choose

1.Which of the following statement is True? ______

A. The beast took the beauty to his castle.

B. The playboy saved the beauty.

C. The beauty did not stay at the beast's castle and left.

D. The beast and beauty did not like to read books.

2. The surprise was given by the beauty to the beast is a ______.

A.rose

B.book

C. kiss

D. skirt

3. How long did the beauty stay in the beast's castle?________

A. One year

B. A day

C. Two weeks

D. Three months

4. Why did the beauty go back, because she _______.

A. did not like the beast

B. was lonely

C. missed her father

D. was scared

5. Only a girl's ______ can break the spell.

A. true love

B. smile

C. rose

D. home

II. Read and answer

1. Did the beast allow the beauty to get into his castle?

2.How did the beauty think of the beast at the beginning? Any changed after that?

3.Did the beauty love the beast?

4. What dream did the beauty make one night?

5.What happened to the beast finally?

Speaking Practice

I. Role Play

Suppose you were the beauty, what would you say when the beast turned into a prince? Use the following functional sentences, you have to add your own expressions when it is necessary.

- Oh, what happened?
- Who are you?
- Do you know me?
- You are a prince?
- I transformed?
- It is true love could break the spell.
- I love you.
- You saved my life

• Look at your face.

II. Problem-Solving

Think of appropriate lines for the beast and the beauty in the picture above.

Translating Practice

I. Translate the sentences into Chinese.

Work in pairs, one student reads the following sentences, and the other translates the sentences into Chinese in spoken way. (Add extra sentences from the scripts if necessary.)

1.I wonder why I didn't see it there before.

2.I have something to show you. But first, you have to close your eyes.

3.I've never seen so many books in my whole life!

4.Take me away from this place, make me forget for a little while.

5.A fairy transformed me into a beast as punishment.

II. Translate the sentences into English.

Work in pairs, one student reads the following sentences, and the other translates the sentences into English in spoken way. (Add extra sentences from the scripts if necessary.)

1. 你一定就是他的女儿了！

2. 有一种甜蜜和几乎善良的感觉。

3. 你想见到你的父亲，是吗？

4. 你知道我们有共同的地方。
5. 这是你的卧室。晚安，我的美人。

III. Delivery Game

The teacher divides the whole class into four or five groups, queuing the students. The teacher writes a long sentence from the script in a piece of paper, just let the first student read and recite it for one minute, and let the student retell the sentence to the second student, the second to the third, when the sentence is delivered to the last student, he/she should write it on the blackboard, and translate it into Chinese. The group which has got great speed and relative accuracy wins.

Writing Practice

Write a summary of *Beauty and the Beast*(II) in 100 words.

"Ws" / "Who"	doing what	whom	where	when

Part Five: Language Skills
Grammar

数词

数词是指表示数目多少或顺序先后的词，数词分为基数词和序数词。表示数目多少的数词叫基数词，如 one，five，ten，thirty，sixty-five 等；表示顺序先后的数词叫序数词，如 first 第一，second 第二，tenth 第十，twenty-third 第二十三，等等。

一、基数词

基数词的写法和读法

(1) 以下是最基本的基数词。如：

one 1，two 2，three 3，four 4，five 5，six 6，seven 7，eight 8，nine 9，ten 10，eleven 11，twelve 12，thirteen 13，fourteen 14，fifteen 15，sixteen 16，seventeen 17，eighteen 18，nineteen 19，twenty 20，thirty 30，forty 40，fifty 50，sixty 60，seventy 70，eighty 80，ninety 90，a/one hundred 100，a/one thousand 1000，a/one million 1000000

基数词 1—12 是独立单词，须逐个记忆。

基数词 13—19 是个位数词的词干后加-teen 构成的。其中 thirteen，fifteen，eighteen，变化不规则。

基数词 20—90 是在十位数词后面加-ty 构成。

(2) 21—99 的表示法。先说“几十”，再说“几”，中间加连字号：twenty-four 24，thirty-two 32，forty-three43，fifty-seven 57，ninety-one 91。

(3) 101—999 的表示法。先说“几百”，后接 and，再加末尾两位数(或末位数)：two hundred and six 206，four hundred and sixty 460，three hundred and forty-five345，nine hundred and ninety-nine 999。

(4) 1000 以上的基数词的表示法。先从右至左数，每三位数加一个逗号。第一个逗号前的数为 thousand（千），第二个逗号前的数 million（百万），然后以一个逗号为基数读，如：

6, 895 six thousand, eight hundred and ninety-five
48,356 forty-eight thousand, three hundred and fifty-six
765, 861 seven-hundred and sixty-five thousand, eight hundred and sixty-one
41, 361, 256 forty-one million, three hundred and sixty-one thousand, two hundred and fifty-six

注意：

① 英语没有“万”这个单位，要表示“万”须借用 thousand，如“一万”用“十千”表示（ten thousand），“十万”用“百千”表示（one hundred thousand）。

② hundred，thousand，million 等词在读数时不带复数词尾-s（用单数形式），如：

three hundred and fifty-five (355)
two thousand and seventeen (2017)

但是，若不是用于读数，而是用于泛指许多，则用复数，这些词不能被具体的数字修饰，但是可以被 many，several，a few 修饰。

Thousands of people 数千人，Millions of workers 数百万工人，several hundreds of 成百上千。

二、序数词

1. 序数词的写法和读法

(1) 以下是最基本的序数词。如：

first 第 1，second 第 2，third 第 3，fourth 第 4，fifth 第 5，sixth 第 6，seventh 第 7，eighth 第 8，ninth 第 9，tenth 第 10，eleventh 第 11，twelfth 第 12，thirteenth 第 13，fourteenth 第 14，fifteenth 第 15，sixteenth 第 16，seventeenth 第 17，eighteenth 第 18，nineteenth 第 19。

注意：

1. 许多序数词是由相应的基数词后加词尾-th 构成的，如 four / fourth，six / sixth，ten / tenth，sixteen / sixteenth。但是 nine 变为序数词是 ninth，而不是 nineth。

2. first, second, third 通常可缩写为 1st，2nd，3rd。

3. 其他。

4. （1）凡是以 th 结尾的序数词可缩写为“基数词+th”，如 4th，5th，9th，11th 等。

（2）表示整十的序数词由相应的基数词将词尾的 y 改为 ieth 即可。如：twentieth 第 20，thirtieth 第 30，fortieth 第 40，fiftieth 第 50，sixtieth 第 60，seventieth 第 70，eightieth 第 80，ninetieth 第 90。

（3）非整十的多位数，将个位数变成序数词即可：twenty-sixth 第 26，thirty-second 第 32，ninety-ninth 第 99，two hundred and thirty-fifth 第 235。

（4）hundred，thousand，million 的序数词形式为 hundredth，thousandth，millionth 等。如：five hundredth 第 500，ten thousandth 第 10000。

注意：这类词前用数字“一”时，这个“一”只用 one，不用 a。如：one hundredth 第 100 （不说 a hundredth）。

Exercises

I. Multiple Choice.

1.______people visit this museum every day.

A. Hundred B. Hundreds C. Hundred of D. Hundreds of

2. There are two ______people in the meeting room.

A. hundred B. hundreds C. hundreds of D. hundred of

3. We can say the number 78,645 in English like this________.

A. seventy-eight thousand and six hundred and forty-five

B. seventy-eight thousand six hundred and forty five

C. seventy-eight thousand six hundred and forty-five

D. seventy eight thousand six hundred and forty-five

5. Monday is the second day, and_____.

A. Tuesday is the fourth B. Thursday is fifth

C. the second day is Tuesday D. the second day is Thursday

5. “The year 1999” should be read “The year _____.”

A. nineteen and ninety-nine B. nineteen ninety-nine

C. one thousand nine hundred ninety-nine D. nineteen hundred and ninety-nine

6. There are ____months in a year. December is the ____month of the year.

A. twelve；twelve B. twelve；twelfth

C. twelfth；twelve D. twelve；twelveth

7. At night we can see ______ stars in the sky.

A. thousands and thousands of B. thousand and thousands of

C. a thousand and thousands D. thousand and thousand

8. There are some _____ in our classroom.

A. hundred of books B. the hundreds of books

C. hundreds of books D. hundred of book

9. I have been to the village ________.

A. a hundred time B. hundred times

C. hundreds of times D. hundred of times

10. There are ____ students in our school.

A. four-hundred and forty-five B. four hundred and forty-five

C. four hundreds and forty-five D. four hundred and forty five

11. The teacher told me to go over _____ lessons.

A. first three B. the three first C. three the first D. the first three

12. Which number is wrong? _______.

A. Ninety B. Ninteen C. Ninth D. Nineteenth

13. There are ________ days in a year.

A. three hundred sixty and five B. three hundred and sixty-five

C. three hundreds and sixty-five D. three hundred sixty-five

14. —How many English books are there on the table? —There is only _____English book on it.

A. a B. an C. one D. the

15. Mr Smith stayed in _____ last night.

A. Room 403 B. the Room 403 C. the 403 room D. 403 the room

16. The road is _________.

A. two thousand and five hundred meters long

B. two thousands meters long

C. long one thousand five hundred meter

D. a thousand and five hundreds meters long

17. Dick , it is _______ time in ______ days that you’ ve made the same mistake.

A. two，three B. second，three C. two，third D. second，third

18. Abraham Lincoln was _______ President of the United States.

A. 16 B. the 16 C. 16th D. the 16th

19. Do you think there is any room for us ________?

A. two B. the two C. second D. the second

20. —How many students are there in your class? —________.

A. Twenty nine B. Thirty and two C. Forty-five D. fifties

II. correct the mistakes.

1. There are three hundreds people in our village. (　　　　)

2. There are hundred of students on the playground. (　　　　)

3. Ten thousands students got together in Beijing Tian’an Men Square. (　　　　)

4. Thousands people are needed to finish the work. (　　　　)

6. The population of this city is about three millions. (　　　　)

III. Translating Practice

Translate the following into English.

1. 一年有 12 个月。

2. 这是我的第一个包。

3. 他在数学比赛中得了第三名。

4. 我们班有 34 个学生。

5. 我的生日是 12 月 21 号。

Translate the following into Chinese.

1. — Are these your books? — Yes, they are.

2. — Are those bears? — No, they are not.

3. — What’s this in English? — It is a toy.

4. — What are those in English? — They are roses.

5. — Is this your umbrella? — No, it isn’t.

Unit Seven
Justice

Part One:	Phonetic Knowledge
Part Two:	Dialogue
Part Three:	Text
Part Four:	Play:Mulan(1)
Part Five:	Language Skills

Part One: Phonetic Knowledge

一、辅音字母组合 gl pl sl

1. 拼读发音方式。

辅音混和音“gl”

辅音混和音“gl”的特点是辅音组合。在这个辅音组合里，每个辅音依然保持自身的发音。当拼读的时候，这里的两个辅音一定要连读，即从前面的第一个辅音迅速滑到第二个辅音，中间不能停顿。包含辅音混合音“gl”发音的单词如 globe，glad，glass，glare 等。

辅音混和音“pl ”

辅音混和音“pl”的特点是辅音组合。在这个辅音组合里，每个辅音依然保持自身的发音。当拼读的时候，这里的两个辅音一定要连读，即从前面的第一个辅音迅速滑到第二个辅音，中间不能停顿。包含辅音混合音“pl”发音的单词如：place，plate，plat，plane 等。

辅音混和音“sl”

辅音混和音“sl”的特点是辅音组合。在这个辅音组合里，每个辅音依然保持自身的发音。当拼读的时候，这里的两个辅音一定要连读，即从前面的第一个辅音迅速滑到第二个辅音，中间不能停顿。包含辅音混合音“sl”发音的单词如：slow，slide，sleep，slim，slice 等。

2. 听一听，学一学下列字母组合的拼读发音。

(1) glove　glue　gloom　glee　glory　gleeful

(2) plain　pleasant　plump　play　plant　plenty

(3) slum　sly　slang　slam　slippery　sliver

3. 仔细听，然后做句子一口气快读练习。

(1) Glen is gleeful that his father has got a new job at the glass factory.

(2) Glen was very glad to get a pair of boxing gloves.

(3) Wear lain clothes when you travel by plane to the grass plains of Canada.

(4) Look at our world. There are plastic bags, plastic boots and plastic chairs.

(5) She is a slim girl with a short sleeved sweater.

(6) Don’t slam the door, the baby’s sleeping.

二、辅音字母组合 gr　pr　tr　dr

1. 拼读发音方式。

辅音混和音“gr”

辅音混和音“gr”的特点是辅音组合。在这个辅音组合里，每个辅音依然保持自身的发音。当拼读的时候，这里的两个辅音一定要连读，即从前面的第一个辅音迅速滑到第二个辅音，中间不能停顿。包含辅音混合音“gr”发音的单词如 green，grape，greenhouse，grandpa，grade 等。

辅音混和音“pr”

辅音混和音“pr”的特点是辅音组合。在这个辅音组合里，每个辅音依然保持自身的发音。当拼读的时候，这里的两个辅音一定要连读，即从第一个辅音迅速滑到第二个辅音，中间不能停顿。包含辅音混合音“pr”发音的单词如 press，problem，property，price 等。

辅音混和音“tr”

辅音混和音“tr”的特点是辅音组合。在这个辅音组合里，每个辅音依然保持自身的发音。当拼读的时候，这里的两个辅音一定要连读，即从前面的第一个辅音迅速滑到第二个辅音，中间不能停顿。包含辅音混合音“tr”发音的单词如 tree，trousers，train 等。

辅音混和音“dr”

辅音混和音“dr”的特点是辅音组合。在这个辅音组合里，每个辅音依然保持自身的发音。当拼读的时候，这里的两个辅音一定要连读，即从前面的第一个辅音迅速滑到第二个辅音，中间不能停顿。包含辅音混合音“dr” 发音的单词如：drama，drug，driver，drag 等。

2. 听一听，学一学下列字母组合的拼读发音。

(1) grade grandma grass grape group green

(2) praise prawn pressure prize princess prince

(3) traffic trade treasure travel truck train

(4) drop drink dress dream drawer drum drain

3. 仔细听，然后做句子一口气快读练习。

(1) Grandpa and grandma have grown green vegetable for grand thirty years.

(2) Greg is a grumpy, greedy man.

(3) The preacher practices preaching.

(4) That’s a pretty high price to pay for a present.

(5) Try to transfer from the train to the tram.

(6) The trucks and trams are stuck in the traffic.

(7) He was drowsy after he took some drugs.

(8) Drew needs to get a driving license before he can drive.

Part Two: Dialogue

Dialogue 1

Mike: Excuse me, Mrs. Brown. Can I speak to you for a few minutes?

Lisa: Yes, of course, Mike. What’s up?

Mike: It's about my wife. She's ill and has to go to hospital tomorrow.

Lisa: Yes, I know that. Is your wife's illness serious?

Mike: The doctor says it's just a minor operation. But it has to be done as soon as possible. And the problem is my daughter, the baby. You see, both our parents live far away, my wife will be in hospital for several days, so that's nobody to look after her.

Lisa: You mean you need a few days off to look after your baby while your wife is in hospital?

Mike: Yes, that's it. Will that be all right?

Lisa: Yes, I'm sure it will. Mike, all I want to do now is to make sure there's someone to take your place where you're away. How long did you say you'd need?

Mike: Just a few days. My wife should be out of hospital by next Wednesday, so I can be back on Thursday.

Lisa: Well, perhaps you'd better stay at home on Thursday just to give your wife a few extra days to rest after the operation.

Mike: That's very kind of you, Mrs. Brown.

Lisa: Don't mention it.

Words and Expressions

minor ['mainə] *adj.* 较小的

as soon as possible 尽快

look after 照顾

Decide whether the following statements are True (T) or False (F).

1. [ ] Mike is asking for several days off to look after her wife.
2. [ ] Mike's wife is very ill and has to go to hospital for a long time.
3. [ ] Mike's and his wife's parents live far away.
4. [ ] Mike has to look after his baby girl because his wife is going

to a business trip.

5. [ ] Lisa advises Mike to stay at home for a few extra days.

Dialogue 2

Mike: Hello. This is Mr. Frank speaking.

John: Hello, Mr. Frank. This is John here. I wonder if it is possible for me to come in a bit late tomorrow.

Mike: What's up? Nothing wrong, I hope.

John: No, no. It's just my mother returning from a long trip tomorrow morning, and I'd like to go and meet her. Would you mind if I come in at 9:30?

Mike: What time is your mother coming?

John: The train gets in at 8:10. It means I'd be about one hour late for work. Would that be all right?

Mike: Well, John, you know tomorrow morning's meeting is very important and you must attend it. So … I mean, isn't there anyone else in the family, who could go?

John: No, I'm afraid there isn't. I'm the only one with a car. I hope you don't mind.

Mike: All right. I suppose you will have to go then. We'll put the meeting off to ten o'clock. Try not to be too late.

John: Right. Thank you very much. Goodbye.

Mike: Goodbye.

Words and Expressions

attend [ə'tend] *v.* 出席

suppose [sə'pəʊz] *v.* 认为

Decide whether the following statements are True (T) or False (F).

1. [ ] John will be late for work because his wife is ill.
2. [ ] John will be one and a half hours late for work.
3. [ ] John must attend the meeting because the meeting is very important.
4. [ ] John is only one with a car in the family.
5. [ ] Mike puts the meeting off to ten o'clock because of John's late.

Dialogue Three

Roger: Say, Lisa, you've been coming home late these days. What are you busy doing?

Lisa: Nothing important. I've been working overtime lately.

Roger: Then how many hours do you work each day now?

Lisa: 12 hours including 5 hours overtime.

Roger: Goodness! That's tough indeed! Do you think your health can afford?

Lisa: I don't care. I need money.

Roger: Surely you will be paid extra for overtime, but do you think it's really worthwhile?

Lisa: Yes, I think so. When I work overtime I'm paid time and a half.

Roger: Oh, yes. Money comes faster in that way than otherwise. Maybe I should find a job with a lot of overtime, too.

Lisa: But jobs with a lot of overtime are quite limited. Employers usually don't like to pay for overtime work if they can manage.

Roger: That's true. Overtime comes only incidentally, such as when someone's sick or having a day off, or when the workload is heavy, and must be finished in time. Well, I'll try to look for chances.

Lisa: But, remember, Roger, it's not practicable in the long run. After all it's not our goal.

Words and Expressions

tough [tʌf] *adj.* 艰苦的
afford [ə'fɔːd] *v.* 受得起
worthwhile [wɜːθ'waɪl] *adj.* 值得做的
employer [ɪm'plɒɪə] *n.* 雇主
incidentally [ɪnsɪ'dent(ə)lɪ] *adv.* 偶然地
workload ['wɜːkləʊd] *n.* 工作量
practicable ['præktɪkəb(ə)l] *adj.* 行得通的
work overtime 加班
in the long run 长远

Decide whether the following statements are True (T) or False (F).

1. [ ] Lisa has been coming home late these days because she went shopping.
2. [ ] Lisa works 5 hours every day.
3. [ ] Lisa has been working overtime because she needs money.
4. [ ] Jobs with a lot of overtime are quite easy to find.
5. [ ] Roger never wants to work overtime.

Dialogue 4

(In Mr. Smith's office)

Smith: I hate to do this to you, Jenny, but I'm going to have to ask you to put in some more overtime.

Jenny: Does it have to be this afternoon, Mr. Smith? I've already made plans.

Smith: Well, I would have preferred to do it today because the task is rather important. Would you please change your plans?

Jenny: Well, OK.

(In the tea room)

Jenny: You won't believe who's been elected to do overtime on the Smith account! Me! I've already logged in 20 hours of overtime!

Lisa: Wow! Why so much? I thought they were getting you an assistant.

Jenny: They were supposed to, but so far nobody's turned up, and I'm left on my own to do the work. This is the first break I've had all day.

Lisa: They're really running you into the ground. Why don't you ask for some time off? You could take a long weekend and go away somewhere.

Jenny: We'll see.

Words and Expressions

prefer [prɪ'fɜː] *v.* 宁愿

rather ['rɑːðə] *adv.* 相当

elect [ɪ'lekt] *v.* 挑选

assistant [ə'sɪst(ə)nt] *n.* 助手

on someone's account 为了某人的缘故

run into the ground 把……做过头

Decide whether the following statements are True (T) or False (F).

1. [ ] Mr. Smith is asking Jenny to work overtime.
2. [ ] Jenny refused to work more because she has been working more than 20 hours.
3. [ ] Jenny has got an assistant so she is very happy.
4. [ ] Jenny works very hard, and she has never had a break so far.
5. [ ] Lisa is going away somewhere for a holiday.

Part Three: Text

I am cleaning the toilet now.

I am sweeping the floor.

The boy is flying a kite.

The teacher is telling a funny story to his students.

Mary is looking out of the window and thinking.

She is surfing the web to get some information.

We are discussing the question.

We are airing our room now.

They are enjoying their lunch in their dining room.

They are boiling some eggs in the kitchen.

It is raining outside and there are not many people on the street.

The sun is rising and it is becoming warmer and warmer.

Words and Expressions

toilet ['tɔɪlɪt] *n.* 厕所，盥洗室

Eg. 1. I clean my bathroom sink and toilet and shower every time I use it.

每次用完之后，我都要清理浴室的下水道、厕所以及沐浴。

2. It's unclear who first invented the toilet.

不清楚是谁第一个发明了厕所。

sweep [swiːp] *vt.* 扫除

Eg. 1. Sweep the room out well.

把这房间好好打扫一下。

2. I can't sweep without a broom.

没有扫帚我无法扫。

kite [kaɪt] *n.* 风筝

Eg. 1. He tried to fly his kite.

他试图放飞他的风筝。

2. Are you trying to mend you kite?

你在试图修好你的风筝吗？

funny ['fʌnɪ] *adj.* 有趣的，好笑的，滑稽的

Eg. 1. He looked so funny, we all roared with laughter.

他看上去那么滑稽，我们都哈哈大笑。

2. We need someone funny to do this work.

我们需要一个滑稽的人来做这个工作。

surf [sɜːf] *vt.* 在……冲浪

Eg. 1. Can you surf the Web and play an online game?

你能够在网上冲浪、玩网络游戏吗？

2. We surf the Web.

我们上网冲浪。

web [web] *n.* 网

Eg. 1. A spider can spin a web.

蜘蛛会结网。

2. I found this on the web.

这是我在网上找到的。

information [ɪnfə'meɪʃ(ə)n] *n.* 信息，资料

Eg. 1. The book contains much new information.

这本书有很多的新信息。

2. What can we do with this information?

我们能够利用此信息做什么？

discuss [dɪ'skʌs] *vt.* 讨论；论述

Eg. 1. We will discuss that matter after lunch.

午饭后我们要讨论那件事。

2. Do we need to discuss this question?

这个问题还用得着讨论吗

air [eə] *vt.* 使通风，晾干

Eg. 1. We air the bedrooms every day.

我们每天给卧室通通风。

2. Can you air all the rooms for me?

能帮我给所有房间通通风吗？

boil [bɒɪl] *vt.* 煮沸，烧开

Eg. 1. Stir in the rice and boil until just done, about 10 minutes.

一边加入大米一边调和，直到煮沸，大约 10 分钟。

2. And boil it again, and so forth.

然后再次煮沸，如此反复。

kitchen ['kɪtʃɪn; -tʃ(ə)n] *n.* 厨房；炊具

Eg. 1. Take it to the kitchen.

把它拿到厨房去。

2. I mop the kitchen floor twice a week.

我一星期两次用拖把拖厨房的地板。

street [striːt] *n.* 街道

Eg. 1.We must make a turn at the next street.

我们必须在下一个街口掉转车头。

2. They live on the other side of the street.

他们住在马路的另一边。

rise [raɪz] *vi.* 上升；增强

Eg. 1.Fear caused his hair to rise.

恐惧使他的毛发竖立起来。

2. We can choose to rise together.

我们可以选择共同崛起。

Language Focus

I. Make a sentence with the words given below.

1. is / homework / his / he /doing
2. she / TV /watching / is
3. are / to /other / each / they /smiling
4. baby / the / playing / cat / with/ is /a
5. we / cleaning /the /are / classroom

II. Translating

Put Chinese into English.

1. 太阳正在升起。
2. 这条狗在追一只猫。
3. 他们在听音乐。
4. 我妈妈现在在厨房里做饭。
5. 我妹妹在地板上玩。

Put English into Chinese.

1. My cousin is taking a shower in the bath room.
2. The students are dancing on the playground.
3. The children are counting their pocket money.
4. We are worrying about our future.
5. The workers are building another new skyscraper.

III. Reading Comprehension

Choose the best answer to each of the following questions or incomplete sentences.

It is a Saturday night. Smith and Anita are talking in the living room. Smith is sitting on the sofa and watching a football match on TV. His wife, Anita, is ironing some clothes. Smith is describing the match to Anita. They are commenting on the match from time to time. They are talking happily. Their son, John is playing computer games on his ipad. He is playing cheerfully because he can only play computer games for 30 minutes on Saturday night according to the family rules. Their daughter, Mary is doing her homework in her bedroom. She is studying hard. She is a diligent student.

1. What is Anita doing? ______.

A. Watching TV

B. playing computer games

C. ironing some clothes

D. studying

2. What are Smith and Anita doing? ______

A. ironing some clothes

B. watching TV

C. studying

D. talking and commenting

3. What is John doing? ______

A. studying hard

B. playing computer games

C. watching football match

D. talking with classmates on the phone

4. Why is John playing computer games cheerfully? ______

A. Because he is allowed to play computer games for the whole night

B. Because he likes to play computer games very much

C. Because he likes his ipad

D. because he is only allowed to play computer games on Saturday night.

5. Which adjective can be used to describe Mary? ______

A. pretty

B. diligent

C. happy

D. cheerful

Part Four: Play

Mulan (I)

Characters:

Narrator	旁白
General	将军（李香的父亲）
Li Shang	李香（新将军）
Mulan	木兰
King	（敌军）的国王
Emperor	皇帝
Messenger	信使
Pat	木兰的父亲
Solider A	士兵 A
Solider B	士兵 B
Neighbors	邻居

Narrator: Long time ago, the war broke out in China. The natives wanted to get the land back, which had belonged to them before. However, the Emperor didn't allow such a ridiculous thing happened, so the war finally broke out. So the Emperor decided to recruit soldiers.

Narrator: Unexpectedly, Mulan's father, who was old and weak, was chosen. Knowing that her father was not qualified to the mission, Mulan decided to dress herself as a man to join the army instead of her father.

Narrator: During the time in the army, she became acquainted with the captain, Li Shang, and she was deeply moved by his care for her. After they won the war, she told the truth frankly to him, and Li Shang asked the king to spare her life for disguising herself as a soldier. In time, they fall in love with each other, got married and lived happily after then.

Scene 1

General: Get out. The land doesn't belong to you.

King: Your land? (to his Prime Minister)...Hey, he says this is his land. Hahaha.

General: We just want to get our land back.

King: Go to hell, you barbarians.

General: Attack!

King: Fire! Kill them all.

General: Just wait and see. My son, Li Shang, will revenge himself on you.

Solider: Your majesty, we are losing. What can we do?

Emperor: Even if the odds are against us, we must keep going on. Now, what we can do is to recruit more soldiers.

Messenger: Pat.......Ouch, what are you doing? Are you Pat?

Pat: Yes.

Messenger: OK. I am the messenger from our great general, Li Shang. This letter is confidential. Please read it carefully.

Mulan: What's up? Daddy, you look so pale, what's going on?

Pat: Nothing....

Mulan: Look!

Pat: What...

Mulan: My father is old and weak. My brother is too young to join in the army. What can I do?

Neighbors: What can she do?

Mulan: What can I do?

Neighbors: You can go to the army instead of your father.

Mulan: But I'm a girl.

Neighbors: Why not? You look like a man.

Mulan: Right! Good idea! I can't see the reason why a girl can't be a soldier to defend her own country.

Scene 2

Narrator: Mulan began her life in the army.

Solider A: Hey, don't cut in. Line up.

Solider A: Attention! This is our general, Li Shang.

Li Shang: Just want you to follow three "A" s. (to the solider) Tell them what three "A" s.

Solider A: The three "A" s are, are, are,… I don't know, sir.

Li Shang: The three "A" s are "Action, ability, and agility". Understand?

Soliders: Yes!

Li Shang: Good! ... Dismissed.

Soldier A: Soldiers, follow me!

Soldiers: One, two, three…

Mulan: Ouch!

Solider A: Are you out of breath for running for such a short time?

Solider B: You are a sissy boy.

Soldiers: Sissy boy.

Soldier A: Look! He is so thin and so weak. How can our country depend on him?

Soldiers: Ha, ha, ha!

Li Shang: Hey, men! There is no time for you to chat!

Li Shang: Are you OK.?

Mulan: I'm all right.

Li Shang: Go to see the doctor and then take a rest under the tree.

Mulan: He is really a good guy. I am wondering which girl will be lucky enough to marry him.

Soldier A: Hey! Soldiers. It's time for dinner.

Soldier B: Oh....food! Food! (to Mulan) Hey, here is nothing for you. Get away!

Li Shang: You are inferior to others in all aspects.

Li Shang: This is for you.

Mulan: Thank you. Sir!

Li Shang: Go and eat there.

Mulan: He is really a good man. In order not to disappoint him, I'll do my best to become stronger.

（师生改编剧本）

Words and Expressions

native ['neɪtɪv] *n*. 当地居民

allow [ə'laʊ] *v*. 允许

ridiculous [rɪ'dɪkjʊləs] *adj*. 荒谬的

recruit [rɪ'kruːt] *v*. 征募

soldier ['səʊldʒə] *n*. 士兵

unexpectedly ['ʌnik'spektidli] *adv*. 出乎意料地

qualified ['kwɒlɪfaɪd] *adj*. 合格的

mission ['mɪʃ(ə)n] *n*. 任务

join [dʒɒɪn] *v*. 参加

during ['djʊərɪŋ] *prep*. 在……的期间

acquainted [ə'kweɪntɪd] *adj*. 熟识的

captain ['kæptɪn] *n*. 上尉

frankly ['fræŋklɪ] *adv*. 真诚地
spare [speə] *v*. 饶恕
disguise [dɪs'gaɪz] *v*. 伪装
general ['dʒen(ə)r(ə)l] *n*. 将军
barbarian [bɑː'beərɪən] *n*. 野蛮人
attack [ə'tæk] *v*. 攻击
fire ['faɪə] *v*. 开火
revenge [rɪ'ven(d)ʒ] *v*. 报仇
odd [ɒd] *n*. 奇怪的人
messenger ['mesɪn(d)ʒə] *n*. 信使
confidential [kɒnfɪ'denʃ(ə)l] *adj*. 机密的
carefully ['keəfəlɪ] *adv*. 小心地
pale [peɪl] *adj*. 苍白的
reason ['riːz(ə)n] *n*. 理由
attention [ə'tenʃ(ə)n] *n*. 立正！（口令）
action ['ækʃ(ə)n] *n*. 行动
ability [ə'bɪlətɪ] *n*. 能耐
agility [ə'dʒɪlətɪ] *n*. 灵活
dismissed [dis'mist] *v*. 解散
sissy ['sɪsɪ] *adj*. 娘娘腔的
chat [tʃæt] *v*. 聊天
marry ['mærɪ] *v*. 结婚
inferior [ɪn'fɪərɪə] *adj*. 差的
aspect ['æspekt] *n*. 方面
disappointed [dɪsə'pɒɪnt] *v*. 使失望
long time ago 很久前
break out 爆发
belong to 属于
decide to 决定
fall in love 坠入爱河
each other 互相
get out 滚出去

go to hell	见鬼去吧
Your majesty	陛下
What's up?	出了什么事?
What's going on?	怎么了?
cut in	插嘴
line up	整队
out of breath	上气不接下气
enough to	足以

Listening Practice

I. Bingo game

Work in groups, one student read about the script of *Mulan*(I), other students listen carefully, when they hear the adjective from the script, say "Bingo", and write the word in the form quickly, and then he/she wins. And take turns, and change the words into Verbs, Nouns, etc.

Words	adjective	verbs	nouns	prepositions	adverbs	conjunctions
student 1						
student 2						
student 3						
student 4						
student 5						

II. Dictation

Listen to the passage three times and supply the missing information.

Narrator: ____1____, the war ____2____ in China. The natives wanted to get the land back, which had ____3____ them before. However, the king didn't allow such a ____4____ thing happened, so the war finally broke out. So the king decided to ____5____ soldiers.

Narrator: ____6____, Mulan's father, who was old and weak, was chosen. Knowing that her father was not qualified to the ____7____, Mulan decided to dress herself as a man to join the army ____8____ her father.

Narrator: During the time in the army, she became ____9____ the captain, Li

Shang, and she was deeply moved by his care for her. After they won the war, she told the truth frankly to him, and Li Shang asked the king to spare her life for disguising herself as a soldier. In time, they fall in love with ___10___, got married and lived happily after then.

Reading Practice

I. Read and choose

1. Which of the following statement is True? _______

A. Mulan decided to dress herself as a man to join the army instead of her father.

B. This story happened in Old India.

C. Mulan's father was killed during the war.

D. Li Xiang was Mulan's brother.

2. Unexpectedly, _______, who was old and weak, was chosen to join the army.

A. Mulan's little brother

B. Mulan's father

C. Li Xiang

D. Mulan

3. Mulan decided to _______.

A. join the army instead of her father

B. let her father go

C. against the Emperor's order

D. Both B and C

4. The three "A" s are _______.

A. action

B. ability

C. agility

D. Both A, B and C

5. Mulan thought Li Shang was a (an) ______ guy.

A. arrogant

B. kind

C. selfish

D. ugly

II. Read and answer

1. Who is Li Xiang? Is he Mulan's little brother?
2. Why does Mulan join the army instead of her father?
3. Where does Mulan get trained?
4. If you were Mulan, would you fall in love with Li Xiang?
5. What are the three "A" s?

Speaking Practice

I. Role Play

Suppose you were Mulan's father, would you let Mulan join the army instead of you or do it yourself? Use the following functional sentences, you have to add your own expressions when it is necessary.

- What can I do?
- I am old and weak.
- You're a girl.
- Shut up!
- Go to the army instead of me!
- Leave me alone!

II. Problem-Solving

Think of appropriate lines for Mulan and her father in the picture above.

Translating Practice

I. Translate the sentences into Chinese.

Work in pairs, one student reads the following sentences, and the other translates the sentences into Chinese in spoken way. (Add extra sentences from the scripts if necessary.)

1. However, the king didn't allow such a ridiculous thing happened, so the war finally broke out.
2. Knowing that her father was not qualified to the mission, Mulan decided to dress herself as a man to join the army instead of her father.
3. During the time in the army, she became acquainted with the captain, Li Shang, and she was deeply moved by his care for her.
4. I can't see the reason why a girl can't be a solider to defend her own country.
5. I am wondering which girl will be lucky enough to marry him.

II. Translate the sentences into English.

Work in pairs, one student reads the following sentences, and the other translates the sentences into English in spoken way. (Add extra sentences from the scripts if necessary.)

1. 国人们希望收回曾经属于他们的土地！
2. 出乎预料的是，木兰的父亲，一位体弱的老人也被选上了。
3. 这时，他们相爱并结婚，从此幸福地生活在一起。
4. 我是大将军李香的信使，这是封绝密信，请仔细阅读。
5. 你各个方面都比别人差！

III. Delivery Game

The teacher divides the whole class into four or five groups, queuing the students. The teacher writes a long sentence from the script in a piece of paper, just let the first student read and recite it for one minute, and let the student retell the sentence to the second student, the second to the third, when the sentence is delivered to the last student, he/she should write it on the blackboard, and translate it into Chinese. The group which has got great speed and relative accuracy wins.

Writing Practice

Write a summary of *Mulan*(I) in 100 words.

"Ws" / "Who		doing what	whom	where	when

Part Five: Language Skills

Grammar

数词的用法

一、年龄表示法

（1）一般直接用基数词表示，如：Her son is eighteen. 她的儿子18岁。

（2）用“基数词 + years old”表示，有时可将 years old 换成 years of age。如：eighteen years old/ eighteen years of age。

（3）用“基数词-year-old”表示，如：18-year-old。

（4）用“at the age of +基数词”表示“在……年龄”。如：She got

married at the age of eighteen.她 18 岁的时候结婚了。

（5）用“of＋ 基数词”表示，如：girl of 18. 十八岁的女孩。

（6）用“aged +基数词”表示，如：He was a boy aged about eighteen. 他是一个大约 18 岁的男孩。

（7）用“be in one’s +几十的复数形式”表示某人大概的年龄。如：He went to the United States in his fifties. 他五十多岁时去了美国。He became a professor in his forties. 他四十多岁时成了教授。

二、时刻表示法

（1）表示几点钟用基数词加 o’clock，o’clock 可以省略。

5:00 读作 five o’clock 或 five。

（2）表示几点过几分，在分钟后加 past，再加小时。

five past nine 九点过五分

half past six 六点半

a quarter past five 五点过一刻

（3）表示几点差几分，在分钟后面加 to，再加小时。

ten to eight 差十分八点（七点五十分）

a quarter to twelve 差一刻十二点（十一点四十五分）

有时也直接以小时、分钟为单位分别读出数字。

14:03 fourteen o three

18:30 eighteen thirty

23:55 twenty-three fifty-five

如果不以 24 小时计，那就需要用 a.m.表示上午，p.m.表示下午了。

三、年、月表示法

（1）世纪可以用定冠词加序数词加世纪 century 表示。

the sixth（6th）century 公元六世纪

the eighteenth（18th）century 公元十八世纪

注意：用百位数整数表示的世纪比这一百位阿拉伯数字本身多一个世纪。

（2）年代由定冠词及基数词表示的世纪加十位整数的复数形式构成。

in the 1930's（in the thirties of the twentieth century 或 in the nineteen thirties）
在 20 世纪 30 年代
in the 1860's（in the sixties of the 19th century 或 in the eighteen sixties）
在 19 世纪 60 年代
It was in the 1960's．那是在 20 世纪 60 年代。
（3）表示某年代的早期、中期和晚期，可以在定冠词后、年代前添加 early，mid-，late。
in the early 1920's 在 20 世纪 20 年代早期
in the mid-1950's 在 20 世纪 50 年代中期
（4）年、月、日表示法
①年份用基数词表示，一般写为阿拉伯数字，读时可以 hundred 为单位，也可以世纪、年代为单位分别来读。
1949 读作 nineteen hundred and forty-nine 或 nineteen forty-nine
1800 读作 eighteen hundred
2018 读作 twenty hundred and eighteen 或 twenty eighteen
1909 读作 nineteen hundred and nine 或 nineteen o nine
表示在哪一年，一般在年数前加介词 in，使用 year 时，year 放在数词之前。
in the year twenty eighteen.在 2018 年。
但是，通常采用 in 加表示年份的阿拉伯数字。如 in 2018
②月份，在哪个月用介词 in 加第一个字母大写的月份词表示。例如：in May 在五月； in July 在七月。简便起见，月份与日期连用时，月份常用缩写形式表示。缩写形式除 May，June，July 外，其他的月份都由其前三个字母表示，但 September 除外。
January——Jan．一月 February——Feb．二月 March——Mar．三月
April——Apr．四月 May——五月， June——六月，

July——七月， August——Aug. 八月 September——Sept. 九月 October——Oct. 十月 November——Nov. 十一月 December——Dec. 十二月

注：这里缩写形式后面加点不能省略，因为它是表示缩写形式的符号。

③日期用定冠词 the 加序数词表示。在哪一天要添加介词 on。

Teachers' Day is on Sept. 10.

教师节是九月十日。（读作 September tenth）

此句也可以表示为 Teachers' Day is on the 10th of September.

May 5 五月五日（读作 May fifth），也可以表示为 the fifth（5th）of May

Mar. 1（st） 三月一日（读作 March first 或 the first of March）

（5）表示不具体、不确切的时间，如世纪、年代、年份、月份时，用介词 in 表示，表示具体确切的某一天用介词 on。通常情况下，morning，afternoon，evening 等词前用介词 in。但是，当这些词前后有一修饰限定的词作为定语，把它们限定为某一天早晨、下午或晚上时，介词 in 应改为 on。这里的修饰限定词可以是介词短语、名词、形容词、定语从句等。

On a cold morning，the old man died in his house.

在一个寒冷的早晨，这个老人死在自己的房子里。

The accident happened on the afternoon of July 7.

这次事故发生在 7 月 7 日下午。

We are to have a small test on Monday morning.

星期一早晨我们将进行一次小测验。

四、分数表示法

分数是由基数词和序数词一起来表示的。基数词做分子，序数词做分母，除了分子是“1”以外，其他情况下序数词都要用复数形式。

3/4 three fourths 或 three quarters

1/3 one third 或 a third

24/25 twenty-four twenty-fifths

3 1/4 three and one fourth 或 three and one quarter

1/2 a half

五、小数表示法

小数用基数词来表示，以小数点为界，小数点左首的数字为一个单位，表示整数，数字合起来读；小数点右首的数字为一个单位，表示小数，数字分开来读；小数点读作 point，o 读作 zero 或 o〔ou〕，整数部分为零时，可以省略不读。

0.5 zero point five 或 point five 零点五

10.2 ten point two 十点二

5.67 five point six seven 五点六七

1.03 one point o three 一点零三

六、百分数表示法

百分数用基数+percent 表示

50％ fifty percent 百分之五十

3％ three percent 百分之三

0.12％ zero point one two percent 百分之零点一二

七、加减乘除表示法

（1）“加”用 plus，and 或 add 表示；“等于”用 is，make，equal 等词表示。

2+3=?

How much is two plus three?

4+3=9

Four plus three is nine.

2+3=5

Two and three is equal to five.

Two and three makes five.

（2）“减”用 minus 或 take from 表示。

10－6＝? How much is ten minus six?

10－6=4

Ten minus six is four.

Take six from ten，we get four.

（3）“乘”用 time 或 multiply 表示。

$2 \times 4 = ?$

How much is two times four?

$2 \times 4 = 8$

Two times four is eight.

Multiply two by four，we get eight.

（4）“除”用 divide 的过去分词形式表示。

$16 \div 4 = ?$

How much is sixteen divided by four?

$16 \div 4 = 4$

Sixteen divided by four is four.

Exercises

I. Multiple Choice.

1. The old professor still works hard though he is _________.

A. in his sixty B. in his sixties C. in sixties D. in the sixty

2. This classroom is ________ ours.

A. three times big as B. as three times big as

C. three times as big as D. as big three times as

3. Which of the following is wrong? ________

A. He is a fifteen-year-old boy. B. He is at the age of 15.

C. He is a boy of 15. D. He is fifteen year old.

4. ________, Coca-Cola began to enter China's market.

A. In 1970's B. In 1970s C. In the 1970s' D. In the 1970s

5. There was no bus in that small town. We had a ________.

A. ten miles walk B. ten-mile walk

C. ten mile's walk D. tenth mile walk

6. ________ of them are dining at school.

A. Twelve B. Twelfth C. The twelve D. The 12th

7. It's 7:17 is read ________.

A. seven and seventeen B. seven seven

C. seven one seven D. seven seventeen

8. Four ________ one is three.

A. plus B. minus C. times D. divided by

9. Forty-two ________ seven is six.

A. plus B. minus C. times D. divided by

10. ________ is less than ________.

A. One-third; two-thirds B. One-third; two-third

C. First-three; first-threes D. One-third; one-three

11. What's the date today? It is ____.

A. Friday B. time to go C. cloudy D. June 4th

12. He said he was going to be free in ______.

A. one and a half hour B. one hour and half

C. one and half hours D. an hour and a half

13. He joined the army on ______ of May 1980.

A. 1 st B. the 1 C. first D. the first

14. Is Sunday the ____ day of the week?

A. a B. one C. once D. first

15. March _____ is Women's Day.

A. eighth B. ninth C. tenth D. eight

16. September is the _____month of the year.

A. nineth B. ninth C. nine D. the twelveth

17. December ____ is Christmas.

A. twenty-five B. twenty-fifth

C. twentieth-five D. twenty-five

18. Another way of saying Lesson 12 is __________.

A. Lesson ten-two B. Lesson Ten-second

C. the Twelfth Lesson D. Twelfth lesson

19. May is ____ of a year.

A. the fifth months B. the fifth month

C. the five months D. the five month

20. The train from Shanghai will arrive ________.

A. in quarter past six

B. in a quarter past six

C. at quarter past six

D. at a quarter past six

II. Read the following in English.

1. 15－11= 4
2. 2+8=10
3. 7×5=35
4. 25%
5. 1 1/2

III. Translating Practice.

Translate the following into English.

1. 她在 90 年代初期离开了家乡。
2. 这个是在 17 世纪 50 年代发明的。
3. 我们的学校 12 点下课。
4. 1997 年 4 月 2 日是我的生日。
5. 这个老人八十多岁时去世。

Translate the following into Chinese.

1. The woman became a famous singer in her thirties.
2. We often get up at 6 o' clock.
3. Christmas Day is on December 25th.
4. The earth is forty-nine times the size of the moon.
5. The output is 12 percent higher this year than that of the last year.

Unit Eight
Patriotism

Part One: Phonetic Knowledge

Part Two: Dialogue

Part Three: Text

Part Four: Play: Mulan(II)

Part Five: Language Skills

Part One: Phonetic Knowledge

一、辅音字母组合 sm　sn　st　sw

1. 拼读发音方式。

辅音混和音“sm”

辅音混和音“sm”的特点是辅音组合。在这个辅音组合里，每个辅音依然保持自身的发音。当拼读的时候，这里的两个辅音一定要连读，即从前面的第一个辅音迅速滑到第二个辅音，中间不能停顿。包含辅音混合音“sm”发音的单词如 smoke，smooth，smash，smother 等。

辅音混和音“sn”

辅音混和音“sn”的特点是辅音组合。在这个辅音组合里，每个辅音依然保持自身的发音。当拼读的时候，这里的两个辅音一定要连读，即从前面的第一个辅音迅速滑到第二个辅音，中间不能停顿。包含辅音混合“sn”发音的单词如 snake，snail，sniff, snatch, snooker 等。

辅音混和音“st”

辅音混和音“st”的特点是辅音组合。在这个辅音组合里，每个辅音依然保持自身的发音。当拼读的时候，这里的两个辅音一定要连读，即从前面的第一个辅音迅速滑到第二个辅音，中间不能停顿。包含辅音混合音“st”发音的单词如 star，student，stop，style 等。

辅音混和音“sw”

辅音混和音“sw”的特点是辅音组合。在这个辅音组合里，每个辅音依然保持自身的发音。当拼读的时候，这里的两个辅音一定要连读，即从前面的第一个辅音迅速滑到第二个辅音，中间不能停顿。包含辅音混合音“sw”发音的单词如 sweet，swim，Sweden 等。

2. 听一听，学一学下列字母组合的拼读发音。

(1) small smart smell smog smuggle smother

(2) snow sneeze snip snowflake snowdrift

(3) station star steak stair statue studio

(4) switch swing swallow swarm sway swear

3. 仔细听，然后做句子一口气快读练习。

(1) There was a strong smell of smoke in the small room.

(2) There's a smart smock she's wearing.

(3) Sniff some snuff then sneeze.

(4) She sniffs and sneezes and snores when he snoozes.

(5) Stop stupid students sticking stickers on the stairs.

(6) Steven's stepson stole stamps from the stationery store.

(7) My father made me a garden swing and I swing on it every day.

(8) He can swim 600 meters but he's never swum in the sea.

二、辅音字母组合 sc sk sp

1. 拼读发音方式。

辅音混和音“sc”

辅音混和音“sc”的特点是辅音组合。在这个辅音组合里，每个辅音依然保持自身的发音。当拼读的时候，这里的两个辅音一定要连读，即从前面的第一个辅音迅速滑到第二个辅音，中间不能停顿。包含辅音混合音“sc”发音的单词如 school，scarf，score 等。

辅音混和音“sk”

辅音混和音“sk”的特点是辅音组合。在这个辅音组合里，每个辅音依然保持自身的发音。当拼读的时候，这里的两个辅音一定要连读，即从前面的第一个辅音迅速滑到第二个辅音，中间不能停顿。包含辅音混合音“sk”发音的单词如 sky，skirt，skip 等。

辅音混和音“sp”

辅音混和音“sp”的特点是辅音组合。在这个辅音组合里，每个辅音依然保持自身的发音。当拼读的时候，这里的两个辅音一定要连读，即从前面的第一个辅音迅速滑到第二个辅音，中间不能停顿。包含辅音混合“sp”发音的单词如 spoon，sport，spy，speed 等。

2. 听一听，学一学下列字母组合的拼读发音。

(1) scam scarf scour scandal screw

(2) skittle skate sketch ski skill

(3) speak spin spit spade space

3. 仔细听，然后做句子一口气快读练习。

(1) The school teacher scolded the school children.

(2) I scorched my scarf on the fire.

(3) I like skiing and skating.

(4) The skinny girl in the skirt skipped and skated.

(5) The spaceman spoke Spanish from the spaceship.

(6) People who play sport are called sportsmen and sportswomen.

Part Two: Dialogue

Dialogue 1

Mike: Mr. Smith, can you spare me a few minutes?

John: Of course. What is it?

Mike: Well, I'm grateful for the opportunity to work for you and I enjoy doing so. I hope you'll agree that, in the past two years I've worked for you, I've become an integral member of your team and accomplished a great deal. For example, in the last six months alone, I've worked out a big deal.

John: Yes. That's true.

Mike: However, I'm still working for the initial salary on which we agreed two years ago. As I recall, We also agree to renegotiate my salary in two years based on my accomplishments, and that time has come.

John: Now I see what you mean. You want to apply for a raise?

Mike: Indeed. In light of my accomplishments and as per our agreement, I'm respectfully requesting an immediate pay rise of six percent.

John: Okay. I will put your demand into consideration.

Mike: Thanks a lot, Mr. Smith.

John: That's all right.

grateful ['greɪtfʊl] *adj*. 感谢的
integral ['ɪntɪgrəl] *adj*. 构成整体所必需的
recall [rɪ'kɔːl] *v*. 回忆
renegotiate [riːnɪ'gəʊʃɪeɪt] *v*. 重新协商
accomplishment [ə'kʌmplɪʃm(ə)nt] *n*. 成就
respectfully [rɪ'spektfʊlɪ] *adv*. 尊敬地
immediate [ɪ'miːdɪət] *adj*. 直接的
consideration [kənsɪdə'reɪʃ(ə)n] *n*. 考录
work out 解决
base on 以……为根据
in light of 根据
as per 按照

Decide whether the following statements are True (T) or False (F).

1. [ ] Mike is John's boss.
2. [ ] Mike is asking for a day off.
3. [ ] John has been working for the company for more than two years.
4. [ ] They both agreed to renegotiate Mike's salary based on his accomplishments.
5. [ ] John will consider Mike's demand.

Dialogue 2

Jenny: Hey, Lisa, How was your trip to New York?

Lisa: Great, I was able to do some sight-seeing as well as meet the new clients.

Jenny: So all in all it was a very successful trip?

Lisa: Yep. The real reason I came to see you was to see if you could help me get reimbursed for my business expenses.

Jenny: No worries. How much do you need to be reimbursed? It's also company policy to check all receipts before we can pay you.

Lisa: No worries, I've got them all right here.

Jenny: I'll need you to complete this form, including all expenses.

Lisa: When will I be able to pick up the money?

Jenny: If you come back after lunch, I should be able to give it to you.

Lisa: Great. I'll see you then. Bye.

sightseeing ['saɪtsiːɪŋ] *n.* 观光
reimburse [ˌriːim'bəːs] *v.* 报销
expense [ɪk'spens] *n.* 消费
policy ['pɒləsɪ] *n.* 政策
all in all 总而言之
pick up 获得

Decide whether the following statements are True (T) or False (F).

1. [ ] Lisa was able to do some sight-seeing and meet the new clients on her business trip.
2. [ ] Generally speaking, Lisa had a very successful trip.
3. [ ] Lisa is trying to get reimbursed for her business expenses.
4. [ ] Jenny needs a form and all receipts.
5. [ ] Lisa won't get her money until next week.

Dialogue 3

Jenny: Has the financial review been completed yet?

Susan: Yes, it has, our accountants managed to finish it last week.

Jenny: What was the outcome for the company's last financial year?

Susan: Good, as forecasted, the company profits increased by 10%.

Jenny: How did the market react to that news?

Susan: Positively, the stock was up by 3.5% last time I looked.

Jenny: How was it that you managed to complete the financial review as well as the new business plan? I mean, your department must've really been burning the mid-night oil.

Susan: Ah, yes. We did have to put in a fair few extra hours.

financial [faɪ'nænʃ(ə)l] *adj*. 财务的
review [rɪ'vjuː] *n*. 回顾
accountant [ə'kaʊnt(ə)nt] *n*. 会计师
outcome ['aʊtkʌm] *n*. 结果
forecast ['fɔːkɑːst] *v*. 预测
react [rɪ'ækt] *v*. 反应
positively ['pɒzətɪvlɪ] *adv*. 乐观地
stock [stɒk] *n*. 股票
burn the mid-night oil 熬夜

Decide whether the following statements are True (T) or False (F).

1. [ ] Jenny is the accountant in the company.
2. [ ] The outcome for the company's last financial year is very positive.
3. [ ] The company profits increased to 10%.
4. [ ] The stock was up to 3.5% last time Jenny looked.
5. [ ] Susan's department had to work overtime.

Dialogue 4

Worker: Have you applied for your visit to be on a business trip in the

United States yet?

Jenny: Yes I have. I handed in my application forms two weeks ago and I'm going for an interview next week.

Worker: Good luck!

Jenny: The application forms are quite complicated. It took me a few hours to fill it out. The hardest thing was getting all the necessary documents. That took me almost two weeks.

Worker: What kind of documents did you need to present?

Jenny: I had to show documents relating to incumbency certification, business license and so on.

Worker: Why do you think so many people have their applications rejected?

Jenny: I think that they don't complete the forms correctly or they don't include all the required documents. The embassy is very strict about it. You have to be quite careful.

Worker: Why are they stricter with Chinese people than with other nationalities?

Jenny: That's simple. Many people break the rules regarding their visa conditions.

complicated ['kɒmplɪkeɪtɪd] *adj*. 复杂的
present [prɪ'zent] *v*. 呈现
incumbency [ɪn'kʌmb(ə)nsɪ] *n*. 在职
reject [rɪ'dʒɛkt] *v*. 拒绝
regarding [rɪ'gɑːdɪŋ] prep. 关于

Decide whether the following statements are True (T) or False (F).

1. [ ] Jenny has applied for a visit to the U.S.
2. [ ] Jenny is waiting for the interview.
3. [ ] The application forms are very difficult and take Jenny a few days.

4. [ ] However, getting all the necessary documents is not difficult at all.
5. [ ] Many applications have been rejected due to the lack of the required documents.

Part Three: Text

Are they swimming in a swimming pool?

No, they aren't. They are swimming in a river.

Are they all drinking lemonade?

No, they aren't. Some are drinking lemonade. Some are drinking tea.

Are you preparing for your presentation?

Yes, I am. I am reading books and taking notes.

Is she making a shopping-list now?

Yes, she is. She needs to buy a lot of things this week.

Is he playing the guitar in the next room?

Yes, he is. He practices playing the guitar every day.

Is it snowing outside?

Yes, it is snowing heavily. It is the first snow this year.

Are the doctors listening to the report in the meeting room?

No, they aren't. They are having a rest.

Are they doing their assignments?

No, they aren't. They are repairing the computer.

Words and Expressions

pool [puːl] *n.* 水塘

Eg. 1. Jump in, Mary. The water is warm in the pool.

跳下来吧，玛丽。池里的水很暖和。

2. Diving into the swimming pool, he splattered water on me all over.

他往游泳池里跳时，溅了我一身水。

lemonade [leməˈneɪd] *n.* 柠檬水

Eg. 1. They had one bottle of lemonade.

他们只带了一瓶柠檬水。

2. Lemonade is my favorite.

柠檬水是我的最爱。

presentation [prez(ə)nˈteɪʃ(ə)n] *n.* 展示；陈述

Eg. 1. My presentation should clarify any questions that you might have.

我的陈述应该可以澄清你可能有的疑问。

2. So what equipment will you need for your presentation?

那你们在展示时需要什么设备吗？

heavily ['hevɪlɪ] *adv.* 沉重地；猛烈地

Eg. 1. The soldier has been wounded in the arm and he was bleeding heavily.

这名战士手臂已受伤，他正在大出血。

2. I shut the door so heavily that it fell on my head.

我关门那么重以致它掉到了我的头上。

report [rɪ'pɔːt] *n.* 报告；报道

Eg. 1. Have you looked at their report?

你看过他们的报告了吗？

2. His report aroused the interest of all.

他的报告引起了大家的兴趣。

assignment [ə'saɪnm(ə)nt] *n.* 任务；作业

Eg. 1. Today we have an assignment.

今天，我们有一项作业。

2. How would you grade the assignment?

你将如何为这个作业评分？

repair [rɪ'peə] *vt.* 修理；恢复

Eg. 1. Yes we can repair this world.

是的，我们能补救这个世界！

2. It will take a long time to repair a broken marriage.

要使破裂的婚姻重新恢复需要很长时间。

Language Focus

I. Make a sentence with the words given below.

1. is / father / his / cooking /? no /isn't /he /reading /is /he
2. she / selling /fruits / is? yes / is /she
3. are / playing /they / now / tennis?
4. speaking / with / you / are / on /phone /the /him?
5. bird / is /the /the / in /flying /sky? is /it /yes

II. Translating

Put Chinese into English.

1. 她在做纸花吗？　不，她正在写作业。

2. 他没有学习，他在玩电脑游戏。
3. 学生们正在操场上跑吗？　是的，所以他们不在教室。
4. 学生们正在考试吗？　是的，他们正在教室考试。
5. 她在找钱包吗？　是的。

Put English into Chinese.

1. Is she driving? Yes, she is. So she can not answer your phone.
2. Are you waiting for your friends? No, I am waiting for my brother.
3. Is your mother sweeping the floor? No, she isn't. A robot is sweeping the floor.
4. Is he sleeping at home? No, he isn't. He is hiking with his friends.
5. Are you staying at home now? Yes, I am. Ok, I will go to visit you.

III. Reading Comprehension

Choose the best answer to each of the following questions or incomplete sentences.

It is Sunday morning. There are many people in the park. Some women are dancing to music from a broadcaster. Some boys are playing the guitar and singing songs together. They are having a concert. Some old men are playing chess under a big tree. Sometimes, They argue with each other. There is a lake in the middle of the park. Some young people are jogging around the lake. Some family members are boating on the lake. A beautiful girl is sitting on a bench near the lake. She is listening to English programs. There are also some animals in the park. Some squirrels are jumping from trees to trees. Some pigeons are either walking on the grass or flying in the park. A dog is chasing a cat. It is peaceful and harmonious in the park.

1. Some women are ______.
A. listening to music
B. having concert
C. singing songs
D. dancing to music

2. Some boys are ______.
A. playing the guitar
B. singing songs

C. having a concert

D. A, B and C

3. ______ argue with each other

A. Some young people

B. Some old men

C. a beautiful girl

D. some squirrels

4. What is a beautiful girl doing? ______

A. listening to English program

B. practicing English

C. sitting on a bench

D. A and C

5. Some pigeons are ______.

A. jumping from tree to tree

B. walking on the grass

C. flying in the park

D. B and C

Part Four: Play

Mulan (II)

Characters:

Narrator	旁白
General	将军（李香的父亲）
Li Shang	李香（新将军）
Mulan	木兰
King	（敌军的）国王
Emperor	皇帝
Messenger	信使
Pat	父亲
Solider A	士兵 A
Solider B	士兵 B
Neighbors	邻居

Scene 3

Narrator: After being humiliated and insulted by others, she was ashamed of her weakness. So Mulan tried every way to strengthen herself. She lifted weights and did push-ups.

Narrator: After a few months of hard training...

Solider A: Sir! Sir! Our enemies are coming back again.

Li Shang: What? Those barbarians are returning? Hey, soldiers! Take up your weapon and follow me. It's time to fight.

Soldiers: Fight!

Mulan: Hey! Wake up! Don't sleep! Where are the other guys?

Soldier A: They....are...fighting!

Mulan: What! Guys! Wait for me!

Scene 4

Li Shang: Do you still remember General Lee? You killed him ruthlessly. I'm his son, Li Shang.

King: I've killed too many people. It doesn't bother me to kill one more so that you can see your father in the hell soon.

Li Shang: Ha! You talk too much, you ugly barbarian. Now it is my chance to take revenge on you.

King: You? Ha, ha, ha. Impossible!

Li Shang: Watch out, I'll kill you all.

King: Oh yeah? You're still wet behind the ears. How can you bear us and kill us all? You are dreaming.

Li Shang: Just wait and see if I can't. Soldiers, fire!

King:My brave soldiers, go! Ha, ha, ha. Now you are under my control. Surrender?

Li Shang: Just kill me. I'd rather die than surrender.

King: Do you look down upon me? Get him! Get him now!

King: It...it is impossible.

Mulan: Are you all right? Li, I'm sorry.

Li Shang: Why did you kiss me? Are you a gay?

Mulan: No. In fact, I am a girl.

Li Shang: According to the law, a woman can't be a soldier. What you have done is a big crime! Have you ever thought of that?

Mulan: I know, but for my old father and young brother, I have to make such a decision.

Li Shang: Hum.....I'll try to save you.

Emperor: My brave soldiers. Congratulations! We are brought to glorious victory by my captain, Li Shang. You deserve a good reward. Come ahead, my hero! Tell me what you want.

Li Shang: I want nothing except the soldier's life. She is a girl, but she has saved us and the whole country.

Emperor: She is a heroine. Oh, I just can't wait to see her.

Li Shang: This is her. She asks for your mercy because of her violation against the law.

Emperor: Why should I kill her? She has become a good example for our people. I should reward her instead of killing her.

Mulan: Thank you, your majesty.

Li Shang: Though this is a sudden proposal, would you marry me?

Mulan: I'm so glad to hear that. But I have to go back home to ask my father first. Will you go to my hometown with me?

Li Shang: Of course, my dear.

Mulan: Let's go.

Scene 5

Mulan: Father, I'm back.

Pat: Mulan, it's really you?

Mulan: Yes, it's been a long time.

Kid: Sis, we are missing you everyday.

Mulan: Oh, my brother. You are grown up.

Pat: Who is the gentleman?

Mulan: This is General Li.

Li Shang: Sir, can I have the honor to ask your permission to marry your daughter?

Pat: Of course. When are you going to get married?

Li Shang: Soon.

Pat: How soon?

Li Shang: How about now?

Everybody: Great!

（师生改编剧本）

Words and Expressions

humiliate [hjuː'mɪlieɪt] *v.*羞辱；使丧失尊严

insult [ɪn'sʌlt , 'ɪnsʌlt] *v.*辱骂；侮辱；冒犯

ashamed [ə'ʃeɪmd] *adj.*惭愧；羞愧

strengthen ['streŋθn] *v.*加强；增强

weight [weɪt] *n.*重量；分量
push-up ['pʊʃ ʌp] *n.*俯卧撑
barbarian [bɑː'beəriən] *n.*没有文化的人；粗野的人
ruthless ['ruːθləs] *adj.*残酷无情的；残忍的
bother ['bɒðə(r)] *v.*使(某人)烦恼；打扰
crime [kraɪm] *n.*罪行；不道德的行为
deserve [dɪ'zɜːv] *v.*值得；应得
reward [rɪ'wɔːd] *n.*奖励；回报
heroine ['herəʊɪn] *n.*女英雄
proposal [prə'pəʊzl] *n.*求婚
permission [pə'mɪʃn] *n.*准许；许可

Listening Practice

I. Bingo game

Work in groups, one student read about the script of *Mulan*(II), other students listen carefully, when they hear the adjective from the script, say "Bingo", and write the word in the form quickly, and then he/she wins. And take turns, and change the words into Verbs, Nouns, etc.

words	adjective	verbs	nouns	prepositions	adverbs	conjunctions
student 1						
student 2						
student 3						
student 4						
student 5						

II. Dictation

Listen to the passage three times and supply the missing information.

Narrator: After being __1__ and __2__ by others, she was __3__ of her__4__. So Mulan tried every way to__5__herself. She lifted __6__ and did __7__.

Narrator: After a few months of hard __8__.

Solider A: Sir! Sir! Our enemies are __9__ again.

Li Shang: What? Those ___10___ are returning? Hey, soldiers! Take up your weapon and follow me. It's time to fight.

Reading Practice

I. Read and choose

1. Which of the following statement is True? _______

A. Mulan was very popular among the soldiers.

B. Mulan was strong enough to kill the enemies when she first got to the army.

C. Mulan did many ways to strengthen herself.

D. Mulan was in love with one of the soldiers.

2. Li Shang revenged on _______.

A. King

B. General Lee

C. Mulan

D. Mulan's father

3. According to _____, a woman can't be a solider.

A. the Emperor

B. the law

C. Li Shang's order

D. Mulan's will

4. The Emperor was very _____ for Mulan's behavior.

A. happy

B. angry

C. sad

D. upset

5. Li Shang should get _______'s permission to marry Mulan.

A. Mulan's brother

B. the Emperor

C. General Li

D. Mulan's father

II. Read and answer

1. Who was General Li? Was he Li Shang's friend?

2. Why did Li Shang revenge himself on the King?
3. Where did Li Shang and Mulan go at the end of the story?
4. If you were Li Shang, would you be surprised to see Mulan in girl's clothes?
5. How did Mulan save Li Shang's life?

Speaking Practice

I. Role Play

Suppose you were Mulan, when you knew Li Shang was in danger, would you go for help, or save his life by all yourself ? Use the following functional sentences, you have to add your own expressions when it is necessary.

- Help, help.
- I am here to save you.
- Run away.
- He is in danger!
- Are you all right?
- It is me, Mulan.

II. Problem-Solving

Think of appropriate lines for Mulan in the picture above.

Translating Practice

I. Translate the sentences into Chinese.

Work in pairs, one student reads the following sentences, and the other translates the sentences into Chinese in spoken way. (Add extra sentences from the scripts if necessary.)

1. After being humiliated and insulted by others, she was ashamed of her weakness.
2. So Mulan tried every way to strengthen herself. She lifted weights and did push-ups.
3. It doesn't bother me to kill one more so that you can see your father in the hell soon.
4. We are brought to glorious victory by my captain, Li Shang. You deserve a good reward.
5. I want nothing except the soldier's life. She is a girl, but she has saved us and the whole country.

II. Translate the sentences into English.

Work in pairs, one student reads the following sentences, and the other translates the sentences into English in spoken way. (Add extra sentences from the scripts if necessary.)

1. 拿上你们的武器，跟我来！
2. 现在，是我报仇的机会了。
3. 根据法律，女孩是不能参军的。
4. 我应该奖赏她，而不是杀了她！
5. 虽然这是一个仓促的求婚，但是你能嫁给我吗？

III. Delivery Game

The teacher divides the whole class into four or five groups, queue the students. The teacher writes a long sentence from the script in a piece of paper, just let the first student read and recite it for one minute, and let the student retell the sentence to the second student, the second to the third, when the sentence is delivered to the last student, he/she should write it on the blackboard, and translate it into Chinese. The group which has got great speed and relative accuracy wins.

Writing Practice

Write a summary of *Mulan*(II) in 100 words.

"Ws" / "Who"			doing what	whom	where	when

Part Five: Language Skills

Grammar

介词

介词是一种用来表示词与词，词与句子之间的关系的词。在句中不能单独做句子成分。介词和它的宾语构成介词词组，在句中作状语、表语、补语或介词宾语。

一、表示时间的介词

1. in，on，at.

（1）in 表示较长时间，如世纪、朝代、时代、年、季节、月，以及早、中、晚等。

例如：in the 20th century，in the 1950s，in summer，in the morning，in May，in 2012，in his forties，in an hour 等。

（2）on 表示确定的时间，如某日，某日的上午、下午、晚上，星期几，或一般节日等。

例如：on January 1st，on Monday，on New Year's Day，on a fine morning，on Sunday afternoon，on a rainy evening，on the night of May 5，on Teachers' Day，on Children's Day 等。

（3）at 表示某一时刻或较短暂的时间，用于表示时间“点”，或泛指圣诞节、复活节等。

例如：at 4 o'clock，at noon，at the end of，at 4:20，at the beginning of，at the age of，at Christmas，at night 等。

2. by，until，till

（1）by 表示“在……之前，到……为止”

You must finish your homework by ten o'clock.

你必须在 9 点前完成家庭作业。

（2）till 与 until 都有“直到……”或“直到……为止”之义，till 多用于口语，且不能放在句首。表示期限时通常用介词 by，until，till 表示“不迟于”“在……之前”。

例如：They had seen two matches by the end of last night.

到昨晚为止他们已经看了两场比赛了。（这里 by 可以换成 till 或 until）

注意：在肯定句中谓语动词要用延续性动词。在否定句中，not…until 译成“直到……才”谓语动词用非延续性动词。

例如：I waited for my classmate until she came back.

我一直等到我同学回来为止。

I didn't go to bed until my mum came home.

直到我妈妈回来我才上床睡觉。

3. in，for，during，through

（1）in 表示“在……时间内”“在……时间后”。

例如：Do you work in day time or at night ?

你在白天工作还是晚上工作？

He’ll be back in a month.

他一个月后回来。

（2）for 后接一段时间，谓语动词只能用延续性动词。

例如：She has learned English for 8 years.

她已经学英语 8 年了。

（3）during 表示“在……期间”。

例如：He traveled to a lot of cities during those years.

这些年他去了好多个城市。

（4）through“自始自终”“从头到尾”。

例如：Our teacher went on working through the night.

我们的老师工作了一整夜。

4. 表示时间的起点用 since 或 from

例如：He has worked in the factory since three years ago.

三年前他就开始在这个工厂工作。

From now on, I will get up at 6 o’ clock every morning.

从现在开始，我要每天早晨 6 点起床。

5. before，after

before 表示“在某时刻或某件事之前”，after 用在时刻或某件事之后。

例如：We must leave before 8 o’ clock.

8 点钟之前我们必须离开。

After breakfast, he hurried to school.

早餐后，他匆忙上学去了。

二、表示地点方位的介词

1. 表示方位的介词：in、on、to

In 表示“在……内”，on 表示“与……相邻”，to 表示“在……之外，又不相邻”。

Taiwan is a beautiful island and it’s to east of Fujian.

台湾是一个美丽的岛屿，与福建隔海相望。

2. 表示“在……之上或之下”的介词

（1）above，over，on 在……之上，above 指在……上方，不强调是否垂直，over 指垂直的上方，不直接接触，on 表示某物体上面并与之接触。

例如：The airplane is flying above my head.

飞机从我头顶飞过。

There is a bridge over the river.

河上有座桥。

He put his book on the desk.

他把书放在桌子上。

（2）below，under 在……下。under 表示在……下面，正下方。below 表示在……下，不一定在正下方。

例如：There is a cat under the table.

桌子下面有一只猫。

The ship disappeared below the horizon.

那条船消失在地平线下。

3. 表示“用”的介词

in，by 和 with 的用法：表示工具的使用、利用、运用，用 with；表示材料、方式、方法、度量、单位、语言、声音等的“用”，用 in；表示方式、方法、手段等，后常接无冠词的名词或动名词，意为“通过，靠，用”时，用 by。

例如：He is writing a letter with a pen.

他用钢笔写信。

He wrote the letter in ink.

他用墨水写信。

Read the text in a loud voice.

大声读课文。

Tell me the story in English.
用英语讲故事。

Don’t judge a person by appearances.
勿以貌取人。

He made a living by teaching.
他以教书为生。

by 还可以表示交通路线或工具，后接名词不用冠词，意为“乘，坐”。
例如：go by bus / plane / train 乘汽车（飞机、火车）去
travel by land / sea / air 陆上（海上、空中）旅行

4. between，among

一般说来，between 表示两者之间，among 用于三者或三者以上的中间。
例如：You are to sit between your father and me.
你坐在我和你父亲中间。

He is always happy among his classmates.
他和同学们在一起总是很开心。

5. 表示“关于”的 about 和 on

两者都有“关于”的意思，不过前者为一般用词，而后者为较正式的“论述”。
例如：He told me about something important.
他告诉我一些重要的事情。

He wrote a book on history.
他写了一本关于历史的书。

Exercises

I. Multiple Choice

1. Mary dropped in ____ Mr Smith, but he wasn’ t at home.

A. on　　B. at　　C. to　　D. of

2. This is a common mistake ____ students.

A. between B. over C. among D. about

3. I don't think Xiao Li is ____ the other students ____ mathematics.

A. after，on B. after，with C. behind，in D. behind，at

4. We go to school ____ a bike.

A. in B. on C. by D. at

5. It's very kind____ you to repair the bike ____ me.

A. for，for B. of，of C. of，for D. for，of

6. Fresh air is good ____ your health.

A.at B.for C.of D.to

7. He will come ____ three days.

A. before B. after C. in D. later

8. He will return____three o'clock.

A. after B. in C. on D. at

9. I agree ____ what you said.

A. to B. on C. with D. at

10. The plane flew ____ the city.

A. across B. past C. through D. over

11. His teacher was angry ____ him ____ his being late.

A. at，with B.at，for C. with，for D. with，about

12. My uncle lives ____ Queen Street. His room is ____ the fifth floor.

A. at；on B. in；at C. on；in D. of；to

13. Many people are still ____ the habit of writing silly things ____ public places.

A. at；at B. in；in C. into；of D. during；at

14. —Do you go there ____ bus? —No, we go there ____ a train.

A. in；on B. on；on C. by；in D. by；with

15. I made the coat ____ my own hands. It was made ____ hand, not with a machine.

A. in；in B. in；with C. with；by D. with；with

16. The population of the world has grown very fast ____ four hundred years.

A. for past the B. in the pass C. in the past D. for past

17. We returned to our hometown___.

A. next week B. in the last week C. last week D. for a week

18. Great changes have taken place___.

A. in the last few year B. in the last few years

C. last year D. on the last year 3

19. Children wake up very early ____ the morning of Christmas Day.

A. in B. on C. for D. at

20. He suddenly returned____ a rainy night.

A. on B. at C. in D. during

II. Fill in the blanks with correct preposition.

1. She usually gets to school _______ 7:30 in the morning.
2. Can you come here ______ the morning of April 5?
3. We have worked in this city ______ about 5 years.
4. I must go now. My parents are waiting _______ me at the bus stop.
5. Lucy is a good student. She often helps her classmates ______ their lessons.
6. Look! Lily is lying ________ the beach and enjoying the sun.
7. Most ______ us are doing very well _______ maths.
8. Don’t forget to say “Thank you” when someone opens the door ________ you.
9. Hawaii is famous _________ its beautiful beaches.
10. I have borrowed some books _______ our school library.

III. Translating Practice

Translate the following into English.

1. 直到一月份他才回来。
2. 昨晚我们一直等到 10 点钟。
3. 两个小时后我将完成这项工作。
4. 我的铅笔盒在李磊的课桌上。
5. 河上有座桥。

Translate the following into Chinese.

1.The Greens have lived in China for three years.

2. He wrote the letter in ink.

3. She returned to her country after five years.

4. There is a big tree behind our classroom.

5. I usually go to school by bike.

Unit Nine
Devotion

Part One: Phonetic Knowledge

Part Two: Dialogue

Part Three: Text

Part Four: Play: The Boy and the Tree

Part Five: Language Skills

Part One: Phonetic Knowledge

辅音字母组合 th ph wh ch sh

1. 拼读发音方式。

复合字母构成的单音"th"

复合字母构成的单音"th"是两个（或三个）辅音字母在一起只发一个音，改变了原有辅音自身的发音。"th"发浊音，舌尖放在上下牙齿中间，声带振动，气流从牙齿和舌头之间的缝隙里冲出来，如 they，their，this，that，these，those，than。另外，如果舌尖放在上下牙齿中间，声带不振动，气流从牙齿和舌头之间的缝隙里冲出来，也形成声音，但是它是清音。如 think，thank，thirty，throat 等。

复合字母构成的单音"ph"

复合字母构成的单音"ph"是两个（或三个）辅音字母在一起只发一音，改变了原有辅音自身的发音。"ph"发清辅音，与字母"f"一样，即唇齿摩擦辅音。发音时下唇轻触上齿，气流由唇齿间通过，形成摩擦音。发音时送气强，但声带不振动。发这个音时，一定要记得轻轻咬着嘴唇，把手放在嘴巴前，感受气流的冲击。

复合字母构成的单音"wh"

复合字母构成的单音"wh"是两个(或三个)辅音字母在一起

只发一个音，改变了原有辅音自身的发音。“wh”的发音可能比较容易混淆，对不同地方的人，“wh”的发音会有一些不同。但现在美式发音里，公认的说法是，一般来说，“wh”与字母“w”的拼读音相同，但在字母“o”前，读字母“h”的拼读音，如 when，what，whale，who，whole 等。

复合字母构成的单音“ch”

复合字母构成的单音“ch”是两个辅音字母在一起只发一个音，改变了原有辅音自身的发音。“ch”发音情况如下：舌尖顶在上齿龈后，先不发音，然后舌尖离开上齿龈，双唇略向前突起，并收圆，气流从舌头和硬腭和上齿龈之间缝隙流出，发出声音。声带不振动，发音送气。如 chocolate，cheap，chip，China 等。

复合字母构成的单音 “sh”

复合字母构成的单音“sh”是两个辅音字母在一起只发一个音，改变原有辅音自身的发音。“sh”发音情况如下：舌前端接近上齿龈，舌身向上抬向硬腭，气流从舌和硬腭及上齿龈之间的缝隙流出，舌前端和硬腭摩擦成音。声带不振动，发音送气。如 sharp，fish，cash 等。

2. 听一听，学一学下列字母组合的拼读发音。

(1) Thursday think thin teeth they that thus this these

(2) phone telegraph physics phoenix elephant

(3) wheel where which while white whether whirl

(4) China chance check each beach touch teacher

(5) ship sheep she shoulder push wash wish polish

3.仔细听，然后做句子一口气快读练习。

(1) They went to the theatre on Thursday.

(2) She thought that they threw away the thick thermometer.

(3) Philip has a nephew who is a physicist.

(4) Frank and phoebe laughed at photographs of pheasants, elephants and fish.

(5) Which is the white whale?

(6) Who is whistling and whispering in the white room?
(7) Each child chooses a chair on the beach.
(8) Children like chicken and chips.
(9) Shane is washing dishes and polishing the shelves.
(10) Sharon is a fashionable girl and she's shy.

Part Two: Dialogue

Dialogue 1

Jenny: Excuse me, Mr. Smith. Have you read the report I gave you?
Smith: Oh, I have talked over the plan with the assistant managers.
Jenny: Would you give some directions about the plan of developing the new product in our firm?
Smith: In my opinion, developing the new product is potential and will produce a great economic benefits. However, the management strategy and the fund accumulation are not very concrete. In addition, something should be done carefully about the market investigation and the sale forecasting.
Jenny: I see. Thank you. Mr. Smith, we'll correct and perfect the report according to your advice.
Smith: By the way, Jenny, please give me the materials you've got about the product of the department in other companies. You'd better make the best use of time to make good preparations for the work.
Jenny: That's right. I will report what we've done to you whenever necessary.
Smith: All right. Thank you.

Words and Expressions

firm [fɜːm] *n.* 公司
potential [pə'tenʃl] *n.* 潜能
economic [ˌiːkə'nɒmɪk] *adj.* 经济的
strategy ['strætədʒɪ] *n.* 策略

accumulation [əkjuːmjʊ'leɪʃ(ə)n] *n.* 积聚
concrete ['kɒŋkriːt] *adj.* 有形的
investigation [ɪn,vestɪ'geɪʃ(ə)n] *n.* 调查
material [mə'tɪərɪəl] *n.* 材料
assistant manager 副经理
in my opinion 我的观点
in addition 此外
sale forecasting 销售预测
by the way 顺便说说

Decide whether the following statements are True (T) or False (F).

1. [ ] Mr. Smith read the report with the assistant managers.
2. [ ] Mr. Smith thought developing the new product was useless.
3. [ ] The management strategy and the fund accumulation are not very concrete in Jenny's report.
4. [ ] Jenny rejected Mr. Smith's advice.
5. [ ] Mr. Smith suggested that Jenny should make the best use of time to get everything ready for the work.

Dialogue 2

Green: Jenny, Miss Johnson tells me you were looking for me.

Jenny: Yes. Sorry to bother you, Mr. Green. I don't think it's anything too important. It's about Mr. Zhang Jie of MTC Co. Ltd. He's made an order for 15,000 sets of WI printers from our company.

Green: Great!

Jenny: But he is asking for a four percent higher discount than we normally give.

Green: Oh! And you want to know what to do?

Jenny: Not really. I guess he's just trying it on. They have already got a higher discount than others. I'd better check with you, just in case you reach a verbal agreement with him. You know, there's nothing in the file about it.

Green: No, you're right. He's just trying it on.
Jenny: By the way, does MTC get a higher discount than anyone else?
Green: What do you think?
Jenny: I think it probably doesn't matter, as long as Mr. Zhang Jie thinks they do.
Green: That's right!

Words and Expressions

discount ['dɪskaʊnt] *n.* 折扣
verbal ['vɜːb(ə)l] *adj.* 口头的
make an order 订购
in case 万一

Decide whether the following statements are True (T) or False (F).

1. [ ] Mr. Zhang Jie made an order for 15,000 printers from Mr. Green's company.
2. [ ] Mr. Green made a verbal agreement with Mr. Zhang for an extra 4% discount.
3. [ ] Mr. Zhang Jie is working for MTC Co. Ltd.
4. [ ] Mr. Zhang Jie has already got a higher discount than others from Mr. Green's company.
5. [ ] Mr. Green finally agrees to give Mr. Zhang higher discount.

Dialogue 3

Green: Jenny, could you come in? I'd like to have a word with you.
Jenny: OK, Mr. Green. What's up ?
Green: Well, it's hard to say…But I'm sorry to tell you that our company has decided to let you go.
Jenny: What? Let me go? Why?
Green: Concerning your work performance during this half year, our board is not satisfied with your work attitude.

Jenny: Mr. Green, would you give me some details?

Green: Er… According to your sales manager, it seems that you don't work hard and take initiative to sell the cars, and the results seem to be frustrating. I don't think you forget the relative articles in the employee contract, Jenny.

Jenny: But, sir, I…

Green: I'm sorry, Jenny. It's all been decided and nothing can be changed.

Jenny: Hm… Is there a severance package?

Green: We offer three months' severance.

Words and Expressions

performance [pə'fɔːm(ə)ns] *n.* 表现

attitude ['ætɪtjuːd] *n.* 态度

initiative [ɪ'nɪʃɪətɪv] *n.* 主动

frustrating [frʌ'streɪtɪŋ] *adj.* 令人沮丧的

severance ['sev(ə)r(ə)ns] *n.*离职补偿金

be satisfied with 对……感到满意

employee contract 劳动合同

severance packages 离职补偿金

Decide whether the following statements are True (T) or False (F).

1. [ ] Jenny is a very hard-working girl.
2. [ ] The board is not happy with Jenny's work attitude.
3. [ ] Jenny is asked to leave the company.
4. [ ] Jenny gets three months' severance.
5. [ ] Mr. Green is quite happy with Jenny's work.

Dialogue 4

Jenny: Excuse me. I'd like some information on how to get into an American university.

Counsellor: Well, first, you write and get an application form. Then you send it in with a copy of your school records and an affidavit support.

Jenny: And do I need to take any tests?

Counsellor: Yes, you have to take TOEFL.

Jenny: And what about this visa? When can I apply for it?

Counsellor: Well, you can't apply for the visa until you get a letter of acceptance and an I-20 form from a university.

Jenny: I see. And one more thing. Are foreign students allowed to work in the States?

Counsellor: They'll only let you work in summer. And you'll need to get permission from the U.S. Office of Immigration to do that. During the school year, you're not allowed to work unless the work experience is part of your school program.

Jenny: Thank you very much.

Counsellor: You're welcome.

Words and Expressions

affidavit [ˌæfɪ'deɪvɪt] *n.* 宣誓书
acceptance [ək'sept(ə)ns] *n.* 接纳
permission [pə'mɪʃ(ə)n] *n.* 许可
immigration [ɪmɪ'ɡreɪʃn] *n.* 移民
U.S. Office of Immigration 美国移民局

Decide whether the following statements are True (T) or False (F).

1. [ ] Jenny is asking some information about how to get into an American university.
2. [ ] Jenny is suggested to get an application form first.
3. [ ] Jenny has to take TOEFL test.
4. [ ] Foreign students are allowed to work during the school year.
5. [ ] Jenny could apply for a visa as long as she gets a letter of acceptance and an I-20 form from a university.

Part Three: Text

What are you doing?

I am jogging with some of my friends in the central park.

What are you doing?

I am writing a letter to the ambassador.

What are they doing?

They are interpreting for an international conference.

What are they doing?

They are enjoying the soap opera.

What is he doing?

He is delivering a speech.

What is he doing?

He is sipping the wine.

What is she doing?

She is translating the passage

What is she doing?

She is chewing gum.

Words and Expressions

jog [dʒɒg] *vi.* 慢跑；轻推

Eg. 1. If you hate to jog, try a team sport or play some tennis.

如果你讨厌慢跑，那就尝试团体性运动或打网球。

2. I hear you jog every day.

我听说你每天都进行慢跑锻炼。

ambassador [æm'bæsədə] *n.* 大使；使节

Eg. 1. I prepare breakfast for the ambassador and his wife.

我给大使和他的夫人准备早餐。

2. The ambassador refused to all interviews.

该大使拒绝了所有记者对他的采访。

interpret [ɪn'tɜːprɪt] *vt.* 说明；口译

Eg. 1. Will you please interpret for me?

你能为我翻译一下吗?

2. Would you like me to interpret for you?

要不要我来帮你翻译?

international [ɪntə'næʃ(ə)n(ə)l] *adj.* 国际的

Eg. 1. I have my own license and an international license.

我有一张自己所在州的和一张国际的驾驶执照。

2. We are in an international market.

我们身处在一个国际市场上。

conference ['kɒnf(ə)r(ə)ns] *n.* 会议；讨论会

Eg. 1. China has sent her delegates to the conference.

中国已派遣她的代表出席会议。

2. I have telephone conference almost every night.

我差不多每天晚上都有电话会议。

soap [səʊp] *n.* 肥皂

Eg. 1. A This soap lathers well and quickly.

这肥皂起泡沫又多又快。

2. They are like soap and water.

它们就像肥皂和水一样。

opera ['ɒp(ə)rə] *n.* 歌剧；歌剧院

Eg. 1. I think she was also an opera singer.

我觉得她可能还是一个歌剧歌手。

2. I love jazz and opera. And also hip-hop.

我喜欢爵士乐和歌剧，还有嘻哈音乐。

deliver [dɪ'lɪvə] *vt.*发表；递送

Eg. 1. It is impossible to deliver this letter because the address is illegible.

由于地址字迹不清，信件无法投递。

2. The professor is delivering a speech.

这个教授在发表演说。

sip [sɪp] *vi.* 啜饮

Eg. 1. She is sipping black tea.

他在啜饮红茶。

2. She was sitting at the table sipping her coffee.

她坐在桌边呷着咖啡。

translate [træns'leɪt; trɑːns-; -nz-] *vt.* 翻译；转化

Eg. 1. My friend will translate for me.

我朋友将给我当翻译。

2. So she took me along to translate.

所以她拉上我帮她翻译。

passage ['pæsɪdʒ] *n.* 一段（文章）

Eg. 1. Kindly explain this passage.

请把这一段文字解释一下。

2. In order that every student might understand it, the teacher explained that passage again and again.

为了使每个学生都能理解，老师一遍又一遍地讲解那一段。

chew [tʃuː] *vt.* 嚼碎，咀嚼

Eg. 1. He even learned to chew tobacco.

他甚至学会了咀嚼烟叶。

2. Mouse starts to chew.

老鼠开始咀嚼。

gum [gʌm] *n.* 口香糖；树胶

Eg. 1. She swallowed her gum.

她把口香糖给吞下去了。

2. He was a guy who chewed gum all the time.

他是一个整天嚼着口香糖的家伙。

Language Focus

I. Make a sentence with the words given below.

1. is / what / wearing / he?	wearing /is /a /coat / blue / he
2. they /what /are /doing?	editing / are / books / they
3. what / you / are /doing?	making / I / my / year / new / am / plan
4. are / you / whom / with / talking?	talking /my / I / am / with /the/ doctor
5. she / what / is /doing?	is/ translating / she / novel / the

II. Translating

Put Chinese into English.

1. 你在干什么？　我在和朋友吃饭。
2. 你们在干什么？　我们在备考。
3. 你在哪里喝酒？　我在酒吧喝酒。

4. 你在和谁说话？　我在和一个亲戚说话。

5. 他们在干什么？　他们在学习新技能。

Put English into Chinese.

1. Where is he standing?　He is standing in front of the line.

2. Where is she studying?　She is studying in a famous university of Brazil.

3. Where is she living?　She is living in Inner Mongolia.

4. What are you thinking?　I am thinking about my learning strategy.

5. What are you doing?　I am trying to make a model plane by myself.

III. Reading Comprehension

Choose the best answer to each of the following questions or incomplete sentences.

Today's story is about Bater. He is a student from Inner Mongolia. He is now studying at Northwest Minzu University in Lanzhou. He is studying computer science. He is living in the dormitory with his classmates. There are four students in the dormitory. They are Bater, Zhaxi, Liu Ming and Li Wei. Bater and Li Wei are studying computer science. Zhaxi and Liu Ming are studying mathematics. Now it is 10 p.m. All the four students are in the dormitory. Bater is talking with his parents on the phone. Zhaxi is reading a book on mathematics. Liu Ming is making his study plan for the new semester. Li Wei is watching a soap opera on his mobile phone. They are living happily in the dormitory.

1. What is true about Bater ______.

A. Bater is from Inner Mongolia

B. Bater is studying computer science

C. Bater is studying in Lanzhou

D. A, B and C

2. Whom is Bater living with? ______

A. his parents

B. his brothers

C. his relatives

D. his classmates

3. who are studying mathematics ______.
A. Bater and zhaxi
B. Bater and Li Wei
C. Zhaxi and Liu Ming
D. Bater and Liu Ming
4. What is Zhaxi doing now?______
A. He is reading a book on mathematics
B. He is reading a book on computer science
C. He is watching a soap opera
D. He is making a study plan
5. What is Liu Ming doing? ______
A. He is watching a soap opera on the mobile phone
B. He is making a study plan for new semester
C. He is talking with his parents on the phone
D. He is reading an interesting book.

Part Four: Play

The Boy and the Tree

Characters:

Aside 旁白

Tree 树
Boy 男孩

Scene 1

Aside: A long ago, there was a huge apple tree. A little boy loved to come and play around it everyday. He climbed to the tree top, ate the apples, took a nap under the shadow…he loved the tree and the tree loved to play with him.

Aside: As time went by…the little boy had grown up and he no longer played around the tree everyday. One day, the boy came back to the tree and he looked.

Tree: Come and play with me.

Boy: I am no longer a kid, I don't play around trees anymore. I want toys. I need money to buy them.

Tree: Sorry, but I don't have money…but you can pick all my apples and sell them. So, you will have money.

Aside: The boy was so excited. He grabbed all the apples on the tree and left happily. The boy never came back after he picked the apples. The tree was sad.

Scene 2

Aside: One day, the boy returned and the tree was so excited.

Tree: Come and play with me.

Boy: I don't have time to play. I have to work for my family. We need a house for shelter. Can you help me?

Tree: Sorry, but I don't have a house. But you can chop off my branches to build your house.

Aside: So the boy cut all the branches of the tree and left happily. The tree was glad to see him happy but the boy never came back since then. The tree was again lonely and sad.

Scene 3

Aside:One hot summer day, the boy returned and the tree was delighted.

Tree: Come and play with me!

Boy: I am sad and getting old. I want to go sailing to relax myself. Can you give a boat?

Tree: Use my trunk to build your boat. You can sail faraway and be happy.

Aside: So the boy cut the tree trunk to make a boat. He went sailing and never showed up for a long time.

Scene 4

Aside: Finally, the boy returned after he left for so many years.

Tree: Sorry, my boy, but I don't have anything for you anymore. No more apples for you.

Boy: I don't have teeth to bite.

Tree: No more truck for you to climb on.

Boy: I am too old for that now.

Tree: I really can give you anything…the only thing left is my dying roots.

Boy: I don't need much now, just a place to rest. I am tired after all these year.

Tree: Good! Old tree root is the best place to lean on and rest. Come, come, sit down with me and rest.

Aside: The boy sat down and the tree was glad and smiled with tears…

Aside: This is a story of everyone. The tree is our parent. When we were young, we loved to play with mom and dad…When we grew up, we left them…only came to them when we needed something or when we were in trouble.

Aside:No matter what, parents will always be there and give everything they could to make you happy.

Aside: You may think the boy is cruel to the tree but that how all of us are treating our parent. Time is too slow for those who wait, too swift for those who fear, too long for those who grieve, too short for those who rejoice, but for those who love, time is eternity.

（师生改编剧本）

Words and Expressions

huge [hjuːdʒ] *adj*. 巨大的

climb [klaɪm] *v*. 爬

top [tɒp] *n*. 顶部

nap [næp] *n*. 打盹儿

shadow ['ʃædəʊ] *n*. 阴凉处

toy [tɒɪ] *n*. 玩具

pick [pɪk] *v*. 捡，拾起

excited [ɪk'saɪtɪd] *adj*. 兴奋的

grab [græb] *v*. 攫取

return [rɪ'tɜːn] *v*. 返回

shelter ['ʃeltə] *n*. 庇护所

branch [brɑːn(t)ʃ] *n*. 树枝

lonely ['ləʊnlɪ] *adj*. 寂寞的

delighted [dɪ'laɪtɪd] *adj*. 欣喜的

relax [rɪ'læks] *v*. 放松

trunk [trʌŋk] *n*. 树干

sail [seɪl] *v*. 航行

faraway ['fɑːrəweɪ] *adj*. 遥远的

bite [baɪt] *v*. 咬

anything ['enɪθɪŋ] *pron*. 任何事

dying ['daɪɪŋ] *adj*. 枯萎的

root [ruːt] *n*. 树根

rest [rest] *v.* 休息

tired [taɪəd] *adj.* 疲倦的

smile [smaɪl] *v.* 微笑

tear ['tɪə] *n.* 眼泪

parent ['peər(ə)nt] *n.* 父母

cruel [krʊəl] *adj.* 残酷的

treat [triːt] *v.* 对待

swift [swɪft] *adj.* 迅速的

fear [fɪə] *v.* 害怕

grieve [griːv] *v.* 悲痛

rejoice [rɪ'dʒɒɪs] *v.* 高兴

eternity [ɪ'tɜːnɪtɪ] *n.* 永恒

a long ago 很久以前

as time go by 随着时间的流逝

no longer 不再

not …anymore 不再

chop off 砍掉

since then 从那以后

go sailing 去航行

show up 露面

for a long time 很长时间

lean on 靠在……上

no matter what 不管什么

Listening Practice

I. Bingo game

Work in groups, one student read about the script of *The Boy and the Tree*, other students listen carefully, when they hear the adjective from the script, say "Bingo", and write the word in the form quickly, and then he/she wins. And take turns, and change the words into Verbs, Nouns, etc.

words	adjective	verbs	nouns	prepositions	adverbs	conjunctions
student1						
student2						
student3						
student4						
student5						

II. Dictation

Listen to the passage three times and supply the missing information.

A little boy loved to come and play around with an apple tree every day. He ___1___ to the tree, ate the apples, took a ___2___ under the ___3___. He loved the tree and the tree loved to play with him. ___4___, the little boy had grown up and he ___5___ played around the tree every day. But he came back when he needs something, like toys, a ___6___, and a boat. The apple tree gave the boy everything he had, such as apples, ___7___, and trunks. When the boy got old, he came back again to the apple tree, and leaned on the ___8___. This is a story of everyone. The tree is our ___9___. ___10___, parents will always be there and give everything they could to make you happy.

Reading Practice

I. Read and choose

1. Which of the following statement is True? ______

A. The apple tree gives whatever he can to the boy.

B. The boy loves the apple tree deeply.

C. The apple tree asks a lot from the boy.

D. The boy is very generous.

2. When the boy wants toys, the apple tree give ______ to the boy.

A. apples

B. branches

C. trunk

D. root

3. The boy uses the apples tree's _____ to build a boat.

A. apples

B. branches

C. trunk

D. root

4. Every time when the boy comes back to the apple tree, the apple tree are very _______.

A. delighted

B. sad

C. lonely

D. fear

5. The apple tree is like our _____, and gives us whatever we ask.

A. sister

B. teacher

C. parent

D. grandparent

II. Read and answer

1. Who is the boy? Does he love apple tree?
2. Why does the boy come back to the apple tree?
3. Where does the little boy lean on when he gets old?
4. If you were the little boy, what would you like to do, keep asking from apple tree or give something back to apple tree?
5. What does the apple tree give to the boy?

Speaking Practice

I. Role Play

Suppose you were the apple tree, would you give everything you have to the boy, even if he seldom comes back to see you? Use the following functional sentences, you have to add your own expressions when it is necessary.

- Hi, my boy, nice to see you.
- What do you need?
- I miss you so much.

- Where have you been?
- I am lonely.
- When will you come back again?
- Stay with me, please.

II. Problem-Solving

Think of appropriate lines for the boy in the picture above.

Translating Practice

I. Translate the sentences into Chinese.

Work in pairs, one student reads the following sentences, and the other translates the sentences into Chinese in spoken way. (Add extra sentences from the scripts if necessary.)

1. A long ago, there was a huge apple tree. A little boy love to come and play around it every day. He climbed to the tree top, ate the apples, took a nap under the shadow.
2. As time went by…the little boy had grown up and he no longer played around the tree every day.
3. So the boy cut all the branches of the tree and left happily. The tree was glad to see him happy but the boy never came back since then.

4. This is a story of everyone. The tree is our parent. When we were young, we loved to play with mom and dad...When we grew up, we left them...only came to them when we needed something or when we were in trouble.
5. Time is too slow for those who wait, too swift for those who fear, too long for those who grieve, too short for those who rejoice, but for those who love, time is eternity.

II. Translate the sentences into English.

Work in pairs, one student reads the following sentences, and the other translates the sentences into English in spoken way. (Add extra sentences from the scripts if necessary.)

1. 来和我一起玩。
2. 他摘下树上所有的苹果，高高兴兴地离开了。
3. 一个炎热的夏天，男孩回来了，苹果树十分开心。
4. 我真的可以给你所有，但是我只剩下枯萎的根了。
5. 无论发生什么，为了让你开心，你的父母永远在那儿，给你他们所有的一切。

III. Delivery Game

The teacher divides the whole class into four or five groups, queue the students. The teacher writes a long sentence from the script in a piece of paper, just let the first student read and recite it for one minute, and let the student retell the sentence to the second student, the second to the third, when the sentence is delivered to the last student, he/she should write it on the blackboard, and translate it into Chinese. The group which has got great speed and relative accuracy wins.

Writing Practice

Write a summary of *The Boy and the Tree* in 100 words.

"Ws" / "Who"	doing what	whom	where	when

Part Five: Language Skills
Grammar

形容词和副词的比较级与最高级

绝大多数形容词有三种形式：原级、比较级和最高级，以表示形容词说明的性质在程度上的不同。

一、形容词的原级

用以修饰名词表示事物特征的词，形容词的原级形式就是词典中出现的形容词的原形，如 poor 穷的， tall 高的， great 伟大的，glad 高兴的，bad 坏的，good 好的等。

副词：用来修饰动词、形容词、其他副词、全句或名词词组及句子的词。如：much early，soon quickly，good enough，much better。

二、比较级的定义

大多数的形容词都有三个级别：原级、比较级、最高级。其中比较级表示“更……”，用于两者之间的比较，用来说明“前者比后者更……”，比较级前面一般用 much，even，a little，a lot 修饰，其中 even，much 只能修饰比较级。

三、比较级和最高级的构成

规则变化：

1. 单音节词和少数双音节词的比较级和最高级的构成

一般情况在词尾加-er 或-est new。

long- longer-longest　new- newer- newest

以 e 结尾的词加-r 或-st。

fine -finer - finest　　late -later -latest

以“辅音+y” 结尾的词 变 y 为 i 再加-er 或-est early。

happy - happier - happiest　　early - earlier - earliest

重读闭音节的词末尾只有一个辅音字母先双写辅音字母，再加-er 或-est。

hot - hotter - hottest　　thin - thinner - thinnest　　fat - fatter - fattest

2. 多音节词和部分双音节词在其前面加 more 或 most

如：useful - more useful - most useful　　difficult - more difficult - most difficult　　delicious - more delicious - most delicious

3. 形容词的比较级和最高级不规则变化

如：good - better - best　　well - better - best　　ill - worse - worst

bad - worse - worst　　many - much - more - most　　little - less - least

四、比较级的用法

（1）形容词最高级前通常必须用定冠词 the，副词最高级前可不用。形容词 most 前面没有 the，不表示最高级的含义，只表示“非常”。

The Sahara is the biggest desert in the world.

撒哈拉是世界上最大的沙漠。

It is a most important problem. = It is a very important problem.

这是一个很重要的问题。

（2）“否定词语+比较级”，“否定词语+ so…as”结构表示最高级含义。

Nothing is so easy as this. =Nothing is easier than this. =This is the easiest thing.

没有什么比在这个更简单的了。

（3）和 more 有关的词组

the more… the more… 越……就越……

The harder you work，the greater progress you'll make.

你越努力，就会取得越大的进步。

（4）more B than A = less A than B 与其说 A 不如说 B

He is more lazy than slow at his work. = He is less slow than lazy at his work.

他在工作中与其说慢不如说懒。

（5）no more… than… 与……一样，不比……多

The officials could see no more than the Emperor.

官员们看到的不比皇帝多。

（6）no less… than… 与……一样

He is no less diligent than you.

他和你一样勤劳。

（7）more than 不只是，非常

She is more than kind to us all.

她对我们非常友好。

（8）当比较的对象 A 与 B 情况对比相同时，要使用以下结构：

主语+谓语（系动词）+as+形容词/ 副词原形+as+从句。

I study English as hard as my brother.

我同我兄弟一样学习努力。

原级结构中可插入表达倍数的词，表示为“为……若干倍”，当与有表示倍数比较的词在一起时候等，他们的位置是倍数词+as…as…，或倍数词+more… than…。如：

This river is twice as long as that one. 这条河的长度是那条河的两倍。

Exercises

I. Multiple Choice.

1. Which does Jimmy like _____ , Chinese or Art?

A. well B. best C. better D. much

2. The Changjiang River is one of _____ in the world.

A. the longest river B. longest rivers

C. the longest rivers D. longer rivers

3. The box is _________than I wanted.

A. biger B. the biger C. bigger D. the bigger

4. My moon cake is nicer _____ his.

A. like B. with C. for D. than

5. You are fatter than _____ .

A. he B. his C. him D. he is tall

6. He jumps _____ of the three.

A. far B. further C. farthest D. furthest

7. My hair is longer than _____ .

A. my sister B. Kate C. my brother's D. Lucys'

8. There are _____ paper here .Please bring some.

A. little B. less C. fewer D. a little

9. The pen is _____ than that one.

A. more cheap B. cheap

C. much cheaper D. quite cheaper

10. Tom speaks Chinese _____ better than Jimmy.

A. more B. very C. a lot of D. much

11. There are _____ girls in Class Two than in Class Four.

A. more B. nicest C. most D. best

12. It's too _____ for you to do that.

A. easy B. more dangerous C. harder D. the easiest

13. Who has _____ apples now, Jim, Lily or Lucy?

A. much B. biggest C. better D. the most

14. You have more rulers than me. But_____ are nicer than _____.

A. mine，yours B. mine，your C. my，yours D. my，your

15. Tingting is _____than Meimei, but Meimei is _____ than Tingting.

A. all，stronger B. taller，strongest

C. tallest，strong D. taller，stronger

16. Mother is _____ in my family.

A. busy B. busier C. the busiest D. more busy

17. There are _____ in the park on Sunday.

A. more children B. a lot of people

C. much men and women D. many peoples

18. —This blue sweater is too big for me. —Will you please show me a ___ one?

A. small B. smaller C. the smallest D. smallest

19. No one is _____ Mary in the class.

A. so tallest as B. as taller as C. so high as D. so tall as

20. This bike is _____ than that one.

A. twenty yuan dear B. twenty yuan dearer

C. dear twenty yuan D. dearer twenty yuan

II. Fill in the blanks with the appropriate form of the given words.

1. Your classroom is _____ (wide) and _____ (bright) than ours.
2. There are _____ (few) hours of sunlight a day in winter than in summer.
3. Which do you like _____ (well) , Maths or Chemistry?
4. This is the _____ (good) film I have ever seen.
5. Africa is the second _____ (large) continent.
6. What he said made his mother much _____ (angry) .
7. I'm not as _____ (careful) as he.
8. We've got as _____ (many) books as we need.
9. Practice as _____ (much) as you can.
10. They have done _____ (much) work with _____ (little) money.

III. Translating Practice

Translate the following into English.

1. 这是我见过的最高的建筑物。
2. 我的个子和玛丽的个子一样高。
3. 汤姆不如杰克那么热心肠。
4. 你越努力，就越优秀。
5. 这次考试他得了全班最高的成绩。

Translate the following into Chinese.

1. This is the most interesting book that I have ever read.
2. Who is the tallest, Tom, Jack, or David?
3. She is the second tallest student in our class.
4. Mobile phones are very popular now and they are cheaper than before.
5. The air in Beijing is getting much better now than a few years ago.

Glossary

Unit One　Honesty

New Words

Dialogue

recommend [rekə'mend] *v.* 推荐

spicy ['spaɪsɪ] *adj.* 辣的

hamburger ['hæmbɜ:gə] *n.* 汉堡包

probably ['prɒbəblɪ] *adv.* 很可能

heartburn ['hɑːtbɜːn] *n.* 胃灼热

monster ['mɒnstə] *n.* 残忍的东西

mustard ['mʌstəd] *n.* 芥末

lettuce ['letɪs] *n.* 生菜

reserve [rɪ'zɜːv] *v.* 预约

certainly ['səːt(ə)nli] *adv.* 当然

private ['praɪvɪt] *adj.* 私人的

look forward to 期待

reservation [rezə'veɪʃ(ə)n] *n.* 预约

expect [ɪk'spekt] *v.* 期待

correct [kə'rekt] *adj.* 正确的

buffet ['bʊfeɪ] *n.* 自助餐

regular ['regjʊlə] *adj.* 定期的

special ['speʃ(ə)l] *n.* 特色菜

charge [tʃɑːdʒ] *v.* 收费

alcoholic [ælkə'hɒlɪk] *adj.* 含酒精的
stomach ['stʌmək] *n.* 胃

Text

yurt [jʊət; jɜːt] *n.*圆顶帐篷
round [raʊnd] *adj.* 圆的
appearance [ə'pɪər(ə)ns] *n.* 外貌，外观
stressful ['stresfəl] *adj.* 紧张的；有压力的
degree [dɪ'griː] *n.* 学位
style [staɪl] *n.* 风格；时尚
fantastic [fæn'tæstɪk] *adj.* 极好的，不可思议的
website ['websaɪt] *n.* 网站

Play

emperor ['empərə(r)] *n.* 皇帝，君主
vain [veɪn] *adj.*自负的
spread [spred] *vt.& vi.*（使）传播；（使）散布
shady ['ʃeɪdɪ] *adj.* 成荫的；阴暗的；名声不好的
fool [fuːl] *vt.*愚弄，欺骗
weave [wiːv] *vt.* 编织；编排
parade [pə'reɪd] *v.*游行 *n.*游行；检阅；炫耀
marvelous ['mɑːvɪləs] *adj.*不可思议的；非凡的
impatient [ɪm'peɪʃnt] *adj.*不耐烦的；热切的
long ago 从前
far away 遥远
pace up and down 走来走去；徘徊
dressing room 更衣室；化妆室
from time to time 时不时，经常

Unit Two Truth

New Words

Dialogue

count [kaʊnt] *v*. 计数
promise ['prɒmɪs] *v*. 许诺
damned [dæmd] *adj*. 糟糕的
ruin ['ruːɪn] *v*. 毁灭
store [stɔː] *n*. 商店
camp [kæmp] *n*. 露营
wonderful ['wʌndə(r)fl] *adj*. 极好的
vacation [və'keɪʃn] *n*. 假期
indoor ['ɪndɔː] *adj*. 户内的
receptionist [rɪ'sepʃ(ə)nɪst] *n*. 接待员
registration [redʒɪ'streɪʃ(ə)n] *n*. 登记
sign [saɪn] *v*. 签名
miscalculation [ˌmɪskælkjə'leʃən] *n*. 误算
fee [fiː] *n*. 费用
acceptable [ək'septəb(ə)l] *adj*. 可接受的
bill [bɪl] *n*. 账单
receipt [rɪ'siːt] *n*. 收据
wake-up call 电话叫醒服务
room attendant 客房服务员

Text

New Words

mobile ['məʊbaɪl] *adj*. 可移动的

laptop ['læptɒp] *n.* 膝上型轻便电脑，笔记本电脑

advice [əd'vaɪs] *n.* 建议；忠告

formal ['fɔː m(ə)l] *adj.* 正式的

education [ˌedʒʊ'keɪʃn] *n.* 教育

field [fiːld] *n.* 领域，田野

graduate ['grædʒʊeɪt] *n.* 研究生；毕业生

degree [dɪ'griː] *n.* 等级；学位

Play

New Words

design [dɪ'zaɪn] *v. n.* 设计；图案

undoubtedly [ʌn'daʊtɪdlɪ] *adv.*无疑；毋庸置疑地

outfit['aʊtfɪt] *n.*一套服装

equal ['i:kwəl] *vt.*等于；比得上

tiny ['taɪni] *adj.*极小的，微小的

stitches [s'tɪtʃɪz] *n.*（缝纫或编织中的）一针（stitch 的名词复数）；缝法

lacework ['leɪswɜ:k] *n.*网状物，花边

brilliant ['brɪliənt] *adj.*才华横溢的；明亮的

loom [lu:m] *n.*织布机

naked ['neɪkɪd] *adj.*裸体的，裸露的

Your Majesty　陛下

hurry up　赶快

put on　穿上

go on　继续

look at　看着

be dressed in　穿着……

has nothing on　什么都没穿

Unit Three　Wisdom

New Words

Dialogue

knowledge　['nɒlɪdʒ] *n.* 知识
continue [kən'tɪnjuː]　*v.* 继续
online [ɒn'laɪn] *adv.* 在线的
several ['sevrəl] *adj.* 几个的
cautious　['kɔːʃəs] *adj.* 谨慎的
fussy ['fʌsɪ] *adj.* 大惊小怪的
further ['fɜːðə] *adj.* 更进一步的
caution　['kɔːʃ(ə)n] *n.* 小心
personal ['pɜːs(ə)n(ə)l] *adj.*个人的
reveal　[rɪ'viːl] *v.* 透露
escort ['eskɔːt] *v.* 护送

client　['klaɪənt] *n.* 客户
gown　[gaʊn] *n.* 长袍
flyover ['flaɪəʊvə] *n.* 立交桥
underground [ʌndə'graʊnd] *n.* 地铁

Expressions

by any chance　碰巧
go straight　直走
traffic lights　红绿灯
common sense　常识

Text

computer [kəm'pjuːtə] *n.* 计算机，电脑
desktop ['desktɒp] *n.* 桌面，台式机
sunglasses ['sʌnglɑːsɪz] *n.* 太阳镜

famous ['feɪməs] *adj*. 著名的
actor ['æktə] *n*. 演员，男演员
pop [pɒp] *adj*. 流行的；通俗的；热门的
fans [fæns] *n*. 狂热者，粉丝（fan 的复数形式）
numerous ['njuːm(ə)rəs] *adj*. 许多的，很多的
camera ['kæm(ə)rə] *n*. 照相机；摄影机

Play

mystery ['mɪstri] *n*. 秘密，谜
consider[kən'sɪdə(r)] *vt*.& *vi*. 考虑；认为
ordinary['ɔːdnri] *adj*. 普通的；一般的
astonished [ə'stɒnɪʃt] (astonish 的过去式和过去分词) *adj*. 吃惊的
rub [rʌb] *vt*. 擦，摩擦
pretend [prɪ'tend] *vi*. 装扮；假装
drag [dræg] *vt*. 拖拽；拖地而行
bow [bəʊ] *vi*. 弓；鞠躬
wink [wɪŋk] *vi*. 使眼色；递眼色

Unit Four　Being Yourself

New Words

Dialogue

honestly ['ɒnɪstlɪ] *adv*. 真诚地
sincere [sɪn'sɪə] *adj*. 诚挚的
enthusiastic [ɪn,θjuːzɪ'æstɪk] *adj*. 热情的
brave [breɪv] *adj*. 勇敢的
active ['æktɪv] *adj*. 活跃的
considerate [kən'sɪd(ə)rət] *adj*. 体贴的
go ahead 继续
skate [skeɪt] *v*. 滑冰

bunch [bʌn(t)ʃ] *n.* 群
bowl [bəʊl] *v.* 打保龄球
seaside ['siːsaɪd] *n.* 海边
stand [stænd] *v.* 忍受
swear [sweə] *v.* 发誓
sense [sens] *n.* 观念
responsibility [rɪˌspɒnsə'bɪlətɪ] *n.* 责任
seriously ['sɪərɪəslɪ] *adv.* 认真地
through [θruː] *adj.* 完结的
obvious ['ɒbvɪəs] *adj.* 明显的
impose [ɪm'pəʊz] *v.* 欺骗
explain [ɪk'spleɪn] *v.* 说明
cousin ['kʌz(ə)n] *n.* 堂（表）兄弟姐妹
gut [gʌt] *n.* 胆量
stand up 放鸽子
drop by 顺便拜访

Text

relatives ['relətɪvz] *n.* 亲属
progress ['prəʊgres] *n.* 进步，发展
milk [mɪlk] *vt.* 榨取；挤……的奶
cookie ['kʊkɪ] *n.* 饼干；小甜点
select [sɪ'lekt] *vt.* 挑选；选拔
poem ['pəʊɪm] *n.* 诗
organize ['ɔ:gənaɪz] *vt.* 组织
Spanish ['spænɪʃ] *n.* 西班牙语；西班牙人
spare [speə] *adj.* 多余的

Play

defeat [dɪ'fi:t] *vt.* 挫败；击败
breath [breθ] *n.* 呼吸；呼吸力

amaze [ə'meɪz] *vt.* 使大为吃惊，使惊奇
underestimate [ˌʌndər'estɪmeɪt] *vt.* 低估；看轻
evil ['i:vl] *adj.* 邪恶的，罪恶的
embrace [ɪm'breɪs] *n.* 拥抱
disappear [ˌdɪsə'pɪə(r)] *vi.* 不见，消失
wedding ['wedɪŋ]*n.* 婚礼；婚宴
feast [fi:st] *n.* 宴会；盛会
come to life 苏醒
fight with 和……战斗
pass test 通过考试，通过考验
wedding feast 婚宴

Unit Five Love

New Words

Dialogue

costume [kɒstjuːm] *n.* 服装
church [tʃɜːtʃ] *n.* 教堂
especially [ɪ'speʃəlɪ] *adv.* 特别
senior ['siːnɪə] *n.* 较年长者
evening service 晚礼拜
turkey ['tɜːkɪ] *n.* 火鸡
stuffing ['stʌfɪŋ] *n.* 填充物
ham [hæm] *n.* 火腿
yam [jam] *n.* 甘薯
corn [kɔːn] *n.* 玉米
carrot ['kærət] *n.* 胡萝卜
pumpkin ['pʌmpkɪn] *n.* 南瓜
Thanksgiving Day 感恩节
Chinese Spring Festival 中国春节

get-together 聚会
forward ['fɔːwəd] *v*. 转寄
kindness ['kaɪn(d)nɪs] *n*. 仁慈
patience ['peɪʃ(ə)ns] *n*. 耐心
realize ['rɪəlaɪz] *v*. 实现
joyous ['dʒɒɪəs] *adj*. 令人高兴的
occasion [ə'keɪʒ(ə)n] *n*. 时刻
up and down 起起伏伏

Text

tomato [tə'mɑːtəʊ] *n*. 番茄，西红柿
secret ['siːkrɪt] *n*. 秘密；秘诀
case [keɪs] *n*. 箱子
listen ['lɪsn] *vi*. 听，倾听
Classical ['klæsɪk(ə)l] *adj*. 古典的；经典的
together [tə'geðə] *adv*. 一起；同时
sound [saʊnd] *vi*. 听起来

Play

castle ['kɑ:sl] *n*. 城堡
shining ['ʃaɪnɪŋ] *adj*. 光亮的；华丽的
handsome ['hænsəm] *adj*. 英俊的，健美的
absolutely ['æbsəlu:tli] *adv*. 绝对地；完全地
delicious [dɪ'lɪʃəs] *adj*. 美味的，可口的
spoiled[spɔɪld] *adj*. 被宠坏的
transform [træns'fɔ:m] *vt*. 变换；改变
fail[feɪl] *vt*.& *vi*. 失败，不及格
success [sək'ses] *n*. 成功，成就
forgive [fə'gɪv] *vt*.& *vi*. 原谅；饶恕
match [mætʃ] *n*. 相配的人（或物）

Unit Six　Inner Beauty

New Words

Dialogue

quarrel ['kwɒr(ə)l] *v.* 吵架
outrageous [aʊt'reɪdʒəs] *adj.* 粗暴的
shower ['ʃaʊə] *n.* 淋浴
stereo ['sterɪəʊ] *n.* 立体声系统
accomplish [ə'kʌmplɪʃ] *v.* 完成
holler ['hɒlə] *v.* 大声叫喊
down in dumps　垂头丧气
cool down 平静下来
let bygones be bygones 既往不咎
suitcase ['suːtkeɪs] *n.* 手提箱
describe [dɪ'skraɪb] *v.* 描绘
leather ['leðə] *n.* 皮革
particularity [pə,tɪkjʊ'lærɪtɪ] *n.* 特质
initial [ɪ'nɪʃəl] *n.*(名字的) 首字母
handle ['hænd(ə)l] *n.* 把手
hand in 交上
capital letter 大写字母
personality [pɜːsə'nælɪtɪ] *n.* 个性
approach [ə'prəʊtʃ] *v.* 着手处理
enthusiastically [in,θjuːzi'æstikəli] *adv.* 满腔热情地
organized ['ɔːgə,naɪzd] *adj.* 做事有条理的
extremely [ɪk'striːmlɪ] *adv.* 极其
capable ['keɪpəb(ə)l] *adj.* 有才干的
persistent [pə'sɪst(ə)nt] *adj.* 坚持的
co-operative [kəu'ɔpərətiv] *adj.* 合作的

electrical engineering 电机工程
aware of 意识到
embassy ['embəsɪ] *n.* 大使馆
contact ['kɒntækt] *v.* 联系
approve [ə'pruːv] *v.* 批准
instruction [ɪn'strʌkʃ(ə)n] *n.* 指示
document ['dɒkjʊm(ə)nt] *n.* 文件
log on 登录
take it easy 放轻松
relate to 有关

Text

homework ['həʊmwɜːk] *n.* 家庭作业
supper ['sʌpə] *n.* 晚餐，晚饭；夜宵
Australia [ɔ'streljə] *n.* 澳大利亚，大洋洲
mountain ['maʊntən] *n.* 山；山脉
visit ['vɪzɪt] *n.* 访问；参观
grandparent ['græn(d)peər(ə)nt] *n.* 祖父母
interview ['ɪntɚˌvjʊ] *v.* 面试；接见
employee [ɪm'plɔɪi;ˌemplɔɪ'iː] *n.* 雇员；从业员工
company ['kʌmp(ə)nɪ] *n.* 公司

Play

mean [miːn] *adj.* 吝啬的；刻薄的
coarse [kɔːs] *adj.* 粗糙的；粗鄙的；粗野的
unrefined [ˌʌnrɪ'faɪnd] *adj.* 粗俗的；不文雅的
shudder ['ʃʌdə(r)] *vt.& vi.* 战栗；发抖
ignore [ɪg'nɔː(r)] *vt.* 忽视，不顾
favorite ['feɪvərɪt] *n.* 特别喜欢的人（或物）
alarming [ə'lɑːmɪŋ] *adj.* 使人害怕的，扰乱人心的
common ['kɒmən] *adj.* 普通的；通俗的
spell [spel] *n.*咒语，魔法

Unit Seven Justice

New Words

Dialogue

minor ['mainə] *adj.* 较小的
as soon as possible 尽快
look after 照顾
attend [ə'tend] *v.* 出席
suppose [sə'pəʊz] *v.* 认为
tough [tʌf] *adj.* 艰苦的
indeed [ɪn'diːd] *adv.* 的确
afford [ə'fɔːd] *v.* 受得起
worthwhile [wɜːθ'waɪl] *adj.* 值得做的
employer [ɪm'plɒɪə] *n.* 雇主
incidentally [ɪnsɪ'dent(ə)lɪ] *adv.* 偶然地
workload ['wɜːkləʊd] *n.* 工作量
practicable ['præktɪkəb(ə)l] *adj.* 行得通的
work overtime 加班
in the long run 长远
prefer [prɪ'fɜː] *v.* 宁愿
rather ['rɑːðə] *adv.* 相当
elect [ɪ'lekt] *v.* 挑选
assistant [ə'sɪst(ə)nt] *n.* 助手
on someone's account 为了某人的缘故
run into the ground 把……做过头

Text

toilet ['tɔɪlɪt] *n.* 厕所，盥洗室
sweep [swiːp] *vt.* 扫除

kite [kaɪt] *n.* 风筝
funny ['fʌnɪ] *adj.* 有趣的，好笑的，滑稽的
surf [sɜːf] *vt.* 在……冲浪
web [web] *n.* 网
information [ɪnfə'meɪʃ(ə)n] *n.* 信息，资料
discuss [dɪ'skʌs] *vt.* 讨论；论述
air [eə] *vt.* 使通风，晾干
boil [bɒɪl] *vt.* 煮沸，烧开
kitchen ['kɪtʃɪn; -tʃ(ə)n] *n.* 厨房；炊具
street [striːt] *n.* 街道
rise [raɪz] *vi.* 上升；增强

Play

native ['neɪtɪv] *n.* 当地居民
allow [ə'laʊ] *v.* 允许
ridiculous [rɪ'dɪkjʊləs] *adj.* 荒谬的
recruit [rɪ'kruːt] *v.* 征募
soldier ['səʊldʒə] *n.* 士兵
unexpectedly ['ʌnik'spektidli] *adv.* 出乎意料地
qualified ['kwɒlɪfaɪd] *adj.* 合格的
mission ['mɪʃ(ə)n] *n.* 任务
join [dʒɒɪn] *v.* 参加
during ['djʊərɪŋ] *prep.* 在……的期间
acquainted [ə'kweɪntɪd] *adj.* 熟识的
captain ['kæptɪn] *n.* 上尉
frankly ['fræŋklɪ] *adv.* 真诚地
spare [speə] *v.* 饶恕
disguise [dɪs'gaɪz] *v.* 伪装
general ['dʒen(ə)r(ə)l] *n.* 将军
barbarian [bɑː'beərɪən] *n.* 野蛮人
attack [ə'tæk] *v.* 攻击

fire ['faɪə] *v*. 开火
revenge [rɪ'ven(d)ʒ] *v*. 报仇
odd [ɒd] *n*. 奇怪的人
messenger ['mesɪn(d)ʒə] *n*. 信使
confidential [kɒnfɪ'denʃ(ə)l] *adj*. 机密的
carefully ['keəfəlɪ] *adv*. 小心地
pale [peɪl] *adj*. 苍白的
reason ['riːz(ə)n] *n*. 理由
attention [ə'tenʃ(ə)n] *n*. 立正！（口令）
action ['ækʃ(ə)n] *n*. 行动
ability [ə'bɪlətɪ] *n*. 能耐
agility [ə'dʒɪlətɪ] *n*. 灵活
dismiss [dis'mis] *v*. 解散
sissy ['sɪsɪ] *adj*. 娘娘腔的
chat [tʃæt] *v*. 聊天
marry ['mærɪ] *v*. 结婚
inferior [ɪn'fɪərɪə] *adj*. 差的
aspect ['æspekt] *n*. 方面
disappoint [dɪsə'pɒɪnt] *v*. 使失望
long time ago 很久前
break out 爆发
belong to 属于
decide to 决定
fall in love 坠入爱河
each other 互相
get out 滚出去
go to hell 见鬼去吧
Your majesty 陛下
What's up? 出了什么事？
What's going on? 怎么了？
cut in 插嘴

line up 整队
out of breath 上气不接下气
enough to 足以

Unit Eight Patriotism

New Words

Dialogue

grateful ['greɪtfʊl] *adj*. 感谢的
integral ['ɪntɪgrəl] *adj*. 构成整体所必需的
recall [rɪ'kɔːl] *v*. 回忆
renegotiate [riːnɪ'gəʊʃɪeɪt] *v*. 重新协商
accomplishment [ə'kʌmplɪʃm(ə)nt] *n*. 成就
respectfully [rɪ'spektfʊlɪ] *adv*. 尊敬地
immediate [ɪ'miːdɪət] *adj*. 直接的
consideration [kənsɪdə'reɪʃ(ə)n] *n*. 考虑
work out 解决
base on 以……为根据
in light of 根据
as per 按照
sightseeing ['saɪtsiːɪŋ] *n*. 观光
reimburse [ˌriːim'bəːs] *v*. 报销
expense [ɪk'spens] *n*. 消费
policy ['pɒləsɪ] *n*. 政策
all in all 总而言之
pick up 获得
financial [faɪ'nænʃ(ə)l] *adj*. 财务的
review [rɪ'vjuː] *n*. 回顾
accountant [ə'kaʊnt(ə)nt] *n*. 会计师
outcome ['aʊtkʌm] *n*. 结果

forecast ['fɔːkɑːst] *v.* 预测
react [rɪ'ækt] *v.* 反应
positively ['pɒzətɪvlɪ] *adv.* 乐观地
stock [stɒk] *n.* 股票
burn the mid-night oil 熬夜
complicated ['kɒmplɪkeɪtɪd] *adj.* 复杂的
present [prɪ'zent] *v.* 呈现
incumbency [ɪn'kʌmb(ə)nsɪ] *n.* 在职
reject [rɪ'dʒɛkt] *v.* 拒绝
regarding [rɪ'gɑːdɪŋ] *prep.* 关于

Text

pool [puːl] *n.* 水塘
lemonade [lemə'neɪd] *n.* 柠檬水
presentation [prez(ə)n'teɪʃ(ə)n] *n.* 展示；陈述
heavily ['hevɪlɪ] *adv.* 沉重地；猛烈地
report [rɪ'pɔːt] *n.* 报告；报道
assignment [ə'saɪnm(ə)nt] *n.* 任务；作业
repair [rɪ'peə] *vt.* 修理；恢复

Play

humiliate [hjʊ'mɪlɪeɪt] *v.* 羞辱
insult [ɪn'sʌlt] *v.* 辱骂
ashamed [ə'ʃeɪmd] *adj.* 惭愧的
weight [weɪt] *n.* 重量
ruthlessly ['ru:θlisli] *adv.* 无情地
surrender [sə'rendə] *v.* 投降
glorious ['glɔːrɪəs] *adj.* 光荣的
heroine ['herəʊɪn] *n.* 女英雄
mercy ['mɜːsɪ] *n.* 宽恕
violation [vaɪə'leɪʃn] *n.* 违反

proposal [prə'pəʊz(ə)l] *n.* 求婚
honor ['ɒnə(r)] *n.* 荣誉
push-up 俯卧撑

Unit Nine Devotion

New Words

Dialogue

assistant manager 副经理
in my opinion 我的观点
in addition 此外
sale forecasting 销售预测
by the way 顺便说说
discount ['dɪskaʊnt] *n.* 折扣
verbal ['vɜːb(ə)l] *adj.* 口头的
make an order 订购
in case 万一
performance [pə'fɔːm(ə)ns] *n.* 表现
attitude ['ætɪtjuːd] *n.* 态度
initiative [ɪ'nɪʃɪətɪv] *n.* 主动
frustrating [frʌ'streɪtɪŋ] *adj.* 令人沮丧的
severance ['sev(ə)r(ə)ns] *n.* 离职补偿金
be satisfied with 对……感到满意
employee contract 劳动合同
severance packages 离职补偿金
affidavit [ˌæfɪ'deɪvɪt] *n.* 宣誓书
acceptance [ək'sept(ə)ns] *n.* 接纳
permission [pə'mɪʃ(ə)n] *n.* 许可
immigration [ɪmɪ'ɡreɪʃn] *n.* 移民
U.S. Office of Immigration 美国移民局

Text

jog [dʒɒg] *vi*. 慢跑；轻推
ambassador [æm'bæsədə] *n*. 大使；使节
interpret [ɪn'tɜːprɪt] *vt*. 说明；口译
international [ɪntə'næʃ(ə)n(ə)l] *adj*. 国际的
conference ['kɒnf(ə)r(ə)ns] *n*. 会议；讨论会
soap [səʊp] *n*. 肥皂
opera ['ɒp(ə)rə] *n*. 歌剧；歌剧院
deliver [dɪ'lɪvə] *vt*. 发表；递送
sip [sɪp] *vi*. 啜饮
translate [træns'leɪt; trɑːns-; -nz-] *vt*. 翻译；转化
passage ['pæsɪdʒ] *n*. 一段（文章）
chew [tʃuː] *vt*. 嚼碎，咀嚼
gum [gʌm] *n*. 口香糖；树胶

Play

huge [hjuːdʒ] *adj*. 巨大的
climb [klaɪm] *v*. 爬
top [tɒp] *n*. 顶部
nap [næp] *n*. 打盹儿
shadow ['ʃædəʊ] *n*. 阴凉处
toy [tɒɪ] *n*. 玩具
pick [pɪk] *v*. 捡，拾起
excited [ɪk'saɪtɪd] *adj*. 兴奋的
grab [græb] *v*. 攫取
return [rɪ'tɜːn] *v*. 返回
shelter ['ʃeltə] *n*. 庇护所
branch [brɑːn(t)ʃ] *n*. 树枝
lonely ['ləʊnlɪ] *adj*. 寂寞的
delighted [dɪ'laɪtɪd] *adj*. 欣喜的

relax [rɪ'læks] *v.* 放松
trunk [trʌŋk] *n.* 树干
sail [seɪl] *v.* 航行
faraway ['fɑːrəweɪ] *adj.* 遥远的
bite [baɪt] *v.* 咬
anything ['enɪθɪŋ] *pron.* 任何事
dying ['daɪɪŋ] *adj.* 枯萎的
root [ruːt] *n.* 树根
rest [rest] *v.* 休息
tired [taɪəd] *adj.* 疲倦的
smile [smaɪl] *v.* 微笑
tear ['tɪə] *n.* 眼泪
parent ['peər(ə)nt] *n.* 父母
cruel [krʊəl] *adj.* 残酷的
treat [triːt] *v.* 对待
swift [swɪft] *adj.* 迅速的
fear [fɪə] *v.* 害怕

大学英语情境式教学教材

第二册答案

Unit One Honesty

Part Two: Dialogue

Dialogue 1

1. F 2. T 3. F 4. T 5. F

Dialogue 2

1. F 2. F 3. F 4. T 5. F

Dialogue 3

1. F 2. F 3. F 4. T 5. F

Dialogue 4

1. T 2. F 3. F 4. F 5. F

Part Three: Text

Language Focus

I. Make a sentence with the words given below.

1. He has a very good job.
2. I have two cows and five horses.
3. Batu has a factory in his city.
4. They have different approaches to gardening.
5. She has no money in her pocket.

II. Translating

Put Chinese into English.

1. I have a new pen.
2. They have lots of money.
3. I have fish for dinner.
4. She has an old car.
5. He has no idea.

Put English into Chinese.

1. 他每天在家吃午饭。

2. 他们每天上英语课。

3. 我们有一些苹果。

4. 她有一双蓝眼睛。

5. 露西有一个双胞胎妹妹。

III. Reading Comprehension

Choose the best answer to each of the following questions or incomplete sentences.

1. D　　2. B　　3. B　　4. D　　5.C

Part Four: Play

Listening Practice

I. Bingo game

Omitted

II. Dictation

Listen to the passage three times and supply the missing information.

1. emperor　　2. vain　　3. clothes　　4. from time to time　　5. shady

6. left　　7. return　　8. followed　　9. discussed　　10. parade

Reading Practice

I. Read and choose

1. A　　2. B　　3. C　　4. D　　5. D

II. Read and answer

Omitted

Speaking Practice

I. Role Play

Omitted

II. Problem-Solving

Omitted

Translating Practice

I. Translate the sentences into Chinese.

1. 很久以前，在很远的地方，住着一位皇帝。
2. 他不时地换衣服。
3. 我们用一种特殊的材料和秘密的方法发明了一种新布料。
4. 皇帝踱来踱去，走了十分钟，到了织布房，他身后跟着半个宫廷的人。
5. 看看（它的）颜色，感受一下（它的）重量。

II. Translate the sentences into English.

1. The king was very vain and could think nothing but his clothes.
2. Can we fool the Emperor who loves his clothes?
3. We have invented a new kind of clothes made of special materials and secret methods.
4. The king sent me to check the progress of clothes making.
5. There is no need to trouble your hard-working tailor any more.

III. Delivery Game

Omitted

Writing Practice

Omitted

Part Five: Language Skills

I. Fill in the blanks with " have, has ".

1.have	2.has	3.have	4.have	5.has
6.have	7.have	8.have	9.has	10.has

II. Correct the Mistakes.

1. Have—has; 2. has—have; 3. have—has; 4. have—has; 5. have—has

III. Translating Practice.

Translate the following into English.

1.He has many good friends.

2. We have some beautiful flowers.

3. What shall we have for dinner?

4. XiaoMing has a headache.

5. Can I buy a new bag?

Translate the following into Chinese.

1. 我有一个新电脑。
2. 我每天都吃早餐。
3. 每个人有两只手。
4. 我们今晚要举行生日派对。
5. 他们每天都有英语课。

Unit Two Truth

Part Two: Dialogue

Dialogue 1

1. T 2. F 3. F 4. T 5. F

Dialogue 2

1. F 2. F 3. T 4. F 5. T

Dialogue 3

1. F 2. T 3. T 4. T 5. F

Dialogue 4

1. T 2. T 3. T 4. T 5. F

Part Three: Text

Language Focus

I. Make a sentence with the words given below.

1. Do you have any books?
2. Do you have any advice for me?
3. Do you have any brothers or sisters?
4. I think their bikes are very beautiful.
5. I am very interested in this book.

II. Translating

Put Chinese into English.

1. My brother has a new pencil box.
2. Do you have a mobile phone?
3.Does Mary have any brothers or sisters?
4. Do we have English class today?
5. Does he have any comments?

Put English into Chinese.

1. 你有吃的东西吗？
2. 你有关于历史的书吗？
3. 你在新加坡有朋友吗？
4. 她有蓝眼睛吗？
5. 她有电脑吗？

III. Reading Comprehension

Choose the best answer to each of the following questions or incomplete sentences.

1. C　2. B　3. A　4. D　5. B

Part Four: Play

Listening Practice

I. Bingo game

Omitted

II. Dictation

Listen to the passage three times and supply the missing information.

1. weavers	2. highly	3. put on	4. dressed	5. parade
6. crowded	7. child	8. nothing	9. man	10. naked

Reading Practice

I. Read and choose

1. D　2. D　3. A　4. B　5. D

II. Read and answer

Omitted

Speaking Practice

I. Role Play

Omitted

II. Problem-Solving

Omitted

Translating Practice

I. Translate the sentences into Chinese.

1. 哇，看，多漂亮的设计啊！多漂亮的颜色！
2. 快点，请穿上新衣服，陛下！
3. 穿上我的漂亮的新衣难道我不是最帅的吗?
4. 镇上的人都听到了他那套奇装异服的消息，都想见他。
5. 哦，天哪，听着！一个孩子说他什么都没穿！

II. Translate the sentences into English.

1. The new clothes will be ready soon.
2. Your majesty, this is your new dress!
3. It is said that only the really smart people will see this dress.
4. Many people are crowded on both sides of the street.
5. This is true! No clothes! The king is naked!

III. Delivery Game

Omitted

Writing Practice

Omitted

Part Five: Language Skills

I. Fill in the blanks with " don't, doesn't ".

1. don't; 2. doesn't; 3. doesn't; 4. don't; 5. don't

6. doesn't; 7. don't; 8. doesn't; 9. doesn't; 10. doesn't

II. Sentence pattern transformation.

1. (1) don’t; have (2) Do; you; have

2. (1) doesn’t; have (2) Does; have

3. (1) doesn’t; have (2) Does; have

4. (1) don’t; have (2) Do; have

5. (1) don’t; have (2) Do; you; have

III. Translating Practice.

Translate the following into English.

1. don't have classes on Saturday.

2. Does Lily have a toy car?

3. Does he have an English book?

4. What do you have for breakfast?

5There is no milk in the bottle.

Translate the following into Chinese.

1. 你有一座大房子吗？

2. 他有一块橡皮吗？

3. 他们有什么？

4. 他们有多少部电话？

5. 她没有一个姐妹。

Unit Three Wisdom

Part Two: Dialogue

Dialogue 1

1. T 2. T 3. T 4. T 5. F

Dialogue 2

1. F 2. T 3. T 4. T 5. T

Dialogue 3

1. T 2. F 3. F 4. T 5. F

Dialogue 4

1. F 2. F 3. T 4. T 5. T

Part Three: Text

Language Focus

I. Make a sentence with the words given below.

1. Do you have many books?
2. How many bags does Lily have?
3. He does not have any toys.
4. We have many beautiful pictures.
5. She has two good friends.

II. Translating

Put Chinese into English.

1. How many classes do you have this week?
2. How many English books does he have?
3. He studies English every day.
4. How many brothers and sisters does Mary have?
5. I have nothing to say.

Put English into Chinese.

1. 你有多少辆自行车？
2. 她对跳舞没有信心。
3. 我只有一个问题。
4. 他有多少只鸡？
5. 我们有几个部门？

III. Reading Comprehension

Choose the best answer to each of the following questions or incomplete sentences.

1. C　2. A　3. B　4. C　5. A

Part Four: Play

Listening Practice

I. Bingo game

Omitted

II. Dictation

Listen to the passage three times and supply the missing information.

1.Lamp	2. appeared	3. master	4. wish	5. world
6. obey	7. killed	8. dragon	9. kingdom	10. agree

Reading Practice

Read and choose

1. C　2. A　3. D　4. A　5. D

Read and answer

Omitted

Speaking Practice

I. Role Play

Omitted

II. Problem-Solving

Omitted

Translating Practice

I. Translate the sentences into Chinese.

1. 我会服从你的。
2. 哇……我想做公主也没那么好。
3. 你的意思是你住在这盏灯里，当我擦它的时候，你会出来做我告诉你的一切！
4. 没有什么好哭的。
5. 先生，我来这里是为了给你女儿找一个更有价值的丈夫。

II. Translate the sentences into English.

1. Well, first of all, my wish is to get some good clothes and new shoes.
2. He looks up and down at Genie and his magic lamp.
3. Have you considered my suggestion?
4. He is a brave and glorious knight with mysterious magic.
5. A dragon has hurt the lives of many villagers in our kingdom.

III. Delivery Game

Omitted

Writing Practice

Omitted

Part Five: Language Skills

I. Fill in the blanks with “do, does, don't, doesn't”.

1. Does;does

2. Do;don't

3. Do;

4. Does;

5. Do;do

6. Do:do

7. Does;

8. Do;don’t

9. don’t;Do

10.Do;don’t

II. Sentence pattern transformation.

1.（1）否定句 I don’t have a soccer ball.

（2）一般疑问句 Do you have a soccer ball?

2.（1）否定句 she doesn't play the piano.

（2）一般疑问句 Does she play the piano?

3.（1）否定句 My parents don't like vegetables.

（2）一般疑问句 Do your parents like vegetables?

4.（1）否定句 He doesn't like eating eggs for breakfast.

（2）一般疑问句 Doe she like eating eggs for breakfast?

5.（1）否定句 They don't watch football games on TV.

（2） 一般疑问句 Do they watch football games on TV?

III. Translating Practice.

Translate the following into English.

1. Do you want to be a doctor?

2. Does his friends play football every day?

3. Where is Tom from?

4. I don't live here.

5. Mary doesn't like swimming.

Translate the following into Chinese.

1. 他们放学后踢足球吗？
2. 他放学后干什么？
3. 他不知道我的名字。
4. 汤姆玩电脑游戏吗？
5. 他不喜欢冰淇淋。

Unit Four Being Yourself

Part Two: Dialogue

Dialogue 1

1. F 2. F 3. F 4. F 5. T

Dialogue 2

1. T 2. F 3. T 4. T 5. F

Dialogue 3

1. T 2. T 3. T 4. F 5. T

Dialogue 4

1.T 2.T 3.F 4.T 5. F

Part Three: Text

Language Focus

I. Make a sentence with the words given below.

1. Daniel watches TV every evening.
2. I do my homework every day.
3. We go to school every morning.
4. John comes from Canada.
5. She is a good student.

II. Translating

Put Chinese into English.

1. We all like swimming.
2. Herdsmen milk cows every day.
3. He studies English every day.
4. They study painting in their spare time.
5. We often go to the playground to play football after class.

Put English into Chinese.

1. 莉莉晚饭吃西红柿。
2. 我每天六点起床。
3. 她每天都做运动。
4. 地球绕着太阳转。
5. 她母亲在一所中学教英语。

III. Reading Comprehension

Choose the best answer to each of the following questions or incomplete sentences.

1.C 2. C 3. C 4. C 5. A

Part Four: Play

Listening Practice

I. Bingo game

Omitted

II. Dictation

Listen to the passage three times and supply the missing information.

1. defeat 2. Genie 3. village 4. long sharp 5. breathing
6. magic 7. disappeared 8. dead 9. test 10. amazed

Reading Practice

I. Read and choose

1. B 2. A 3. D 4. D 5. C

II. Read and answer

Omitted

Speaking Practice

I. Role Play

Omitted

II. Problem-Solving

Omitted

Translating Practice

I. Translate the sentences into Chinese.

1. 你说过你会为我做任何事，不是吗？
2. 太好了。今晚跟我到村子里来……我们必须一起打败那条龙。
3. 龙在喷火，鼻子里冒出浓烟。
4. 它很漂亮，比我期望的要漂亮得多。
5. 我想这一定是你愚蠢朋友的末日。

II. Translate the sentences into English.

1. Dear boy, nice to meet you!
2. You look terrible. What happened?
3. Come on! We don't have much time.
4. We are going to plan the wedding feast, my children!
5. Aladdin and his magic Genie fought with the dragon.

III. Delivery Game

Omitted

Writing Practice

Omitted

I. Multiple Choice

1. B	2. C	3. A	4. D	5. D
6. A	7.C	8. B	9. B	10. B
11. B	12 . C	13. B	14. C	15. D
16. A	17. C	18. D	19. A	20. C

II. Write the plural form of the following words.

mouse (mice), man (men), sheep (sheep), tooth (teeth), child (children), boy (boys), belief (beliefs), roof (roofs), wolf (wolves), life (lives), piano (pianos), photo (photos), potato (potatoes), zero (zeros), box (boxes)

III. Translating Practice.

Translate the following into English.

1. How many teeth do you have?
2. He has three kids.
3. There are a lot of boxes in the classroom.
4. Could you play the piano?
5. There are many mice in this restaurant.

Translate the following into Chinese.

1. 他有一些白头发。
2. 中国 80% 的人是农民。
3. 我的眼镜去哪了？
4. 这有几双新鞋子。
5. 我的新裤子太长了。

Unit Five Love

Part Two: Dialogue

Dialogue 1

1. T 2. T 3. T 4. F 5. T

Dialogue 2

1. T 2. F 3.F 4. T 5. T

Dialogue 3

1. F 2. T 3. T 4. F 5. F

Dialogue 4

1. F 2. T 3. T 4. T 5. T

Part Three: Text

Language Focus

I. Make a sentence with the words given below.

1. Do you like to drink orange juice?
2. Does he get up early in the morning?
3. Do you want to swim this afternoon?
4. Do you read books in your free time?
5. Does he like his work?

II. Translating

Put Chinese into English.

1. Do you smoke?
2. Does she like the book?
3. Do they go to school every day?
4. Does he listen to music on weekends?
5. Do we have bread for breakfast?

Put English into Chinese.

1. 你想通过大学英语四级考试吗?
2. 你学英语吗？
3. 他们放学后踢足球吗？
4. 他喜欢游泳吗？
5. 他们经常在宿舍看电视吗？

III. Reading Comprehension

Choose the best answer to each of the following questions or incomplete sentences.

1. D 2. B 3. C 4. C 5. C

Part Four: Play

Listening Practice

I. Bingo game

Omitted

II. Dictation

Listen to the passage three times and supply the missing information.

1. faraway 2. castle 3. spoiled 4. lost 5. move
6. diamond 7. rose 8. found 9. appeared 10. happened

Reading Practice

I. Read and choose

1. C 2. C 3. B 4. D 5. A

II. Read and answer

Omitted

Speaking Practice

I. Role Play

Omitted

II. Problem-Solving

Omitted

Translating Practice

I. Translate the sentences into Chinese.

1. 从前，在一个遥远的地方，一个年轻的王子住在一座闪闪发光的城堡里。
2. 外面很冷，我又饿又困。
3. 别以貌取人，年轻人！
4. 年轻人，你心中没有爱。
5. 谁会爱上一头丑陋的野兽？

II. Translate the sentences into English.

1. Who is knocking at the door?
2. The old man came home and told his daughter what happened.
3. I was caught by a wild animal when I picked roses for you.
4. I am a handsome boy and you are a beautiful girl,so we are very well matched.
5. She is the most beautiful girl in the world.

III. Delivery Game

Omitted

Writing Practice

Omitted

Part Five: Language Skills

I. Multiple Choice

1. B	2. B	3.A	4. D	5. C
6. D	7. C	8. C	9. D	10. D

11. B 12 . A 13. C 14. A 15. B

16. C 17. B 18. D 19. B 20. C

II. Fill in the blanks with "/ 、a 、an 、the"

1. /, the 2. / , the 3. the, /, the 4. a, an, the 5. /, / 6. an, the

7. an, a 或 the, the 8. a 9. an ,the, a 10. a, The

III. Translating Practice

Translate the following into English.

1. There was a heavy rain last night.
2. Zhang fei is their monitor.
3. She is a doctor.
4. There is an apple on the table.
5. There is an old woman over there.

Translate the following into Chinese.

1. 我们在这里等了半个小时。
2. 学生们放学后经常踢足球。
3. 他们经常在餐馆吃晚饭。
4. 史密斯夫妇正在愉快地交谈。
5. 熊猫生活在中国。

Unit Six Inner Beauty

Part Two: Dialogue

Dialogue 1

1. F 2. T 3. T 4. F 5. T

Dialogue 2

1. F 2. T 3. F 4. F 5. T

Dialogue 3

1. T 2. F 3. T 4. F 5. T

Dialogue 4

1. F 2. F 3. T 4. T 5. T

Part Three: Text

Language Focus

I. Make a sentence with the words given below.

1. What does she like?
2. What time does he get up every morning?
3. What do you know?
4. How do you learn English so well?
5. What do you like to drink?

II. Translating

Put Chinese into English.

1. Where does your father work?
2. How is your brother?
3. Which book does she like?
4. What color is his sweater?
5. When do you go home?

Put English into Chinese.

1. 你每天怎么上学？
2. 我能为你做些什么？
3. 你为什么起得这么早？
4. 你在哪个班?
5. 你从哪里来?

III. Reading Comprehension

Choose the best answer to each of the following questions or incomplete sentences.

1. D 2. A 3. B 4. B 5. C

Part Four: Play

Listening Practice

I. Bingo game

Omitted

II. Dictation

Listen to the passage three times and supply the missing information.

1. playboy 2. mean 3. touched 4. book 5.in common

6. missed 7. dream 8. die 9. alone 10. love

Reading Practice

I. Read and choose

1. A 2. B 3. C 4. C 5. A

II.Read and answer

Omitted

Speaking Practice

I. Role Play

Omitted

II. Problem-Solving

Omitted

Translating Practice

I. Translate the sentences into Chinese.

1. 我想知道为什么我以前没在那里看到它。
2. 我有东西给你看。但首先，你必须闭上眼睛。
3. 我这辈子从没见过这么多书！
4. 带我离开这个地方，让我暂时忘记。
5. 一个仙女把我变成了野兽，作为惩罚。

II. Translate the sentences into English.

1. You must be his daughter!
2. There is a sweet and almost kind feeling.
3. You want to see your father, don't you?
4. You know we have something in common.
5. This is your bedroom. Good night, my beauty.

III. Delivery Game

Omitted

Writing Practice

Omitted

Part Five: Language Skills

I. Multiple Choice

1. D	2. A	3. C	4. B	5. B
6. B	7. A	8. C	9. C	10. B

11. D 12. B 13. B 14. C 15. A

16. A 17.B 18.D 19. A 20. C

II. correct the mistakes.

1. hundreds-hundred; 2. hundred-hundreds; 3. thousands- thousand;

4. Thousands-Thousands of; 5. millions-million

III. Translating Practice.

Translate the following into English.

1. There are 12 months in a year.
2. This is my first bag.
3. He won the third place in the math contest.
4. There are 34 students in our class.
5. My birthday is on December 21st.

Translate the following into Chinese.

1. 这些是你的书吗？—是的。
2. 那些是熊吗？—不，它们不是。
3. 这个用英语怎么说？—它是一个玩具。
4. 那些用英语怎么说？—它们是玫瑰。
5. 这是你的伞吗？—不，它不是。

Unit Seven Justice

Part Two: Dialogue

Dialogue 1

1. T 2. F 3. T 4. F 5. F

Dialogue 2

1. F 2. F 3. T 4. T 5.T

Dialogue 3

1. F 2. F 3. F 4. F 5. F

Dialogue 4

1. T 2. T 3. F 4. T 5. F

Part Three: Text

Language Focus

I. Make a sentence with the words given below.

1. He is doing his homework.
2. She is watching TV.
3. They are smiling to each other.
4. The baby is playing with a cat.
5. We are cleaning the classroom.

II. Translating

Put Chinese into English.

1. The sun is rising.
2. The dog is after a cat.
3. They are listening to music.
4. My mother is cooking in the kitchen now.
5. My sister is playing on the floor.

Put English into Chinese.

1. 我表弟正在浴室洗澡。
2. 学生在操场上跳舞。
3. 孩子们正在数他们的零花钱。
4. 我们在担心我们的未来。
5. 工人们正在建造另一座摩天大楼。

III. Reading Comprehension

Choose the best answer to each of the following questions or incomplete sentences.

1. C　2. D　3. B　4. D　5. B

Part Four: Play

Listening Practice

I. Bingo game

Omitted

II. Dictation

Listen to the passage three times and supply the missing information.

1.long time ago　2. broke out　3. belonged to　4. ridiculous　5. recruit

6. unexpectedly　7. mission　8. instead of　9.acquainted with　10. each other

Reading Practice

I. Read and choose

1. A　2. B　3. A　4. D　5. B

II. Read and answer

Omitted

Speaking Practice

I. Role Play

Omitted

II. Problem-Solving

Omitted

Translating Practice

I. Translate the sentences into Chinese.

1. 然而，国王不允许这种荒唐的事情发生，于是战争终于爆发了。
2. 木兰知道父亲不具备参军的条件，决定把自己打扮成一个男人，代替父亲参军。
3. 在部队服役期间，她结识了上尉李尚，李尚对她的关心使她深受感动。
4. 我不明白为什么一个女孩不能成为保卫自己国家的战士。
5. 我想知道哪个女孩会幸运地嫁给他。

II. Translate the sentences into English.

1. The natives wanted to get the land back, which had belonged to them before!
2. Unexpectedly, Mulan's father, a frail old man, was chosen.
3. At this time, they love each other and get married, and live happily ever after.
4. I am the messenger of General Li Xiang. This is a top secret letter. Please read it carefully.
5. You are worse than others in all aspects!

III. Delivery Game

Omitted

Writing Practice

Omitted

Part Five: Language Skills

I. Multiple Choice

1. B	2. C	3. D	4. D	5. B
6. A	7. D	8. B	9. D	10. A
11. D	12. D	13. D	14. D	15. A
16. B	17. B	18. C	19. B	20. D

II. Read the following in English.

1.Fifteen minus eleven is four./take eleven from fifteen, we get four.

2.Two plus eight equals ten./two and eight is ten/two and eight make ten.

3. Seven times five is thirty-five./Multiply seven by five， we get thirty-five.

4. Twenty-five percent.

5. One and a half.

III. Translating Practice.

Translate the following into English.

1. She left home in the early 90s.

2. This was invented in the 1650s.

3. Our school finishes class at 12 o'clock.

4. My birthday is on April 2, 1997.

5. The old man died in his eighties.

Translate the following into Chinese.

1. 这个女人三十多岁时成了著名的歌手。

2. 我们通常 6 点起床。

3. 圣诞节在 11 月 25 日。

4. 地球是月球的 49 倍大。

5. 今年的产量比去年增加了 12%。

Unit Eight Patriotism

Part Two: Dialogue

Dialogue 1

1. F 2. F 3. F 4. T 5. T

Dialogue 2

1. T 2. T 3. T 4. T 5. F

Dialogue 3

1. F 2. T 3. F 4. F 5. T

Dialogue 4

1. T 2. T 3. F 4. F 5. T

Part Three: Text

Language Focus

I. Make a sentence with the words given below.

1. Is his father cooking? No, he isn't. He is reading.
2. Is she selling fruit? Yes, she is.
3. They are playing tennis?
4. Are you speaking with him on the phone?
5. Is the bird flying in the sky? Yes, it is.

II. Translating

Put Chinese into English.

1. Is she making paper flowers? No, she's doing her homework.
2. He didn't study. He was playing computer games.
3. Are the students running on the playground? Yes, so they are not in the classroom.

4. Are the students taking the exam? Yes, they are taking the exam in the classroom.

5. Is she looking for her wallet? Yes.

Put English into Chinese.

1. 她在开车吗？是的，她是。所以她不能接你的电话。
2. 你在等你的朋友吗？不，我在等我弟弟。
3. 你妈妈在扫地吗？不，她没有。一个机器人正在扫地。
4. 他在家睡觉吗？不，他没有。他正在和朋友们一起徒步旅行。
5. 你现在待在家里吗？是的，我是。好的，我去看你。

III. Reading Comprehension

Choose the best answer to each of the following questions or incomplete sentences.

1. D　2. D　3. B　4. D　5. D

Part Four: Play

Listening Practice

I. Bingo game

Omitted

II. Dictation

Listen to the passage three times and supply the missing information.

1. humiliated　2. insulted　3. ashamed　4. weakness　5.strengthen

6. weights　7. push-ups　8. training　9. coming back　10. barbarians

Reading Practice

I. Read and choose

1. C　2. B　3. B　4. A　5. D

II. Read and answer

Omitted

Speaking Practice

I. Role Play

Omitted

II. Problem-Solving

Omitted

Translating Practice

I. Translate the sentences into Chinese.

1.被别人羞辱和侮辱后，她为自己的软弱感到羞愧。

2.所以木兰想尽一切办法来使自己强壮。她举重做俯卧撑。

3.我不想再杀一个人，这样你很快就能看到你父亲在地狱里。

4.我的队长李尚带领我们取得了辉煌的胜利。你应该得到很好的奖励。

5.除了士兵的生命，我什么都不要。她是个女孩，但她拯救了我们和整个国家。

II. Translate the sentences into English.

1. Take your weapons and follow me!
2. Now, it's my chance to get revenge.
3. According to the law, girls are not allowed to join the army.
4. I should reward her, not kill her!
5. Although this is a vulgar proposal, can you marry me?

III. Delivery Game

Omitted

Writing Practice

Omitted

Part Five: Language Skills

I. Multiple Choice

1. A	2. C	3. C	4. B	5. C
6. B	7. C	8. D	9. C	10. D
11. C	12. A	13. B	14. C	15. C
16. C	17. C	18. B	19. B	20. D

II. Fill in the blanks with correct preposition.

1. at	2. on	3. for	4. for	5. with
6. on	7. of, in	8. for	9. for	10. from

III. Translating Practice.

Translate the following into English.

1. He did not return until January.
2. We waited until ten o'clock last night.
3. I'll finish the work in two hours.
4. My Pencil case is on Li Lei's desk.
5. There's a bridge over the river.

Translate the following into Chinese.

1. 格林一家已经在中国生活了三年。
2. 他用墨水写了这封信。
3. 五年后她回到了自己的国家。
4. 我们教室后面有一棵大树。
5. 我通常骑自行车上学。

Unit Nine Devotion

Part Two: Dialogue

Dialogue 1

1. T 2. F 3. T 4. F 5. T

Dialogue 2

1. T 2. F 3. T 4. T 5. T

Dialogue 3

1. F 2. T 3. T 4. T 5. F

Dialogue 4

1. T 2. T 3. T 4. F 5. T

Part Three: Text

Language Focus

I. Make a sentence with the words given below.

1. What is he wearing?	He is wearing a coat.
2. What are they doing?	They are editing books.
3. What are you doing?	I am making my year plan.
4. Whom are you talking with?	I am talking with the doctor.
5. What is she doing?	She is translating the novel.

II. Translating

Put Chinese into English.

1. What are you doing? I'm eating with my friends.

2. What are you doing? We are preparing for the exam.

3. Where do you drink? I drink in a bar.

3. Who are you talking to? I'm talking to a relative.

4. What are they doing? They are learning new skills.

Put English into Chinese.

1. 他站在哪里？他站在队伍前面。
2. 她在哪里学习？她在巴西一所著名大学学习。
3. 她住在哪里？她住在内蒙古。
4. 你在想什么？我在考虑我的学习策略。
5. 你在做什么？我想自己做一架模型飞机。

III. Reading Comprehension

Choose the best answer to each of the following questions or incomplete sentences.

1. D 2. D 3. C 4. A 5. B

Part Four: Play

Listening Practice

I. Bingo game

Omitted

II. Dictation

Listen to the passage three times and supply the missing information.

1. climbed 2. nap 3. shadow 4. as time went by 5. no longer

6. house 7. branches 8. tree root 9. parents 10. no matter what

Reading Practice

I. Read and choose

1. A 2.A 3.C 4. A 5. C

II. Read and answer

Omitted

Speaking Practice

I. Role Play

Omitted

II. Problem-Solving

Omitted

Translating Practice

I. Translate the sentences into Chinese.

1. A long ago, there was a huge apple tree. A little boy loved to come and play around it every day.

He climbed to the tree top, ate the apples, took a nap under the shadow.

2. As time went by…the little boy had grown up and he no longer played around the tree every day.

3. So the boy cut all the branches of the tree and left happily. The tree was glad to see him happy but the boy never came back since then.

4. This is a story of everyone. The tree is our parent. When we were young, we loved to play with mom and dad…When we grew up, we left them…only came to them when we needed something or when we were in trouble.

5.Time is too slow for those who wait, too swift for those who fear, too long for those who grieve, too short for those who rejoice, but for those who love, time is eternity.

II. Translate the sentences into English.

1. 来和我一起玩。
2. 他摘下树上所有的苹果，高高兴兴地离开了。
3. 一个炎热的夏天，男孩回来了，苹果树十分开心。
4. 我真的可以给你所有，但是我只剩下枯萎的根了。
5. 无论发生什么，为了让你开心，你的父母永远在那儿，给你他们所有的一切。

III. Delivery Game
Omitted

Writing Practice
Omitted

Part Five: Language Skills
I. Multiple Choice

1. C	2. C	3. C	4. D	5. C
6. C	7. C	8. A	9. C	10. D
11. A	12. A	13. D	14. A	15. D
16. C	17. A	18. B	19. D	20. B

II. Fill in the blanks with the appropriate form of the given words.

1. wider, brighter	2. fewer	3. better	4. best	5. largest
6. angrier	7. careful	8. many	9. much	10. the most, less

III. Translating Practice.
Translate the following into English.
1. This is the tallest building I have ever seen.
2. My height is as tall as Mary's.
3. Tom is not as warm-hearted as Jack.
4. The harder you work, the better you will be.
5. He got the highest score in the class in this exam.

Translate the following into Chinese.
1. 这是我读过的最有趣的书。
2. 谁最高？汤姆，杰克，还是大卫？
3. 她是我们班第二高的学生。
4. 现在手机很流行，而且比以前便宜。
5. 北京的空气比几年前好多了。